CONTEMPORARY SOCIAL THEORY

General Editor: ANTHONY GIDDENS

This series aims to create a forum for debate between different theoretical and philosophical traditions in the social sciences. As well as covering broad schools of thought, the series will also concentrate upon the work of particular thinkers whose ideas have had a major impact on social science (these books appear under the sub-series title of 'Theoretical Traditions in the Social Sciences'). The series is not limited to abstract theoretical discussion – it will also include more substantive work on contemporary capitalism, the state, politics and other subject areas.

CONTEMPORARY SOCIAL THEORY

General Editor: ANTHONY GIDDENS

Theoretical Traditions in the Social Sciences

This new series introduces the work of major figures in social science to students beyond their immediate specialisms.

Published titles

Barry Barnes, *T. S. Kuhn and Social Science*
David Bloor, *Wittgenstein: A Social Theory of Knowledge*
Julian Roberts, *Walter Benjamin*
Dennis Smith, *Barrington Moore: Violence, Morality and Political Change*

Forthcoming titles

Ted Benton, *Althusser and the Althusserians*
Chris Bryant, *Positivism in Social Theory*
John Forrester, *Jacques Lacan*
John Heritage, *Garfinkel and Ethnomethodology*
Athar Hussain and Mark Cousins, *Foucault*
Bob Jessop, *Nicos Poulantzas*
Harvey J. Kaye, *The British Marxist Historians*
James Schmidt, *Maurice Merleau-Ponty and Social Theory*
Robin Williams, *Erving Goffman*

Beyond the State?

Dominant theories and socialist strategies

Boris Frankel

MACMILLAN PRESS
LONDON

First published 1983 by
THE MACMILLAN PRESS LTD
London and Basingstoke
Companies and representatives throughout the world

ISBN 0 333 29420 3   (hard cover)
ISBN 0 333 29421 1   (paper cover)

Typeset in 10/12pt Times by
MULTIPLEX

Printed in Hong Kong

SSH

Contents

Preface

In recent years there have been a number of debates on the nature of
capitalist states and the related questions of the causes of widespread
socio-economic depression and 'alternative strategies'. Much dissatis-
faction has been expressed with those writings which concentrate
heavily on either 'class-theoretical' or 'capital-logic' analyses of states;
little has been done to transcend the traditional conceptual divisions
between 'the State', 'Civil Society' and 'the Economy'. While I have no
wish to eliminate the concept of 'state' or reduce all social life to 'the
State', I have developed a set of categories which go beyond 'economism',
'ideologism' and the reduction of state institutions to mere political/
administrative 'superstructures'. When Lenin and Gramsci were writing,
state theory was relatively undeveloped as nation-states were emerging
from the disintegration of European empires. Today, the role and nature
of national and local state institutions are threatened by supra-national
organisations and social institutions. Yet too many authors have over-
emphasised the phenomenon of 'world capitalism' as if the death or
irrelevancy of the nation-state had already been confirmed by the
existence of transnational corporations. In rejecting the crude forms of
'economism', mono-causal explanatory models of the crisis-collapse of
capitalist societies, etc., Marxists have not yet successfully developed
concepts which explain the nature of complex state institutions and the
interconnections between local, national and supra-national social
forces and organisations. Rather than write off the complex social
institutions operating at the local and national level, I argue that no
adequate understanding of current crises can be acquired, or radical
strategies developed, unless the complex roles of state institutions are
recognised. Hence I am concerned with breaking down overgeneralised
notions of the 'the State', 'world capitalism' and other traditional
concepts.

This book is the outcome of several years' research of political economic issues and participation in debates over radical strategy. Readers will find that I engage in simultaneous discourse with state theorists, political economists, sociologists and political activists. The book may be read in at least two ways. Those wishing to understand the theoretical and epistemological bases of my analysis of state institutions should pay close attention to the chapters in Part I. On the other hand, those readers who wish to gain a quick, but limited, understanding of my analyses of the role and nature of state institutions and critique of existing radical strategies can begin reading Parts II and III. The book is *not* a textbook, and various parts assume that the reader has a certain degree of familiarity with the issues discussed. Nevertheless, the book has an integrated and elaborate thesis developed over the three parts and I have tried to write in a style which is accessible to all the various audiences mentioned above. Special thanks go to Belinda Probert, who improved innumerable passages in the book and generally provided invaluable criticisms. I would also like to thank Tony Giddens for his valuable editorial help and constructive criticisms; Alan Roberts, Peter Beilharz and Julian Triado who laboured very hard over different versions of the book; Anne Doble and Rob Watts who commented upon a couple of chapters in an early draft; Susie Reichwald and Helen Lennox who spent long hours typing the different versions of the manuscript; Steven Kennedy at Macmillan for his help in producing the book. Finally, a special thank you to my mother Tania for her invaluable general support.

May 1983   B. F.

Definitions

State and State Institutions

Too many people use the term 'state' in a loose manner as designating everything from a whole society, a government, to a specific territory or executive officialdom. While this book devotes considerable space to analysing the nature and role of state institutions, two preliminary definitions are in order. First, I do *not* use the concept 'state' as a synonym for nation, society or country. Instead, I use the concepts 'nation-state', 'society' or 'country' whenever I discuss officially recognised territorial and social entities. Many societies or territories are recognised as being 'nation-states' but have no internal social unity, while others have unity but little or no independence. Second, I endeavour to avoid the use of the concept 'state' as a synonym for elected or non-elected government. The concept 'state institutions' designates all those non-privately owned and non-voluntary public institutions – whether administrative, legal, military, educational, cultural – as well as all those producing commodities or engaged in social welfare and other activities and services. The terms 'government' or 'regime' are used when referring to those hierarchically supreme elements within state institutions (at local or national levels) responsible for executive policy-making, e.g. the Cabinet, as opposed to the millions of workers employed in numerous state institutions.

1
Identifying the Problems

In 1972, while discussing issues in politics and aesthetics with Herbert Marcuse, I asked him whether he believed rock music should have a place in any future socialist society. Grimacing, he responded bitingly: 'I hope it withers away, preferably before the State'. Perhaps, Marcuse would have preferred even 'rock music' (*circa* 1972) to punk and new wave ten years later. But it is doubtful that he would have ever lost his strong desire to see 'the State' 'wither away'. Like many radicals, Marcuse used the term 'the State' to mean the repressive apparatuses of the army, police, courts, and the bureaucratic apparatuses of administration and representation. But contemporary state institutions comprise far more than these repressive and bureaucratic institutions which Marx and Lenin wished to see 'wither away'. As I will show later on, the very concept of 'the State' is a highly loaded and ideological concept – when used by either the Left or the Right. The aim of this book is to go beyond the concept of 'the State' and to examine what can or should 'wither away', if socialists are committed to a social order which maximises freedom and equality.

Never before have so many governments struggled to maintain their credibility in the face of widespread cynicism, disbelief, hopelessness and resignation. It is difficult to estimate whether governments are surviving deep-seated social crises because of mass support for their policies, or because inactive majorities have ceased to believe in the possibility of a better future. In fact, it is difficult to think of many other historical periods which have witnessed such a profound discrediting of dominant values and ideologies in so many countries. Despite the proliferation of numerous social movements actively fighting against all forms of oppression, exploitation and irrationality, bourgeois and Orthodox Marxist explanations of the nature of contemporary societies continue to dominate, despite their inability to motivate the masses, let alone resolve current crises.

In earlier decades, many people believed in the Soviet Union or China as 'new civilisations', or in the 'welfare state', 'higher education' and other such gradualist reforms as the path to equality, or in variations of Keynesian and monetarist policies which would bring back the 'affluent society' and end 'stagflation'. Today, it is mainly the 'faithful' or 'born again' who believe in the discredited panaceas of the past – which are still repackaged for present consumption. Apart from the active oppositional minorities in most countries, the majority remains relatively passive, suffering, or defensively opting for what they mistakenly believe to be survival tactics. As Brecht put it (while writing during the dark period of the Second World War): 'History shows that peoples do not lightly undertake radical changes in the economic system. The people are not gamblers. They do not speculate. They hate and fear the disorder which accompanies social change. Only when the order under which they have lived turns to an indubitable and intolerable disorder do the people dare, and even then nervously, uncertainly, again and again shrinking back in turn, to change the situation'.[1]

But what constitutes an intolerable disorder? The Solidarity movement emerged within a context of 'planned' disorder. The ruling party had created chaos in the name of 'rational planning'. But the recourse to Western technology and market mechanisms by so many Communist governments (as a substitute for socialist democracy) will fail just as surely as Tseng Kuo-Fan's attempt to save Confucianism from Western corruption failed during the nineteenth century. While the Confucian mandarins hoped that Western technology would protect the Confucian ethic (without contaminating it), the rulers of state institutions in communist countries preside over populations and party members who no longer believe in a strong and clear socialist ethic which is identifiable and distinct from the ever-changing party line – let alone an ethic capable of resisting 'Western decadence'. The vacuum created by the absence of a Marxist or socialist ethic in Communist countries was most visible during the debates within Solidarity (in 1981) over the alternative to bureaucratic state institutions. Would market mechanisms, democratic planning and/or self-management, or the complete destruction of state institutions clear up the mess created by party bureaucrats? Although the context was different, the confused answers by Solidarity members were not so different from the various proposals put forward by radical opponents of monetarism in capitalist countries. The unanimous ethical condemnations of poverty, unemployment, bureaucracy, inequality and repression are unfortunately not matched by any consensus about what should be the nature and role of state institutions in an alternative society - or whether there should be any state.

Rather than a contribution to the existing widespread cynicism and hopelessness, this book is an attempt to confront and evaluate some dominant misconceptions of what is called 'the State', and the political objectives derived from these misconceptions. Marx analysed the nature of capitalist production in order to overcome the inadequate views of the utopian socialists. It was not the utopian socialists' descriptions of the horrors of capitalism which Marx objected to, but rather their explanations of the causes, as well as the solutions which they advocated. The critique which Marx made of the utopian socialists has been made of Marx himself in recent decades. Writers on the Left have tried to construct a Marxist theory of state institutions (which Marx had not completed), while anti-Marxists have criticised the so-called naïveté of revolutionaries by pointing to the triumph of the bureaucrats over the revolutionaries once the fight at the barricades had been won.

Today, there is no shortage of written and audio-visual material depicting the horrors of poverty, unemployment, urban decay, nuclear threat, ecological destruction and mass oppression and discrimination. There is also no shortage of alternative policies such as expanded public sectors, workers' plans, co-operatives, self-managed communes, and numerous manifestos proclaiming the need for societies without oppression, discrimination and irrational waste. But how many of these alternative policies are based upon an adequate understanding of the nature and role of state institutions? How many of these alternative policies are based upon the mistaken beliefs - that expanded public sectors are compatible with private accumulation, that self-managed enterprises can resolve the major problems of social welfare and material distribution without state institutions, that socialism can guarantee maximum social equality and political freedoms without parliaments, courts, territorial defence and other institutions necessary for the over-coming of gross inequality and intolerance? At the moment many of the dominant conceptions of alternatives to capitalist and Communist societies are based upon varieties of market socialism or 'mixed economies' (e.g. a larger public sector), or at the other extreme upon some form of stateless socialism characterised by self-managed councils or other such alternatives to bureaucratic vanguard parties and social-democratic corporatism.

The desire for a society which can regulate itself without state institutions is shared by many people of the Left and the Right. Most anarchists, and many self-management socialists, share with conservative free enterprisers a belief in 'the State' as enemy number one. In reality, most defenders of laissez-faire favour the maintenance of repressive state apparatuses and all forms of state subsidies which protect or enhance private accumulation. On the opposite side, advocates of self-management are divided between those who oppose all forms of state institutions, and others who believe in the necessity of new socialist state institutions which will redistribute resources to regions and populations less fortunate. The whole debate amongst radicals over plan or market, decentralisation or central planning, ultimately boils down to one's position on the future role of state institutions and whether a more just and free society can exist without a state. Therefore, any political strategy which is based on superficial analyses of existing state institutions is most unlikely to be convincing when it comes to persuading people about the nature of any future societies. The viability of any socialist society is directly related to the comprehension of the present. Yet there can be little hope of a better future so long as fundamental misconceptions about the nature and role of state institutions continue to dominate the theory and practice of contemporary social movements.

Twenty years after the 'renaissance of Marxism', it is clear that the Left has not advanced significantly beyond orthodox theories of 'the State' first developed by Marx, Lenin and Gramsci (an issue I will discuss in Chapter 2). Certainly there have been invaluable critiques of economism and other simplistic accounts of the relationship between state institutions and capitalists. But most of the writings on 'the relative autonomy of the State', how capitalist states assist and defend private accumulation, the nature of Ideological State Apparatuses and other related contributions, have been attempts to revive and refine Marxism rather than put forward a radical reappraisal of the role and nature of states. Much of the energy invested in 'state theory' during the 1970s was directly or indirectly related to a defence or critique of 'Eurocommunist' political strategy. By this I mean that a focus on the role of states in maintaining bourgeois hegemony, and a refusal to reduce the 'political' to the 'economic', provided the theoretical justification for the strategy of gradual, proletarian 'counter-hegemony' within state institutions under the name of 'historical compromise' or 'alternative economic strategy'. While 'Eurocommunists' and 'Eurosocialists' have been distancing themselves from orthodox Marxism–Leninism, this has not been due to any radical reappraisal of the role and nature of states. On the contrary, many socialists have fallen back upon traditional bourgeois analyses of the role and limits of the 'public sector': witness for example the incorporation of recycled neo-Keynesian policies into what masquarade as 'alternative programmes'. Yet most revolutionary Marxists and anarchists have little reason to feel smug, as they have equally failed to come to grips with a world which no longer corresponds to the 'classical texts'.

Today we are witnesses to a perverse relationship between theory and practice. The revival and implementation of monetarist doctrine by the political Right leads one to ask: are these conservative ideologies cynically invoked (in public) by Thatcher, Reagan and others as justifications for policies which they privately defend in more ruthless terms? Or are conservatives sincerely, but naïvely pursuing a 'model' of private capitalist society which is unworkable, because it is a self-deluding ideological fiction? Similarly, we must ask of revolutionaries and reformers – when they picture the future states as playing an alternative role (in planning agreements, market socialism, etc.) or as altogether abolished (in models of self-management, council communism and various anarchist ideals) – is this window-dressing (in the case of 'Eurosocialists' and 'Eurocommunists' perhaps to disguise 'Eurocorporatism') or naïve unrealism (in the case of the advocates of 'stateless socialism')? While there is no shortage of critiques of key aspects of orthodox Marxism – for example, the problematical theories of 'crisis-collapse', the transformation of value into price, or the neglect of vital issues relating to gender, environment, bureaucratic authority, national movements and so forth – the 'renaissance of Marxism' has failed to produce a radical reconsideration of the traditional divisions between 'the State'. 'Civil Society' and 'the Economy'.

The classical Marxian notion of the capitalist mode of production fails to deal with all the non-market jobs and roles of state institutions. For example, it is well known that millions of people in capitalist societies work in state institutions or are dependent on state-run welfare schemes; it is also well known that most wage-workers are not blue-collar factory operatives. Yet many radical programmes are still largely based on models of the social division of labour which ignore the majority of non-surplus-value-producing workers – both paid and unpaid. These historically unreal radical programmes generally fail to address themselves to the enormous problem of how socialist societies could provide alternative employment and welfare provision to all existing state employees and dependents, when they advocate the abolition of state institutions.

While many conservatives promote an idealised and distorted conception of capitalist societies for defensive reasons, what excuse have radicals to offer for their misconceptions? If radicals continue, however sincerely, to base their alternatives to existing societies on a set of concepts often no more valid than the ideal-typical images of capitalism championed by their conservative opponents, the future is indeed bleak.

The gap which exists between the dominant conservative and radical notions of 'the State' on the one hand, and the reality and practices of institutions on the other hand, is partly attributable to the long neglect of state theory by most writers on the Left and Right. It was only in the 1970s that non-radical scholars rediscovered 'the State' and invested their energy in 'public policy' studies – many of which were simply exercises in crisis-management to protect capitalist interests. In contrast, most Marxian writings on state institutions were in fact expositions of Marx, Engels, Lenin, Gramsci, etc. on 'the State', rather than substantially new analyses of contemporary state institutions. As an invaluable revival of an almost lost tradition, these Marxian writings cannot be over-estimated. Nevertheless, the vast majority of radical analyses of capitalist states have left many vital areas (such as the future role of state institutions) almost untouched.

During the past thirty years we have already witnessed a 'crisis in Marxism' at two different levels. It was initially a crisis of the party – a crisis associated with the rejection of the *organisational* experiences and consequences of Stalinism at domestic and international levels. Recently this organisational crisis has been matched by a *methodological* crisis – a by-product of the 'renaissance of Marxism' itself. Once the old mechanical Marxism, as well as the dogma of Soviet Marxism, had been successfully challenged in the 1960s and 1970s, it was only a matter of time before every aspect of Marxism was challenged. Unfortunately, many people who totally rejected Marxism did so on superficial or uninformed grounds. Many of these same people found their real home on the political Right – e.g. the French 'new philosophes'. Those who remained committed to a socialist revolution, but who found significant aspects of Marx to be either wrong or insufficiently radical, have found themselves marginalised by many labour movements which have never really been very revolutionary.

The revival of radical state theory in the late 1960s went hand in hand with the growth of the New Left. But the boom in state theory had peaked by the end of the 1970s, as the 'Eurocommunist' parties failed to transform 'the relatively autonomous' apparatuses from within. In the early 1980s, state theory appeared to take a secondary role to the Left's preoccupation with immediate socio-economic policies designed to alleviate deep-seated stagnation and social crises. While the various 'Eurocommunist' and 'Eurosocialist' parties have not given up their earlier goal of the 'peaceful' transition from capitalism to socialism, there is a minimal amount of theoretical reflection about the role accorded to state institutions in most 'alternative programmes'. An empirical urgency appears to have silenced many in the Left as theoretical questions have been overwhelmed by the frenetic action of local struggles. Nearly all the local struggles against cuts in social welfare or rising unemployment are tied to national 'alternative programmes' espousing a variety of 'mixed economy' or anti-monopoly capital strategies. In the last part of this book I will examine important aspects of these 'alternative programmes' in order to show why these strategies are based on very inadequate assumptions about the nature of state institutions.

While the student movement, anti-war movement and 'counter-culture' of the 1960s opposed most forms of state authority, it is interesting to note how much of this opposition to state institutions gave way to the political strategies of transforming capitalist states from within. The optimistic anti-authoritarianism of the 1960s and the pedestrian, sombre caution of 'alternative programmes' of the 1970s and 1980s is perhaps well expressed by two authors writing fifty years earlier. In 1926, Paul Valery wrote in *The Persian Letters* that:

> Order is always a burden to the individual. Disorder makes him [*sic*] wish for the police or death. Such are the two extreme conditions in which human nature is not at ease. The individual's wish is for a perfectly enjoyable era, in which he [*sic*] is completely free, yet completely cared for. He [*sic*] finds it toward the beginning of the end of a social system.

> That moment between order and disorder is the reign of delight. Every possible advantage to be had from the regulation of powers and duties has been acquired, and now the first relaxations of the system are to be enjoyed. The institutions still stand. They are great and imposing. But, without showing any visible alteration, their splendid presence is now nearly all they are; their character is no longer sacred, or rather it is now merely sacred; criticism and contempt weaken and empty them of all subsequent value. The body politic quietly loses its futurity. It is the hour of general emjoyment and consummation.

The nearly always spectacular and voluptuous doom of a political structure is celebrated by a bonfire on which everything is heaped which fear had kept from being consumed before. State secrets, private shames, unspoken thoughts, long-repressed dreams, everything from the depths of those over-excited and joyously despairing hearts is brought out and thrown on the public mind.[2]

In the same year that Valery penned these optimistic and joyful aphorisms, Antonio Gramsci was arrested by the Italian Fascist regime. A few years later he was to write (in that often quoted passage from the *Prison Notebooks*), that the crisis in capitalist society 'consists precisely in the fact that the old is dying and the new cannot be born; in this interregnum a great variety of morbid symptoms appear'.[3] The contrast between Valery's and Gramsci's notions of a 'crisis in authority' and disintegration of the old order could not be greater. Valery's 'moment between order and disorder' seems to be a more appropriate description of the 1960s and early 1970s, when the New Left and the 'counter-culture' lit 'a bonfire' and celebrated everything which was 'brought out and thrown on the public mind'. On the other hand, Gramsci's 'interregnum' seems to fit the 'stagflation', terrorism, threat of nuclear holocaust, monetarism, 'Eurocommunism' and 'alternative economic programmes' of recent years. Marcuse's celebration of the 'counter-culture' and New Left in *An Essay on Liberation* (1969)[4] is light-years distant from Lasch's *The Culture of Narcissism* (1979)[5] or Foucault's preoccupation with surveillance and control in *Discipline and Punish* (1975).[6]

The current manifestation and preoccupation with 'morbid symptoms' in all spheres of political economy and culture has produced a climate in which political strategies and social relations are once again closely tied to particular hopes and fears derived from notions of 'the State'. Having been a diligent reader of state theory for the past decade, I will build my analysis of state institutions upon the numerous contributions made since Miliband and Poulantzas revived this neglected area in 1968.[7] My analysis departs from the majority of books and articles on state theory and capitalism in that I am not concerned with textual exposition of the ideas of Marx, Engels, Lenin and Gramsci; I do not subscribe to the political strategy of 'Eurocommunism' or 'alternative economic programmes' as do most writers who accept a version of 'the relative autonomy of the state' thesis; and I do not accept most of the prevailing negative interpretations of 'the State' which indiscriminately depict complex apparatuses as the epitome of repression. Finally, I reject as

naïve or unacceptable the dominant views (within the Left) of the role
(or even disappearance) of state institutions in future socialist societies
held by various self-management socialists, 'workerist' parties and market
socialists. But in order to construct an alternative to these perspectives,
it is first necessary to identify some of the major weaknesses in orthodox
and neo-Marxist analyses of state institutions.

Dominant Misconceptions of States

In a recent reflection upon some of the weaknesses in his very valuable
book – *The Fiscal Crisis of the State* – James O'Connor criticises the
functionalist formulations he made on the 'relationship between state,
economy and society'.[8] He goes on to note, with almost innocent amaze-
ment, that in Italy Marino Regini also 'cannot find any clear "logic of
action of the State" whether it be "capital logic" or "accumulation/
legitimation logic"'.[9] That O'Connor and many other Marxists should
only now discover this – that state institutions do not function according to clear, *a priori* criteria – symptomises the deeply intrenched misconceptions of 'the State' permeating contemporary schools of thought.
That O'Connor can reject this functionalism and yet continue to talk of
distinct spheres of 'state, economy and society', is evidence of the even
more deeply entrenched notions of 'the State', 'Civil Society' and 'the
Economy' restricting radical theory and practice – an unnecessary burden
I will discuss in the next chapter. For the moment, let me explain why
the functionalist misconception of a clear 'logic of action of the State'
goes hand in hand with the equally misconceived concepts of 'the State'
as ideal type, as subject, as thing, and as derivative part of capital.

The state as ideal type

Ideal types of the 'modern state', the 'capitalist state', the 'authoritarian
state', the 'totalitarian state', the 'exceptional state' and many other such
models only too evidently pervade conservative, liberal and radical
social theories alike. In non-Marxian political analyses, it is not unusual
to find many Weberians and others basing their social evaluations upon
a variation of the 'modern state' theme – which is synonymous with the
phenomena of bureaucratisation and 'modernity' – regardless of whether
these state institutions are in capitalist of communist countries.[10] A
state is supposedly not 'modern' unless it exhibits certain functional

characteristics of legal-rationality and so forth. Furthermore, many of these 'modern state' analyses depict workers in state institutions as essentially bureaucratic administrative personnel, thus overlooking the actual variety and complexity of state sector workers – occupationally, structurally and politically. There is a tendency to contrast a 'modern state' with a 'traditional state' – thus reducing 'the State' to an ideal type consisting of specific 'modern' roles and functions. Accusing radicals of naïveté, many so-called *Realpolitik* analysts use the Weberian concept of the 'modern state' to promote anti-socialist critiques based on paternalistic resignation to the existing organisational structures of the 'modern world'.

The desire to construct models and ideal types of 'the State' is no less keen in many radicals. Countless analyses of particular state institutions have been based on models of the 'capitalist state' which have been constructed out of the fragmentary comments made by Marx, Engels, Lenin and Gramsci. The historical specificity of a given capitalist society was forsaken in the quest to theorise the functions and roles of the 'capitalist-state-in-general'. These models of the 'capitalist state' paralleled the equally misconceived notion of a single world-wide 'capitalist mode of production' – a misconception I will discuss later on in the book. Instead of speaking of a 'traditional' and a 'modern state', many Marxists contrasted an ideal-typical 'feudal state' with an equally overgeneralised model of the 'capitalist state'.[11] Once these homogeneous, ahistorical models of 'the State' were accepted, it was not surprising to see a limited political practice fail to respond to or account for the actual complexity of historically specific state policies. Many radicals have taken as a finished reality the attempts of capitalist classes to create a boundaryless 'world mode of production' and a 'capitalist-state-in-general', and thus ignored the actual historical unevenness and non-identical nature of state institutions in so many capitalist societies. During the 1970s it was not unusual to read radical works on state theory which attempted to classify and construct model after model in neo-Marxian versions of bourgeois social science – thus failing to learn the lessons of ahistorical 'modernisation' theory and other such exercises in obsessive abstractionism. Each 'normal' or 'exceptional' capitalist state apparatus had to be constantly adjusted, in order to fit in with actual social relations which constantly transcended and defied the strait-jackets which Left- and Right-wing model-builders tried to impose in neat and functional terms.

The state as subject

The erroneous belief in a clear 'logic of action of the State' is particularly evident in all those analyses which misconceive complex social relations within state institutions and reduce the latter to subjects or persons. There are two common versions of this dominant misconception: (1) 'the State' as identifiable subject; and (2) 'the State' as impersonal subject. The confusion of state institution with the physical existence of prominent government figures or 'heads' of state, has a long tradition which periodically manifests itself in political assassination. To remove the 'head' of state is merely the extreme version of a popular misconception which blames individual leaders (e.g. Thatcher or Reagan) for class policies. The personification of 'the State' obscures the complexity of state institutions, blurs the differences between temporary, elected or non-elected leaders and long-standing institutions employing millions of people, and often gives rise to conspiratorial and irrational conceptions of social power.

It is ironic that the other common version of 'the State as subject' does not necessarily rely upon identifiable persons. The misconception of state institutions as impersonal subjects which can act, or have a will, takes various forms in bourgeois and Marxian social analyses. Each time the question, 'Does the State have autonomous power?' is posed, or endless comments about the so-called inherent interest of 'the State' are made, one can almost be sure that state institutions are being misconceived as subjects or actors which have an individual or collective will. Most liberal and conservative theories have focussed on the conflict between 'the State' and the individual. In social contract theory, 'the State as subject' implicitly or explicitly enters into a contract with other subjects. Similarly, in Marxian analyses (departing from Engels's observations), 'the State as subject' is clearly evident in the notion of the capitalist state as the 'ideal collective capitalist' – a super-subject which embodies the unified collective will of the capitalist class. This fictitious collective will elevates the 'ideal collective capitalist' above the intra- and inter-class struggles – of which state employees are constituent participants – and creates the false image of 'the State' as a unified, homogeneous actor. A related but even cruder misconception of state institutions is to be found in those radical analyses which reduce both 'the State' and 'capital' to subjects.[12] Thus, 'the State' or 'capital' compete or collude with one another; complex social relations are reduced to two super-subjects which have almost omnipotent powers to defeat or outmanoeuvre 'the proletariat'. The reality of administrative disorder, competing departments, clashes between local, regional and national state institutions is somehow overlooked. The even greater divisions between capitalists are also neglected. If 'capital' or 'the State' does this, or does that, the contradictory policies and practices emanating from both capitalist enterprises and state institutions disappear from view and only the 'monolithic powers' of the collective subject remain.

Finally, it is quite common for the party in Communist countries to be confused with the state apparatuses. When dissidents demand the emancipation of 'Civil Society' from 'the State', they are often demanding the end to one-party dominance over all facets of both social life and state activities, rather than the overthrow of 'the State as dictatorial subject'. The misconception of the conflict between 'the State as subject' and the individual thus has its parallel in Communist countries with the reduction of the party and 'the State' to a super-subject preventing pluralist institutions. When people are classified as 'enemies of the State', we know that they are merely enemies of the ruling party or group. My point is not to defend dictatorial party policies and bureaucratic powers in capitalist and Communist countries, but to indicate why misconceptions of state institutions as subjects effectively prevents people from either grasping the complexity of class or party oppression, or positing viable alternatives to existing state institutions – which are all reduced to the derogatory term 'the State'. For while particular individuals carry out policies in the name of 'the State', this does not at all mean that states have a collective will, interest or consciousness which transcends the living individuals who constitute state practice. If one ceases to believe that the structures have an 'impersonal' life of their own, or that identifiable persons are equivalent to whole states, then the misconception of 'the State as subject' loses its analytic and explanatory force.

The state as thing

The misconception of state institutions as instruments or things has been widely criticised by many writers during the 1970s.[13] To conceive of state institutions as passive things – which can be wielded or manipulated by the ruling classes in capitalist countries – is merely the opposite side of the same misconception which gave rise to 'the State as subject'. Instead of 'the State' as an active subject which intervenes and has a will of its own, 'the State as thing' is a passive, homogeneous entity. Once again, the complex social relations characterising a multitude of state institutions are obliterated. Once seen as a homogeneous thing, it is not surprising that state institutions are then misconceived as either being neutral (like the misconceived analyses of 'science and technology'), or mere puppets of external forces. Needless to say, a thing can be seized, smashed, made to work in a good or bad way, as there is no need to come to terms with the complex internal relations of actual state insti-- tutions as constituent elements of historical social forces.

The state as derivative part of capital

Linked to the misconception of states as things are many, but not all, those analyses which treat state institutions as by-products of class decisions made in the capitalist boardrooms, or of class struggle waged by workers. By concentrating on the accumulation of private capital, various Marxists such as Mandel, Baran and Sweezy tended to reduce state institutions to things. Focussing on what happened 'outside' state institutions, they reduced states to 'superstructural' epiphenomena of fundamental processes in the 'the Economy' or 'base'. State institutions have thus been depicted in many radical analyses as little more than appendages or instruments of monopoly capital or mere administrative 'superstructures' derived from 'the Economy'. I will later examine some of the weaknesses in orthodox Marxian concepts of capital accumulation, extended reproduction and the concept of 'the Economy' which fail to explain the nature and role of state institutions.

A new generation of 'derivative' theorists of state institutions emerged during the 1970s.[14] Largely free of the instrumental, mechanical and crude economic determinism of earlier generations of Marxists, they nevertheless attempted to explain the nature of state institutions by reference to the logic of capital accumulation. But the state institutions which came into existence before the domination of capitalist classes, and the social relations which preoccupy state administrations in the areas of racism, gender and sexuality, ecology and militarism – to name several important policy areas – cannot all be completely reduced to the process of capitalist accumulation. The vital mediation of private capitalist relations in all the latter areas does not in itself enable us to 'derive' state institutions solely from 'the logic of capital'. Most of the contemporary 'derivation' theorists are uncritical of Marx's analysis of capitalism and strive to construct a 'capital-logic' theory of 'the State'. In this respect, they leave the old categories of 'the State' and 'Civil

Society' largely untouched – and proceed to 'derive' state institutions from the classical 'anatomy of Civil Society' first attempted by Marx. Intentionally or unintentionally, state institutions continue to be misconceived as mere administrative 'superstructures' outside 'the Economy'. The millions of state workers who produce no surplus-value, and even those who produce commodities exchanged on the market, are somehow reduced to 'non-economic', 'superstructural' phenomena – even though it is highly unlikely that any single capitalist society would survive a 50 per cent reduction in state sector goods and services, let alone return to some mythical condition of pure capitalist accumulation.

In criticising the various misconceptions of states as ideal types, subjects, things or derivative parts of capital, I do not want to suggest that we cannot use the concept 'state' at all. I am mainly concerned to highlight the manner in which dominant misconceptions are embedded within that seemingly innocent generalisation – 'the State'. While it is perfectly reasonable to speak of the French state, or the Turkish state, or any such shorthand term which implies a set of historically specific social institutions and relations, it is quite another matter to invoke concepts of 'the State' and 'the capitalist State' as if they were self-evident or empirically visible and similar in all societies and over long periods of time. Once we begin to examine how particular state institutions in one society are based on specific historical social struggles or developments, it becomes increasingly important to understand why political strategies and solutions to current crises are not as easy to duplicate in other societies – as model-builders would have us believe. The history of the Second, Third and Fourth Internationals has been a history of domination by generalities such as 'the capitalist State' or the 'world capitalist mode of production'. Outside the Left, the generalisation of 'the State' has been used to conjure up images either of an impartial 'umpire' defending the interests of all citizens, or of a quintessential tyrant constantly threatening the individual.

The immoral/moral/and amoral state

In most non-Marxist political theories, 'the State' is often represented as the embodiment of morality or immorality. For example, in liberal theories 'the State' is admonished to 'keep out of the bedroom', while in contrast, conservatives wish 'the State' to protect 'decency' by enforcing censorship and strict moral guardianship. Fascists have proclaimed 'the State' as the highest moral subject, whereas liberals and anti-socialists have warned against the tyrannical immorality of the 'collectivist State' and the 'totalitarian State'. What is common to many of these theories is the depiction of state institutions as passive things which should not interfere in the affairs of private citizens, or as active subjects which defend or advance the highest moral code. Whether 'the State' is depicted as a good or bad moral subject, most non-Marxian theories pay scant attention to the social classes dominating state institutions and instead convey the impression that it is 'the State' – as an autonomous subject – which is to be blamed for unacceptable policies or praised for upholding the 'public interest'.

In contrast to the moral/immoral view of 'the State', an influential tradition of *Realpolitik* analysis puts forward the cynical and 'pragmatic' misconception of state institutions as amoral subjects. The belief that states are guided by an inherent amoralism, known and justified as 'reasons of state', goes back to Machiavelli's *The Prince*. Whereas Machiavelli was writing for a real subject – a Florentine prince – no complex set of contemporary state institutions can be reduced to a single subject which determines policy according to some amoral logic of 'pure power' or 'survival'. The moment one identifies actual people in different departments, parliaments, statutory bodies, nationalised industries, educational institutions – to name just a few of the numerous apparatuses which make up capitalist states – we need to ask the following questions: do all the people working in the above institutions have identical views? If not, why is it that certain individuals or social class representatives have more power to make state policy? Why do certain elements or institutions within a particular national state complex (e.g. a treasury of defence department) have more power than other apparatuses of the same national state structures? Who or what determines which people are eligible to make state policies? How did the people who made these rules manage to dominate state institutions in the first place? And finally, how do these people maintain and justify their dominance of state institutions, assuming there is freedom to question these decision-makers in the first place?

While many politicians may justify policies in opportunistic terms, this does not mean that there is a homogeneous, coherent internal logic governing 'the State'. The onus is on all *Realpolitik* amoral analysts to show why particular so-called 'reasons of state' are not in fact merely ideological justifications for specific class, individual or group interests – rather than the autonomous interests of 'the State'. Furthermore, the belief that a subject – 'the State' – exercises 'pure power' or 'pure force' is equally erroneous. *Realpolitik* analysts would have us believe that state goods, services and policies all flow from amoral 'reasons of state', rather than from social struggles (involving conflicting moral priorities) over the allocation of resources or suppression or tolerance of alternative policies. To elevate 'the State' to a position above moral conflict is to obscure the reality of social struggle which involves state apparatus workers as much as all other citizens. Ultimately, the ideological distortion of state institutions into inherently amoral, self-serving subjects is aimed at predetermining the future – as it is claimed *all* states will be governed by cynicism (or 'reasons of state') despite the naïve beliefs and expectations of democrats and socialists.

The state as the epitome of repression

In recent years, an avalanche of works has submerged both radical and conservative movements with the image of state institutions as unremitting vehicles of repression and tyranny. So many writers have focussed on the way states develop surveillance, or interfere in every facet of 'private' life, that the history of the modern world appears as the unfolding of a bureaucratic, paternalistic monster. The 'therapeutic State', the 'Behemoth', the concepts of 'tutelage', 'governmentality', 'iron cage' and depersonalisation and 'narcissism'[15] all confirm – in subtle or crude terms – the suffocation and loss of individual autonomy which 'the State' as super-subject inherently promotes. I would like to emphasise very strongly that I am not trying to deny or cover up all the numerous forms of repression, bureaucratic controls, pain, isolation, depersonalisation and trivialisation of existence which writers such as Foucault depict. Rather, in criticising such interpretations of state institutions, I am rejecting the one-sided historical (and often ahistorical) analyses of life since the eighteenth century as the history of negative, 'rationalising' and domineering forms and structures.

Although radical critics of the prison, school and hospital, or of 'narcissism' and 'therapeutic paternalism', are strong opponents of the conservative forces which also attack 'big government', there is a practical convergence here between radicals and conservatives. This 'convergence' is to be seen in the one-dimensional attacks made upon hard-won social welfare services – because they are all supposedly forms of 'tutelage' or bureaucratic paternalism. When the unemployed and the poor fight to retain even these meagre and far from humane services, the limits of the abstract theories of 'the State' as the epitome of repression are revealed. Not only is it wrong to reduce all state-run services and facilities to manifestations of 'unfreedom' or 'rationalisation', but the critics of 'the State' as super-subject which crushes the individual ego are left with a chasm between the awful present and a better future. For if contemporary history is really the unrelenting, inherent unfolding of bureaucracy, surveillance or whatever, then the only hope for the future is a society without any states, administration or nation-wide institutions. I will later argue that this concept of stateless socialism will probably only guarantee unfreedom and inequality. For the causes of current problems are not reducible to an abstract notion of 'the State' as some independent bureaucratic entity. Only detailed historical analysis of each particular state institution, the delivery and administration of goods and services, and the definition of social and individual problems (and their causes) will enable us to evaluate social relations rather than abstract 'states'. Despite all the horrific practices of state institutions, in many contexts it is both misleading and politically dangerous to attribute contemporary social problems to some inherent 'logic' of repression unavoidably associated with the abstract generalisation known as 'the State'.

The state as reproducer of capitalist hegemony

Until very recently, the dominant view amongst most Marxists – whether they were followers of Gramsci, the Frankfurt School, Althusser or Soviet Marxism – was that the 'capitalist State' existed solely to defend and reproduce the capitalist mode of production. This unambiguous functionalism was conveyed in moral and amoral analyses. In moral terms, Marxists analysed all the practices of state institutions in maintaining alienation, reification, authoritarian social and legal rules, racism, sexism and general cultural and moral impoverishment of the working class. In amoral terms, structural Marxists – rejecting the moral critiques of 'humanists' – proceeded to analyse state institutions in terms of the roles and functions they played on behalf of capitalists. Neither 'humanists' or 'anti-humanists' devoted much energy to analysing the contradictory roles and practices of state institutions – because most Marxists subscribed to misconceived notions of 'the State' as ideal type, subject, thing or derivative part of capital. Consequently, the struggles which resulted in new state services, laws and other important gains, were nearly always depicted in negative or functional terms as 'band-aids' for capitalism, irrelevant reforms, or merely forms of co-optation of the proletariat. It was only in the late 1970s – after the counter-offensive waged by monetarists – that the moral and amoral reproductive functionalism was slowly rejected. Two important contributions to a richer, more complex analysis of capitalist state institutions emerged: first, an examination of the historical differences between capitalist societies in order to understand why socio-political struggles have resulted in significantly different levels of social welfare, legal rights, etc. (both within the OECD, and between the OECD and non-OECD capitalist countries); and second, an examination of what is meant by 'bourgeois hegemony' – that is, whether the dominant relations in capitalist countries were being unambiguously reproduced by state institutions – or whether in fact there were continual struggles over the administrative definition of citizens, rights and social powers. More will be said about the contradictory role of state institutions, when I discuss the historical development of local and national Electoral Processes in Part II.

In short, most of those radical theories, in which state institutions can only reproduce capitalist hegemony, have been unable to explain why it is that capitalist classes have so vehemently attacked the existence of particular state-run goods and services. In fact, state institutions in capitalist countries have not just reproduced capitalist relations – although this has been their predominant role – but they have also undermined the reproduction of dominant social values and practices. Bourgeois relations are not in a static, ready-finished form which state administrators (and the bourgeoisie themselves) are consciously agreed upon and reproduce. There is no ahistorical 'capitalist State' which exists above or outside social struggles and consciously reproduces capitalist relations in an all-knowing manner as a super-subject.

Private capitalist production presupposes the existence of private property, the existence of wage-workers who do not own or control the means of production and distribution and the domination of societies by commodity-exchange production. But detailed historical analysis shows that no two capitalist societies possess or have possessed a common 'political order' or set of state institutions. It is the very non-identical nature of state institutions in capitalist societies which I will analyse in later chapters. Capitalist businesses have flourished under monarchies, republics, fascist regimes, military dictatorships and other forms of states. In so far as each of the latter forms of state institutions defended and assisted capitalist classes (thus maintaining capitalist social relations as the dominant social order), it is legitimate to speak of these states as capitalist states. Beyond this general characteristic of defending and reproducing capitalist social classes there is such an enormous variety of roles carried out by particular state institutions, such an enormous variety of historically specific structures and set of practices within state institutions, that it is not possible to reduce this historical complexity to a general model of 'the capitalist state'. As capitalist classes do not have consistent or uniform interests – locally, nationally or internationally – it is necessary to analyse the specific social conflicts between and among classes in order to understand the contradictory roles and structures of local, national and supra-national state institutions.

A Brief Outline of Main Themes to be Discussed

This book is divided into three parts – each part having a central theme. In Part I I endeavour to show why key categories in Marxian and radical political economy (such as Departments I and II, 'world-system' and long waves) are either in need of serious revision, or should be completely rejected. Too many writers are still content to rely upon basic concepts such as 'Civil Society', without fully probing the adequacy of their explanatory power. Marxists and other radicals not only divide social life into arbitrary and confusing realms known as 'the State', 'Civil Society' and 'the Economy', but they also derive their explanations of the causes of crises from these arbitrary realms. State institutions are constantly discussed as if they are merely non-economic repressive and ideological administrative 'superstructures' which 'intervene' in, yet are not part of this vague realm called 'Civil Society'. The private sector is equated with 'the Economy' and the 'political business cycle' is conceived in narrow economistic and positivistic terms. Hence, the whole thrust of Part I is to show how many radicals perpetuate the false dichotomy between the 'economic' and the 'political' by largely ignoring the vital and inseparable roles of state institutions in 'civil life'.

In Part II I develop a new set of categories which attempt to overcome the artificial divisions between 'the State', 'Civil Society' and 'the Economy'. Within what I call Electoral, Production, Credit and Food Production Processes, are to be found social relations which are organised either within state-run or privately-run institutions. Social change is not determined by 'laws of motion' or other monocausal theories. Each Process (or set of institutions and relations) has its own history and is to be found at local, regional, national and supra-national levels. The interrelated nature of each Process is established in direct contrast to the homogenising and blurring models of 'world capitalism'. More importantly, I try to show how each local, national and supra-national Process is desynchronised with other local, national and supra-national Processes. The inability of capitalist classes or their agents to 'synchronise' or co-ordinate social relations within separate Processes is a principal cause of contemporary social crises. In short, the new concepts of Electoral, Production, Credit and Food Production Processes attempt to show the integral role of state institutions in all major facets of life without reducing all social phenomena to either 'state' or 'mode of production'; nor do I discard the many valuable insights Marxism has to offer, despite the serious weaknesses in Marxian analyses of states. This book is not another anti-Marxian apology for 'post-industrial society'.

Once the nature of local, national and supra-national Processes is established, I proceed to show how the desynchronisation of Electoral, Production, Credit and Food Production Processes affects existing radical alternatives to capitalist and official Communist societies. Part III is subdivided into chapters which critically evaluate the viability of 'alternative programmes' proposed by many European and non-European socialists. The hegemony of traditional categories such as 'Civil Society' also leads, I argue, to equally dangerous and unreal expectations as to the viability of various forms of stateless socialism based on workers' councils, self-sufficient collectives and other 'anti-state' organisational forms. At the moment, radicals are either subscribing to well-intentioned but indiscriminate forms of 'anti-statism', or pragmatic and illusory notions of market socialism as the alternative to capitalist and Communist societies. One of the main theses which I argue for, is the need to postulate an alternative to contemporary capitalist societies which comes to terms with the existing division of labour (especially the millions of people who work in state institutions), and the role of state institutions in socialist planning and redistribution.

I have no desire to defend existing state institutions, but I do believe that any socialist society which is based on the absence of new socialist state institutions (which I will discuss), or on variations of 'mixed' plan and market, is doomed to failure. The vague socialist ideals about 'direct producers' running society, the geographical ambiguity as to whether a socialist society will be local, nation-wide or on a world scale, the questions as to whether there will be laws, police, central planning, decentralised control or one world-centre are also discussed. The concepts of Electoral, Production, Credit and Food Processes are developed, not simply to expain better the nature of capitalist societies, but equally importantly, to comprehend which social relations could lead to a perpetuation or revival of the crises resulting from the desynchronisation of Processes – a condition which, ironically, socialists may imagine they are overcoming. In other words, how can any socialist society avoid the horrors of existing capitalist and Communist societies, maximise egalitarian self-determination and freedom for all races and gender, minimise or eradicate the abuse of the environment and of other species, transcend technical rationality, and yet have responsible social administration and the viable reproduction of socially determined goods and services? In recent decades radicals have attacked the failure of the Old Left to change its views on gender, environment, technology, authority, unpaid labour and so forth. But how can these radical new needs and social relations be realised if we are not clear about the viability of self-managed institutions, their co-ordinating mechanisms, or their geographical sovereignty? If we do not have socialist state institutions: will wage-labour continue to exist? Will coercive institutions be necessary? Will representative structures be abolished? Will internationalism and non-parochialism be attainable via small, self-managed communes? Will scarcity, intolerance, institutionalised discrimination and national chauvinism, somehow 'wither away' with 'the State'? I argue that these vital questions cannot be left floating in mid-air or postponed until after the revolution. State institutions will *not* 'wither away', and therefore the key issue is: what kind of new state institutions can we build which will maximise socialist values and yet prevent the recurrence of the 'morbid symptoms' resulting from the crises of desynchronised Processes in contemporary capitalist societies?

To recognise the role and nature of states is therefore to come to terms with social institutions which continue to remain mystifying. It has taken decades for Marxists to reject the vulgar economism which reduced states to 'superstructures' hanging 'above' 'the Economy' – as 'heaven' did above life on earth for fundamentalist Christians. The next step is to recognise how everyday life is reproduced within particular state institutions. The retention of various traditional categories of 'the State' deflects attention away from entrenched social forces, maintains illusions about how these class forces can be either overthrown, or co-opted into 'transitional' alliances, and perpetuates illusions about the possible 'withering away of the State'. While it is not possible to discuss all aspects of state institutions in one book, I hope that my critique of various dominant concepts and theories will prove useful to a wide range of theorists and activists.

Part I
Abandoning the 'Sacred Cows' of Marxian Orthodoxy

2
Against the 'Holy Trinity' of 'The State', 'Civil Society' and 'The Economy'

Just as the concepts 'democracy' or 'socialism' have been abused and muddied, so too the traditional concepts of 'the State', 'Civil Society' and 'the Economy' have lost their original meaning and their structural relationship with one another. While many people may be clear about what 'the State' or 'the Economy' means, there is much confusion concerning the realm of 'Civil Society'. From the seventeenth century on, the notion of *'civitas'*, 'commonwealth', 'Civil Society', *'bürgerliche Gesellschaft'* gained prominence in the writings of Hobbes, Locke, Kant, Smith, Hegel, Marx and many others. 'Civil Society' has been depicted as a realm where private property, labour, class divisions and all relations to do with the market are manifested. It has also been characterised as a realm which is separate from 'the State', the private 'family' and 'the Economy'. Kant and others discussed 'Civil Society' as a 'public sphere' where it was hoped man [sic] could exercise his reason. 'Civil Society' was thus seen as being synonymous with the market or 'the Economy', or on the other hand, as a sphere which linked the family and individual to 'the State' via spiritual and rational discourse, toleration and civic duty. Depending on whether one saw 'Civil Society' as (a) conflict-ridden market relations – the war of all against all; (b) a natural outgrowth with principles of its own; or (c) a realm where reason or religious toleration could flourish in opposition to the absolutist monarch and/or feudal corporate structure, so too particular notions of 'the State' followed suit. For example, one could believe 'the State' was independent of 'Civil Society' and 'the Economy' and existed 'above' the self-interested relations in the latter realms. Or one could believe, as Marx did, that 'Civil Society' 'evolves directly from production and commerce and in all ages forms the basis of the state'.[1]

While early political economists such as Adam Smith, or philosophers such as Locke and Hegel, essentially praised or defended the newly emerging bourgeois 'Civil Society', socialist revolutionaries have been preoccupied with analysing capitalist societies in order to overthrow their market relations. In recent decades, non-Marxists have departed from the orthodoxy of eighteenth-century 'social contract' theory by adding new categories such as 'public sector', 'private sector', 'political system' and so forth. These new categories have only compounded the confusion surrounding the 'holy trinity'. Whether 'the State' is the same as the 'public sector', whether the 'political system' comprises both institutions within 'Civil Society' and 'the State', or whether 'the Economy' implies only the 'private sector' – these are merely a few of the prevalent confusions dominating contemporary social science. With Marxists the confusion and disagreements concerning the nature and role of 'the State', let alone the relationships among the 'holy trinity' (e.g. can one still speak of distinct realms of 'the State' and 'Civil Society'?) are perhaps even more consequential than the confusions within the ranks of non-Marxists. This is because the socio-political goals put forward by radicals are inseparably tied to the partial or total rejection of existing institutions and social values.

Since the 1960s, radicals of many varieties have continually attacked 'statist' notions of socialism. Some equate 'statism' with Leninism/ Stalinism; other critics see anything short of complete decentralised self-management as 'statist'. Now, all critiques of 'statist' solutions involve a notion, explicit or implicit, of 'boundaries' (or lack of 'boundaries') between 'the State', 'Civil Society' and 'the Economy'. Alvin Gouldner and Agnes Heller, for example, have expressed a very strong anti-Leninist/anti-statist perspective. Writing in the light of experiences of Stalinism, Gouldner argued: 'No emancipation is possible in the modern world, however, without a strong civil society that can strengthen the public sphere and can provide a haven from and a center of resistance to the Behemoth state'.[2] Or as Heller warns: 'Where there is a state, the public and private spheres can be unified only at the cost of tyranny. Whoever wants to avoid tyranny has to reconsider what kind of relations have to exist between state and society, the public and private spheres'.[3]

If one did not know that these words date from the 1970s, one could be forgiven for thinking that Gouldner and Heller were writing in the seventeenth or eighteenth centuries. Both are anchored firmly within the traditional dichotomy of 'the State' and 'Civil Society' – especially the Kantian concern with a rational 'public sphere'. It is a typology which was originally based on the defence of private property – and hence individual liberty – against 'the State'. If tyranny is the inevitable outcome of the 'unification' of the 'public' and 'private' spheres, then either socialism cannot excape becoming synonymous with the 'Behemoth state' (if traditional notions of 'public' and 'private' are retained), or else the 'private sphere' (that is 'Civil Society' and 'the Economy') must be completely redefined, abandoning the bourgeois definition which rested upon the material basis of private property.

It would be a serious error to think that a dispute over the definition or nature of 'the State', 'Civil Society' and 'the Economy' can only be an abstract semantic game. The events in Poland during 1980 and 1981 were 'concrete' illustrations of how theoretical concepts involving the nature of 'the State' and 'Civil Society' may vitally affect social struggles. A number of Polish supporters of Solidarity, as well as sympathetic foreign observers, described the emergence and campaigns of Solidarity as a battle of 'Civil Society Against the State' – to use the title of one recent article.[4] People discussed the Solidarity movement in terms of 'Civil Society' reconstituting itself, of a new 'social contract' which would clearly establish an autonomous sphere of 'Civil Society' which 'the State' had not been able to dissolve in previous decades.[5]

While it was clear at one level that the Solidarity movement was struggling for greater self-management and democratic control against a corrupt and dictatorial party and bureaucracy, it was not clear what was meant by the term 'Civil Society', or how this 'sphere' could be separate from 'the State' and 'the Economy'. For Solidarity was not based on private-property owners, wishing to re-establish a 'private sector' which would be autonomous *vis-à-vis* 'the State'. On the contrary, the vast majority of Solidarity members (apart from small farmers) were struggling for control of institutions which were all part of 'the State' – that is, state-owned enterprises, cultural institutions, universities, social welfare centres and so forth. Solidarity members (apart from the Church), along with the ruling party and the bureaucracy, were simultaneously part of 'the State', of 'Civil Society' and of 'the Economy', as defined in classical bourgeois and Marxist terms.

The struggle to redefine 'private' and 'public' spheres in Poland has been brutally if temporarily interrupted. Yet the continued use of concepts such as 'Civil Society', to describe a 'sphere' in society which is free of party domination, leaves many theoretical and practical problems unsolved. It is not unusual to find many opponents of one-party dictatorship proclaiming the need for pluralist social institutions. As state institutions are dominated by the ruling party, 'the State' is depicted as a monolithic subject which swallows 'Civil Society'. But state institutions entail far more than political administration.

Consequently, it is important not to confuse the demand for freedom from the party, with freedom from 'the State'. For 'the State' and 'Civil Society' are not opposing subjects.[6] Free institutions can only be created by liberating enterprises, cultural institutions and welfare institutions (which are all part of communist states) from dictatorial party control rather than from 'the State' as a self-interested subject. It is clear that Solidarity and other movements in Communist countries have actually attempted to gain control of all state-owned enterprises and cultural institutions (in the name of 'Civil Society') and to redefine the relationship between 'public' and 'private', while adhering to traditional bourgeois categories. These categories of 'the State', 'Civil Society' and 'the Economy' are not even relevant to capitalist societies – let alone to countries such as Poland.

If one wishes to retain a clearly defined 'private' sphere which is not equivalent to the 'private' sphere in capitalist societies, then it is imperative that social relations within this new socialist 'private' sphere be based on values and material conditions which do not derive their meaning from the ownership of private wealth. Many characteristics of 'bourgeois individualism' cannot be simply transferred to a socialist society, for they are rooted in a set of specific historical relations supposedly delineating the boundaries between 'the State' and 'Civil Society'. I will later attempt to show why even capitalist societies, and the state institutions within these societies, do not conform to the ideal-typical categories of 'the State', 'Civil Society' and 'the Economy'.

The continued use of categories such as 'Civil Society', I would contend, conjures up false political objectives which divert people away from the difficult tasks of confronting and changing the nature of both capitalist and Communist societies. Several potentially incompatible objectives arise from the plethora of anti-statist/anti-Leninist reformulations of socialist strategy and ethics in capitalist and Communist countries. As there is no agreement between various anarchist, self-management, Trotskyist, 'Eurocommunist', 'Eurosocialist' and other movements concerning the immediate or long-term objectives of socialist struggle, any particular definition of 'the State', 'Civil Society' and 'the Economy' poses the following problems: can one have a 'socialist private sphere'? Can one have a pluralist political system? Can one retain the existence of a pluralist democracy without state institutions based on constitutions, laws, rights, police and so forth? How could equality be maximised in a self-managed society if pluralism guaranteed private-property rights? How could freedom and equality be achieved in a self-managed society, if this society had no state institutions to defend the underprivileged and redistribute the unequal resources which were self-managed? If self-management without socialist state institutions became the dominant organisational principle, how could there be any retention of a 'public sphere' (and socialist morality)? Would society revert to a new form of 'feudalism' if it were reorganised into an infinite number of self-referring, decentred communities? These and many other questions are both abstract and empirically immediate. The answers we give depend, implicitly or even explicitly, on whether we accept or reject deeply-entrenched notions about the nature of 'the State', 'Civil Society' and 'the Economy'.

Marxist Disagreements over the Concept of 'Civil Society'

Although socialists have used the concepts 'Civil Society' and 'the State' very extensively, little has actually been written about these 'spheres' – apart from the numerous expositions of what Marx or Gramsci said about 'Civil Society', etc. It is possible to identify within socialist theory several broad conceptions of the relations between 'the State', 'Civil Society' and 'the Economy'. The first school, an orthodox Marxism, tends to follow the 'base/superstructure' division, which equates the market (or 'the Economy') with 'Civil Society', while 'the State' is reduced to the political/administrative 'superstructure'. The second school, represented by writers such as Poulantzas, rejects the division between 'Civil Society' and 'the State' and regards this artificial division as merely a 'juridical' distinction.[7] According to this latter school, people may be legally defined as independent, voting citizens, but this 'juridical' distinction only disguises the class nature of society. Instead of analysing the relation between 'Civil Society' and 'the State', Poulantzas, Althusser and others emphasised the dominant 'mode of production' which necessitated a 'juridical' division of 'public' and 'private' life. By focussing on the dominant capitalist 'mode of production', the family, school, church and media were all reconceptualised as 'ideological state apparatuses' whose roles were functionally to reproduce the capitalist 'mode of production'. Within this framework, 'Civil Society', 'the State' and 'the Economy' are all blended together; not only are the differences between privately-owned businesses and state-owned enterprises lost, but all institutions are reduced to a part of 'the State' – or, conversely, 'the State' is reduced to a part of the 'mode of production'.[8] While the first school of orthodox Marxism posits a mechanical and arbitrary division between the 'base' and the 'super-structure', the second school, in its attack on 'mechanical Marxism', virtually obliterates the differences between state apparatuses and other social institutions.

How 'Civil Society' and 'the State' interpenetrate has also been analysed by Habermas, Negt, Kluge and other German Marxists.[9] Writing in the late 1950s and early 1960s, Habermas sought to come to terms with the structural change of the 'public sphere' (*Öffentlichkeit*) under the conditions of 'late capitalism'. This 'public sphere' was seen as an institutionally-organised 'space' (consisting of journals, political movements, etc.) where 'public opinion' manifested itself. Standing between the private organisation of material production and private social life on the one hand, and the organisational form of state institutions on the other hand, the early bourgeois 'public sphere' mediated the relationship between 'the State' and 'Civil Society' (market) without being equivalent to either. According to Habermas, it is the growth of monopoly capitalism and the 'social welfare state mass democracy' which results in the transformation of the 'public sphere'; large corporate institutions interact with state institutions to construct or manufacture a new 'public sphere' via 'public relations' professionals. Technology and science become the new ideology as private social life is repoliticised due to mass 'state intervention'. Habermas's analysis of the bourgeois 'public sphere' led other writers, such as Negt and Kluge, to argue that he had overlooked the emergence of an alternative proletarian 'public sphere' which opposed the dominant bourgeois 'public sphere'.[10] Thus, while the concept of 'public sphere' illuminated important aspects of bourgeois hegemony, it did not radically challenge the traditional categories of 'Civil Society', 'the State' and 'the Economy'. Because the category 'public sphere' made it possible to focus on questions of 'public reason' – e.g. symbolic structures, public discourse, manipulation, legitimation procedures and so forth – little attention was paid to whether 'the Economy' was synonymous with the private market ('Civil Society') or whether it also embraced millions of state workers and state institutions. The concept of 'public sphere' was too ambiguous. In focussing on the development of the capitalist 'culture industry', the socialisation of hitherto private family practices by the 'welfare state' and so forth, the analysts of '*Öffentlichkeit*' fluctuated from a position which saw no differences between state institutions and society (given the new and multiple forms of interpenetration), to one which disputed the existence of a single dominant mass culture or 'public sphere', thus raising the possibility that several sub-cultures or 'public spheres' could co-exist.

In Habermas's later works such as *Legitimation Crisis*, the separate realms of 'the State', 'Civil Society' and 'the Economy' are reconceptualised into system theory concepts of the 'political sub-system', 'socio-cultural sub-system' and 'economic sub-system'. While there are exchanges between each 'sub-system', they are nevertheless subjected to a different organising principle and a different type of crisis. For example, 'the State' or 'political sub-system' can experience a rationality crisis, while the 'socio-cultural sub-system' or 'Civil Society' can experience a motivation crisis. However, 'the State' cannot experience an economic crisis, and the 'economic sub-system' cannot experience a legitimation crisis. This artificial compartmentalisation of social relations perpetuates the old base/superstructure dichotomy without the mechanistic pitfalls or economic determinism of vulgar Marxism. In trying to come to terms with the complexity of contemporary state institutions, Habermas moves beyond monocausal crisis theory without moving beyond the traditional view of state institutions as mere political/administrative 'superstructures'. I will discuss some of the weaknesses of this crisis theory in chapter 10.

Finally, another school (which is particularly influenced by Gramsci), also attempted to come to terms with the seemingly overlapping relations between 'Civil Society' 'the State' and 'the Economy'. Authors such as Anderson[11] and Urry[12] reject the simple dichotomy of 'base' and 'superstructure' as well as the reductionism implied in all-embracing concepts like 'Ideological State Apparatuses'. Instead, 'Civil Society' is conceived as mediating between 'the State' and 'the Economy' playing even more complicated roles. For example, John Urry argues that there are 'three different aspects of civil society: the sphere of circulation, the sphere of reproduction and the sphere of struggle'.[13] From this perspective Urry sees the 'circuits interlinking civil society and the state ... as complex and contradictory, and therefore that notions of base/superstructure or of the economic/political/ideological, should be placed once-and-for-all in the dustbin of history'.[14] While Urry's goal of a non-reductionist analysis is admirable, he actually works with the very dichotomy between 'the economic' and 'the political' which he wants to consign to the 'dustbin of history'. There is evident in the very title of his book (*The Anatomy of Capitalist Societies, The Economy, Civil Society and the State*) a concept of 'the Economy' as essentially a 'private' economy which 'the State' vitally assists and protects, but from which it is clearly distinct.

Before I consider further this dichotomy of 'the economic' and 'the political', I will note how both schools – the analysts of the 'public sphere', and writers such as Anderson and Urry – shift their emphasis away from a clearly-defined realm or sphere of 'Civil Society', to a context or situation of perpetual flux, mediation and interconnection. It is not clear what belongs to 'the State' and what remains 'private' or part of 'Civil Society', nor whether these traditional categories have any real meaning at all following their alleged transformation in the period of 'monopoly capitalism'.

The continued use by Marxists of categories which divide societies into realms of 'Civil Society', 'the State' and 'the Economy' clashes with their admirable critique of the artificial bourgeois division between 'the economic' and 'the political'. When Vincent Navarro asserts the 'need to break with the bourgeois distinction between political and economic, public and private, political and civil, objective and subjective struggles',[15] he simply repeats a call made by Marxists for decades – without any real changes in their fundamental way of analysing capitalist states. Navarro himself reverts to the old division between 'the economic' and 'the political', by narrowly defining states as being concerned only with 'technical–administrative' functions, 'mediating and consensual' functions, and 'coercive' functions.[16] Similarly, Urry can provide a good critique of the 'state-derivation' theorists, yet go to the other extreme – and exclude capital-accumulation apparatuses – by reducing 'the State' to simply a unified, coercive, bureaucratic, law-applying apparatus determined by class conflict.[17]

An even clearer example of how unable many Marxists are to overcome the dead weight of the past, appears in a recent article by Ellen Meiksins Wood – 'The Separation of the Economic and Political in Capitalism' – which the editors of *New Left Review* hailed as 'an original and far-reaching investigation'.[18] Wood, like many Marxists, ably shows that the private-production process has a 'political' and 'juridical' dimension; yet she has a typical blind spot when it comes to understanding the nature of state institutions. According to Wood, capitalism is marked by a 'specialized economic sphere', and 'the State' is something 'which stands *apart* from the economy even though it *intervenes* in it'.[19] One wonders which century she and other Marxists are living in. Somehow, the mass employment of millions of workers, in state institutions and in the production of goods and services by states, is conceived only in 'political–administrative–coercive–ideological' terms, while 'the Economy' remains synonymous with the market, 'Civil Society' or the 'capitalist mode of production'.

In rejecting the separate and artificial realms of 'the Economy' and 'the State', it is not necessary to cease speaking of 'the economic' or 'the political' provided that one does not equate 'the political' solely with activities in state institutions or 'the economic' solely with activities in the market. Since the 1960s, we have been used to thinking of 'the political' as being much more than party politics or the actions carried out by state administrators. Just as the 'personal is political', so too, we must broaden our understanding of 'the economic' to include unpaid labour in the home as well as the millions of workers employed in state institutions who produce a large variety of goods and services. Rather than constantly modify and redefine the 'holy trinity', it is, I would contend, far better to abandon these traditional categories which, originating in non-Marxian theory, have become an unnecessary burden for Marxists to carry. It is quite possible to preserve the distinction between state-run institutions and privately owned or administered institutions, without having to fit all these institutions into separate realms. In the following chapters I will discuss those Marxist and radical theories of crises which are based on the false assumption that 'the Economy' in capitalist societies is solely the private capitalist production process. I will also analyse the weaknesses inherent in all those theories which assume the existence of a single 'world capitalist market' or 'world-system'. These theories have implicitly or explicitly extended all the erroneous notions of states as 'superstructures' from the national to the world level.

3
From 'Civil Society' to 'World Capitalism': The Reduction of State Institutions to Non-Economic 'Superstructures'

Following Marx's 'anatomy of Civil Society', Marxian crisis-theorists have generally focussed on 'the Economy' and either ignored or reduced states to secondary 'superstructures'. According to many radicals, the capitalist 'mode of production' transcended individual nations and became a single 'world capitalist mode of production' with a 'centre' and a 'periphery'; this 'world capitalism' or 'world-system' is then interpreted as having distinct 'stages' and subject to deep historical long waves of expansion and stagnation. Thus, the 'laws of motion' of capitalist production in 'Civil Society' become the 'laws of motion' of the single 'world-system'. The marginal and secondary roles which state institutions play in these 'global economy' analyses are the direct outcome of theories which misconceive states as 'external' to 'the Economy'. The traditional division of particular societies into 'the State', 'Civil Society' and 'the Economy', is now projected onto the whole world. In this chapter I will discuss why Marx's theory of crises emerging from the relations between Departments I and II fails to explain the role and nature of state institutions. I will then show how Marxian preoccupation with private surplus-value production has produced highly dubious theories such as the 'world-system' and long waves analyses.

Within volume 2 of *Capital*, Marx put forward a theory of simple and extended social reproduction which is inseparable from his whole theory about how crises occur within capitalist modes of production. If most contemporary Marxists readily acknowledge that state institutions are not just 'superstructures' passively reflecting activities in the economic 'base', then why have so few of them bothered to investigate whether Marx's analysis in *Capital* adequately takes into account the numerous roles and structures of capitalist states? Certainly, there have been long historical debates (involving people such as Luxemburg,

Mandel and many others[1]) concerning the disproportional relations between Departments I and II, the role of military and luxury goods production and other technical issues. But little has ever been said about whether Marx's schema is worth retaining, given its failure to incorporate production and services emanating from state institutions. While Ian Gough has attempted to show how state production could be incorporated in Marx's schema,[2] the result is far from satisfactory, as I will discuss later.

Marx's Notion of Departments I and II

In volume 2 of *Capital* (edited posthumously by Engels), Marx spends over 130 pages carefully elaborating the relations and exchanges between Departments I and II under conditions of simple and extended reproduction. According to Marx, 'The total product, and therefore the total production, of society may be divided into two major departments'.[3] The capitalist enterprises in Department I make commodities which are the means of production (e.g. machinery) needed to make commodities for consumption. The other great Department consists of capitalist enterprises which produce commodities 'having a form in which they pass into the individual consumption of the capitalist and the working class'.[4] Marx subdivides Department II into IIa, the mass of articles consumed by all classes, and IIb, luxury articles which are not consumed by the proletariat.[5]

When Marx analyses the intricate and mediated exchanges between capitalists in Departments I and II, capitalists and workers in Department I, capitalists and workers in Department II, workers in Department I and capitalists in Department II, and so forth, he uses a model in which *private* capitalists production is the *total* sphere of production and exchange. His single brief mention of state institutions (concerning taxes) is only to show that the wage paid to workers in Department II 'passes through many channels (shop-keepers, house owners, tax collectors, unproductive labourers, such as physicians, etc., who are needed by the labourer himself)',[6] before ending up in the hands of capitalists in Department II. Similarly, in his whole analysis of extended reproduction, Marx concentrates on showing how the credit and circulation process mediates between all participants in Departments I and II; the effects of hoarding, speculation, interruption of money capital and of course, disproportional accumulation in one or the other Departments are treated only to illuminate the inherent contradictions of capitalist production.

Underlying Marx's whole work in the three volumes of *Capital* is the basic premise that 'all that the working-class buys is equal to the sum total of its wages, equal to the sum total of the variable capital advanced by the entire capitalist class. This money flows back to the capitalist class by the sale of its product to the working class'.[7] Given this premise, it is not surprising that Marx should concentrate solely on *private* capitalist production in Departments I and II. After all, since workers cannot purchase the means of production, it is logical for Marx to analyse the manner in which the consumption of individual capitalists and workers falls out of step with the tempo of accumulation in Department I. If the majority of individual consumers are not capitalists, then capitalists producing articles of consumption in Department II will be able to buy more means of production from capitalists in Department I, only if the conditions of the working-class are improved so that their consumption increases. But if their conditions improved, would this be at the expense of surplus-value extraction and private capitalists' profits? Thus, the nature of class struggle and the inherently opposed interests (as well as the partial mutual dependency) of capitalists and workers, so long as capitalism existed, were elaborated by Marx in an immensely rich and penetrating study of the 'anatomy' of capitalist relations.

But his whole analysis of relations in private capitalist production now poses a problem, given that class struggles, technological change, etc. have altered the nature of both capitalist enterprises and capitalist classes, not to mention the nature and social profile of working-classes. While Marx had to note only a tiny minority of unproductive state officials, the working-class in most OECD countries does not constitute the 'sum total of variable capital advanced by the entire capitalist class'. Roughly a quarter to over a third of the paid working-class of leading capitalist countries is employed by non-capitalist enterprises in local and national state institutions. Large numbers of people on welfare benefits are also sustained out of general tax revenue (collected from all classes), rather than from only wages advanced by capitalist classes. Certainly, these people cannot generally afford to purchase means of production – but neither can their welfare income be classified as variable capital, since this category has meaning only in its *relation* to *constant capital* within Marx's whole theory of the *organic composition of private capital*. State institutions are *not* operated according to the logic of the ratios of variable and constant capital, and hence do not obey the law of the tendency of the rate of profit to fall which governs private enterprises. In order to grasp the exchanges and relations between capitalist enterprises and the workers in state institutions (and the welfare recipients dependant on state institutions), and also between workers in private enterprises and in state sectors, etc., the concept of total production within the framework of Marx's Departments I and II would have to be revised.

Not only do most state-employed workers not fit into Marx's category of variable capital, but also the presence of large nationalised industries – many of them financed partly out of general revenue, and constituting significant portions of industries in countries such as Italy, France, Austria or particularly India – poses the problem of how they relate to capitalists in Departments I and II, not to mention whether they can be fitted into the latter categories. This problem is unnecessarily cumbersome and the solutions tend to be arbitrary (see, for example, Gough's classification[8]).

Two other important historical developments have also added problems to Marx's original scheme. The first is the transformation of science and technology since Marx's death, which makes the old division between means of production and commodities for individual consumption less clear than in the past. For example, electricity, gas, oil and now solar and wind power are both used in production and individually consumed. Telecommunications, electronics, chemicals, computerisation (some of the largest contemporary industries) could all be subdivided into component parts belonging to Departments I and II – just as they could also resist such classification, given the number of commodities which are both used in production and individually consumed. Secondly, given the nature of technological changes and corporate diversification, it is quite common to see monopoly sector businesses operating enterprises belonging to both Departments I and II, thus complicating the theory of disproportionality between growth in Department I and growth in Department II.

I agree that this latter complication can often be minimised, if we know which subsidiary of a giant corporation is producing what and when. However, internal corporate enterprise calculation and accountancy practices, numerous forms of state subsidy, research and technical overlaps, all add major difficulties which Marx's theory did not anticipate. For example, military production contributes directly and indirectly to production in Departments I and II via the utilisation of technological innovations. Also, it is difficult to separate corporations clearly into

Departments I and III (Mandel's Department of military production[9]), as some of the largest military producers (such as General Electric) are also leading producers of consumer goods in so-called Department II.[10]

Uncritical Applications of Marx's Theory

The difficulties arising when one retains Marx's schema become apparent with two of the best orthodox Marxists, Aglietta and Mandel, who have used Marx's model in creative attempts to explain contemporary capitalist societies. In his extensive application of Marx's theory of Departments of production to the history of American capitalism, Aglietta writes as if all social relations can be assimilated into Departments I and II without the slightest conceptual indigestion. Aglietta's *A Theory of Capitalist Regulation*[11] is strong on theory but weak on American historical material – which partly explains why the book is mainly devoted to an explication of orthodox Marxian and Gramscian categories. The book's main thrust is to show that disproportionate development in Department I as compared to Department II underlies the periodic crises of American capitalism. Department I has been the driving motor of capitalist accumulation, especially after 1961 when rapid accumulation in this Department 'broke the dynamic equilibrium of expansion of the two departments',[12] thus giving rise to the serious crises of the 1960s and 1970s. Aglietta says very little about the state sector in the United States, and does not even provide any significant discussion of whether military expenditure belongs to Department III – a notable omission given the size of military production in the United States of America and the whole debate involving Mandel and others on whether the rate of profit has been seriously affected by armament production. Aglietta produces a book which blurs the differences between capitalist enterprises and state institutions by forcing all state workers and state dependents, along with workers in private enterprises into the same category – as consumers of Department II.

In so far as all state workers and dependents are consumers, it is true that they consume goods and services produced largely by capitalists. But states also produce goods and services which are consumed by workers and dependents. The complicated exchanges and relations between state institutions and members of social classes are not equivalent to exchanges between capital and labour in the private market. In Aglietta's all-embracing use of Departments I and II, American state institutions are reduced to mere transmission belts between Departments

I and II, or mechanisms whereby social consumption is improved and finance capital is assisted in its historical concentration and centralisation. Aglietta sheds little light on why state institutions do not operate according to the law of value, simply because he sees these institutions as merely derivative reflections of private enterprise.[13]

In contrast to Aglietta who attributes particular importance to the faster growth of Department I than Department II, Mandel wavers between agreement upon the disproportional developments (analysed by authors such as Aglietta), and an almost cavalier indifference. 'It matters little,' he says, 'whether the slump begins in one or the other of these two Departments. Empirically, it may be noted that most often it begins in Department II. This was the case for the 1974–75 recession (automobiles). *But this empirical fact expresses no particular intrinsic logic*. There have been and can be over-production crises that begin simultaneously in both Departments and others – less frequently – which begin in Department I, that of producer goods.'[14] This is indeed an amazing conclusion, since the whole notion that Department I expands faster than Department II (because the working-class cannot buy more than its total wages) breaks down if Mandel is right and Aglietta and other Marxists are wrong. Mandel's 'flexibility' is even more striking, given his whole analysis (in *Late Capitalism*) of long waves and technological innovation in Department I – in other words, of the causes for the emergence of monopoly capitalism, fascism and imperialism as solutions to blockages on the expansion of heavy producer goods from Department I capitalists during the twentieth century. Yet Mandel is also prepared to state that from a technical point of view there 'is nothing extraordinary or magical in this two-department scheme. It is just the most elementary conceptual tool – an extreme simplification intended to bring out the underlying assumptions of equilibrium (or equilibrated, proportionate growth) under conditions of commodity production'.[15] Mandel goes on to suggest alternative models with as many as nine departments![16]

One wonders why Mandel did not use this more complicated nine-department model in books such as *Late Capitalism*, rather than Marx's 'most elementary' two-Department model? Mandel's answer is that the two-Department model is not just a simple analytic tool, but a model which corresponds to a social structure. Accordingly,

the choice of *these* two Departments as basic sub-divisions of the mass of commodities produced is not at all an arbitrary one, but corresponds to the essential character of human production in general – not merely its specific expression under capitalist relations of production . . . . The two Departments of Marx's reproduction schemes are nothing other than the specific *capitalist* form of this general division of human production, insofar as they 1) take the generalised form of commodities, and 2) assume that the workers (direct producers) do not and cannot purchase that part of the commodity mountain which consists of tools and raw materials.[17]

Mandel's resort to external, ontological metaphysics is even more startling than his honest admission that Marx's two-Department model is the 'most elementary'. First of all, it is unacceptable to argue that these two Departments are part of the human condition. The question here, whether the direct producers can or cannot purchase the means of production, is only relevant to those societies where classes are divided along the lines of wealth, ownership and exclusive control. Those barriers to capitalist accumulation which Marx, Aglietta and Mandel himself analysed would not be applicable to socialist societies organised along lines of collective social ownership and planned production. Even those non-capitalist dictatorships in Eastern Europe are untroubled by falling rates of profit due to disproportional growth in so-called Departments I or II, because they are not subject to the logic of private accumulation. Either the two-department model has an *intrinsic logic* applicable to capitalist production only, or it has none at all.

Given its historical inapplicability to non-capitalist societies, the question remains: does the two-Department model accurately correspond (as Mandel states) to capitalist social structures? Once Mandel admits that more sophisticated analytical tools can be developed to explain exchange relations in capitalist societies, then by his own argument Marx's analysis of the 'specific capitalist form of this general division of human production' fails to stand the test. Whereas Aglietta proceeds with unquestioned orthodoxy, Mandel, in not ignoring the many contemporary changes in capitalist societies, is thereby led to cast a giant cloud over the methodological credibility of Marx's two-Department model. Yet, like Aglietta, Mandel also treats capitalist states as derivative bodies, in that he considers them only in terms of how they supplement income (in order to sustain purchases in Department II),[18] or assist general accumulation in Department I through military contracts, subsidies and so forth. In this view, crises are essentially produced in private sectors while states are evaluated only in terms of what they do for the capitalist class. Thus it is not logically possible, in this derivative analysis, for state institutions to create crises or to act in any other manner than to *reproduce* capitalist accumulation; to admit an alternative conception of capitalist states would entail abandoning the two-Department model based on private production as the sum total of *all* production within capitalist societies.

Recent Attempts to Modify Marx's Theory

While Aglietta and Mandel give minimal attention to the role and internal structure of capitalist state sectors, Gough tries to rescue Marx's two-Department model by confronting the problem directly. He thus attempts to answer his orthodox critics (such as Fine and Harris) by constructing a synthesis of O'Connor's and Marx's categories, in order to distinguish those state sector activities which create means of production and wage-goods from those that do not. Gough tries to solve the problem of where to fit state sector production such as the production of electricity (a good which could belong in either Department I or II), as well as social services which could be consumed as Department II goods or as unreproductive Department III services. It appears that what Gough calls Department III, is a synthesis of Marx's Department IIb (luxury goods), Mandel's Department III (military production) and O'Connor's state sector social consumption and social expenses[19] (i.e. welfare services as well as legitimating functions to maintain social harmony) – all 'economically unreproductive'.[20] But there remains the whole problem of marketable and non-marketable goods and services, as well as the relation of variable and constant capital which is not duplicated in state institutions. While Gough valiantly tackles these problems, he fails to convince me that the intricate exchanges between Departments I and II, which Marx worked out on the basis of the law of value, can be retained (without major distortions) once state institutions become inextricably bound up with the production process. For example, how does one accurately measure socially necessary labour time, given the division between wages and *non-wage* state-produced services and goods, which are consumed so unevenly by the proletariat (depending on whether they are young, old, single, married, etc.)? How can one calculate the relation between constant and variable capital in different private enterprises, when these are vitally mediated and reproduced partially through general revenue subsidies and services –

e.g. health, education, labour retraining, infrastructure costs, tax and numerous other forms of subsidies and allowances?

Orthodox Marxists such as Fine and Harris argue against Gough that state workers are paid for out of the surplus-value produced in the capitalist sector. This is partially true, but ignores the fact that many private enterprises engage in exchanges with state institutions rather than exchanges only with capitalists in Departments I or II. Revenue is also raised from many private enterprises which do not extract surplus-value from workers (see the analysis of Production Processes in chapter 7) or from workers who do not produce surplus-value (including state workers). The argument here is not that state workers totally finance themselves. It is rather that the way surplus-value is distributed between productive and unproductive capitalists or between state institutions and workers, is hardly a mechanical or simple slicing of a metaphorical cake.

Just as Althusserians argue that 'the economic is determinant in the last instance', so too, orthodox value-theorists postulate that the level of surplus-value is determinant in the last instance. At the time when Marx said that the workers could not purchase more than their wages, this was valid in so far as historical class struggles had only begun to create what is now called the 'welfare state', in which governments appropriate some of the surplus (e.g. tax on profits) from capitalists and distribute it to the proletariat in the form of social services and public goods. While workers still pay the largest proportion of all 'welfare state' expenditure, nevertheless, the limited appropriation of surplus from capitalists has resulted in class struggles over the size of the 'social wage'. The financing of state sector workers through higher taxation, increased debt and other methods is too infinitely intricate to be reduced to exchanges between Marx's two Departments.

Either one accepts the orthodox position on value theory and extended reproduction, or one has to reconceptualise capitalist societies in categories other than Departments I, II and III. It is possible to grasp the processes of private capital accumulation, the nature of class struggles and the role of state institutions without trying to fit all of these complex social interactions into the 'sacred' categories which Marx developed. In a world marked by numerous states (with their elaborate apparatuses employing millions of people), as well as supranational state institutions and transnational private corporations, the difficulty of applying Marx's scheme becomes even more evident. Rosdolsky argued that 'Marx studied the reproduction of social capital only in its "basic form" ;[21] and quoted Marx's refusal to include any analysis of external trade in his scheme as it would only complicate rather than resolve the problem of relations between Departments I and II.[22] While Rosdolsky tried to defend Marx by arguing that his scheme was only in its 'basic form' (a condition which does not seem to deter Aglietta and Mandel), contemporary Marxists must be able to show how international exchanges and relations between both private enterprises and national state institutions can be explained within the categories of Departments I and II. When we recall the numerous studies of imperialism including Mandel's and Aglietta's works which treat the expansion of capital accumulation beyond national boundaries, we will hardly be convinced by discussions of a 'world capitalism' in which Departments I and II engulf a boundaryless world consisting of just *one* world mode of production.

I have already indicated why Marx's schema of Departments of Social Production is inadequate for any comprehension of national state institutions. Not only did Marx fail to examine the complicated exchanges between state institutions and private capitalist enterprises, but he also gave no clear analysis of the geopolitical dimensions within which the two Departments of Social Production operated. Consequently, many Marxists continue to discuss the 'capitalist mode of production' as if it were simultaneously a world phenomenon as well as one at national levels. If one uses the theory of Departments of Social Production as encompassing the sum total of exchanges between capitalists and workers, then it must be made clear how all the enterprises in the world or in a particular nation fit into this scheme. The truth is than in a world of both capitalist and non-capitalist modes of production, elaborate supra-national state institutions, complex credit processes involving transnational enterprise calculation, currency exchanges, not to mention an infinite variety of national and local state institutions which employ millions of people and subsidise variable and constant capital according to quite different national criteria – in such a world, Marx's theory of extended reproduction is woefully inadequate. It is not surprising then that we have yet to read any Marxist calculus, within the parameters of Marx's original scheme, of flows between transnational enterprises and of other supra-national exchanges – to mention just one problem area.

The attacks by orthodox Marxists on O'Connor and Gough are revealing, in that they throw light on the 'scientistic' tendency associated with Marx's theory of extended reproduction. Many Marxists still believe that *Capital* can be used as some kind of manual or tool-kit because Marx's analysis is equivalent to a natural science. The division of products into Departments I and II is bound up with the 'laws of motion of capital', since a theory of crisis depends on understanding the exchanges or proportional relations between these Social Departments. It is not surprising to find in the orthodox Marxists a positivist understanding of 'crisis' and class struggle. For example, Fine and Harris attack Gough for not being able to distinguish an 'economic crisis' from a 'general crisis'.[23] Similarly, Folin attacks O'Connor's categories as Keynesian and yet admits that all state sector investment and administration 'is above all *political* in character'.[24] Folin, Fine and Harris seem to work on the basis that capitalism functions according to 'economic' laws while state institutions work according to 'political' or 'general social' laws. Once again we see the old dichotomy of the 'economic' and the 'political' rearing its head. Since Marx's theory of the Departments of Social Production is based on the traditional division between 'the State' and 'Civil Society', it is no accident that so many Marxists still uphold it – continuing as they do in the mistaken belief that states are mere political/administrative 'superstructures'.

Against the Notion of a Single 'World Capitalist Mode of Production'

Most bourgeois economic theories and public policy analyses operate at the level of the nation-state or national economy. Imperialism, class struggle, transnational corporate penetration are either denied or given only token recognition, as they cannot be comfortably accommodated within the context of notions such as free competition, neutral states or beliefs that 'stagflation' is mainly caused by increases in the price of oil, or in the money supply, or in the level of wages, or in all three! On the other hand, Marxists have by and large either neglected the nation-state (because of their long-standing failure to investigate state institutions), or rejected the idea of a 'national political economy' by starting their analyses at the level of 'the capitalist mode of production'. This pattern was largely set by Marx, whose major works were concerned to establish the 'laws of motion' of 'the capitalist mode of production' as a 'world process', rather than analyse particular social formations (within whose boundaries private capital first developed). Although Marx also stressed the historical importance of national laws and wage rates in determining the cost of variable capital (especially the specific historical level of morality and social needs), the thrust of his work was in the direction of explaining the *particular* as a variation of the *general* laws of capitalist production. It is this tendency which has predominated in Marxist analyses to this day. As Trotsky put it: 'Marxism takes its point of departure from world economy, not as a sum of national parts but as a mighty and *independent reality* which has been created by the international division of labour and the world market, and which in our epoch imperiously dominates the national markets'.[25]

While it would be ludicrous to deny the growing interdependence of capitalist countries, this massive historical growth in international trade is not equivalent to the existence of a single 'world market'. Because there is no such thing as a 'capitalist-state-in-general', it also follows that there is no such thing as an 'independent reality' of a *singular* world-wide 'capitalist mode of production'. This conclusion follows when we pursue the other important element in Marx's thought – namely, that capital has meaning only as a social relation. Hence, if we take seriously the idea that capitalist production is a process emanating historically from particular social relations (rather than from the international division of labour and the world market), it will follow that there is no one 'world pattern' of social relations which in turn produces *one* capitalist mode of production. Rather, there is a world of nation-states and national markets in which capitalist enterprises compete under different conditions and with different modes of production, largely determined by the class forces in various nation-states – from non-capitalist societies which have strict control over foreign capitalist investment (such as Cuba or China), to developing capitalist countries with minimal controls or 'open-door' policies (e.g. the Philippines under Marcos's regime). To admit that there has been a historical tendency to create 'a new international division of labour' and one 'world market' should not make us forget the reality of capitalist accumulation and exchange, which takes place within the confines and explicit social conditions of a world more fragmented by barriers and obstacles than united by the 'invisible hand' of a single and open market.

The problem with many analysts of 'world capitalism' is that there is a tendency to misconceive local and national state institutions (with their millions of workers, specific laws and organisational structures) as no more than geographical entities which are linked by one market – just like many cities in a single nation. It is common to read radicals proclaiming the autonomy of transnational corporations *vis-à-vis* nation-states, of one market with a 'centre' and a 'periphery', of the irrelevance of balance-of-payments deficits as artificial 'national' facts, of the general reduction of 'economic activity' to capital and labour as basic units which traverse the 'world economy' – as if state institutions were little more than fictitious, token boundaries or functional tools for 'capital', e.g. 'the colonial state' or 'the social-democratic state'.[26] But once we reject the idea that states are ideal types, things, subjects or mere derivative parts of capital, it is no longer possible to believe that there is a homogeneous or single 'world mode of production'. For each specific local, regional or national state institution promotes or negates the relative or absolute extraction of surplus-value.

Instead of recognising that state institutions are integral parts of national economies, most 'world-system' and 'world mode of production' theorists perpetuate the old 'base/superstructure' dichotomy. It is very common to see radicals conceive 'world capitalism' as a 'system' which is characterised by sharpening contradictions between the 'world political system' (i.e. territorial units governed by historically specific states) and the 'world economy'.[27] This reduces state institutions to 'non-economic', political–administrative 'superstructures' struggling over their nation's share of the 'world economic' cake. Two serious errors flow directly from this fundamentalist dichotomy. The first error is that the belief in 'accumulation on a world scale' is taken to an absurd extreme; the second error is that class struggle is conceived in simplistic and sweepingly generalised terms.

If one focusses primarily on the relations between 'capital' and 'labour' as they battle across the 'world stage', it is not surprising that all roles and structures associated with state institutions will be reduced to secondary by-products of this larger class struggle. As it is not clear whether most Marxists are referring to the world, or to national modes of production, when they use the concept 'capitalist mode of production', it is no accident that the national mode becomes submerged in the 'world-system' perspective. If a singular 'world-system' is supposed, why not analyse the 'world pool of surplus-value' which is extracted from 'labour' by 'capital'? This is precisely what writers such as Amin and Palloix attempt, when they subdivide the working-class, peasantry and other classes into a 'world' consisting of a 'core' and a 'periphery'.[28] Although Amin advocates a study of particular rates of exploitation, it is not clear how one could even begin to calculate the 'world surplus-value pool'. Given the decisive size and complexity of national state institutions, the vital assistance and subsidy given to private enterprises (which varies from country to country), it is not at all clear how one could calculate the size of a 'national surplus-value pool' let alone a 'world surplus-value pool'. For if one does *not* accept that 'there is only one single process of capital accumulation taking place on a world scale in the capitalist economic system',[29] then the size and relation of particular state institutions requires a detailed analysis in order to determine the source and distribution of surplus-value in a world so unevenly divided between numerous societies.

Linked to the simplistic metaphysics of a 'world pool of surplus-value' is the reduction of complex social relations to sloganistic caricatures. For example, Harris believes that there is a 'world ruling class', while according to Wallerstein, 'there are two kinds of politics in the modern world-system: the class struggle between bourgeois and proletarian, and the political struggles among different bourgeois'.[30] This type of simplistic reductionism completely blurs the significant differences between numerous pre-capitalist classes and those classes existing in capitalist societies, not to mention the diverse range of non-capitalist social groups and social strata in Eastern Europe, China, Cuba, Angola and so forth. But then 'world-system' theorists do not even agree on whether Communist countries are part of the 'world capitalist mode of production' and on whether they belong to the 'core' or the 'periphery'.[31] I will later show how important it is to recognise historically specific Electoral Processes. If one misidentifies wage-workers by narrowing and reducing the latter to only those who produce surplus-value, then it will not be surprising if the alternatives to capitalist society will be as unrealistic as analyses of existing capitalist societies.

Long Waves - The New Metaphysics

The preoccupation of 'world-system' theorists with a homogeneous 'world pool of surplus-value' also derives from their concentration on large transnational corporations and 'world factories', at the expense of the vast majority of capitalist businesses which have no assembly lines and are small, local enterprises. As the focal point is monopoly capitalism, any theory of a 'world-system' or 'world capitalist mode of production', not surprisingly, explains the past and the present as the unfolding of 'stages' of the 'world-system'. Once the uneven and diverse histories of particular social classes and state institutions are incorporated under the homogenising categories of 'stages', the next level of refined mystification can be promoted, namely, the documentation of supposedly uniform or interconnected long waves which determine the fortunes of each 'stage' of the 'world-system'.

Just as there is no unity between 'world-system' analysts on whether Communist countries are part of the 'system', whether they parasitically absorb the surplus-value produced in the 'periphery' or contain a class structure which is analogous to classes in capitalist countries, etc., so too the long wave theorists disagree on the nature, the cause and even the length of long waves. In recent years there have been numerous definitions and redefinitions of what constitutes a long wave. Originally long waves were conceived by Kondratieff and others to be long historical periods of sustained economic expansion followed by periods of stagnation and depression. If historical development could be charted as the unfolding of long waves of expansion, then much of the pre-occupation by social analysts with day-to-day short-term events could be placed in a more illuminating perspective. Politically, the significance of long waves could be seen in the claims which long wave theorists made in relation to predicting new depressions or upswings in the 'capitalist world' – thus determining whether conditions were favourable or unfavourable for revolution. The revival of long wave theory in the 1970s has not been confined to the Left. Many bourgeois economists have also used long wave theory either to justify austerity measures as necessary (if the new period of expansion is to take place in the late 1980s or early 1990s), or as a guide to short-term speculative activity on the stock-market.

In contrast to Marx, who attempted to explain the accumulation of capital and the inherent barriers to this accumulation (by constructing a theory of exchanges between Departments I and II), long wave theorists do not all confine themselves to just the 'capitalist world economy' and are not all Marxists. Long wave theorists are divided in explaining periods of expansion, some attributing them to internal (endogenous) 'economic' factors, others to exogenous or 'extra-economic' factors such as wars and revolutions. No long wave theorist has much to say on the specific historical nature and role of state institutions. Considering the grand and sweeping explanations supposedly provided by long wave theory, it is worth probing the various patterns of historical development which this body of theory uncovers. I will try to show why long waves cannot adequately explain historical phenomena, and why long wave theories involve various confusions, omissions and demand a great deal of historical juggling when they try to fit multiform local and national social relations and events into homogeneous waves of expansion and stagnation. Long waves do not determine the historical analysis; rather, like sound waves, they bend around and bounce off the pre-existing notions of the world with which long wave theorists begin.

It seems that with each new long wave theorist who studies the 'historical sea', ever-new patterns, swells or fluctuations are discovered. For example, Kondratieff traces the first upswing from 1789 and puts the length of this wave at sixty years. The second long wave is, however, only forty-seven years long, and the third even shorter – a mere twenty-four years.[32] In contrast, Mandel argues (in his work written in 1978) that long waves are of twenty to twenty-five years' duration[33] and that it is not possible to speak of long waves existing before 1826, 'the year of the first modern crisis of overproduction of industrial goods'.[34] Yet in an earlier work, Mandel argues that long waves begin at the end of the eighteenth century, last approximately fifty years, 'of which we have experienced four up till now'.[35] Wallerstein and Hopkins outdo both Kondratieff and Mandel by arguing that 'logistics' or long cycles begin in 1450 (although the original French theory of 'logistics' goes all the way back to the ninth or tenth centuries!).[36] Bergesen, another 'world-system' theorist, disagrees and opts for two long cycles: 'the first lasted 410 years (1415–1825), the second only 143 years (1826–1969), and if the trend holds, the third will be even shorter'.[37]

Given the widespread disagreement over the length of long waves, it is not surprising to find that long wave theorists read 'into' cycles as many different concepts and 'histories' as do readers of tea-leaves. While it is true that Mandel does not use long waves to predict the future, others such as Rostow, Hobsbawm and Wallerstein predict an upswing in the 1990s.[38] Most importantly, there is no agreement about what long waves are, what they are supposed to tell us and why they occur. Rostow agrees with Kondratieff that long waves are periods of expansion. But with Rostow it is the availability or scarcity of food, raw materials and energy sources which determines price levels, and the expansion or deceleration of growth.[39] Mandel rejects Kondratieff and Rostow's approach and argues that long waves are not about the history of price and money movements. Rather they are 'movements involving output of commodities and sales of commodities'.[40] Barr sees long waves mirroring the four phases of an ideal-typical business enterprise – i.e. the procurement phase, the productive consumption phase, the realisation phase and the accumulation phase.[41] However, Bousquet, Wallerstein, Cronin and Bergesen are even further removed from prices and overproduction. For these people, long waves are about periods of hegemony and competition among 'core' powers,[42] movements affecting 'core–periphery' relations,[43] cycles affecting the level of class struggle[44] or cycles of 'colonial rule'.[45] 'World-system' theorists such as Wallerstein, Bousquet, Bergesen or Hopkins reduce long waves to 'political' phenomena. While they use terms such as 'accumulation of capital', there is no evidence that they either understand or rely upon a Marxian theory of extended reproduction. What makes accumulation possible? Are there particular relations between constant and variable capital? Does a long wave begin with expanded accumulation in Department I or in Department II (if one accepts Marxian extended reproduction categories)? All these questions remain unanswered and untheorised in the generalised 'political' notions of long waves.

The point which I wish to emphasise strongly here is that the application of long wave theories evades serious historical and conceptual problems, by ignoring the role of the great variety of state institutions, or making them secondary in ideal-typical models of the 'world capitalist mode of production'. Wallerstein and others discuss 'accumulation' as if the logic of extended reproduction (Departments I and II) were unproblematical. The history of the 'world-system' is periodised into long waves of expansion and recession, while the processes of accumulation traverse, without the slightest bother, centuries of widely divergent class relations, pre-capitalist and capitalist, and of completely different state institutions. If long waves are perceived as the movement of what Kondratieff and Mandel call 'extra-economic' factors, then, as I have outlined, each writer can call anything – whether it be changes in hegemony or colonial rule, or changes in music, climate or religion – a 'long wave'!

While claiming to be sensitive to the historical specificity of various 'core' or 'peripheral' societies, 'world-system' theorists reduce long waves to historical ideal types similar to models of the 'capitalist-state-in-general'. Long waves thus take the form of abstract cycles superimposed on actual historical societies, or conversely, social formations are all fitted in to the movement of these ideal-type waves. Unless the 'world-system' theorists specify the relationships between the 'internal' changes in Departments I or II and the larger 'external' changes in core-periphery relations or colonial cycles, then the origins of each new wave and the 'internal' dynamics of each wave will have little to do with 'capital accumulation'. The problem with 'world-system' theorists, and with many Marxists who work with the notion of a single, world-wide 'capitalist mode of production', is that they fail to grasp why the re-production of capitalist relations, and even more importantly, their *non-reproduction*, does *not* take place within *one* 'mode of production'.

Mandel's Attempt to Wed Long Wave Theory to Marxism

Whereas Wallerstein *et al.* 'sociologise' concepts of capital accumulation, Mandel runs into major problems when he tries to wed Marx's theory of Departments I and II to the 'extra-economic' causal factors behind long waves. Mandel operates with a fundamentally narrow 'productionist' view of class struggle.[46] This is evident in his belief that upturns in long waves 'cannot be deduced from the laws of motion of the capitalist mode of production by themselves ... [but] these imply a whole series of *non-economic* factors like wars of conquest, extensions and con-tractions of the area of capitalist operation, *inter-capitalist competition, class struggle*, revolutions and counter-revolutions, etc.'[47] [my emphasis]. Given Mandel's definition of 'non-economic', has he reduced capitalist accumulation to a process devoid of class struggle? What can the 'laws of motion of capitalist production' be, if variable capital (and hence class struggle), along with inter-capitalist competition, are 'non-economic' factors? Precisely what is this 'internal logic of capitalist laws' which explains the 'cumulative nature of each long wave'?[48]

If we examine Mandel's 'internal logic' of capitalist production it can be seen that, in the first phase of a long wave, 'technology under-goes a revolution' leading to a cheapening of constant capital in Depart-ment I; above-average profit rates and general accelerated activity are also accompanied by above-average productive investment. The depletion of the industrial reserve army of labour leads to greater worker militancy, and thus to increased effort by capitalists to extract relative surplus value from workers, especially in Department II consumer goods enterprises. Once the above-average rate of technological innovation and development in Department I has slowed down, the increase in the organic composition of capital results in declining rates of profit in Department II.[49]

In this explanation of long waves Mandel repeats a very common error associated with 'scientistic Marxists': the reduction of class struggle to 'non-economic' relations or the elevation of 'laws of motion of capital' above social relations. This error is also evident in the way he isolates technology from general social conditions or what Mandel calls 'extra-economic' factors. While Mandel denies Rowthorn's accusation that he attributes long waves to 'technological revolutions',[50] he does not adequately answer Rowthorn by explaining why new technological innovations cannot be ongoing discoveries (sustained by state subsidies) rather than periodic bursts of creativity. For if new technology continually cheapens the costs of constant capital, why does expansion of a long wave have to come to a halt?[51] Mandel appears to be unaware that he is undermining the very basis of his explanation of the origin and periodisation of long waves. For when he argues that 'extra-economic' factors determine the upswings of new waves, he also needs to defend the notion that the *durations* of long waves are based solely on the *'internal logic'* of capitalist production. According to Mandel,

> to deny that once a new long wave is under way the inner logic of capitalism (i.e. the laws of motion of the system) must of necessity command the further trend of events is to deny that these laws of motion are operative in any real sense whatsoever. If one believes that not just once every fifty or sixty years, but continuously, external non-economic forces determine the development of the capitalist economy, then one rejects out of hand Marx's entire economic analysis.[52]

Here we have the 'scientific truth' – the 'laws of motion' of 'capitalism' have a cycle of fifty to sixty years. Disbelief is 'unMarxian'.

Mandel has been swamped by his own long waves. If wars, revolution, counter-revolution, class struggle are all 'outside' the 'internal logic' of capitalist accumulation, why not admit the influence of sun spots (as Jevons did) and numerous other 'extra-economic' factors in determining when a long wave begins? After all, 'extra-economic' factors *do* enter *continuously*; how then can Mandel arbitrarily pick out one set of 'extra-economic' factors as opposed to another set? As Rowthorn points out, there are more than enough historical facts to dispute in Mandel's periodisation.[53] Further, Mandel acknowledges that, after 1914, 'the nature of the long wave will be significantly different from the nature of the long wave seen during the period of historical rise and expansion of the capitalist system'.[54] If it is true that 'capitalism' has changed, then just what are these 'internal laws of motion of capitalist production' which, according to Mandel, must determine all subsequent phases of the twenty- to twenty-five year long wave?

Mandel's artificial division of the 'internal laws' into the 'economic', and the 'non-economic', is evident when he argues that: 'there is a long cycle of class struggle, (or to be more precise, a long cycle of rise and decline in working-class militancy and radicalisation) that is relatively independent of the long waves'.[55] This argument confirms Mandel's derivative conception of state institutions as 'superstructures', and his scientistic division of capitalist relations into 'economic laws' and 'non-economic' class struggle. For how can above-average rates of profit and the expansion of investment, in either Department I or Department II, be autonomous of the 'long cycle of rise and decline in working-class militancy'? Either working classes are militant and win higher wages, better 'social wage' conditions, the implementation of laws on health, safety, environmental control, consumer protection and so forth (all affecting rates of profit, taxes and investment options), or capitalists are able to defeat the workers and eliminate such obstacles to profitable accumulation. It remains a mystery how 'internal laws of motion of capitalism' can be conceptualised as independent of 'the long cycle of working-class militancy'. Further, Mandel does not even consider the millions of people employed in state institutions who cannot be strictly incorporated into these traditional Marxian 'internal laws' of *private* accumulation. In other words, Mandel has not established how extended reproduction in Departments I and II operates independently of 'non-economic' factors. Consequently, he has also failed to establish why we should agree with his set of dates marking the development of long waves from 1826. While Wallerstein *et al.* have argued that long waves began as far back as 1450, Mandel's dichotomy of 'economic' and 'extra-economic' gives us no more cogent reason to subscribe to his notion of long waves, than any of the other dozen or so versions can offer.

Major Weaknesses in Long Wave Theory

In conclusion, I would like to point out a few other weaknesses characterising most long wave theories.

Lacking any substantial analysis of local, national and supranational state institutions, long wave theorists somehow assume that states cannot determine or modify the nature of long waves in various countries – simply because waves are either self-regulating or determined by 'economic' and 'extra-economic' factors. It is true that Gordon includes state institutions as one of his thirteen 'agencies of accumulation', but his concept of 'the State' is basically one which reduces it to 'non-economic', 'political–administrative' roles.[56] Wallerstein, also, constantly uses the term 'state', but only territorially to divide the 'world-system' into countries or nation-states, rather than to analyse in detail the role of state institutions in the reproduction or negation of particular social relations.[57]

It is very interesting to note that all long wave theorists somehow conclude that we are currently going through a period of stagnation and/ or that the conditions for the next upswing have been laid and the 1990s will witness the next long wave (if there is to be a next one). Yet in order to know that the 1990s will be the period of the next upswing, it is necessary to go back to 1450, 1789, 1826 or whatever. For how can one know when the next long wave is to take place unless one knows when the *first* one occurred? To argue that the 1970s and 1980s can only be explained if we understand the causes of the first long wave in the fifteenth, eighteenth or nineteenth centuries is *a priori* deterministic nonsense. Long wave theorists may reply that, as each long wave has different causes and is of a new character, it is not necessary to go back to the original wave. If this is true, then why should we expect an upswing in the 1990s? Why not in the 2050s or the 2070s? What is the point of arguing for long periodisations if the original wave has no relation to the next wave? Either the focus on the 1990s is meaningful because of what occurred in 1450, 1789 or 1826, or long wave theory becomes simply vacuous.

Not only does the original long wave predetermine the division of future history into periods of stagnation or upswing, but – even less convincingly – the original long wave in pre-capitalist Europe (e.g. 1450) determined the future of the *whole* world, both European and non-European, capitalist and non-capitalist, or so 'world-system' theorists would have us believe. Why not begin with ancient Chinese, Persian or Aztec long waves? But it is not just that long wave theories tend to be thus 'Eurocentric'. For if one believes (as Kondratieff did) that long waves arise out of internal 'economic' factors, then (as Trotsky argued), an examination of the uneven development of countries, with their individual internal contradictions, would result in any uniform long cycle crumbling into dust.[58] On the other hand, if long waves can be anything from 'core–periphery' relations to 'colonial cycles', then what guarantees that these various 'non-economic' long waves will occur uniformly and be applicable to all societies?

Finally, long wave theorists have used long waves to predict business booms and slumps or to construct a 'total' view of 'capitalism'. All those capitalists who buy or sell stock on the basis of long wave predictions are risking financial loss; similarly, all those revolutionaries who emphasise the 'global' signs of expansion or collapse must still confront the reality, in which developments within local and national Processes are determined by specific historical social forces rather than by generalised waves of accumulation or militancy. Certainly, supranational connections and influences have created similar conditions in more than one country – the Great Depression of the 1930s, for example. But long wave theory would have to explain why each capitalist society met the Great Depression with quite different 'remedies' (from Nazism in Germany to Social Democracy in Sweden or the Front Populaire in France), and why there are no causal factors or origins commons to the end or to the beginning of what appear to be periods of general growth or decline. We can concede that particular countries such as the United States have a disproportionate influence upon developments in other countries, without having to endorse the existence of long waves. It is rather the desynchronisation of local, national and supra-national Electoral, Production, Credit and Food Production Processes (see Part II), which helps to explain not only the uneven developments within each society, but also why the past, present and future of an infinitely complex 'world' cannot be reduced to homogeneous ideal types whose 'internal' and 'external' dynamics have yet to be established. Perhaps the most surprising aspect of long wave theory is not its reduction of state institutions, diverse social classes and modes of production to cyclical patterns, but rather the popularity of this theory. What has to be explained is not just long waves, but how and why so many prominent Marxists and non-Marxists[59] have fallen for, and continue to be fooled by, this superstitious and superficial nonsense.

4
Electoral Struggles: The Limits of 'Political Business Cycle' and 'Class-Theoretical' Analyses

The temptation to reduce historically complex and non-repeatable social developments to precise 'laws', or to an 'intrinsic logic' of long waves, is still very widespread today. Having criticised the new metaphysics of 'world-system' theory and long wave theory, let me complete the picture by concentrating on those analyses which either perpetuate economistic notions of 'the political', or reduce electoral politics to secondary struggles. All the weaknesses manifest in the division of social life into 'the State', 'Civil Society' and 'the Economy' become particularly evident when analyses are made of elections and their effect on what is called 'the Economy'. First, a long tradition of bourgeois and Marxian political economy has operated with the concept of a 'business cycle' which continually goes up and down at certain intervals. From the 'business cycle' we have seen the emergence of larger, transnational cycles known as long waves. At the national level, cyclical theory has manifested itself in the form of the 'political business cycle'. Second, as most contemporary political economy tends to be far more 'economic' than 'political-economic', elections have also been partially analysed in 'class-theoretical' terms. Within the 'class-theoretical' school one can distinguish between strategic, humanist and structuralist analyses of elections. If we are to overcome the artificial realms of 'the State', 'Civil Society' and 'the Economy', it is important to recognise the narrow economistic manner in which 'electoral politics' has been treated in 'political business cycle' theories as well as the elevation of elections to 'superstructural' or secondary phenomena in strategic, humanist and structural 'class-theoretical' analyses.

Weaknesses in the 'Strategic', 'Humanist' and 'Structural' Analyses

Historically, radicals have given minimal attention to the electoral contestation between bourgeois and social-democratic parties. Leninists have always evaluated party politics and parliamentary systems in *'strategic'* terms rather than with any deep interest in the ups and downs of accumulation processes of national 'political business cycles'. Although there have been many books and articles by Soviet and Western Marxists on the 'economic cycle in capitalist systems' and on whether Keynesian economics has eradicated crises in capitalism since the Great Depression,[1] nearly all of these analyses concentrate on the 'internal' contradictions of the *private* production system and tend to marginalise or treat as 'super-structural' all party-political activity. In so far as orthodox Marxist–Leninists treat capitalist states as instruments wholly under the absolute control of the bourgeoisie, electoral conflict is reduced to a superficial marketing tussle between different 'brand names' of the same bourgeois product. Participation by revolutionaries in elections has been approved of at different historical periods for a variety of reasons: to propagate the revolutionary message, to bolster united or popular fronts against reactionaries, to attempt to win a majority of votes, or to challenge the hegemony of conservative communist or social-democratic parties within the ranks of the working-class.

The narrow 'strategic' evaluation of electoral politics has accordingly varied from intense opposition to enthusiastic participation. During the Third Period (1928–35) of major confrontation between the Comintern and Social democracy, 'electoral politics' was often unfavourably contrasted with 'revolutionary insurrectionism'. Attacking Hilferding's and Kautsky's modification of Marx's and Engels's notion of 'the capitalist State', the Comintern argued in 1928 that

> once the State is not the instrument [*sic*] of one's class domination . . .
> it follows that in Germany and elsewhere power belongs not to the
> bourgeoisie, but to all classes and all parties; that it belongs to all
> the citizens who make up the State. But if this is how matters stand,
> there can be no question of combatting the State; on the contrary,
> the aim must be to occupy a suitable niche within it. In practice,
> this means coalition governments in which social democracy col-
> laborates with bourgeois parties. It means a bitter struggle against
> the revolutionary proletariat . . . . It means that . . . all that remains
> to be done today is to democratize the State more fully, democratize
> the League of Nations, and pass peacefully, without revolution,
> dictatorship, or bloodshed, into socialism.[2]

The polarisation between revolutionary policies and reformism has continued to the present day with replays under new conditions and with new personalities. This is particularly evident in the polemic over the revolutionary credentials of the 'Eurocommunists', and in evaluations of 'historical compromises' trying to 'democratise the State'.

It should be made clear that 'Eurocommunist' notions of 'democratising the State' are significantly different from the Second International's views, in that they embrace institutions outside 'the State' and are relatively, though not completely, free of the naïvety of the 'evolutionary socialist' path, given the experiences after 1933 and more recently in Chile in 1973. Whereas the orthodox Leninists continued their 'strategic' evaluation of 'electoral politics' in terms of traditional notions of state power, it is also clear that the 'Eurocommunists' equally ignore the non-strategic aspects of 'electoral politics'. One of the main things that preoccupied the 'Eurocommunist' Left during the 1970s, in their period of optimistic growth, was the 'strategic' question of whether the Right would stage a coup d'état should the Left be electorally successful. This problem together with the other organisational problems related to winning a 'niche within the State', far outweighed any consideration of the political economic consequences flowing from the contestation between conservative and labour type parties. Once again, the 'electoral process' was conceived 'strategically' as a 'superstructural' phenomenon rather than as a vital 'process' in the accumulation of private capital.

While the 'strategic' analyses of elections and parliaments were concerned with creating a 'new society' rather than with how existing capitalist states function, most of the 'non-strategic' Marxist analyses of capitalist states also minimised or ignored the contradictory dynamics of electoral politics. During the renaissance of Marxism in the 1960s and 1970s, many writers made indirect comments on the nature of existing capitalist states via the analysis of alienation, exploitation, and commodity fetishism in Marx's writings. The theory of 'alienated politics' was especially influential among the American Left. For example, Bertell Ollman devalued electoral politics by emphasising the similarity between alienated relations in the factory and those governing state institutions. According to Ollman, surplus-value extraction takes place in the political process via the voting system. The relation between workers and their capitalist boss in the factory

is duplicated with citizens and the men who run the machinery of government. Both are value and class relations, and, in each case, alienation occurs through the transfer of use-values. Just as workers give up the use-value of their labour-power, labour, and with it all its products, people, as citizens, give up the use-value of their political activity – of legislating, administering and judging for all – and with it the use-value of the products created by the ensuing political interaction.[3]

The analogy which Ollman makes between the factory and political institutions is only true to the extent that workers and citizens are not in control of either the commodities they produce or their legislatures and state institutions. However, there is a fundamental error in equating voting or political participation with surplus-value extraction. Whereas capitalist production can quite easily flourish without the so-called 'value' extracted via an election – in fact, many capitalists would prefer no elections – the same is definitely not true of real surplus-value which is extracted in the workplace.[4] Ollman repeats the erroneous 'philosophical' interpretation of value theory and thus obscures the important part which 'electoral politics' *actually* play in the rate of surplus-value extraction. But to understand how political struggle affects the rate of surplus-value extraction, it is necessary to go beyond seeing bourgeois politics as merely a realm of alienation.

It would be wrong to believe that it is only 'humanist' Marxists who misunderstand 'electoral politics'. All those Marxists who stressed only the functional role which capitalist states play in reproducing capitalist production also sought to minimise or devalue the non-reproductive or contradictory aspects of electoral politics. These 'derivative' and 'economistic' analyses of state policies were so preoccupied with expounding all those functions and roles which parties and state administrators carried out on behalf of private capitalist production, that this 'blind spot' prevented any balanced perception of social developments after 1945. Just as non-Marxist sociologists perpetrated the myth of the 'end of ideology' during the late 1950s and early 1960s, so too did many radicals succumb to the 'politics of the welfare state'. Marxists generally stressed the similarities between parties, ignored the historical specificity of the post-war period, reduced party-political conflict to 'rhetoric' (behind which supposedly lay common attitudes to capitalism), and by and large treated elections and parties as direct or indirect structural components of 'the capitalist mode of production'. The Althusserian 'structuralists' merely extended the 'strategic' Leninist analyses of 'electoral politics' by focussing on all the structures and apparatuses which maintained 'social cohesion' rather than class conflict. From a different perspective, even Marxists such as Claus Offe considered the 'systemic' analyses of public policy studies (by authors such as Dye) as complementary to the radical idea that party politics was marginal to the workings of the 'capitalist system'. Writing in 1971, Offe argued that 'Party platforms and elections results seem to have no influence on the percentage of the State budget that is spent for welfare purposes or the new welfare programmes that are inaugurated'.[5]

After stressing the structual homogeneity of 'bourgeois politics', Marxists met with a historical rebuff to their one-dimensional analyses of 'electoral politics', as the 'end of ideology' theorists similarly experienced. It was the eruption of major social protest in the 1960s which made a mockery of the 'end of ideology' theorists' belief in social convergence and consensus. Similarly, it was the major crises of 'stagflation' in the 1970s which simultaneously brought the idea of the 'affluent society' to an end (despite the earlier critiques of 'affluence' by Galbraith and many others) and, for Marxists, highlighted the painful awareness that party politics *could* affect welfare budgets. In contrast to the 1960s, it was the followers of monetarism and aggressive conservatism (rather than Left radicals) who sought to break the 'social cohesion' of welfare policies which Marxist reproductive theorists had ahistorically believed to be 'above' party politics. During the thirty years or so after 1945, concessions were won in social struggles, concessions which bourgeois classes in many countries can no longer afford without undermining the profitable accumulation of capital. But even during the period of the growth of the 'welfare state', it would be an historical error to believe that political struggles were irrelevant to the size and benefits available to working-classes in different capitalist societies. Recent studies by Stephens, Esping-Andersen, Castles and McKinlay[6] among others, have shown that the occupation of political office by social-democratic parties, as opposed to conservative-bourgeois parties, *has* made a difference to the nature and extent of state involvement – especially programmes concerned with social welfare. I will return to some of their findings later, in chapter 6. In the meantime, it is worth noting that their analyses are mainly directed on the one hand against revolutionaries (who argue that there is no significant difference between non-revolutionary parties), and on the other hand against public policy writers (such as Wilensky) who argue that welfare is a consensual outcome of general economic policy formed by strong 'corporatist' interest groups. Although Stephens and others provide very useful material which undermines both public policy studies and orthodox Marxist neglect of 'electoral politics', their emphasis is very much on the relationship between welfare spending and party politics. To this extent, Stephens and others leave largely untouched the vital issue of the direct relationship between electoral struggle and private capitalist profitability (except to admire the Swedish labour movement's strategy of pension funds and peaceful transition to socialism). A much more comprehensive notion of the interrelationship between elections, representative institutions and accumulation processes is needed, if elections are not to be seen as pertaining only to the realm of 'the political'.

One of the lessons to be learnt here, from the 'convergence' of 'structural' Marxist and public policy analyses of state institutions and elections, is that there is no substitute for detailed historical analyses of specific social formations. What is of particular interest is the fact that Marxist and public policy analysts could arrive at similar erroneous positions from quite different political perspectives. After beating the ideological drum over how Western political processes were the outcome of free competition and the expression of political parties and groups, many pluralists converted into public policy analysts and went to the other extreme of proclaiming that 'pluralist' political systems produced no different public policies to 'non-pluralist' systems; in other words, political struggle was irrelevant to the nature and size of state services. Similarly, after proclaiming the fundamental role of class struggle in the determination of the material conditions of existence, Marxists went to the other extreme and stressed the reproduction of capitalist structures regardless of historical complexity, the organisational strength of classes or the constitutional avenues through which non-revolutionary class struggles could be waged. Politics became virtually irrelevant unless it was 'revolutionary politics'. The 'capitalist mode of production' became the generalised model to describe *all* capitalist societies, to explain away historical differences as marginal or variations of the same mode of production, thus reducing class struggle to some metaphysical metaphor or an as yet unleashed potential force, come the pre-revolutionary breakdown of society.

One might immediately protest that the above remarks are a gross distortion of Marxian analyses. I will simply answer that it is not enough to cite all the *theoretical* works in which Marxists showed their full awareness of the complexity and historical specificity of class struggle. The damning evidence is to be found in the mountain of writings (until very recently) which stressed only the reproductive roles of all non-revolutionary political parties and in the dominance of generalised models which depicted states in instrumental and derivative terms.

The Economism and Positivism of 'Political Business Cycle' Analyses

Given the major neglect by Marxists of electoral politics it is a pity that Kalecki did not fully develop his very perceptive, but limited analysis of the 'political business cycle'.[7] Although Kalecki was to write much more on various problems associated with capitalist societies as well as critiques of economic theories, he never fully elaborated upon the 'political' aspects of his seminal 1943 paper. In differentiating between the fascist 'armament economies' and the other capitalist societies which still had parliamentary systems, Kalecki made the following observations: (1) unemployment was functional for capitalists in that it maintained 'discipline in the factories' and 'political stability' – a condition which was 'more appreciated by business leaders than profits';[8] (2) business disliked government spending policies which tried to solve unemployment by increasing public investment and subsidising mass consumption; (3) capitalists preferred governments to counteract slumps by lowering the rate of interest, reducing income tax and subsidising private investment – all of which would do little to prevent mass unemployment; (4) if governments reduced the rate of interest or income tax in a slump but did not increase them in the subsequent boom, then the boom would last a bit longer but the eventual slump would require even further reductions of interest on tax rates again and again. 'Thus in not too remote a time the rate of interest would be negative and income tax would have to be replaced by an income subsidy. The same would arise if it were attempted to *maintain* full employment by stimulating private investment: the rate of interest and income tax would have to be reduced continuously.'[9]

The dilemma of capitalist state administrators, in attempting to counteract slumps without undermining 'discipline' and 'stability' while also resolving fundamental problems in maintaining the profitability of private capitalist firms, is a familiar story of recent decades. What has to be explained is why public investment, interest rates and tax rates have grown since Kalecki's time, and how struggles within Electoral Processes have determined or influenced the 'political business cycle' in various countries. A more integrated political economic analysis can be constructed by focussing on those social forces and institutional arrangements of particular Electoral Processes' (see chapter 6), which have made policies carried out prior to the 1940s extremely difficult to repeat after 1945 or revive in the 1980s.

Until recently, the only people who have attempted to build upon Kalecki's notion of the 'political business cycle' (with the exception of a few radicals such as Boddy and Crotty)[10] have been liberal and conservative economists and public policy analysts. Writers such as Nordhaus, Frey, Schneider, MacRae and Brittan[11] have investigated in fairly narrow terms the possible correlations between elections and income levels, unemployment rates and inflation rates. Most of these analyses have been largely ahistorical despite their investigation of actual elections in countries such as the United States and Britain. That is, the elections studied have been lifted out of context, and statistics have been mathematically evaluated without substantial analysis of the historical social struggles behind each election. This essentially positivist approach is built upon a Schumpeterian notion of parties and presidents having to bid for voters via promises and performances which raise income while lowering unemployment and inflation rates. According to Frey, an 'empirical analysis of twenty-seven democracies over the period 1960-71 shows that in twenty-one of these countries (among them the UK, USA, Canada and Australia), the growth rate of real disposable income was higher in election years than in non-election years'.[12] Other research showed that tougher austerity measures were adopted in early years of office, while during election years (or in an earlier year, given 'time-lags'), reflationary policies were implemented in order to 'buy' voters.[13] Samuel Brittan extends the mathematical analyses to incorporate an evaluation of such things as minority and majority attitudes to spending programmes and tax cuts, the electorate's short memory and the general effect of changes in currency exchange rates, trade cycle, budget size and money supply.[14]

The problem with most of these 'political business cycle' studies is that they are largely confined to merely establishing the correlations between election years and 'cyclical' economic activity. Consequently, 'economic activity' is treated in ahistorical non-class terms and is reduced to quantitative statistical data subject to limited comparative analogies. Even though booms and slumps may appear outwardly similar (in that base measurements can be made of increases or declines in goods and services), no capitalist accumulation process is shaped and affected by identical or repeatable social relations and forces of production. Therefore, the correlation between reflationary 'economic activity' and election years has not been uniform and, over the last ten years, unemployment rates did not drop during election years (e.g. in Australia in 1975, 1977, 1980 and 1983, Britain in 1979, Canada in 1980, the United States in 1980 and France in 1981). One of the major reasons for these so-called 'anomalies' in the narrowly conceived 'political business cycle' is that no crisis in local or national capitalist Production Processes (see chapter 7) ever repeats itself under the same conditions and hence is not amenable to similar 'curves'. Unfortunately, authors like Nordhaus have tried to evaluate Kalecki's notion of the 'political business cycle' as if 'politics' and 'business' were ahistorical factors which went up and down according to non-social quantitative variables.

The limitation of Kalecki's original paper of 1943 is that he was writing in the shadow of Nazism and the Great Depression, prior to the post-1946 Cold War military budgets and during a period of relatively underdeveloped money capital, with much smaller state sectors and weaker workers' organisations following their historic defeats in the 1920s and 1930s. Most of the non-Marxist 'political business cycle' analysts rejected Kalecki's radical attack on particular historical capitalist systems of the 1930s and 1940s, and consequently failed to grasp the significant historical changes of the last forty years; they instead reduced elections and political struggles to econometric models using mathematical variables based on a combination of voters' behavioural responses to the marketing of policies during election years. In so far as parties and candidates *do* sell policies in order to win elections, there are quite valid reasons for investigating the relationship between elections and the accumulation of capital. What is wrong with the analyses of Frey, Nordhaus and MacRae is that conservative and liberal economic theories, which form the basis of their writings, prevent them from grasping the broader implications of the 'political business cycle', just as bourgeois theories fail to come to terms with the causes of 'stagflation'.

In conclusion, I have tried to highlight the weaknesses of those theories which (a) treat electoral struggles as 'political' events which either have only a marginal effect upon 'the Economy' or are seen in strategic terms alone, or (b) go to the opposite extreme, and minimise the importance of class and other social struggles by reducing elections to quantitative or economistic by-products of the 'business cycle' or 'logic of capital'. In the previous chapters I have tried to combat and expose the problems and blind spots of all those theories which are based on the notion of distinct realms of 'the political' and 'the economic'. My concern is to move beyond the ideal-typical notions of 'the State' without succumbing to the weaknesses manifested in both 'class-theoretical' and 'capital-logic' perspectives. I am not interested in studying elections for the sake of elections, like most non-radical political scientists. Rather, I wish to show how many social struggles are constituent elements of what I call an Electoral Process. It is the degree of freedom permitted in Electoral Processes which has direct and indirect repercussions on Production, Credit and Food Production Processes at local and national levels. Many other people have attempted to analyse all aspects of social life as being 'political'. I wish to build upon this tradition without reducing everything to some vague generality called 'the political'. We have already had radical 'productivist' theories, such as the Italian 'workerist' analyses of Tronti, Bologna, Negri, etc.,[15] which attempt to reduce all social activity outside the factory – education, theatre, housework, sport, leisure – to the workings of a 'social factory'. These economistic analyses conceive most activity in social institutions as functional for capitalists, and hence the contradictory and oppositional elements within the 'social factory' are minimised or ignored. Contemporary social relations cannot be adequately conceptualised in sweeping, all-embracing functional terms such as the 'social factory'. Nor can they be confined to neat and separate realms such as 'Civil Society'. If we are to transcend the artificial divisions between 'the State', 'Civil Society' and 'the Economy' as allegedly distinct realms, then a new set of categories is necessary – a set of categories which recognises the dynamic interrelations and contradictions between individuals and social movements, between public and private institutions, between local and national apparatuses, between national and supra-national autonomy and dependency.

Part II
Towards a New Way of Analysing State Institutions

5
Introducing the Concepts of Electoral, Production, Credit and Food Production Processes

Rather than simply contrast state institutions with private institutions as belonging to separate realms – each governed by inherently different forms of rationality – Electoral, Production, Credit and Food Production Processes are concepts which attempt to explain the overlapping and interdependent relations between state institutions and private institutions. There are, however, social practices such as judicial arbitration or the printing of money which are almost exclusive roles carried out by state institutions in most capitalist countries. But it is difficult to think of many social practices in contemporary capitalist societies which are carried out exclusively by private institutions. This is not to deny that in many capitalist countries such as the United States, state institutions are involved in less commodity production or the operation of cultural institutions and other social practices, compared to state institutions in other capitalist countries such as those in Western Europe. It is precisely these historical differences which make the concepts of Processes valuable analytical tools. Each local, regional and national Electoral, Production, Credit and Food Production Process consists of greater or fewer state-run or privately-run institutions. Whereas the concepts of 'the State', 'Civil Society' and 'the Economy' are nearly always used to delineate private institutions from state-run institutions – i.e. 'Civil Society' and 'the Economy' are supposed to be realms of only *private* activity – the concept of Electoral, Production, Credit and Food Production Processes cut across these traditional and artificial divisions. The notion of Processes does not conflate or reduce all 'non-economic' social institutions to 'the State' (e.g. the family), as do Althusserian concepts of Ideological State Apparatuses. On the contrary, it is very important not to lose sight of those institutions and enterprises which are privately owned or controlled (as I will make clear in subsequent chapters); but it is also important to analyse similar social practices, regardless of whether these are carried on within state or private institutions.

If one rejects the notion that 'the State', 'capital' or the 'proletariat' are subjects which act accordingly to coherent 'interests' (whether conscious or unconscious), then it is important that state and private institutions be seen in a new light. First, it is not possible to avoid economistic analyses (whether crude or subtle) if 'the Economy' is perceived to be separate from 'the State'. This is because 'the Economy' is regarded as being 'determinant in the last instance' or 'the State' has only 'relative autonomy'. Second, it is not possible to avoid attributing to 'the State' a coherent 'interest' if the multiplicity of state institutions are either overlooked or not analysed as part of diverse social processes. For while state administrators may strive for the total co-ordination of all state institutions, or publicly speak in the name of 'the State', there has never been a capitalist state which achieved complete unity of interest. Even in dictatorships historical analysis has shown that particular state institutions and administrators secretly undermined official orders or diverted resources to suit their own varied interests. In 'deconstructing' the so-called coherent 'interest' and nature of 'the State', I am concerned to analyse the role and nature of specific state institutions as constituent parts of Electoral, Production, Credit and Food Production Processes. For if one begins an analysis of state institutions as constituent elements of different Processes - each having different histories, pursuing different interests and characterised by different organisational structures, spheres of jurisdiction and control - then it is possible to better understand the contradictory roles which state institutions play in social development. It is also important to understand the varying capacities of particular governments which try to impose uniform control over diverse national and local state institutions - either through fiscal, legal, military or administrative coercion.

In capitalist societies, one can identify four main Processes or spheres of activity. Each Process can be found in different historical forms at local, regional, national and supra-national levels. Within each of these four different kinds of Processes are to be found a plethora of state and private institutions. Let me describe these four Processes or spheres briefly.

Electoral Processes consist of all those state and private institutions

which are involved with social policies, moral norms, social representation, law enforcement, cultural expression and definitions of citizenship. In chapter 6 I will explain why Electoral Processes are not to be
confused with voting systems. The expression or inhibition of activity
in cultural institutions is vitally affected by the organisation and ever-
changing historical definition of 'private' and 'public' rights. State institutions such as legislatures, city councils, social welfare institutions,
schools, courts, hospitals or television stations not only enforce policies
or disseminate ideas, they also constitute the arenas of social struggle
where churches, trade unions, political parties, employers' organisations,
artists, social movements, families and individuals confront one another.

Not only are Electoral Processes made up of diverse state and private
institutions, movements and organisations, but the very level at which
these forces and relations are organised is of critical importance. At the
supra-national level are to be found such state and privately organised
institutions as the European Parliament, International Labour Office,
United Nations' organisations, religious orders, military and intelligence
installations, and numerous cultural, scientific and political institutions –
both open and secret. At the national level, Electoral Processes are
characterised by the presence or absence of central or federal structures
and organisations. The degree of freedom to participate in decision-
making institutions, or tolerance of social values and practices, defines
the specific historical characteristics of each national Electoral Process.
However, regional and local Electoral Processes often embody values,
practices and institutional arrangements quite at odds with national
Electoral Process institutions and practices. The variety of local historical
institutions, the existence of particular religious, racial, ethnic and other
indigenous social forces all give local and regional Processes their specific
configuration of 'public spheres'. Each local city or region enjoys greater
or fewer state-run institutions, artistic and recreational facilities and
more or less democracy and social tolerance. The history of local and
regional Electoral Processes is also one of conflict and transformation,
as national and supra-national state and private institutions intervene,
or superimpose practices and structures upon local residents and institutions. Conversely, it is the sum total of local and regional Processes
which shape and determine the often fragile nature of particular national
Electoral Process institutions. The complexity of social forces within
local, regional and national Electoral Processes are also manifested in
supra-national institutions, where uniform policy and practice is
extremely difficult to achieve.

The social struggles over policies, laws, forms of representation and cultural expression are interrelated, but not reducible to the practices within Production Processes. Briefly, Production Processes are made up of all those enterprises and institutions which produce goods and services. The vast majority of enterprises are privately owned, but a significant percentage of goods and services – depending on the national Production Process – are produced within state sector institutions. The notion of Production Processes cuts across the artificially separate realms of 'the State' and 'the Economy', just as the concept of Electoral Processes cuts across the separate realms of 'the State' and 'Civil Society'. The constituent role of state institutions in particular national and local Production Processes creates major problems for all those theories which analyse 'the Economy' and the 'business cycle' as a realm or patterned development which 'the State' may 'intervene in' or 'steer', but which nevertheless remains the exclusive domain of private enterprise.

In contrast to organisations and enterprises within Production Processes, the institutions and social forces within Credit Processes do not directly produce goods and services (except banking, insurance and other financial services). Rather, one can divide Credit Processes into all those institutions which create credit or administer finance for the purpose of making profits (e.g. banks, accountancy firms or brokers), and all those institutions involved in the collection and distribution of tax revenue, fiscal budgeting, currency control and so forth. The creation of credit for private businesses, state institutions, social organisations or individuals is not identical with the struggle over the size, nature and distribution of revenue in different local and national Credit Processes. Within Credit Processes it is possible to identify historical developments and conflicts which have produced 'fiscal crises' affecting both state-run and privately-run institutions. Although social relations and institutions within Electoral, Production, Credit and Food Production Processes are interrelated, the problems associated with the raising and distribution of sufficient credit or revenue, cannot be reduced to those relations visible in other Processes.

Finally, the notion of Food Production Processes enables one to distinguish the type of goods produced within Production Processes from the social relations and environmental forces affecting the production of food. Food Production Processes consist of (a) *direct* food producers such as farmers; (b) *intermediate* elements such as the producers of fertilisers and chemicals as well as those involved in the storage, sale and distribution of manufactured and unprocessed food; and (c) all the *indirect* elements of Food Production Processes which affect the quantity and quality of food production as well as species survival – from pollution, raw material extraction, changes in climate to a whole range of other environmental variables. While food production overlaps with other industries in Production Processes, an ecological or food crisis cannot be equated with a crisis in the production of inanimate goods, nor reduced to crises within Credit or Electoral Processes. The historical changes in many intermediate and indirect elements of Food Production Processes, while brought about by capitalist production, now threaten all forms of food production and all species. Failure to provide adequate food (at prices which the majority of a particular population can afford), creates potential disaster for both governments and populations alike.

Just as there are major differences between elements of local, national and supra-national Electoral Processes, so too, it is necessary to note the major differences between institutions in local, national and supra-national Production, Credit and Food Production Processes. At local and regional levels, it is often the case that Production, Credit and Food Production Processes are increasingly dominated by national and supra-national state and private institutions and enterprises. The size, nature and availability of state-produced goods and services, the quality of social welfare and educational institutions, the relative dependency of local and regional authorities upon national budgetary allocations and fiscal revenue, the presence or absence of national food marketing boards, environmental protection agencies or supra-national laws governing fishing or mineral rights in local waters – all determine the social relations and practices within local and regional Production, Credit and Food Production Processes. Similarly, the penetration of local and regional markets by national and supra-national private enterprises, the domination of finance capital and credit facilities by non-local banks, the cartelisation of commodities and food crops, the transformation of local crops and diets by supra-national agribusinesses, the large variations between national and local wage rates, levels of unemployment and rates of investment and inflation, all vitally affect class relations both between classes and within classes. Given that state institutions and private enterprises together constitute the nature of local, national and supra-national Production, Credit and Food Production Processes, I will try to show in subsequent chapters why the uneven historical development of these Processes (at so many levels), has serious implications for class conflict, crisis control and the possible reproduction of particular capitalist societies.

Although distinct social practices are to be found in each specific local or national Process, these Processes are not rigid spheres with strict boundaries. For example, trade unions are part of Production Processes as well as being important organisations struggling over rights and powers within Electoral Processes. Similarly, state-owned banks help finance private businesses as well as provide credit to foreign governments – thus linking private and state-run institutions within Production, Credit and Food Production Processes. The interpenetration of institutions and social relations has long been noted by people unhappy with the concepts of 'Civil Society' and 'the State' as separate realms. Once the focal point has shifted away from 'the State' and 'Civil Society' a polar opposites and separate realms to different kinds of practices making up different kinds of Processes, social life can be analysed in a more dialectical manner. For example, the uneven historical development of particular nation-states and local cultures, the residue of social institutions (e.g. legal and monarchical institutions) which are peculiar to specific Electoral Processes, the varying levels of state-owned industries in particular national Production, Credit and Food Production Processes or the varying powers of local, regional or supra-national institutions in centralised or federal social orders – all these historical developments vitally affect the relationship of forces in one Process with forces in another local or national Process. It is the social conflict and contradictions within each local, national and supra-national Electoral, Production, Credit and Food Production Process which exacerbate the *desynchronisation of Processes* and make it impossible for capitalist societies to avoid major crises. In subsequent chapters I will explain in detail why social relations within each local or national Process cannot be adequately planned or co-ordinated, and why the failure to 'synchronise' relations within and between the different Processes causes many contemporary crises.

Having briefly defined some of the characteristics of Electoral, Production, Credit and Food Production Processes, let me explain how I arrived at the concept of Processes. First, I have always been conscious that capitalist societies are characterised by numerous social and historical differences which manifest themselves at local, regional, national and supra-national levels. Instead of there being a single 'world capitalist mode of production', it is important to recognise that many of the social institutions and social movements within all these fragmented local and national Processes are permanently at odds with one another. Second, if one is not to reduce all these conflicts to impersonal 'structures', it is necessary to reject all those 'scientific laws' which subject social life to a series of cycles or waves which are independent of peoples' activity and consciousness. Third, the phenomenon of desynchronisation comes from volume 2 of *Capital* where Marx attempted to explain a whole range of different activities by analysing the 'circuits' or processes of capital. While Marx's analysis of the capitalist production and circulation process is too limited to explain adequately social relations within state institutions or all those social relations 'outside' the wage-labour process (e.g. family relations), it does serve as a useful departing point. I have therefore reconceptualised Marx's theory of the processes of capital metamorphosis by significantly broadening and modifying the 'circuit' of *private* capital and including all those social relations and forces 'outside' the market.

I share with Marx the basic desire to explain the social relations which reproduce capitalist societies. The difference is that I regard Marx's categories as inadequate not only for analysing how capitalist societies reproduce themselves, but even more so when the *nonreproduction* of dominant social relations is to be explained. Nevertheless, Marx's brilliant analysis of the 'circuits' of *private* capitalist production serves as an excellent basis for grasping the nature of desynchronised Processes. Marx, it will be recalled, was interested in more than simply abstracting the laws and categories of capitalist production. His specific historical analyses of the social relations of capital accumulation were matched by his subdivision of capital itself – into 'money-capital', 'productive-capital' and 'commodity-capital'. In volume 2 of *Capital*, Marx attempted to show how capital underwent a metamorphosis through the different 'processes' or 'circuits' of money, production and circulation of commodities. Each stage of the metamorphosis of capital entailed different relations and problems; during the phase of 'productive-capital', for example, the labour process could be interrupted, while the failure to sell commodities during the phase of 'commodity-capital' would prevent the 'circuit' being completed by the form of 'money-capital'. Given the numerous businesses competing with one another, plus the infinite variety of commodities produced, forms of money borrowed, and complications in circulation processes, Marx attempted to show that each phase of capital operated in a different period of time and space. The individual capitalist cannot control all stages of capital metamorphosis – e.g. the circulation of commodities once they leave the 'productive-capital' phase. Yet the capitalists' goal is to *reduce* the turnover time in each 'circuit' of capital, so that 'money-capital' invested in 'productive-capital' returns to the money form after being sold on the market. The quicker the turnover time, the cheaper the process, the greater the profit; thus more can be invested and produced, and more value realised in the money form.

It was part of Marx's analysis of capitalist production to show that capital always existed in a *desynchronised* or discontinuous form as the successive phases of the 'circuit' were realised (or failed to be realised) at three levels: (a) the micro-level of the metamorphosis of each individual commodity; (b) the 'circuit' of several commodities produced within the same capitalist enterprise; and (c) the macro-level of all capitalist enterprises each embedded within multiple 'circuits' of capital as they constituted the whole capitalist mode of production and exchange. Even when particular capitalist societies experienced what is called a boom period, the sum total of all the capitalists operating could never overcome the *permanent desynchronisation* of time and physical phases of the numerous 'circuits' of capital. Each business at one point or another encountered interruptions, bottlenecks or crises in production or circulation as well as in the availability of 'money-capital', which could prove harmless or ruinous depending on the variables involved. When the capitalist class as a whole experienced interruptions to the numerous individual 'circuits' of capital, a major social crisis manifested itself as a 'depression'. According to Marx, capitalist societies could not avoid major crises in the 'circuits' of capital as an unplanned competitive society was continually subject to desynchronisation of turnover time, which he called the 'anarchy of the market'.

While Marx's theory of *private capital* in its three stages of the 'circuit' serves as one of the points of departure for my notion of Processes, there are good reasons why this classical theory cannot be accepted in its original form. First, hardly any major capitalist enterprise now undergoes a purely private form of capital metamorphosis. This is evident in the numerous indispensable roles which state institutions play in the provision of 'money-capital', the subsidisation of 'productive-capital' and the provision of infrastructural support to facilitate the circulation of 'commodity-capital' (ports, roads and many other services). Second, *social* reproduction entails *far more* than an understanding of the 'circuit' of *private capital* – hence the need to grasp other Processes, especially social relations within Electoral and Food Production Processes – which are constituent elements in the possible reproduction and non-reproduction of capitalist societies. Third, private capitalist enterprises exist in a world divided into capitalist and non-capitalist nations whose interests and social conflicts cannot all be reduced to the logic of capitalist production.

Marx identified the constituent elements in each phase of capital (e.g. all the different aspects of 'commodity-capital' in circulation such as transport, storage, sales), without overlooking the fact that each of these constituent elements denoted a quite different stage or phase in the 'circuit' of capital. While my conception of Processes is much broader than Marx's three forms of capital, it is also possible to distinguish the component elements of each Electoral, Production, Credit and Food Production Process. For example, it is possible to isolate and analyse a particular business, legal institution, social movement, church, farm or whatever, without forgetting the role of this individual social unit within a larger Process. In other words, one can identify and isolate particular state institutions and private institutions as constituent elements of local, national or supra-national Processes without having to establish empirically the existence of a *whole* Electoral, Production, Credit or Food Production Process. Just as one cannot see surplus-value in a commodity (even though one can analyse the separate phases of the production and circulation of value), neither can one empirically observe Electoral or Credit Processes with clear boundaries separating one from the other. But then the notion of distinct realms, as in 'the State', 'Civil Society' and 'the Economy', embodies precisely that artificiality which the notion of Electoral, Production, Credit and Food Production Processes seeks to combat. Marxism has already shown us how to identify an individual at both the micro- or inter-personal level as well as at the macro- or class level – even though one cannot clearly see classes as empirical entities. Similarly, a person may well be employed in a state or private institution, and yet simultaneously be part of an Electoral, Production, Credit or Food Production Process.

In short, Processes are no more empirically visible than concepts such as 'class' or 'the Economy', or the production of surplus-value. Yet, as analytic concepts, I believe they not only overcome existing categorical deficiencies, but also throw new light on the complexity of local, national and supra-national relations. The following analysis of the desynchronisation of the various Electoral, Production, Credit and Food Production Processes is, I believe, one of the first attempts to grasp how the roles and structures of state institutions are integral to capitalist societies, to relate the vital relations 'outside' the factory to the possibilities of particular capitalist societies surviving, and equally importantly, to clarify the simplistic misinterpretations of relations between local, national and international social institutions and classes.

I have stressed the importance of going beyond Marx's analysis of the 'circuit' of private capital if we are to understand the causes of contemporary crises in capitalist societies. Capitalist social relations cannot be faithfully reproduced due to lack of adequate control and 'synchronisation' of local, national and supra-national social forces; hence the future compatibility of the interrelated private and state institutions within capitalist societies is diminished the more that each local or national Process becomes subject to its own separate conflictual or desynchronised social relations. However, it is important to emphasise that Electoral, Production, Credit and Food Production Processes are quite different to Marx's 'stages' of capital. The positivism latent in Marx's desire to specify the 'laws' of capitalist production can have no place in studying the historical development of particular Processes. The social relations which I analyse in different Electoral or Credit Processes, etc. cannot be reduced to inanimate objects such as 'commodity-capital' – despite the fact that social participants within each Process are constantly struggling over the control or nature of numerous commodities and physical objects.

Also, the Processes I am about to discuss are not 'circuits' or cycles. Processes are desynchronised with one another, but they do not undergo a metamorphosis of one stage after another. The social relations within each local or national Process are not reified or quantifiable variables which go up and down in a historical vacuum as do so many ideal-typical models of the 'business cycle'. Although it is possible to identify various activities within particular Processes which occur on a regular basis – elections, government budgets, or quarterly business figures, for example – this does not mean that a whole local or national Electoral or Production Process operates according to cyclical patterns. In fact, the concept of Process is free of the notion of circularity or repetition and hence more aptly conveys the meaning of the social relations and forces I wish to discuss. As I will explain later on, it is not possible to devalorise or write off state institutions or social relations or environmental pollution as one does with commodity capital. Production, Credit, Electoral and Food Production Processes are not subject to mechanical booms and busts. Hence the desynchronisation of social relations within particular local or national Processes leads to crises which are not repeatable or cyclical as in the conventional bourgeois and Marxian analyses of private capitalist production. Poverty of language, plus the deeply ingrained notion of cyclical activity, should not prevent us from thinking of Processes in a *non-cyclical* manner.

I would also like to emphasise that I spell the various Processes with capital letters, not in order to reify these social spheres, but rather stylistically in order to distinguish these new concepts from the conventional use of the term 'process'. Although the 'bourgeoisie are constantly revolutionising the means of production' in local, national and supra-national Processes, it would be a mistake to interpret Processes as having no permanent or relatively unchanged social structures. The concepts of Electoral, Production, Credit and Food Production Processes are not intended to replace deep-seated structures, but rather to replace the traditional notions of separate realms of 'the State', 'Civil Society' and 'the Economy'.

The non-cyclical historical development of each desynchronised local, national and supra-national Process can be documented by careful historical research. While the following chapters will draw upon historical studies to explain the nature of relations within particular Processes, the emphasis will be largely on contemporary historical relations rather than on the historical development of Processes. Nevertheless, it is important to state that the notion of Processes is close to meaningless in pre-capitalist societies. This is because there is an inadequate differentiation of specific institutions, social roles, productive and credit enterprises and division of labour which we find only as capitalist societies begin to develop. Although one can historically trace the early development of particular capitalist enterprises and state institutions (as constituent elements of developing Electoral, Production or Credit Processes), it is only in the nineteenth and twentieth centuries that we witness the emergence (in very uneven chronological order) of numerous local and national Processes in different societies. In short, the history of particular Processes is inseparably linked to the emergence and development of capitalist societies. But as capitalist societies consist of more than *private* capitalist enterprises, the history of Electoral, Production, Credit and Food Production Processes is the history of the emergence and development of both public and private social institutions, of their compatibility and incompatibility, of the social struggles to limit, control or transform these private and public institutions and social relations.

Finally, it may be asked: why are there only Electoral, Production, Credit and Food Production Processes? Why not have a 'Cultural Process' or some other Process? What of all those individuals, families and social organisations which are neither businesses, unions, nor part of state institutions – are they 'outside' Electoral, Production, Credit and Food Production Processes? First, individuals exist on their own or in particular forms of family or group relations. All individuals are simultaneously constituent elements of one or more Process through their occupation, social position or relation to particular institutions. Second, all those institutions and practices which are currently conceptualised under the headings 'the State', 'Civil Society' and 'the Economy', are also constituent elements of Electoral, Production, Credit and Food Production Processes. But as the boundaries between these traditional realms are so misleading and arbitrary, I have introduced the notion of Processes in order more adequately to explain the many overlapping and interdependent social practices carried out by both state-run and private institutions. Many people are attracted to theories which posit clear realms of social action. For example, if I had called local, national and supra-national Processes 'Electoral subsystem' or 'Production sub-system', it is possible that many readers would feel more at home with these system-theory concepts. However, Processes are spheres of social practice which defy the strict boundaries between one sub-system and another.

Because the four Processes embrace all those activities and institutions normally conceptualised as 'the State' or 'Civil Society' (but without the disadvantages and distortions inherent in these concepts), it is not necessary to speak of extra and distinct Processes such as a 'Cultural Process'. For example, historical analyses will show that all forms of cultural expression have been affected or determined by the degree of freedom permitted within Electoral Processes, or the availability of material resources, state subsidies and personal income which make it possible to perform, publish or indulge in social activities and leisure. An individual's class, gender, race or age all determine possible levels of 'cultural capital' which can be acquired or utilised. In this respect all people within capitalist societies are defined by their role and relationship within one or more of the local and national Processes. Formally, they may all be members of a society, but in actuality they are all defined by an act in terms of their dependence on, control of and critical awareness of social relations in one or more of the Processes. For example, the distribution of state funding of the arts, the level of profit in the 'culture industry', censorship and moral controversies over art, plays, films, books, the exclusion of women and blacks from sporting and other cultural activities, the popularity of violent, competitive sports, the barbaric killing of animals in blood sports or the specific social laws which make gambling, divorce, childcare, access to clubs, etc. – these are all forms of social action and policy constituting Electoral, Production, Credit and Food Production Processes. Although one can identify many forms of social activity, e.g. war, sport, etc., I do not believe that these acts justify being called separate Processes or social spheres. In developing the concepts of Electoral, Production, Credit and Food Production Processes I recognise that there is a major risk that the notion of Processes may be trivialised or used in a manner which is quite at odds with my theory. In subsequent chapters I hope that my new concepts will be adequately grounded so as to minimise misinterpretations.

Finally, one cannot reduce individual artistic creations to social structures; this is ultimately true of all individual thought and activity. The concept of particular Processes enables us to comprehend the social context and historical conflicts which make it possible for some people as opposed to others, to have access to or control over resources, or greater or limited life-chances. But why some people become great artists, administrators or athletes cannot be completely reduced to the 'structures'. The concept of Electoral Process enables us to analyse which people are either participants through one or more organisations, or merely inactive victims, consumers or observers.

Many theorists are more preoccupied with thematic issues such as 'mass culture', secularisation, alienation, etc., and leave either untouched or unquestioned basic categories such as 'the State' or 'Civil Society'. The concept of desynchronised local and national Processes can throw new light on these thematic problems, and yet avoid the ahistorical analyses of states so common in theories of 'modernity'. As for the manner and form in which individuals experience personal and social changes, only a detailed study of the interconnections between individual cognitive and moral development, and the roles which ideology and coercion play in preventing, inhibiting or stimulating the participation of individuals in social institutions, will help to explain the specific historical character of local, national and supra-national Processes. If the concepts of Electoral, Production, Credit and Food Production Processes can avoid the problems associated with categories such as 'Civil Society', and yet throw new light on the nature of social contradictions within capitalist societies, then the difficulty of introducing new concepts will have been justified.

6
Overcoming the Dichotomy of 'The State' and 'Civil Society': The Importance of Electoral Processes

I would like to explain why I have chosen the concept Electoral Process in preference to other concepts. I would also like to explain why Electoral Processes are more than the formal electoral or voting system of particular countries and why activities and institutions within Electoral Processes are not simply 'superstructural' phenomena.

Many Marxists have contrasted the formal 'appearance' or ideological notion of individual citizens as free and equal in 'the State', with the 'essence' or reality of 'Civil Society' as a class-dominated realm of exploitation and inequality. Yet, because Marxists are also aware that churches, political parties, media outlets, trade unions, cultural organisations, educational institutions, etc., simultaneously traverse, occupy or function within the so-called separate realms of 'the State' and 'Civil Society', there is no agreement as to where the boundary of one realm finishes and the other begins. For while it is quite important to distinguish between ideological notions of 'abstract citizens' and 'actual', unequal members of social classes, it is quite another thing to believe that these divisions mirror the separate and distinct realms of 'the State' and 'Civil Society'. If states are not to be thought of solely as geographical entities (a common misconception to be found especially in works on international relations), or reduced to elected or non-elected political, legal, bureaucratic and military executives (a common misconception of states as mere 'superstructures'), then the enormously complex roles and practices within state institutions will have to be analysed more comprehensively. It is important not to lose sight of the existence of state institutions as opposed to private organisations. But it is also important to recognise that in many instances there are little or no organisational, ideological and structural differences between state-run and private institutions, just as in many other instances there are fundamentally irreconcilable differences between the latter. The differences between state institutions and private institutions do not exist because one type of institution follows the 'rationality' of 'the State', and the other conforms to the 'logic' of 'Civil Society'. *There is no uniform 'logic' expressed in state institutions.* Rather than discuss 'the State' as a homogeneous subject or thing, it is vital to recognise the different social practices and logic of operation of specific state institutions in Electoral Processes, e.g. legal or parliamentary institutions, as opposed to practices within state institutions in Production, Credit or Food Production Processes (e.g. nationalised industries, treasury departments or food marketing boards).

There are countless studies about how 'Western man' struggled to define individual rights against the tyranny of 'the State'. The dichotomy of 'the State' and 'Civil Society' has affected both Right and Left political analyses, in so far as 'the State' has been depicted as enemy number one. Social and political rights are normally seen as belonging to the realm of 'Civil Society' while 'the State' is defined and circumscribed by the varying strength and plurality of groups existing in 'Civil Society'. The notion of Electoral Processes cuts across this false dichotomy and false history. In reality the historical record is also very much a struggle for democracy and participation within state institutions, rather than simply a struggle of 'Civil Society' against 'the State'. No history of capitalist societies would be complete without recognising the ongoing battles which have taken place in state institutions – in educational institutions, radio and television stations, hospitals, legislatures, public housing estates, etc. – rather than simply 'outside' 'the State' in 'Civil Society'. Many of the institutions which belong to what is traditionally called 'Civil Society' also belong to Electoral Processes. But the crucial difference between the concepts of 'Civil Society' and 'Electoral Process' is that while one cannot have state institutions in 'Civil Society', *there can be no Electoral Process unless state institutions are also constituent elements of each local, national and supra-national Electoral Process.* Conversely, Electoral Processes are not simply another conceptual version of the Althusserian notions of Ideological and Repressive State Apparatuses which blur the difference between state institutions and private institutions. Electoral Processes are the very arenas of social struggle; state institutions within these Processes do not faithfully reproduce the dominant social relations, or express an unambiguous and *a priori* 'logic' which maintains 'social cohesion'.

Just as state institutions do not have a life of their own, so too, there has never been a ready-finished realm known as 'Civil Society' which has either produced the 'superstructures' known as 'the State', or been the victim of ever-increasing 'state intervention'. Rather, the history of Electoral Processes in capitalist societies is the history of public and private institutions which have both been controlled or financed by restrictive, secretive, authoritarian and exclusive social classes, or partially democratised and/or challenged by new social movements, oppressed social classes and new institutions. In many capitalist societies which exist today, the historical period which corresponded to the formation of large numbers of completely independent, private social institutions (separate from the old 'feudal' pre-capitalist orders) either never existed, or lasted only a brief length of time. By the beginning of the twentieth century, many of these private institutions were being organisationally or financially intermeshed with state institutions. For example, the early historical struggles by religious groups for autonomy and freedom from persecution by ruling princes or 'established churches', has not meant that contemporary state institutions are all invariably distinct from religious bodies. While government administrators are generally different personnel to the leaders of religious institutions (hence the old division between 'State' and 'Church'), it is quite common to see clerical and lay religious personnel inseparably involved in the administration of various statutory bodies, or 'private' church schools dependent on state taxes. It is even more common to see religious bodies – whether Catholic, Dutch Reform, Islamic or mixtures known as the moral majority – directly or indirectly seeking to win control over legislatures and other state institutions.

As for that other key institution of 'Civil Society' – 'the family' – we know from historical studies that capitalist industrialisation in its ferocious infancy, often had little room for a separate sphere known as the 'private family'. Workers, whether children or adults, slept, ate and often died in the all-consuming factories. The depopulation of the countryside, the masses of nomadic or relatively unsettled peasant and early proletarian populations, the growth and disappearance of a large servant class, the mass migration of millions to other countries, the growth and minimisation of child labour – all made the experience of 'family life' something quite different to what is currently called 'the family'. Certainly, many capitalist societies were characterised by well-developed kinship relations or family life. But it is also true that in many other capitalist societies, the emergence of a 'settled' private family sphere enjoyed by members of all social classes, was something which only developed with the improvement of working conditions (won by class struggle) and the corresponding growth of state-run institutions such as schools, public transport and housing and recreational facilities. If 'Civil Society' is supposed to constitute that realm where the material conditions of everyday life are reproduced, then the history of urban life in capitalist societies is incomprehensible without acknowledging the massive role played by local and national state institutions – not as mere regulatory structures – but as active constituent elements of 'civic life'.

Although the concept 'electoral' is generally used in contemporary language to mean something to do with voting systems or party politics, I use Electoral in the more traditional and broader sense as embracing the notion of 'the elect', 'the chosen' or 'the privileged'. Leaving behind the religious connotations, Electoral Processes should be understood as involving social struggles over what constitute public and private rights and privileges. Why have certain individuals and groups been appointed, or appointed themselves rather than been elected by others? Who has a say on the vital issues of how social institutions (state or private) are to be organised and what criteria or needs they should try to satisfy? It is no accident that the contemporary notion of 'electoral' has been reduced to a restricted sphere of voting or 'parliamentary politics'. The contemporary 'elector' is no longer a prince determining policies in all spheres of life. Yet in capitalist societies there are few private or state institutions not subjected to challenges and demands for access, accountability and equality made by the 'non-elect' and non-privileged.

In choosing the concept 'Electoral Process', I have deliberately avoided the popular notion of 'political process' because this is widely regarded as being synonymous with the narrow sphere of party politics. Also, the term 'political process' is indiscriminately used and lacks sufficient rigour. One can find a 'political process' in any century in any society, no matter how rudimentary or complex. Everything can be 'political' or, conversely, only official parties and institutions can be seen as 'political'. In other words, the concept 'political process' transcends capitalist countries, and can embrace all types of social formations in a vague and over-generalised manner. Electoral Processes are by and large relevant to emerging and developed capitalist societies and denote, as I will explain later on, the relations between formal state institution and a whole range of social movements and organisations. The notion of Electoral Process also differs fundamentally from the attainment of 'citizenship rights' as analysed by non-Marxists such as Marshall or Bendix.[1] First, authors such as Marshall, Bendix and Dahrendorf emphasise the development of 'citizenship rights' as testimony to the obsolescence of either Marx's theory of class conflict or the passing of industrial capitalist society.[2] In contrast, the notion of Electoral Processes opposes the ideological concept of a post-capitalist, 'post-industrial society' and is based on the central role of class struggle. Second, while including Marshall's focus on 'citizenship rights', the notion of Electoral Processes spreads well beyond the question of changes to the legal and social definition of individuals. The concept of Electoral Processes enables one also to analyse and understand the informal, illegitimate and revolutionary elements within societies; the struggles to democratise both private and state-run social institutions are important in so far as these struggles indicate which areas of social control will be bitterly defended by capitalist classes, and also why the struggle for citizenship transcends the right to have a vote, get social welfare or be treated equally before the law.

To speak of an Electoral Process is to identify the proverbial tip of an iceberg beneath or alongside which go a set of social institutions, consciousness and specific history of social conflicts. I will attempt to show that *the capitalist class (in any capitalist society) can alleviate (but not overcome) profound crisis only to the extent that it can free Production, Credit and Food Production Processes from the constraints of ongoing free Electoral Processes.* At the same time, a capitalist society which lacks free Electoral Processes is in turn deeply affected by those capitalist classes which cannot resolve crises (such as 'stagflation') within their own national boundaries *precisely because they are subject to a free Electoral Process.* The movement of American, West European and other transnational corporations into Brazil, South Korea, Taiwan and other dictatorships is not fully comprehensible, unless we grasp the *relative* freedom of social forces acting within particular Electoral Processes, and the effect of these varying Electoral Processes upon the profitable accumulation of private capital. Of course, the different conditions applying in capitalist societies with free political participation, and in those with fascist or repressive regimes, has been noted for decades. As Kalecki put it so clearly in 1943: 'In a democracy one does not know what the next Government will be like. Under fascism there is no next Government'.[3] In their narrower sense, Electoral Processes are based on the degree of protection and 'political space' afforded by the existence of a freely-elected national parliament and local or regional legislatures.

But just as we can see the historical fragility of formal electoral rights in many capitalist societies, so too can we witness the deep-seated social struggles over the other related historical tendency visible within Electoral Processes. This broader tendency can be best understood, perhaps, as the historical struggle for democratisation and participation *within* social institutions. This broader tendency (so bitterly resisted in the past and the present) is much more than the fight for formal citizenship rights. It is the larger struggle to democratise and redefine the eligibility, the identity and the needs of whole sections of society who have been at one time or another excluded, oppressed, and not even recognised as existing, let alone permitted to participate in making decisions for themselves. Whether it be state-run institutions such as hospitals, schools or administrative departments, or private, non-state organisations such as trade unions, businesses, churches, cultural and sporting groups, or at the micro-level, the structure of family relations, it is impossible to ignore the struggles which have taken place over accountability, representation, non-secrecy, discrimination, autonomy and so forth. To be fully accountable, honest, democratic and non-discriminatory means to require the people running these institutions to face elections, or to consider the views of all those hitherto excluded or represented only tokenly – that is 'formally'. Electoral Processes therefore constitute those spheres where the larger historical tendency of more and more people to demand choice, voice, control, open books and reciprocal, egalitarian rights has been evident in clashes between local and national as well as between national and supra-national forces; it is expressed at the micro-level in the clash between members of different classes, genders, races or age groups. Electoral means to have a say and not just a vote. It embraces the struggle against hierarchical relations which are expressed territorially.

While the demand for a freely elected parliament based on a universal franchise is inseparably related to the broader historical tendency of democratisation just described, the two historical tendencies should not be reduced to one another. In fact, many people engaged in the struggle for self-management, or against the oppression of women, have a profound distrust for what is called 'bourgeois democracy'. Nevertheless, the combined struggles for the extension of participation and accountability at both the formal and informal levels of Electoral Processes are sufficiently threatening to particular ruling classes – who often see no difference between free trade unions, political parties and feminists, animal liberationists, etc., regardless of the hostility the latter groups and movements feel for one another.

One additional related point has to be made. Electoral Processes should not be seen as purely social processes which have a negative or positive relationship to private capital accumulation. While I will be strongly emphasising the relationship between Electoral Processes and capitalist enterprises, the historical developments (within Electoral Processes) of anti-authoritarian, anti-sexist, anti-racist and pro-environmental values and practices clearly transcend the immediate historical question relating to the future of capitalist societies. In this vital sense the concept of Electoral Process is not a new form of economism. Let me now elaborate on some of the key characteristics of Electoral Processes.

Characteristics of Free Electoral Processes

In so far as the level of mass participation reflects the historical struggles against class opposition and religious and social consorship, a free Electoral Process is inconceivable without the corresponding or *a priori* freedom won by organisations such as trade unions, cultural institutions and civil liberties groups. To the overt politicised despotism of everyday life under feudalism (where everyone knew their restricted formal place in the social hierarchy), Marx contrasted capitalist societies in which despotic control was overthrown in the 'public sphere' only to continue inside the enterprises of private capitalist production. Lenin extended Marx's critique of the limited 'guerilla war' carred out by trade unions against the despotic control of capitalists within private enterprises, by delineating the differences between spontaneous, narrow economistic demands and conscious revolutionary politics in and outside the factory. Despite Lenin's mistaken reduction of nearly all trade union activity to non-revolutionary economistic consciousness,[4] both he and Marx were correct in calling for the need to develop broadly-based revolutionary political organisations if capitalist classes were to be overthrown.

In their critique of economism and 'despotism within the factory', Marx and Lenin left subsequent generations of Marxists a heightened sense of the limits of reformism but a poor understanding of how *'non-revolutionary'* consciousness was undermining capitalist social relations. The fight to extend the franchise was merely one aspect of the struggle to extend democracy and civil participation. During the past one hundred years, democracy has been extended very unevenly in various capitalist societies – from the limited right to vote in elections, to greater rights and decision-making powers in community institutions.[5] The fact that mass revolutionary parties have not swept to power in leading capitalist societies is not a sign that consciousness has remained universally trapped at the level of 'trade union economism'. Movements against the oppression of women and blacks, against nuclear war, against the destruction of the environment, against the violation of patient, prisoner, animal and child rights, together with struggles against intolerance, corruption and manipulation, have all radically challenged the notion of democracy and equality within Electoral Processes without overthrowing capitalist production.

Between despotism and the revolutionary barricades may be found a multitude of political freedoms and activity; it is the very uneven attainment of social freedoms and *limited* political control by non-capitalist forces which makes the role of Electoral Processes (in their broadest sense) so crucial in determining rates of private accumulation. Therefore, it is generally easy to see the differences between capitalist societies such as Britain or Sweden (which have free parliamentary institutions), and military dictatorships like those in Chile, Indonesia, Pakistan or Turkey, where voting is either prevented or reduced to token rituals which are tolerated so long as they constitute no threat to the prevailing regimes. Marxists have tended to put 'reformism' into the one boat and blur the important ideological and institutional differences between those countries which have free elections.

It is important to explain why the inclusion of trade union activity, civil liberties and community struggles under the notion Electoral Processes is not simply one of convenience. While these latter forms of struggle preceded, and often continue without direct interest in, or connection to, party-political activity in elections, there would be little scope for trade unions, civil liberty organisations and community groups to be successful (short of overthrowing dictatorial regimes) without the formal sanction of freely-elected parliamentary institutions. The degree of power and freedom permitted in different national parliaments or legislatures, acts as both symbolic and structural guarantor of the degree of freedom and activity in which *non-party* organisations can engage. Conversely, the organisational strength of unions, critical media, educational groups, and other social movements decisively affects the maintenance of a free parliamentary process, since defeats suffered by the former may result in the loss or watering-down of the legislatures' power and of the range of alternative social policies offered at elections. It is in this sense that Electoral Processes are unintelligible if confined merely to elections and voting behaviour.

But it is not just organisations and movements demanding greater freedoms and rights which are part of particular Electoral Processes. Within Electoral Processes are also to be found anti-democratic bodies (from reactionary political movements to business lobby groups, private security organisations and professional criminals), as well as all those state apparatuses preoccupied with the enforcement of law and order – plus a myriad of illegal, corrupt and undercover operations. Military and police apparatuses are part of Electoral Processes because they define the historical possibilities of violent and non-violent change. The constitutional checks and balances on military and paramilitary apparatuses are inseparably related to the balance of class forces within particular Electoral Processes, and to the strategic options open to ruling classes (whether they will tolerate free Electoral Processes or find naked force more attractive).

It should not be forgotten, however, that the members of police and military apparatuses are themselves influenced by developments within Electoral Processes. One has only to think of the attack upon police forces in the United States, Western Europe and Australia, when the police attempted to organise themselves into trade unions shortly before and after the First World War. Police were either sacked en masse (as in Boston in 1919) or prevented from joining trade union movements. We should similarly note the attempts by soldiers in recent years to organise trade unions, the perennial problems of conscript soldiers as a security risk should civil war break out, the need to maintain income parity of military and police personnel *vis-à-vis* other civilian wage levels, and finally, the direct participation of police and other military personnel in elections and their lobbying of legislatures (due to threats of unemployment, cut-backs, investigation of corruption and so forth). Even more dramatically, we have seen in countries such as India, Turkey and the United States police and other paramilitary forces fighting one another in violent confrontations over local and national policies. In Western Europe and North America police chiefs have identified themselves as for or against specific social protest movements, strikes or law-and-order legislation. The democratising tendency within particular Electoral Processes has also witnessed military personnel openly marching in protest against nuclear missiles and war. While there is no disputing the repressive and often brutal roles which police and military have played in the suppression of anti-capitalist movements, those state personnel working within what some choose to call Repressive Apparatuses do not stand 'above' Electoral Processes; their specific historical responses to social conflict and policy issues cannot be taken for granted – as many radicals assume – because not all military and paramilitary forces are committed to some *a priori* ethic or functional role in capitalist societies. In Part III I will discuss the role of military and paramilitary organisations (as non-democratic institutions) and the problems they pose for socialist alternatives.

Of particular importance in understanding the effect of different Electoral Processes on private accumulation are the substantial historical differences and structural connections between wage-workers and other citizens. In Western Europe, Japan and Australia, there are long historical connections between trade union movements and Labour, Social-Democratic and Communist parties. Yet there are major differences between all of these parties and national trade union organisations in such matters as structural relations, size of membership, length of years in government (compare the decades of Social-Democratic dominance in Sweden with the brief years of Federal Labor Party government in Australia), alliance with non-labour parties of the Right, historical suppression by Axis powers and existence under post-war military administration in Austria, Germany and Japan. All of these experiences are in marked contrast to the United States and Canada where the Electoral Processes are characterised by the absence of a major Social-Democratic party, let alone a major Communist Party (the New Democratic Party in Canada is still relatively small). The belated emergence of large industrial unions in the 1930s and 1940s,[6] the subordination of significant sections of Canadian workers to American unions largely outside their control, and major imbalances between the minority of organised workers and the vast majority of unorganised workers (not to mention the larger populations dependent on government welfare), are also important historical differences. It goes without saying that there are vast differences between all those capitalist countries with free Electoral Processes, and all those other capitalist societies with severely limited or completely suppressed free Electoral Processes.

At this point it is important to qualify what I mean by a free Electoral Process. No capitalist society to date has had a completely free Electoral Process. Even countries such as Britain or Sweden have numerous formal and informal legal, material and organisational restrictions on participation within state institutions and private institutions. Yet compared to openly repressive regimes in South Korea or Argentina, one can identify a cluster or combination of relatively free social institutions – political parties, media, educational and cultural institutions, trade unions and social welfare agitational lobbies which function with varying degrees of freedom in most OECD countries. No capitalist country has been able to crush completely or 'domesticate' every institution within Electoral Processes. The concept of totalitarian or panoptican control is an ideal-typical construct rather than an achievable goal. During the most brutal period of Nazi control, or of recent mass terror in Argentina, Uruguay or South Korea, not all opposition was eradicated even though it may have been effectively silenced and eliminated from *public* participation. Generally speaking, it is the state institutional elements within particular Electoral Processes which are effectively purged of any oppositional forces; once these state institutions are controlled by fascists or military juntas, the interrelated *private* organisations and movements within Electoral Processes lose their protective 'political space' and are either crushed, driven underground or forced into exile. Yet for a good example of how impossible it is to control completely all facets of unfree Electoral Processes, consider the active underground (and at times even public) opposition in Spain from 1939 until Franco's death in 1975. The same was true of the opposition forces under Mussolini, the eruption of well-organised underground workers' movements in Japan after 1945 and the present-day struggles in countries such as the Philippines, Indonesia, Brazil, where military regimes have been unable to attain complete 'totalitarian' control.

On the other hand, free, multi-party voting systems have historically co-existed in many countries with strict cultural and social censorship in the arts, media, educational and health institutions. The struggle against religious bigotry and intolerance (especially in the area of sexual relations), has been a central historical feature of all Electoral Processes. These historical struggles confirm the inseparable relationship of cultural institutions (and degree of artistic freedom permitted) to the larger democratising battles waged within Electoral Processes. Rather than 'the State' oppressing 'Civil Society', many struggles have actually involved freeing or secularising state institutions from the influence and control exercised by religious and other private organisations.

Leaving aside the use of coercion, or the degree of censorship in particular local or national Electoral Processes, it is also very important to comprehend the level of 'institutionalisation' or organisational structure of key component elements of Electoral Processes. For example, trade union movements in West Germany, Israel and other countries simultaneously act as defenders of labour and as owners of many businesses.[7] Workers' pension funds are also a major source of new investment capital for capitalist firms (even though these funds are generally not controlled by workers).[8] Significant differences exist between those workers covered by private union pension schemes (which in turn depend on income earned from stocks and bonds), and those people dependent on government welfare schemes. The political response by unions to crises in capitalist firms or local state institutions (e.g. using pension funds to rescue city administrations in the United States), plus the historical restructuring of trade unions and social-democratic parties into more centralised organisations which have closer connections to private businesses and government departments – all indicate that the partial 'integration' of unions and parties is much more structural, rather than merely the betrayal of revolutionary politics by 'reformist' leaders as Trotskyists have argued.[9]

At the supra-national level, the strength of free trade unions in EEC countries is visible in relation to Southern European countries' application to join the EEC. Portugal, Spain and Turkey can be accommodated within the European Economic Community, only to the extent that free Electoral Processes are permitted – thus making possible direct elections to the European Parliament and other bodies. The free Electoral Processes in the EEC are a major inhibition on the production and circulation of private capital. Capitalist classes have to reconcile two incompatibilities: private accumulation with hard-won working-class rights, and national order with transnational instability. It will be interesting to see how 'institutionalised' key component elements of free Electoral Processes in EEC member countries will remain, should potential crises in Spain, Greece or other societies spill over the boundaries of European nation-states.

The Non-identical Nature of Capitalist State Institutions

The effect of particular national Electoral Processes on the reproduction of capitalist social relations stems very much from the historical variety, as well as the organisational limitations of particular state institutions. One has only to think of the deep-seated linguistic, regional and religious divisions which have split countries such as Belgium, India, Canada and Spain, and made it extremely difficult to maintain uniform state regulation, budgetary policy and stable political representation (due to party fragmentation), as compared to Australia, Sweden or Austria. These historical divisions become decisive when stringent 'austerity' measures prove difficult to implement because of divided legislatures, fear of antagonising regional minorities and lack of strong national parties –

all creating added problems for capitalist accumulation.[10] Extra difficulties for all classes are associated with federal systems, as opposed to unitary or centralised state institutions. The duplication and/or sharing of powers by numerous federal, state and local legislatures, administrative organs, statutory bodies and legal authorities in countries such as Australia, Canada, West Germany and the United States not only significantly inhibits the possible 'synchronisation' of Electoral, Production, Credit and Food Production Processes, but also fragments each class, and deprives it of complete control over the workings of particular local and national Electoral Processes (if in fact this were ever possible).

The orthodox Marxian preoccupation with private capitalist production, has also tended to leave analysis of varying state structures, voting systems and statutory bodies to bourgeois political scientists. One does not have to be an American pluralist or 'pressure group theorist' in order to acknowledge that heterogeneity of state institutions so long neglected by Left-wing analysts. One of the traditions in radical analysis exemplifying this neglect is epitomised in America by C. W. Mills, and recently, in reference to the transnational corporate development of the EEC, by Mandel and Poulantzas; it tends to treat legislatures and state institutions as bi-partisan rubber stamps for monopoly capital (despite the existence of 'fractions'), thus ignoring the tremendous veto and countervailing power of non-monopoly capitalists and workers via local, regional and national state administrators, politicians and organisations which espouse the latter's interests.[11] While unitary state structures (e.g. in France or Britain) are also characterised by the sharing of certain central powers with local city, county or regional bodies (thus producing electoral contestation and local governments at odds with central regimes), there are far fewer obstacles in these highly centralised states compared to federal state structures.

The constitutional 'checks and balances' between federal state institutions based in Washington D.C., Bonn, Canberra or Ottawa, and the numerous state or Ländes apparatuses in the remaining areas of the latter societies, means that 'state intervention' is often uncoordinated at best and nullified at worst. Historically, the one political party has never or rarely (with the exception for example of Australia in the 1930s) held office at all federal and state government levels, let alone in all the numerous local city bodies and legislatures. This is most evident in the largest capitalist country, the United States with its fifty states and over 116 000 governmental units, but is also true of nearly all other federal capitalist state institutions. Federal systems also tend to weaken Left parties and union movements because it is difficult to defeat Right-wing officials at every rung of the fragmented federal organisations – especially if a party branch holds office locally and any major attack upon it by the Left could result in a national split.

The well-organised nature of agricultural capitalists has always been a decisive conservative force in the historical determination of voting systems. The bias in favour of conservative parties or candidates is particularly obvious in countries such as the United States or Australia, where the federal structure of upper-house legislatures (such as the Senates) institutionalises a disproportionate amount of power in the hands of small, conservative rural forces. For the large, urban-based working-classes and ghetto poor (as well as the poor in rural areas), this structural discrimination has meant decades of neglect or minimal social reform. I would not like to suggest that the poor in Italy or France are better off because they have centralised state institutions,[12] but one cannot ignore the additional obstacles to Left-wing organisational strength erected by federal institutions within Electoral Processes. Had these historical structural constraints not been present, the fortunes of anti-capitalist forces in these societies might have been entirely different – especially in the United States, where the creation of a major national working-class party has been severely inhibited by the federal system.

While federal systems enable radicals and social reformers to use a variety of institutional sources, they have tended to make it easier for conservative parties to 'pass the buck' (e.g. cut expenditure or avoid responsibility), under the guise of 'New Federalism' or 'state rights' slogans. Capitalist firms are also able to engage in dangerous and shady practices as they hide behind local laws – in the absence of nation-wide standardising legislation. Protracted conflicts between poorer and richer states within federal systems, or within quasi-federal systems such as the EEC, often result in endless *ad hoc* decisions and budgetary compromises. In short, there is such major variation in the power of particular national state institutions constrained by free Electoral Processes, that it is more than dubious to argue (as do many radicals) that 'state intervention', protection and assistance are given to an ideal-typical, homogenised or ahistorical 'capitalist mode of production'.

It is an oversimplification to conceive of 'parliamentary democracy' and 'fascist dictatorship' as a polarised dichotomy, when the historical record of capitalist countries shows the uneven development of capitalist relations based on a wide variety of Electoral Processes. The repressive suspension of free Electoral Processes only tells us that capitalist accumulation can proceed without 'interferences'; but lack of repression does not tell us how the possible reproduction of capitalist social relations is affected by differing Electoral Processes. For example, in the United States of America many city or local governments have power over a whole range of social welfare, police and other budgetary and social policies which local councils would not have in many other capitalist countries. To the degree that local apparatuses are subject to electoral contestation, the ability of a particular capitalist class to avoid complicated public scrutiny or participation in decisive policy areas such as taxation, transport, environmental control and 'social wage' issues is perceptibly reduced compared to highly centralised and less accessible capitalist state structures. In recent years there have been calls by business groups for the abolition of annual state sector budgets at all levels of government. At a recent symposium on the growing incompatibility of free Electoral Processes and private accumulation (or why democracy is 'dysfunctional') the American economist James Buchanan echoed widespread authoritarian sentiments when he said that budgets 'cannot be left adrift in the sea of democratic politics'.[13] By having three- or five-yearly budget outlays, capitalist classes hope to 'immunise' state institutions from the constant flood of social expenditure demands which Electoral Processes make possible when annual allocations and cuts are given unfavourable publicity. The Ash Reforms under President Nixon were symptomatic of attempts to centralise budgetary allocations and minimise all the extraneous congressional modifications to expenditure targets resulting from members of Congress responding to local Electoral Process pressures.[14] With French presidents free of elections for the lengthy period of seven years compared to biennial congressional elections in the United States of America or triennial elections in Australia and New Zealand, the leeway available in different national Electoral Processes varies significantly.

Each local and national Electoral Process has major differences in voting procedures, with proportional, preferential, first-past-the-post and other systems, not to mention varying degrees of property franchise, double-round voting in consecutive weeks, compulsory or voluntary voting, the availability of referendums such as those in various American states which involve mass citizen initiatives, regulations governing advertising and campaign funds, the presence of state-controlled or wholly private media and many other variables – all of which tend either to work in favour of conservative forces, or to facilitate a higher degree of mass participation in policy-making. Even where particular

Electoral Processes are subject to minimal censorship, there are vast differences between the constitutional provisions of particular states. These vary from very weak federal powers in Australia (where even Right-wing governments cannot introduce wage and price controls or Left-wing governments nationalise industry), to the opposite extreme of Portugal where the capitalist class is trying to overturn Left-wing constitutional provisions (enacted after 1974) which limit capitalist enterprises in crucial areas of the Production Process and Credit Process.

Nearly every capitalist society with a multi-layered Electoral Process at central, federal, regional and local levels is characterised by checks and balances and *ad hoc* reforms emerging from historical struggles, not to mention important judicial structures and rights of appeal such as the American Bill of Rights. In West Germany and the United States the elected governments in Bonn and Washington D.C. continually struggle with appointed boards of the Bundesbank and Federal Reserve Board over monetary policy. Most central or federal governments are also unable to control completely the numerous local councils and statutory bodies, which are either subject to their own electoral discipline (if they impose expenditure cuts or increase local property taxes and service charges), or are relatively immune to regular elections in that they are run by non-elected officials. The significance of all these structural checks and balances is attested by the constant attempt of capitalist enterprises to free themselves of the mountain of regulatory and often uncontrollable legal interferences to investment and circulation plans by these state structures, simply because the national and local Electoral Processes are often at odds with the 'efficiency' criteria of non-democratic private corporate institutions.

The significance of particular historical developments within Electoral Processes becomes evident when one considers the *ad hoc* emergence of numerous local state institutions and statutory authorities. In many capitalist cities, for example, hundreds of local boards and authorities responsible for everything from roads and sewage to housing and so on, sprang up from the end of the eighteenth century. These non-democratic institutions were gradually subjected to challenges by local populations and often transformed into elected, accountable bodies.[15] Institutions originally organised on territorial and functional criteria either by central administrations or by compromising social forces wishing to preserve local and regional interests, have all made the notion of a 'capitalist-state-in-general' a historical fiction. What is of particular interest is the fluctuation of historical struggles over the past two centuries as local

Electoral Process institutions were forcibly subordinated to national institutions and then, in an uneven fashion, have attempted to reassert their independence in recent years. Also of interest is the way conservative state administrations have alternated between concentrating power at central levels and devolving powers to local authorities when it has politically suited them – especially to cut social expenditure. These territorial clashes between local, regional and national elements within respective Electoral Processes create additional complications for those political parties and state administrators who wield power through patronage and corruption. In those countries such as Italy, Spain, the United States, where state administration and private interests are mediated via local political bosses, tension between institutions in local Electoral Processes and in national Processes is exacerbated when either local democratic forces clean up traditional political bosses representing a national party, or stringent austerity measures imposed by conservative national administrations severely limit the amount of local patronage which can be distributed.

Electoral Processes and the Reproduction of Capitalist Societies

At this point it should be clearer why Electoral Processes are not mere 'superstructural' phenomena. The production and circulation of commodities are vitally affected by all those legislative and administrative criteria imposed upon private enterprises by environmentalists, civil rights activists, consumer protectionists, freedom of information campaigners and social welfare reformers. While Marxists such as Mandel are partially correct in arguing that public agencies are largely ineffective because they are dependent on the very industries which they are supposed to police,[16] it would be a serious political error to underestimate the trouble these regulatory agencies create for capitalists. The cost of reproducing variable capital (labour power) and investing in fixed capital assets (especially in new plant equipment, mines, etc. or state-subsidised public infrastructures such as airports, freeways, harbours) necessary for the production and circulation of commodities has been seriously affected by the accumulated struggles of different component elements of Electoral Processes such as environmentalists, unions or community groups. One of the best examples of the cost of regulation is the nuclear power industry, which has been reeling from massive delays to construction forced upon it by the anti-nuclear movement in various countries.[17] Food and drug policing has also led to the forced dumping by companies of harmful chemicals in those countries with weak or non-existent regulatory laws.

The presence or absence of 'freedom of information' legislation, ombudsmen, investigative committees or tough company laws requiring the disclosure of directors and assets, etc. all influence the amount of 'elbow room' available to anti-capitalist groups in their struggle to curb business abuses or prevent new investment disasters. The very struggles to open the numerous departments and public apparatuses of capitalist states to public scrutiny, both directly and indirectly, threaten private enterprises and their public administrative allies. Private enterprises have been faced with expensive lawsuits; humiliating disclosures concerning corruption of foreign and domestic governments, costly damage to public relations campaigns after tax avoidance, shoddy production, dangerous pollution or other activities have been revealed. In response a whole industry of academic publications has been commissioned by corporations in recent years, bearing variations on the public relations title of 'the responsible corporation'.

While the growth of regulatory activities and the added costs to capitalists resulting from anti-racist and anti-sexist legislation have been minimal, given that these struggles are only recent historical phenomena,[18] disputes over the funding and size of welfare and warfare budgets are older features of Electoral Processes which have had major effects on private capitalist accumulation. Here authors like Esping-Andersen have important insights to offer in regard to the effect of party politics on the funding of welfare programmes, and the manner in which 'fiscal crises of the state' have hit some states harder than others. Thus in Sweden the Social Democratic Party passed legislation (during their long period in government) requiring employers to bear a significant part of the cost of welfare provisions.[19] According to Esping-Andersen, this latter approach was not pursued by the Social Democrats in Denmark, where there have consequently been major setbacks to welfare programmes as well as loss of traditional working-class support for the Danish SDP because of the 'tax revolt' by people reluctant to bear the burden of increased fiscal costs. Not only was this 'tax revolt' backlash largely avoided in Sweden, but the Social Democrats also retained most of their working-class base during the 1970s and have successfully resisted large cuts to welfare undertaken in other capitalist countries, despite their removal from government office in 1976.[20] The comparison between Sweden and Denmark is illuminating since both countries superficially appear to be similar 'Scandinavian social-democratic countries'. The absence of social reform governments in other capitalist countries is even more striking when one thinks of the dominance of conservative parties in North America, Italy, France (until 1981), Australia or Japan, and the likely effect upon their capitalist classes if welfare levels comparable to those attained by the working-class in Sweden (which is hardly a 'socialist' society) had been implemented in the 1960s and 1970s.

Particularly striking is the institutional structure of the Electoral Process in the United States, where the absence of a strong working-class party has resulted in the periodic evaporation of any massive social protest. The inability of anti-capitalist and social welfare forces to consolidate their position, after the upheavals of the 1960s, has meant that private capitalists were spared a major challenge, despite all the thorns placed in their sides by environmentalists and civil rights activists. That a revamped militarism and reactionary moral majority could assert itself by the end of the 1970s so soon after the traumas of Vietnam, while massive poverty and unemployment continued to grow, is ample testimony to the structural and historical constraints through which particular component forces of Electoral Processes express themselves.

It is not necessary to dwell on the critical role of a particular national 'military–industrial complex', in order to appreciate the serious threat to capital accumulation and imperialist policies that would have resulted had peace and environmental movements been successful in altering the existing pattern of the arms race, wasteful energy use and commodity production. The actual and potential impact of environmental and peace movements on the restructuring of capitalist production (especially since 1973) cannot be minimised. If social movements within Electoral Processes in North America, Western Europe and Japan had succeeded in bringing to power reform parties committed to the implementation of alternative fuel policies (e.g. solar power), and to increases in social welfare expenditure rather than in arms budgets, then accumulation in key sectors of capitalist industry would have been drastically affected. However, the historical record shows massive state subsidy in OECD countries of military production, synthetic fuel production and continued low-cost (but environmentally devastating) open-cut mining and other highly profitable activities.

One could object to the above analysis by arguing in orthodox Marxian terms that institutions in free Electoral Processes are incapable of preventing the logic of capital accumulation, especially in the 'monopoly' or imperialist phase. I would argue that there is no inherent logic of imperialism which is inevitable or irreversible. To recognise the massive power of capitalist enterprises is not to succumb to the belief that 'capital' rules absolutely and without opposition. It is precisely the democratic strength and nature of particular Electoral Processes which determine the options available to particular capitalist classes and trans-national enterprises. Here the uneven historical development of capitalist states, and the presence or absence of free Electoral Processes, is further complicated by the disproportionate power and influence of particular forces within national Electoral Processes. The absence of large oppo-sitional Socialist or Communist parties in the United States and Canada for most of the twentieth century, the failure of large Socialist and Communist parties to win national office in Japan, the very limited success of the Left parties in Italy, France or Britain during the past forty years, the dominance of the Right-wing in West Germany's Social Democratic Party following the destruction of the Left during the Third Reich – all have vitally affected seven of the largest capitalist powers. These countries have been relatively free of non-conservative national governments or very successful anti-capitalist oppositions. The lack of *consistently* successful nation-wide (as opposed to local) challenges by social welfare, peace and other movements, permits conservative forces in these major capitalist societies, and especially in the United States, to intervene in numerous other national Electoral, Production, Credit and Food Production Processes.

On the other hand, social protest movements within one national Electoral Process can influence policies and social relations in other national Processes. For example, the partial victories of anti-war and civil rights groups in the United States limited the American government's capacity to intervene in the late 1970s in Angola, Iran and Nicaragua, prior to the wave of re-militarisation in late 1979 and 1980. Carter's policy of 'human rights' was a direct spin-off from earlier domestic Electoral Process struggles in the 1960s and early 1970s and had a world-wide effect despite its cynical application and abuse by the American government.[21] Similarly, the dissemination of film, television, literature and theatre across national boundaries, makes it very difficult for con-servative local and national regimes to 'immunise' Electoral Processes from the influences of more avant-garde, democratic and liberatory practices emanating from other Processes.

It is important to recognise that Electoral Processes are multi-layered and uneven historical institutional arrangements, setting the elbow-room capitalists have for accumulating, while also determining the defence and attack mechanisms available to anti-capitalist social forces. The conflict between diverse social forces within local, regional, national and supra-national Electoral Processes is one of the decisive reasons for the non-reproduction of many capitalist social relations. It is all these unco-ordinated or poorly co-ordinated elements of free Electoral Processes which go to make the 'political business cycle' in its fullest sense. When all the disparate social forces struggling within particular domestic Electoral Processes reverberate in the council chambers of supra-national state apparatuses (such as the EEC or World Bank), it becomes clear why the notion of a single 'world capitalist mode of production' is of little use in comprehending the actual disparate processes and determinate limits to particular forms of local and national capitalist accumulation.

I have not said anything about the relations between Communist countries and capitalist societies with free Electoral Processes. Suffice to say that specific relations between capitalist countries and the USSR or China add a complication to the internal strains of particular Electoral Processes – especially the clash between those social forces which favour greater trade and social exchanges with Communist countries, and others who see national and transnational capitalist interests furthered by belligerent or competitive military methods. Given the general desynchronisation of Electoral Processes in capitalist societies, and faced with the lack of a united Communist bloc, it is highly likely that the American attempt to control military and economic policy (as it did especially during the 1950s and 1960s) will not only be impossible to revive or sustain, but will aslo lead to even further splits in the 'Western alliance' as particular nations work out their own specific relations with Communist countries.

As with all other policies – whether it be health care or export subsidies – capitalist classes and their political representatives have to wage a constant war to legitimise their plans, or persuade or defeat their opponents. But the desire on the part of many capitalists to do away with the massive problems associated with free Electoral Processes is by no means a united desire. Large sections of the petty bourgeoisie have just as substantial a vested interest in maintaining a voice in free Electoral Processes as they do in periodically demanding the authoritarian suspension of these Processes. It is the fragmentation of Electoral Processes at local, regional and national levels which gives smaller capitalists a chance to participate in a way that is not always available to them in centralised, repressive regimes. This raises, of course, the whole question of political class representation in capitalist state institutions – an issue which space prevents me from analysing in any detail. Other writers have already noted the importance of the 'mass political party', which in its structure often mirrors the major state institutions needed to crisis-manage contemporary capitalist societies.[22] The question as to whether or not political parties are part of capitalist state institutions is, I believe, of secondary importance. It is also a question which arises if one works with the concepts of 'the State' and 'Civil Society'. Far more important is the question of the presence or absence of free Electoral Processes, in which conservative parties contest with Left parties and many other social organisations the actual workings, priorities and future of specific state policies.

The emergence of new mass organisations to crisis-manage capitalist accumulation, such as the combination of military and civilian techno-crats in various Third World countries,[23] is indicative of the need to recognise the importance of a free Electoral Process. Gramsci and sub-sequent Marxists focussed on the tendency of political parties to fuse with state administrative personnel, forming a 'power bloc'. This fusion can also be achieved *without* the existence of free political parties (e.g. by substituting the army for the party as the governing or co-ordinating force); hence it is necessary to understand why even long-serving political parties in free Electoral Processes cannot completely fuse with state institutions so long as they face the risk of being thrown out of office in the next election.

Although Poulantzas made many pertinent observations on the re-lations between 'dominant mass parties' and capitalist state apparatuses, I think he exaggerated the fusion of Western two-party systems or rival parties into a 'single-party centre' lodged in capitalist state institutions. This perspective lacks historical dynamism, in that it blurs the differences between conservative and social-democratic parties and assumes that they have, and will continue to share, a common administrative and political inter-party network in order to run state institutions. The 'corporatist' tendencies which appeared in the mid-1970s are historically atypical of the development of political parties and state institutions within Electoral Processes since the late nineteenth century. The emergence of Thatcher, Reagan, Fraser and others (with their clear-cut reactionary policies), has pushed some national opposition parties further to the Right, but has also widened divisions between parties rather than led to the abolition of alternatives as Poulantazas believed. Within particular Electoral Processes such as the Italian and Austrian, many Christian Democrats or Social Democrats have 'fused' with state administrations (owing to the length of time they have enjoyed in office); but it would be a mistake to interpret these instances as examples of a general 'corporatist' historical tendency. It is mainly in capitalist countries without free Electoral Processes (e.g. Singapore) where the dominant party has 'fused' with state institutions.

Other important social institutions which are intertwined with state institutions range from national church and religious institutions, certain trade union movements (as in Greece), many cultural and welfare institutions – all of which depend to a lesser or greater extent on joint state and private funding, organisational resources and criteria of operation. But even granted these past and present historical examples of 'fusion' between particular state institutions and private organisations, it is not simply the organisational relation of a party to a particular state institution which alone is decisive. Rather, it is the level of democracy and participation within particular free Electoral Processes which influences the relation of *all* parties and non-parties to particular state institutions – thereby determining the context in which capitalist relations may be reproduced or negated.

It is, of course, important to note that like all social classes, the bourgeoisie, because of their historical diversity and organisational strength *vis-à-vis* other classes, are no more likely to evaluate their short- or long-term interests rationally (given that there is no coherent 'class interest' to begin with), or to opt for non-violent solutions simply because their more far-sighted members may advocate them. If the various capitalist social orders were ruled by long-term rational calculation, rather than the short-sighted logic of self-interest, fear and intolerance, then it is doubtful they could remain capitalist. The heterogeneous or hybrid nature of particular capitalist social relations – that is, the specific combination of pre-capitalist and bourgeois social values and practices[24] – becomes decisive when radical or liberal component groups of Electoral Processes fight to extend anti-capitalist practices, combat the historical entrenchment of conservative ideologies, or suffer defeats at the hands of conservative forces trying to curtail or reverse gains already won. These capitalist and non-capitalist conservative social forces will express their authoritarian opposition to particular elements of Electoral Processes (such as radical women or militant unionists) in a variety of ways appropriate to the level of tolerance operating in the capitalist society concerned – from Right to Life movements in the

United States to the killing and jailing of unionists in Malaysia, El Salvador and other countries with weak or non-existent free Electoral Processes. However, the divided attitudes of capitalists towards the maintenance of free Electoral Processes is also very much influenced by the desynchronised state of Production, Credit and Food Production Processes. As capitalist enterprises are affected in quite different ways by their location in or relation to these latter Processes, the retention or overthrow of particular free national Electoral Processes would also very much depend on, or be mediated by, the interconnection of all of the Electoral, Production, Credit and Food Production Processes operating at local and national levels in different capitalist societies.

The interconnections which exist between institutions and enterprises in national and supra-national Production, Credit and Food Production Processes are often less visible within particular Electoral Processes. I am referring here to the numerous military, diplomatic and other secret agreements or alliances plus covert connections between particular state institutions and private organisations. The degree to which social forces and state institutions within local and national Electoral Processes have control and sovereignty over their own institutions, varies dramatically from Electoral Process to Electoral Process.

Finally, when Marx said that at a certain stage of their development the material productive forces of society come into conflict with the existing relations of production, he and other Marxists have generally used the notion of 'fetters' to describe the development of capitalist production within the womb of restrictive pre-capitalist relations. In contrast, the notion of Electoral Processes enables one to grasp the 'fetters' imposed on capitalist production in a period of the *dominance* of private capitalism rather than the opposition of feudal social forces to the newly-emerging relations of capitalist enterprises. The point is that contemporary relations within Electoral Processes have not all derived from the rise of capitalist production. While socialist production cannot develop within the 'womb' of capitalist societies, social practices within state institutions and private non-profit-making institutions can exist as 'fetters' on a dominant mode of private production. If relations within Electoral Processes merely reflected the 'logic' of capitalist production, the desynchronisation of Electoral Processes with Production, Credit and Food Production Processes would not only be an irrelevant non-issue, but the whole uneven history of democratising struggles within Electoral Processes would be misconceived as complementary to private enterprises rather than the 'fetters' they really have proved to be. One

must not only be able to identify which relations and policies within
Electoral Processes complement or act as 'fetters' upon private accumulation, but equally importantly, which social forces are practising alternative ideas which threaten to transcend rather than simply restrict capitalist production.

7
Production Processes: Beyond the Separation of 'The State' from 'The Economy'

Production and Credit Processes are comprehensible as social practices which are simultaneously linked, but relatively autonomous of each other. The increasing integration of local, regional, national and *supranational* levels of these Processes should not blind us to the *historical reality, that nationally organised activities still predominate over international exchanges.*

In recent decades Credit Processes have become much more integrated and dependent on international fluctuations than Production Processes. This is visible in the growth of such activities as the Eurodollar and Eurobond markets, or the effects of currency exchange rates and interest rates, which all reverberate in the internal workings of domestic national Credit and Production Processes. On the other hand, *Production Processes are still governed more by the level of national and local class struggles* (which affect the cost and nature of labour power – wage rates, skills, welfare provisions as well as investment policies via tariff protection, and particular forms of state subsidies), even though international commodity exchange and supranational business pressures have grown enormously in recent decades.

In the previous chapter I tried to show how free Electoral Processes have historically restricted private capitalist classes. It is also necessary to modify Marx's analysis of the causes of crises in capitalist societies by emphasising the historical nature of local and national Production Processes. It will be recalled that Marx argued that the 'ultimate reason for all real crises always remains the poverty and restricted consumption of the masses'.[1] While accepting this proposition with certain qualifications (e.g. the role of governments in supplementing the capacity of the masses to consume via income and welfare schemes), I would also add the following major modification. *One of the ultimate barriers* to capitalist accumulation remains the national restrictions on enterprises in national Production Processes whose labour processes and markets are constantly under threat of control or penetration by private enterprises and state institutions from other national Production Processes. It is in this sense that the desire to create a 'world capitalist mode of production' clashes daily with the reality of deeply entrenched social forces within local and national Processes.

If capitalist state institutions are heavily involved in the related but distinct Production and Credit Processes, it is not possible to explain crises in these Processes by a monocausal theory. Contrary to the orthodox Marxist view; it is not possible to account for 'stagflation' by explaining *all* the contradictions within Processes in terms of the law of value. Similarly, it is not possible to explain major crises solely in terms of a distribution problem arising from the struggle over the size of wages and profits, or a realisation crises due to underconsumption, or a disproportionality crisis between Departments I and II. On the contrary, one must examine how the law of value (or any of the other monocausal theories) affects certain parts of Production and Credit Processes. This is not to argue that Credit Processes are completely independent of Production Processes, as some economists assume when analysing the quantity of money supply. Rather, it is to reject reductionist analyses which interpret multiple forms of social activity through the prism of a *single* law or form of social conflict.

Production and Credit Processes cannot be explained solely by 'law of value' or any other monocausal crisis theory, because each Process is made up to a lesser or greater extent of (i) private capitalist units of production, circulation or credit creation; and (ii) state-owned units of production, servicing and credit creation. Hence the relation between Production and Credit Processes at local, national and supra-national levels is complicated by the fundamental differences in the social relations which govern the operation of private as compared to state-owned units. These opposing relations and objectives are a consequence of the conflicting needs, either to realise or support profit-maximising activities, or to carry out non-profit, non-exchange-value production and distribution of goods and services – conflicting priorities which result from specific levels of national and local social struggles in Electoral Processes. Hence the 'law of value' is not *directly* applicable, or able to explain crises in those sectors of Production or Credit Processes which are not involved with commodity-exchange-value production (i.e. various state-run services), even though it is correct to say that each national 'public sector' is inextricably bound up with the capitalist enterprises accumulating in that same geographical area. But unless the private and state sectors of these Processes are kept analytically distinct, one will simply reduce capitalist states to 'derivative' spheres of the 'capitalist mode of production', and one of the principal causes of desynchronisation will be overlooked.

Major Characteristics of Production Processes

Just as Electoral Processes involve social groups (such as trade unions and civil rights organisations) as well as particular state institutions, e.g. legislatures and local councils, so Production Processes are more than simply the *private* industrial enterprises of particular capitalist countries. Moreover, Production Processes are *not* merely those industrial enterprises which produce surplus-value. In this sense I do *not* equate Production Processes with Marx's concept of 'productive-capital' (i.e. the process whereby money is deployed in enterprises to make commodities, thus adding or producing value). Rather, Production Processes embrace all those enterprises and institutions which manufacture and circulate goods and services via market *and* non-market mechanisms. This includes all those commodities produced, sold or serviced by private enterprises, together with all those exchange commodities (produced by nationalised, state-run industries) as well as all those use-values goods and services (e.g. welfare services) not determined by the principle of profit-making. In other words, Production Processes comprise (1) all those workers (whether employed by private enterprises or within state institutions) who either directly produce surplus-value, help circulate goods, guard or administer commodity production, or produce, administer, service or distribute non-marketable goods and services; (2) all those capitalist units involved in the processing and manufacture of raw materials, semi-finished and finished commodities (here there are overlaps with Food Production Processes) as well as the circulation of goods (here there are overlaps with Credit Processes), and the provision of services for other capitalists and private consumers.

The all-embracing category of Production Processes enables us to comprehend the conflict taking place between the private and state sector component parts of local and national Production Processes. It also demarcates the *production* of private commodities for exchange and public use-value goods and services from the *financing* of the latter (which concerns the nature of Credit Processes). Yet it is not possible to completely separate 'money-capital' from Production Processes, because it is quite common for large corporate enterprises to be simultaneously involved in the manufacture of commodities as well as the provision of credit or finance. Nevertheless, it is important to distinguish the relatively autonomous Processes whereby the production of exchange-value and use-value goods and services (in both private and state national sectors) are subject to conflicts and contradictions which are related to, but also quite different from, the local, national and international contradictions associated with the provision or restriction of finance or credit. The 'circuits' of 'money-', 'productive-' and 'commodity-capital' which Marx analysed as the basis of the *reproduction* of *private* capitalist production, are therefore no longer adequate to an understanding of turnover time and how crises emerge in capitalist societies given the substantial interconnection and involvement of state institutions in Production and Credit Processes.

Production Processes within each capitalist society are the combined result of specific domestic and foreign historical developments. Each national and local Production Process has been determined by the uneven historical emergence of enterprises and institutions from pre-capitalist social conditions (in both chronological and geographical senses). The size and nature of particular national Production Processes also partially determines the specific structure and development of other local and national Production Processes, e.g. through imperialist domination. By the end of the 1970s it was clear that the Production Processes in many but not all OECD countries, had developed the following characteristics: (1) a monopoly or oligopoly sector of private capitalist units which operated at national and transnational levels, characterised by highly organised sales markets, capital-intensive production and greater control over commodity prices; (2) a competitive or small-scale capitalist sector which constituted the vast majority of capitalist enterprises, even though this numerical superiority was not matched by actual dominance of production and exchange. These small-scale enterprises (incorporating many small family businesses and self-employed entrepreneurs) were generally labour-intensive, had limited access to national and transnational markets and were much more subject to price determinations outside their own control as well as being subject to the full thrust of competitive market pressures; and finally (3) a state or 'public sector' which varied in size and scope depending on whether it was a federal or unitary series of institutions, statutory bodies and nationalised industries – which in turn depended on the presence or absence of free Electoral Processes and specific historical developments – e.g. the nationalisation of parts of private industry in Austria after 1945 as a result of military occupation. These state sector elements of Production Processes were also predominantly character- ised. by labour-intensive production, and were subdivided between wage-earning labour and non-wage welfare and other recipients who were significant consumers of services produced.[2] Welfare recipients do not produce goods or income unless they are also part-time or full- time ('moonlighting') wage earners. (This is also true of all private investors living off dividends, rent or speculative transactions, e.g. the sale of shares.) The level of income which welfare populations receive and spend, makes them part of Production Processes even though they derive their income in different ways to unproductive capitalist investors. The same is true of military personnel and other unproductive ad- ministrative employees.

In most non-OECD capitalist societies such as Brazil, India, Mexico, the Philippines and South Korea, the actual size and roles of state sectors are quite different from most OECD capitalist countries in that they have, among other things, poorly developed 'welfare state' com- ponents.[3] The non-capitalist classes of non-OECD countries have been less successful in winning larger social expenditures and free Electoral Processes. Furthermore, the non-OECD capitalist societies also contain large pre-capitalist social classes based on varying forms of rural peasant or tribal production, which are subordinated to the expanding and dominant capitalist and state sector elements of the Production Processes of their respective social formations.

This is not the place to give an exposition of the nature of monopoly, competitive and state sectors, let alone a description of the rich variety of Third World capitalist formations. An impressive and extensive radical literature already exists on such topics as cartels and other marketing practices of transnationals, the emergence and transformation of occupations, segmented labour markets, sexual, racial and social discrimination, specific state assistance and subsidisation of industries in the form of research and development, structural reorganisation of markets, de-industrialisation, tariff and tax preferences, penetration and breakdown of less developed national and local Production Processes, welfare cuts, urban crises, the conservative organisational delivery of welfare services, structural unemployment and so forth.[4] Instead of reviewing these illuminating analyses, I will rather concentrate on pointing out how the forces and social relations within Production Processes are moving deeper and deeper into conflict and fundamental incompatibility with developments and needs in the Electoral, Credit and Food Production Processes at local, national and supra-national levels.

Surplus-value-extracting Enterprises and their Relation to Non-value-producing Institutions

A major historical tendency of the last fifty years in leading OECD capitalist societies has been the steady *increase* in the number of workers *not* producing surplus-value embodied in commodities for exchange, and a corresponding *decrease* in the proportion of private capitalist enterprises *extracting* surplus-value from workers. When one takes the combined totals of all those wage-workers involved in the circulation of commodities (e.g. retailing and wholesale merchandising), plus all the service establishments (other than those producing commodities such as food), together with the large state sector administrative services and workers in education, health, transport and so forth, then it can be safely established in Marxian terms that a clear majority of wage-workers in most OECD countries are not engaged in the production of surplus-value. This uneven historical development of non-surplus-value-producing workers and welfare recipients in most OECD countries should be compared with the doubling and quadrupling of *privately* employed surplus-value-producing workers in countries such as Taiwan, South Korea, Brazil and the Philippines since 1950, as a result of the relocation and expansion of capitalist commodity production from their original sites in OECD countries.

Most discussions of the increase in state sector and privately-employed unproductive workers have generally revolved around the classificatory problem of the class location of the new mental and manual workers.[5] Whether a person is a 'new petty bourgeois' or a member of a new 'professional/managerial' or 'intellectual' class is not directly relevant to the problems I am currently discussing. My purpose in distinguishing between surplus-value-producing and non-surplus-value-producing (unproductive) workers, and between capitalist enterprises extracting surplus-value and those operating under other criteria, is to illuminate why the law of value has only *limited explanatory power* when trying to comprehend the relations existing between state institutions and private businesses. According to Marx, even though capital took on the various forms of 'money-capital', 'productive-capital', 'commodity-capital', and even though the amount of time required to circulate commodities (thus realising value) was very important in the total capitalist mode of production, the real 'producer' in the capitalist system was the surplus-value-extracting industrial enterprise, rather than all the other unproductive private businesses (which took a 'slice' of surplus-value as they circulated commodities).

Thus a crisis in capitalism is seen by contemporary orthodox Marxists as being due to a crisis in the rate of surplus-value production *vis-à-vis* all unproductive expenditures and activities. In Yaffe's words,

> If production grows faster in the 'non-productive' sector of the economy than in the 'private' sector, the production of profit, or surplus value, relative to total production, declines more rapidly than before. More surplus value must be produced from a smaller base of productive workers in order that the tendency of the rate of profit to fall is checked. As long as the productivity of labour can be sufficiently increased so as to maintain the rate of profit and finance the non-productive sector, government-induced expenditure will indeed be the 'cause' of high employment and social stability. But this process is self defeating: to cope with the expense of the non-productive sector the exploitability of labour must be steadily raised. This means a higher organic composition of capital and a decline in the exploitable labour force relative to the growing capital. To maintain a state of high employment indefinitely, the non-productive sector must increase faster than total production. But this implies a slow deterioration of private capital expansion which can only be halted by halting the expansion of the non-productive sector.[6]

When one considers the growth in unemployment from cuts to unproductive services and jobs in the state sectors of countries such as Britain or Australia, plus increased state assistance to industry during the past decade so that living labour can be either exploited faster or replaced by capital-intensive production, there appears to be a great deal of logic in the orthodox Marxian concentration on the rate of surplus-value extraction. Ultimately, the capitalist units of production operating in various national Production Processes could not survive if all the leading Production Processes permanently declined. In this case the rate of surplus-value could not be increased despite the massive infusion of direct and indirect assistance from all capitalist states. But in so far as the potential and actual extraction of surplus-value occurs at quite different rates (depending on the industry concerned and the class relations of national social formations, e.g. Italy as opposed to Taiwan), the orthodox Marxian monocausal theory of universal crisis-collapse is prevented from consummation by the historical desynchronisation of Electoral, Production, Credit and Food Production Processes. This is the ironic and double-faced quality of Processes *chronologically and structurally at odds with one another*. On the one hand, the very desynchronisation of Processes prevents capitalist classes from controlling or 'synchronising' antagonistic capitalist relations, while the very historical manner of the desynchronisation at local, national and supra-national levels means that even when capitalist societies experienced almost uniform crisis characteristics during the Great Depression (or to a lesser extent in 1974–5), the after-effects on capitalist enterprises and national bourgeois classes as a whole were by no means uniform. These uneven experiences are echoed in radical theory, as there is no agreement between Marxists on whether the international crises of the 1930s and 1970s were caused by, among other things, a rise in the organic composition of capital, an overproduction crisis leading to a failure to realise value, or a profits squeeze resulting from militant wage demands.

This is not the place to discuss all the empirical controversies surrounding the issue of the tendency of the rate of profit to fall (e.g. can one measure the national rate of surplus-value?, has the organic composition of capital risen or fallen?, etc.). Orthodox Marxists must resolve the following dilemma, if their analysis concerning the relation between productive and unproductive enterprises and workers, is to be plausible. If one is analysing the relationship between the productive and unproductive sectors, then it has to be shown whether the unproductive sector of a *national* social formation, e.g. Britain, is being financed from a 'smaller base of productive workers' labouring within the *same national* formation, or from a diminishing *world* pool of surplus-value-producing workers. Those Marxists who talk about a 'capitalist mode of production' must be able to establish whether they are speaking of a 'world mode of production', or of national modes of production in order to show how the world rate of profit affects each national *unproductive* sector. And they must also show why each national government is constrained by the size of unproductive public sectors if they reject the notion of 'national economies' and reduce the balance of payments to a set of irrelevant paper symbols (according to Marxists such as Laurence Harris), as capital and labour moves across national boundaries.

In order to determine the sources and rate of surplus-value in a particular national Production Process, it would be necessary to analyse in detail the size of each unproductive sector within national Production Processes. The amount of value exported or repatriated to parent companies in and out of national Production Processes must also be known in order to estimate whether particular national state institutions are helping to increase the rate of profit of particular local and national firms or parasitically eating up more than the diminishing pool of surplus-value can withstand. It would be truly amazing if orthodox value-theorists could surmount the major obstacles of corporate secrecy and complex national government budgetary allocations and infrastructural provisions, and document the relationship between productive and unproductive sectors!

Orthodox Marxists point out that the *rate* of surplus-value is important because contemporary capitalist production requires more workers to help *realise* value via sales and circulation than was required by industrial enterprises in the pre-1920s.[7] Hence a crisis in the rate of surplus-value would result in the loss of jobs and bankruptcies in many private circulation enterprises, e.g. shops. There is no doubt that the growth of capitalist production in OECD countries has witnessed a massive increase in unproductive enterprises concerned with circulating and servicing surplus-value-laden commodities, and that many of these businesses go bankrupt when the overproduction of commodities outstrips consumption.[8] But it does not follow that a crisis in the rate of value extraction (in enterprises of a national Production Process) will result in all the other enterprises (both private and state) collapsing like a pack of cards. As no capitalist society is a self-sufficient autarchy, it is important to recognise that profit is made by non-surplus-value-extracting enterprises operating at the supra-national level, e.g. sales, banking services and so forth. To analyse the 'slice' of surplus-value taken by particular nationally based unproductive private enterprises and state-owned institutions, e.g. banks, would be to presume that these unproductive enterprises depend on a pool of surplus-value produced in the same 'national economy'. However, we know that there are major differences between capitalist societies in terms of their degree of dependence on domestic private production for tax revenue and those states which have recourse to external credit sources, e.g. deficit budgeting via foreign borrowing. There are also significant differences between capitalist societies that derive revenue from invisible payments (foreign investment, tourism) as opposed to visible commodity exports and trade relations with non-capitalist societies which are not part of a so-called 'world capitalist' pool of surplus-value.

The notion that national state institutions and private unproductive firms depend solely on the rate of surplus-value extraction from the 'productive' sector of the *same* society is difficult to substantiate; it also fails to explain adequately the actual class struggles surrounding *rates of profit* (as distinct from rates of surplus-value), and the levels of non-profit-making goods and services consumed by non-capitalists. Moreover, as *most* capitalist enterprises do *not* extract surplus-value, but circulate commodities or provide services, their rate of profit is not *directly* determined by the diminishing pool of surplus-value, but by the rate of wages and rate of taxes, and costs of means of operation as expressed in real money or price terms. In opposition to Yaffe's work and other orthodox positions, the financing of unproductive state sectors does *not* depend solely on the rate of exploitation in the 'productive' sector. Most direct income tax and company tax as well as indirect sales and other revenue is raised from businesses and workers who do not extract or produce surplus-value. Therefore, the relation of unproductive state sectors to 'productive' private sectors is not determined by the rate of surplus-value, but rather by the *rate of profit* of *all* private enterprises regardless of whether they extract value, circulate goods or provide services.

The distinction between rate of profit and rate of surplus-value is crucial because the two are by no means equivalent.[9] Given the historical tendency for fewer and fewer firms to extract surplus-value in OECD capitalist societies (as a percentage of the total number of private businesses operating), the relations between particular national state institutions and private sectors is increasingly governed by conflict over factors determining *profit rates* rather than rates of surplus-value extraction. This is because all those businesses which are unproductive cannot increase the *relative* extraction of surplus-value (i.e. increasing the rate of labour exploitation) in order to compensate for reductions in the length of the working day, higher wage costs and general tax increases related to improvements in the 'social wage' (education, health, housing, etc.) flowing from the specific level of class struggles within Electoral Processes over previous decades. Similarly, state institutions operating at national and local levels are also unable to increase relative and absolute surplus-value (except in those state institutions producing exchange commodities) where none has ever been produced in the first place. Even those nationalised industries extracting surplus-value (e.g. power utilities, steel, oil, cars) are not strictly determined by the relation between constant and variable capital. Instead, it is political criteria which govern these nationalised operations in the prices they can charge for gas or steel, or the wage levels they will grant, or particularly the level of capital they may borrow from general tax revenue rather than from market sources. Hence the so-called rise in the organic composition of capital is not the deciding force which determines whether these industries make profits, let alone whether they survive. In state institutions which produce non-exchange goods and services (e.g. 'social wage' goods and services), the concepts of constant and variable capital and organic composition of capital are either irrelevant or secondary.

Put simply, the rate of surplus-value extraction may *not* tell us what the *rate of profit* is for the *majority* of businesses, but knowledge of the *rate of labour exploitation* is crucial to any comprehension of class relations in *all* the *surplus-value-extracting enterprises*.[10] It is not necessary to base one's analysis of crises in Production Processes on Marx's law of the tendency of the rate of profit to fall, in order to indicate why certain historical problems appear to be insoluble short of massive class conflict. The following points are intended to illustrate some of the major problems confronting contemporary Production Processes.

Crisis Tendencies within Production Processes

There is an irreversible trend towards the introduction of more labour-saving means of production in both surplus-value-extracting and unproductive capitalist enterprises. Given the need to reduce the turnover time of the production of commodities, the short life expectancy of new machine tools,[11] the fierce competition between corporations operating across national boundaries and the inability of individual companies to refrain from introducing new products, there can be no prospect of a slowing down or a reversal of the trend to increasing automation, short of the threat of bankruptcy confronting many firms or working-class control over production. Linked to the irreversible trend to greater automation is the low growth or actual decrease in the volume of output of key products such as steel, cars and ships since 1973.[12] While there have been significant changes in the share and penetration of key national commodity markets (e.g. Japanese businesses overtaking American car and steel manufacturers in 1980), there have been no major new labour-intensive industries to replace the near stagnant or declining volume of output – despite brief upswings in production – in industries such as cars and steel which have been the dynamos of capitalist development during the twentieth century.

While outputs of key industries have stagnated or declined in volume, the underutilisation of extensive productive capacities has not resulted in universally falling prices. On the contrary, inflation has been fuelled by the increased ability of companies in the monopoly sectors of OECD countries constantly to increase the prices of most commodities in order to make up for the relative decline in units produced. Hence it is *not scarcity* which has fuelled inflation, but overproduction which was partially disguised by marketing cartels. In contrast to the Great Depression of 1929–32 when American monopoly sector prices dropped 10 per cent (compared to a drop of 60 per cent for competitive sector businesses) the recession between 1973 and 1975 saw monopoly sector prices *rise* by 27 per cent.[13]

The prospect of increasing competition for diminishing markets has led capitalist states increasingly to subsidise the provision of infrastructure, research and development. These increased supports have been necessary to improve the relative extraction of surplus-value in productive enterprises and cheapen the costs of new fixed capital-intensive forces of production. It is difficult to see how state administrators will be able to avoid 'rationalisation' programmes designed to eliminate weak private businesses – especially those in the competitive sectors – or avoid bearing the costs of sustaining a growing number of corporate giants either through outright or indirect nationalisation. Most OECD countries – especially the United States, Britain, Australia, West Germany, Belgium, Italy – are reaching an historical limit to the exploitability of living labour working under conditions averaging a working week of forty hours or less. The social cost of labour (e.g. wages, work conditions) is becoming too high in capitalist societies experiences low or non-existent growth.[14] This is particularly true of those capitalist societies with strong organised unions which are able to resist attacks on real wage levels. The limits of labour exploitability vary from productive to unproductive enterprises in particular Production Processes. In surplus-value-extracting enterprises, the historical reorganisation of work processes in order to increase productivity through speed-ups, shift-work and occupational retraining, is proving unable to offset the decreases in the length of the working day won by workers in previous decades.[15] Major retrenchments of workers, the reduction of wages and the 'disciplining' effect of the depression have by no means reversed the major gains made by workers during the past fifty years.

Even in those capitalist enterprises in countries without free Electoral Processes (such as Argentina) where the working day is longer, harsher and wages much lower than in OECD countries, most factories were operating well below capacity by 1982. Despite the deterioration of wage and work conditions for many workers in recent years, the surplus-value-extracting enterprises in most OECD countries are faced with major crises. Even a massive historical reversal of working-class gains – e.g. extending the working week from forty to fifty or sixty hours, which is highly improbable at the moment – would not resolve the problem of overproduction, though the rate of exploitation were increased dramatically. If anything, an increase in the rate of surplus-value through an extension of the work week, or speed-up of the labour process, would increase realisation problems. For, attacks on wage levels and living standards of workers would lead to a fall in domestic consumption (for example, two-thirds of United States gross national product comes from personal consumption). Only those domestic industries oriented to the export market (e.g. mining, plant construction and other capital goods) would immediately benefit from a reduction in workers' standard of living. Yet even these initial gains would be eventually nullified by a slump in key OECD countries' domestic consumption.

A reduction in the level of real wages would temporarily benefit most capitalists provided that the 'historical level or morality' (Marx's term) could be reversed – i.e. redefining the socially accepted standard of living. Such a redefinition has been partially achieved by the Reagan administration. But the reduction of real wages will either exacerbate social crises by further reducing domestic national consumption of the already overproductive private enterprise sectors, or at best bring only temporary relief to the rate of profit levels. Furthermore, capitalist state institutions have accounted for significant increases in employment rates within national Production Processes since 1945. Any significant decrease in workers' wages and state-administered services (e.g. social welfare, transport, health, education) would bring an end to already sluggish private sector growth rates (despite the optimism of the monetarists) unless there was a massive infusion of money from outside particular social formations in the form of foreign investment, tourism or other income sources.

The inability of unproductive, competitive-sector capitalist enterprises and state institutions to increase the rate of value is also compounded by the limited options available in regard to the replacement of living labour by machinery. This is particularly true of small-scale, unproductive competitive-sector businesses in services and retailing, where the introduction of computers or other labour-saving devices has so far been either impossible due to prohibitive costs, or irrelevant and inadequate due to the nature of the work done in these businesses by humans. However, large unproductive enterprises in monopoly sectors (such as banks and insurance companies) have seized the opportunity of introducing labour-saving technology subsidised by government taxation allowances and exemptions. The concerted efforts of all capitalist enterprises (whether extracting surplus-value or not), to obtain increased state subsidisation of their technical means of operation, together with lower wage costs and reduced taxation, is inherently contradictory and doomed to cancel out any short-lived increase in profits. As the largest portion of most capitalist states' direct and indirect revenue comes from wage-workers and their dependents, it is difficult to envisage a drastic reduction in the number of state sector workers, plus a substantial cut in wages of all workers, leaving adequate tax revenue and workers' consumption to sustain continued growth in most private production, circulation and services.

The shortfall in taxes from the working-classes in OECD countries would either have to be met by inflationary budgeting or collected from the owners of private businesses. Given the competitive nature of international and domestic business, the short life-span of fixed capital, new products and processes would require further subsidisation of automated equipment and R and D from an already diminished tax base. The internal dynamics of Credit Processes will be examined in chapter 8. For the moment it is important to recognise that the historical growth of state sectors in OECD countries since 1945 has been both the cause of delayed crises in capitalist enterprises as well as the means whereby growth was generated until the early 1970s. No class of capitalist firms in a national Production Process can sustain the rate of profit, let alone social stability, by incessantly increasing unemployment and decreasing corporate taxation each time the temporary boom gives way to a deeper slump. In this respect there are ultimately finite limits to the degree to which state institutions can artificially increase the rate of profit.

There has been a strong tendency since the 1970s for capitalist classes to try to reverse post-1945 growth in state sectors (especially those institutions providing social welfare which are largely, but not wholly, unproductive for private capitalists). Such attacks upon state institutions have been accompanied by an increasing reliance on state-organised crisis-management. The divisions which have erupted between those sections of particular capitalist classes who demand a return to so-called laissez-faire, pre-1929 relations between state institutions and capitalist classes, and those who advocate increased planning and control as the solution to crises (e.g. various supporters of the Brandt Commission) is symptomatic of the contradictory nature of capitalist states. But the Weberian image of state bureaucracy as an efficient organisational machine is overshadowed by the reality of most capitalist state bureaucracies exhibiting a clear propensity for *avoiding* the responsibility of crisis-management. This avoidance-reaction to crises is particularly crucial when considering the capacity of capitalist state administrators to plan efficiently. State institutions are not governed by the immediate threat of bankruptcy or loss of profit in the same way as private enterprises within Production Processes; governments can displace crises via processes of bargaining or postpone problems for future administrators and generations. Those state administrators who desire to plan efficiently face the constant risk of becoming *too* efficient and *autonomous* of their capitalist clients (and thereby threatening them), or becoming *subordinate* to private interests and thereby damaging the ideological notion of the 'neutral state' held by a large number of citizens in societies with free Electoral Processes. No national capitalist state administration can increase planning to the extent where freedom of private investment ceases and private units of capitalist production become subordinate to *political* decisions rather than to the relations of private accumulation. Capitalist state administrators cannot plan on behalf of whole capitalist industries or classes in a spontaneous, natural manner in the way of the market's 'invisible hand'. Planning involves discussion, articulation of priorities, and the need to constantly justify these policies in free Electoral Processes where institutions are fragmented by class struggle. The *limited* planning capacity available to capitalist state administrations is restricted by the constant attempt of state administrators and political parties to guarantee state assistance to private enterprises *without* exacerbating mass demands that state policies should be oriented away from private needs and more to public, non-profit use-values and services.[16]

The existence of free Electoral Processes directly, as well as potentially, threatens private accumulation in that any further increase in state planning (necessitated by crises in the rates of profit) would open the doors to greater public scrutiny of private capitalist decision-making (i.e. politicise decisions of production and investment) – a situation bitterly resisted by capitalist classes at the moment. The desire of many capitalists and authoritarian social forces to crush, or restrict activities in free Electoral Processes is constantly evident. Yet the dominant OECD capitalist powers could not crush free Electoral Processes without also savagely reducing wage rates and standards of living. This tactic can only be marginally successful in isolated countries such as Chile, Argentina and so forth, because of their relatively small place in international trade and investment. A massive reduction of living standards in the United States (well beyond what Reagan has already accomplished), Western Europe and Japan would signal the onset of a potential collapse of hundreds of thousands of private capitalist units within Production Processes. One could argue in response that capitalist business survived two world wars and the extensive destruction of private capital. However, it is clear that the largest capitalist war-oriented Production Processes (e.g. in North America) thrived as did private enterprises in many other countries. The difference in the 1980s is that Production Processes in OECD capitalist countries have been based on civilian consumer-production and state-run 'social wage' services, which could not be extensively transformed into military production. Apart from the grave risk of producing another world war (considering the nature of contemporary military products), and the fiscal crises in Credit Processes associated with such a giant transformation (from civilian to military production), one would have to ignore the whole history of post-1945 capitalist developments in key industries such as automobiles, electronics, home and office construction, chemicals and all the other industries and services associated with the latter examples.

Given the fact that most workers do not produce surplus-value, it is important to recognise that class struggles take place both in the sphere of production *and* in the sphere of distribution. With orthodox Marxists it is crucial to grasp the critical role which the rate of exploitation plays in all surplus-value-extracting enterprises. Against orthodox Marxists it is necessary to recognise that distributional struggles over the share of wages or profits is decisive in all non-surplus-value-extracting private and state enterprises and institutions. Furthermore, governments must impose *administrative* ceilings on the level of wages of state sector workers; the theory of the reserve army of the unemployed, whereby the rate of exploitation increases due to the fear of being replaced by the multitudes of unemployed, is not strictly applicable or as effective in state sectors compared to private sectors. This is partially due to the more secure and even permanent nature of many state workers' jobs, plus the historical growth of union militancy amongst more and more state sector workers in national Production Processes. The old relationship between 'capital' and 'labour' has been changed for all those workers employed in state institutions. Instead of confronting individual employers, many of the largest trade unions in countries such as Britain, Australia, etc. confront the full power of governments determined to use their immense resources to break strikes and other workers' campaigns.

While most workers in non-surplus-value-producing jobs (whether in state or private institutions), cannot be analysed according to the theory of the organic composition of capital – that is, the balance between constant and variable capital – they are certainly subject to harsher labour reorganisation methods. The increased discipline resulting from the growth in unemployment and part-time work,[17] plus the threat of new labour-replacing technology, are just two examples of the way most wage-workers are threatened. Finally, all workers are affected by the level of 'social wage' services which form part of the 'historical and moral' (Marx) element needed to reproduce labour power in particular capitalist societies. In so far as the 'social wage' (health, education and other public services) is not a money wage or is not usually obtainable *directly* from private enterprises (because it is largely paid for from general tax revenue or social service contributions, and is administered by state institutions), the distributional struggle between classes is much more than the struggle over money wages earned in the factory, shop or office.

Struggles Internal to Production Processes

Within the private sectors of local and national Production Processes, there are major differences between those businesses which can go 'offshore', survive reductions in national tariff protection, finance expensive retooling requirements, etc., and all those businesses locked into local market forces or dependent on government protection. With the elimination of millions of jobs in the manufacturing industries of national Production Processes,[18] intense rivalry over national protection policies, it is remarkable that there is still such a widespread belief (especially in conservative and social-democratic parties), that an 'export-led recovery' will resolve national unemployment and profit-ability crises. Despite the massive growth in international trade over the past one hundred years (and the vital role which exports play for most countries), by 1980 exports in most leading capitalist countries made up a small percentage of total gross national product (8.2 per cent in the United States, and an average of about 10 per cent for other major capitalist countries).[19] In Japan, out of the millions of businesses oper-ating, a mere nine firms (such as Mitsubishi) accounted for a staggering 48 per cent of exports and 51 per cent of imports in 1979.[20] For leading OECD countries to experience an 'export-led recovery', there would have to be an enormous explosion in international trade – a scenario worthy of science fiction books. Even the most successful new capital-ist countries, e.g. South Korea, Singapore, Taiwan and Hong Kong (which accounted for over 60 per cent of all exports of manufactured goods from the Third World), only collectively accounted for a miniscule 4.10 per cent of the total world manufactured export goods in 1977[21] – and their growth depends on their ability to penetrate very competitive OECD national markets. One writer has already estimated a rate of over 1000 million underemployed and unemployed (in the next twenty years) in Third World capitalist countries.[22]

Turning to state institutions within local and national Production Processes, it is important to recognise that many of the recent reduc-tions in expenditure by governments have been politically disguised – due to social conflict within free Electoral Processes. There have been more cut-backs in public works (e.g. public transport stock, buildings, etc.) than in direct sackings of state sector workers in OECD countries. From an average of 14 per cent of public spending in 1967–9, OECD governments have reduced investment in state sector capital works to less than 10 per cent of public spending since 1974.[23] This reduction will only postpone fiscal crises and create future production bottlenecks as old state sector facilities and services collapse and have to be renewed in response to working-class or capitalist pressure. Thus the various local, regional and national infrastructural and financial incentives given to new business investments may impose additional political problems as existing outdated state sector infrastructure and facilities become dilapidated and threaten both old and new capitalist enterprises in the areas affected. Competitive sector businesses also tend to create more new jobs (because they are labour-intensive and do not move 'offshore') than the heavily subsidised and problem-creating monopoly sector scavengers.[24]

As capitalist state sectors account for anything between 20 and 60 per cent of OECD gross domestic products, intense rivalry has developed within and between national private sectors over the share of particular state institution contracts. This competition is expressed in the growing lobbies of local and regional businesses in various countries, each seeking to gain exclusive tendering rights to their local and regional state sector elements of Production Processes. At the supra-national level this competition between businesses is expressed in the demand by American, Japanese or European governments (on behalf of particular corporations) that other governments open up large national state sector contracts to foreign participation. In 1981, it was estimated that national state institutions purchased about US $130 billion worth of goods – two-thirds of which consisted of contracts worth less than US $167 000 each.[25] According to recent GATT policy, only contracts worth more than US $167 000 can be tendered for by foreign firms. International competition between arms exporters from Western Europe, North America, Israel, Brazil and Japan has been intense for years. With civilian consumer markets failing to maintain adequate growth levels, the added pressure on private enterprises is manifested in the competition for state contracts, whether of a civilian or military nature. The rivalry is heightened by the desire of many corporations to enter the lucrative, but potentially unstable market for state contracts provided by Communist countries. As with military contracts and other tendering to state institutions, trade with Communist countries is not governed solely by market criteria, but rather is highly dependent on or influenced by the nature of particular Electoral Process struggles, and the added contradictions of Credit and Food Production Processes which I will discuss in later chapters.

All the above contradictions between monopoly, competitive and state sectors within Production Processes, and the class struggles over rates of exploitation, distribution of wages and social services, have to be situated within the larger historical clashes and shifts of power between imperialist countries. Much has been written about the historical growth of American imperialism and the challenges to this hegemony by Western European and Japanese capitalists.[26] Of particular interest in recent years has been the steady growth of foreign investment in the United States which reached approximately US $53 billion in 1979 – yet still only a quarter of the massive US $200 billion American businesses have invested abroad.[27] When one considers other factors such as the increasing number of non-American firms in dominant positions, to the rate of research and development expenditure by Japan and West Germany, the level of labour productivity, strength of currency and growth of visible exports – it is clear that American corporations have been seriously threatened on many fronts.[28]

Furthermore, the United States' historical role of 'world policeman' for Western capitalists has also meant that United States state institutions are burdened with fiscal and socio-political costs from which the country's closest rivals – Japan, West Germany, Italy, France, Britain, Sweden – are relatively free. On the other hand, the dominant nature of American foreign investment earned its businesses over US $70 billion in *invisible* earnings (investment income, insurance, administrative services) in 1978, compared to the large *invisible* deficits incurred by Japan and West Germany – the two capitalist countries with the largest surpluses of *visible* commodity exports in recent years.[29]

By the end of the 1970s, transnational corporations accounted for over US $1000 billion worth of international trade via intra-company exports. Of *Fortune* magazine's top 500 non-United States companies in 1980, three-quarters (or 377) belonged to just six countries – Japan, Britain, West Germany, France, Canada and Sweden – and out of these 377 giants many were in fact American subsidiaries, e.g. Ford Motors in Britain or IBM Deutschland – thus making inter-imperialist rivalry intense.[30] Despite the extensive growth of transnational corporations and international trade, most goods and services are produced for consumption within local and national markets. Hence the pressure by monopoly sector companies to violate tariff walls and penetrate national Production Processes. Either way, crises cannot be avoided. If free trade is instituted, many businesses (especially small ones) will suffer; if protectionism is continued or increased, international trade will stagnate or slump. It is most likely that the crises in overproduction of commodities will get worse after each slight recovery from recessions in national Production Processes; this is because of the tendency of private firms to create extra productive capacity without the corresponding long-term markets in which to realise profits.

Given the growing interdependence of leading national capitalist Production Processes, the situation is fast approaching when any advantage which a particular capitalist class wins over its national proletariat will be soon lost. For firms will be unable to capitalise on lower wage rates and higher productivity if the added commodity production fails to penetrate foreign markets due to increased protectionism. The absence of a single 'world capitalist mode of production' is confirmed every day in the bitter struggles over unemployment, tariff protection, state contracts and 'social wage' levels, which go on within local and national Production Processes. It is all these local and national obstacles with which corporations would like to do away. While capitalists may prefer 'greater discipline in the factories' to higher profits, the prospect of bankruptcy or bare survival will see national chauvinism triumph over the abstract and fictitious 'collective capitalist will' if free trade means one country's capitalists are going to suffer at the hands of 'foreigners'.

In conclusion, social forces at local, regional, national and supra-national levels of Production Processes are inherently at odds with one another. Geographically this conflict is particularly visible in uneven regional development.[31] Technically, it is visible in the disproportionate levels of capital-intensive equipment available to monopoly as opposed to competitive sector businesses. Socially, conflicts are expressed in the fragmentation of proletarian classes along local, regional and nationalistic lines, plus the major divisions created by the discrimination and oppression of women, blacks and ethnic minorities who, as workers and as welfare recipients, battle one another over diminishing jobs and state sector budgetary outlays. At the supra-national level, imperialist rivalry is visible in the rush by American, European and Japanese businesses to corner greater shares of existing national markets and to dominate new industries such as computers and communications.

The inability of capitalist classes to resolve contemporary crises is partially due to the fact that each Production Process can no longer be 'rationalised' by 'market forces' alone. This is because the massive state sector elements within Production Processes cannot be destroyed or devalorised in the same way as private capital can be during depressions. Too many people still analyse the private 'business cycle' as if it were the sum total of economic activity in a society. Yet the fortunes of state institutions do not go up and down as private enterprises in the market. State institutions cannot be generally liquidated or absorbed by larger capitalists as happens to private firms. The needs of social groups in Electoral Processes and the needs of private capitalists in Production Processes are often irreconcilable. Even the growing socialisation of the cost of private production by state institutions (to prevent bankruptcy and save jobs) is too controversial and costly in many countries to win overwhelming support. The process of 'administrative recommodification'[32] whereby capitalist states deliberately formulate policies designed to restructure or eliminate whole industries such as textiles, is only viable to the extent that coalitions between local and regional businesses, workers and their supporters in local and regional state institutions are too weak to resist central or federal government directives. Production and Electoral Processes in OECD countries will therefore remain the battle ground for innumerable contestations over the future jobs of millions of workers and profits of millions of small and large businesses. These jobs and/or profits will depend on the out-come of social struggles over the quantity and quality of privately-owned or state-owned enterprises. Bourgeois classes have long recognised that state institutions are simultaneously a threat to private capitalist busi-ness and complementary to it. The question remains: will capitalists survive this historical contradiction or will Production Processes come to be dominated by state-owned enterprises and institutions?

8
From Abundance to Scarcity: Contradictions within Credit Processes

Credit Processes involve social practices and institutions concerned with the financing and budgetary allocation of both private and state-run goods and services. It is the diverse forms of financing goods and services which produce social conflicts within and between private and state institutions as well as between social groups in Credit Processes. The historical struggles within Electoral Processes over the allocation, ownership of, or access to material and immaterial social resources (both private and state-controlled) particularly manifest themselves within the specific relations of Credit Processes. Like Electoral and Production Processes, each Credit Process is the product of earlier historical developments – especially the uneven growth of private finance enterprises, changes in the nature of direct and indirect taxes and revenue raising, and the manner in which local and national Credit Processes have become interrelated with supra-national private and governmental financial sources and co-ordinating institutions, e.g. the International Monetary Fund.

It is possible to see more regularity in certain activities in Credit Processes compared to Electoral and Production Processes; periodic activities such as the collection of taxes, the need to present quarterly and annual private corporate and government accounts, all contribute to the desynchronisation of Credit Processes with other Processes as will become clearer later on. Historically, governments in Europe presented their annual budgets at the end of winter or in early spring after evaluating the effects of the weather on crops and other vital material production. The development of capitalist societies has seriously modified the regularity of financial allocations which were tied to the rhythmic patterns of seasonal production. Credit Processes have not only become very complex, but the regularity of financial allocations and revenue raising has been loosened or desynchronised by the internal conflicts in

Electoral, Production and Food Production Processes trying to satisfy incompatible demands and needs. Even the formality of annual present-ations of government expenditure and revenue accounts has been over-shadowed in many countries by 'mini-budgets', 'emergency budgets' and other ongoing fiscal interventions designed to 'crisis-manage' chronic problems associated with inflation, overproduction, unemployment and accumulated debt. Credit Processes are characterised by the inherent contradictions caused on the one hand by private businesses, state in-stitutions and private citizens having to raise finance for their own operations or needs, while on the other hand, within the same Credit Processes, private finance capitalists and state-owned banks 'live off' the credit or financial problems of other private businesses, state institutions or individuals. The social struggles surrounding revenue raising and financial allocations by state institutions, as well as the internal corporate pressures created by the varying forms of 'credit squeeze' or 'credit crunch', have ushered in a combination of problems which increasingly exhibit crisis tendencies *almost* autonomously of the crisis experienced in Production Processes.

For Marx and orthodox Marxists such as De Brunhoff and Aglietta,[1] the circulation of money is subordinate to the circulation of commodities. As Marx puts it, 'although the movement of the money is merely ex-pression of the circulation of commodities, yet the contrary appears to be the actual fact, and the circulation of commodities seems to be the result of the movement of the money'.[2] In Marx's analysis of the 'circuits' or methamorphosis of capital from 'money-capital' through to 'produc-tive-capital', 'commodity-capital' and then back again to 'money-capital', it can be seen that the quantity of money in circulation is very much dependent on both the nature of commodity production, and the *quantity* of commodities in circulation. The orthodox Marxian approach to money and credit opposes bourgeois or neo-classical economies which claims that the level of supply and demand for money determines the quantity of commodities in circulation. Cutler, Hindess, Hirst and Hussain have already provided us with an excellent discussion of some of the weaknesses in Marx's, Lenin's and Hilferding's analysis of money and finance capital without lapsing into monetarist or other conservative assumptions concerning the relation between money and commodities.[3] Rather than concentrate on the technical debates concerning the role of money, I would like to draw attention to the fact that orthodox Marxists are almost wholly preoccupied with money and credit as constituent elements of *private* commodity production and exchange. But just as one cannot analyse Production Processes by reducing or subordinating non-exchange goods and services of state sectors (e.g. social welfare services) to the 'logic' of private production, so too one cannot fully understand Credit Processes by treating the volume, velocity and role of money and credit solely in terms of *private* capitalist *commodity* production and circulation.

Marxists are only slowly beginning to come to terms with taxation, debt servicing, nationalised industries and other forms of activity carried out by capitalist state institutions which were either unknown to or unwritten about by Marx, Engels, Lenin, Gramsci and other Marxists. As I stated earlier, one has to reconceptualise Marx's 'circuits' of capital in order to grasp the contemporary nature of capitalist societies with their varying state institutions playing constituent roles in Production and Credit Processes. Marx's conceptualisation of the relationship between businesses in Department I (the production of means of production) and businesses in Department II (the production of means of consumption) is clearly inadequate in its neglect of the role of capitalist state institutions. This is particularly apparent when we examine the nature of Credit Processes. The notion of seemingly self-regulating exchange between two Department of *private* enterprises (see my discussion in chapter 3) is seriously at odds with contemporary capitalist societies based on the interrelation of private and state sectors.

Sources of Credit for Private Firms

Just as businesses in particular national monopoly or competitive sectors of Production Processes are governed and affected by different forms of labour processes, local or international markets, levels of state sector subsidy, tariff protection and other factors, so too are private enterprises drastically affected by their source of credit. Businesses are also very much affected by their internal company calculations (e.g. accountancy procedures) and not just their size and location in monopoly or competitive sectors of particular Production and Credit Processes. Whether the enterprise extracts surplus-value or is involved in unproductive servicing or circulation of commodities, the internal operations of each capitalist unit is limited by its degree of influence in particular Credit Processes. The businesses with the lowest degree of credit flexibility and the highest degree of dependency upon external sources are the vast majority of small, competitive sector enterprises. These firms have minimal internal fiscal resources, are generally not listed on stock exchanges, and depend to a large degree on the supply of credit from banks or other large sources of money. Those private enterprises (particularly monopoly sector businesses) that can generate investment funds from internal resources, raise finance by borrowing from the public, e.g. issuing new debentures, shares or other short- or long-term supplies of funds, are in a much better position to withstand major restrictive alterations to local and national state fiscal regulations.[4]

It is also essential to distinguish those countries in which the stock exchange is a major source of new credit or 'money-capital' and those countries where the interlocking of banks and industrial enterprises is more important (e.g. West Germany). Apart from the almost total self-financing of industry in the USSR after 1928, Japan stands out as the only major *capitalist* country which also almost wholly self-financed its own Production and Food Production Processes after 1868. While capitalists within Britain and other countries self-financed much of their own industry in the eighteenth and nineteenth centuries, they long ago opened their doors to significant levels of foreign investment. Those capitalist countries which are dependent on the continued inflow of foreign capital (such as Australia and Canada) tend to be more susceptible to foreign speculation in national stocks and shares compared to the much greater historical control over national Production and Credit Processes in Japan where the penetration of foreign capital has grown in recent years, but has been kept to a minimum.

The flexibility available to enterprises operating at supra-national as opposed to only local levels, is also clearly visible in the minimal use made of the Eurodollar market by small, competitive sector businesses compared to the funding of transnational and other large national corporations. In short, the rate of profit or potential rate of profit of a business is *not solely* determined by all those factors, such as the organisation of the labour process, which I discussed in reference to Production Processes. The availability of varying forms of 'money-capital' (and the price charged for this credit) is in greater or lesser degree *autonomous* of the internal structure and functioning of surplus-value-extracting and non-surplus-value-extracting businesses. Similarly, the incapacity of indigenous local or national bourgeoisies to generate new investment projects in particular cities or regions (such as the establishment of new industries) has historically been partially determined in many countries by the unavailability of sufficient indigenous 'money-capital' rather than the reluctance to invest due to poor profit rates. The phenomenon of credit scarcity should be contrasted to the deliberate investment of 'money-capital' by British and American finance capitalists in foreign countries where the profit rate is higher – despite the fact that numerous businesses in Britain or America are desperate for extra new funds.

It is therefore crucial to distinguish between those businesses which lack an adequate supply of credit, and those corporations which refuse to invest in local and national Production Processes because of the historical nature of class struggle or low rates of return due to excess production capacity. This point is well made by Glyn and Harrison who criticise socialists in Britain for believing that lack of investment funds in private corporations is one of the main causes of the British crisis, rather than recognising that large corporations have refused to invest in unprofitable ventures.[5]

While private capitalists may desire to move money across national boundaries, they are not able to do so 'at will', within a so-called 'world market'. The reality of national state institutions intrudes in the form of varying tax laws, investment controls, currency controls and so forth. Hence an 'average rate of profit' in a particular capitalist society is not the result of internal 'self-sufficient market forces'; the profit rates of particular industries, or rather the profit rates of particular enterprises within these different industries, are partially determined by the ability of each enterprise successfully to limit the costs and controls imposed by states (i.e. taxes, currency rates, company laws – especially in the area of share issues and fund raising). In addition, profit rates are partially affected by each enterprise's autonomy rather than dependence upon private sources of credit supply (i.e. banks, finance companies, insurance firms). Even giant corporations such as Chrysler or International Harvester were seriously affected by increases in interest rate charges on desperately needed loans because of their inability to generate sufficient working capital internally.

Sources of Credit and Revenue for State Institutions

The massive growth of state sector borrowing, together with the proliferation of regulatory codes, investment projects and other public activities carried out by capitalist states, all affect Credit Processes in a manner which the law of value is unable fully to explain. Capitalist state institutions share with the vast majority of businesses the inability to generate internally sufficient funds to cover their operations. Whereas private businesses go bankrupt or are taken over when the going gets tough, when local or national 'fiscal state crises' occur, governments resort to fiscal decisions which redistribute monetary burdens to those social classes or sections of a class which are least powerful. The fluctuating balance of class forces in many OECD countries has prevented drastic solutions (in the last two decades). As a result, the problem of revenue shortfalls is being handed on to future generations and governments (in the form of increased state debt) – a political solution designed to avoid major socio-political conflict in the short-run.

Before outlining the incompatible credit and revenue needs of states and private enterprises, let me first indicate very briefly why there are various options available to capitalist state administrators when it comes to the ability of each state institution (at local or national level) to raise finance in the least costly form possible (both in monetary and political price). One might ask, why confuse taxes and other capitalist states' revenue raisings with credit sought by private businesses? The reason why I have placed the demand for private and public money together with the collection of taxes and the profit-making activity of banks and other finance capitalists, is that all of these elements are dialectically related in a direct and indirect way – through interest rates, debt servicing, currency speculation, profit levels, to the general competition for similar fiscal sources.

The specific structure and division of capitalist states, along centralised, unitary lines or various federal lines with numerous states and local institutions, is an important determinant of the extent of revenue and expenditure co-ordination (or competition and conflict) in particular national Credit Processes. Whether the national state institutions are organised along federal or unitary principles, the bulk of state sector expenditure on both social needs and investment in infrastructure for capitalists is carried out by local and regional institutions (even though the money may be allocated by central or federal governments). The importance of free Electoral Processes is crucial in that the more subnational state institutions are controlled by public elections, the more difficult it is for national state administrators to prevent escalating demands by local and regional structures on revenue and loans. As local state institutions are very heavy borrowers of money, it is crucial to recognise the different conditions governing revenue-raising as well as sources of money available in capitalist countries. These vary from the relative autonomy (from the federal government) of local state institutions in countries like the United States, where borrowing from private markets is possible, to the centralised control of public borrowing in countries such as France where local state institutions have very limited access to private lenders.[6] In Australia, federal constitutional statutes restrict the ability of governments to raise money unless the amounts to be borrowed are mutually agreed upon or bitterly fought over in a Loans Council.

These variations in the autonomy or dependence of sub-national state institutions make the co-ordinated control of Credit Processes extremely difficult. In recent years, local and regional institutions in many countries have increased state sector employment and services at a time when central or federal governments were cutting expenditure. On the other hand, those local and regional state institutions controlled by parties which are not dominant at the national level, have been unable to implement their political programmes due to the central or federal veto of funds, e.g. the conflict between Communist controlled Italian cities and the conservative central government in Rome.[7]

Not only are there major differences between capitalist states in terms of their borrowing options and capacities, but variations in the size and nature of debt servicing are also particularly important, e.g. Japan has the largest part of its state budget financed by government bonds.[8]

The proportion of particular capitalist states' revenue coming from income tax, company tax, capital gains tax or indirect taxes (such as sales tax) is largely determined by the level of class struggle in particular Electoral Processes. Before discussing taxation, it is particularly important to note that the specific historical conditions of local and national Credit Processes are determined by numerous factors, including the size of nationalised industries, the political effects of inflation in earlier decades, the extent of corruption which erodes revenue collection, the emergence of black markets or the amount of 'moonlighting' in the workforce, and the degree of influence of supra-national institutions such as the IMF, EEC and other agencies such as the Asian Development Bank on national state administrations. For example, the amount of money needed by British nationalised industries (for new investment or simply to run existing facilities) has been sufficiently burdensome that an equivalent number of nationalised industries in the United States would have necessitated a budget deficit of double the size of United States deficits legislated in the late 1970s.[9] In West Germany the historical fear of high inflation producing major social conflict has led to a 'social-psychological' response to inflation. It is possible that in Germany there could be far greater political repercussions if inflation reached a quarter or half of recent Israeli levels of 130 per cent or more – simply because of the sensitivity of forces within the German Electoral Process to events prior to 1933, rather than because of the actual damage caused by double-digit inflation figures. The existence of quite different rates of inflation in national Credit Processes is further evidence of the non-existence of a homogeneous 'world economy' or 'world market', despite the fact that supra-national factors are very important in determining particular national rates of inflation.

There is no need to repeat all the arguments and all the findings of various Left and Right political analysts concerning tax systems. A mountain of literature and daily commentary on the level of taxes, tax avoidance, tax revolts, and so forth are indicative of the growth of awareness of the inequity of taxation levies and class responses to what are perceived to be either intolerable burdens on low income earners, or 'big government' suffocation of 'individual initiative and hard work'. In OECD countries there is, for historical reasons, not only quite a *range* of taxes levied at central, local and regional levels, but also a wide range of tax *rates*. The presence or absence of direct levies apart from income tax (such as social security payments), is important in that those countries which finance welfare services from general tax revenue are faced with political choices not encountered by those countries which separate income taxes from social security taxes. For example, if the lowest income tax rates are 30 per cent or more (as in Australia) this severely restricts tax options compared to those countries with income tax rates beginning at 10 or 17 per cent. Income tax rates have to be analysed in relation to the way in which 'social wage' services are financed. Pensions are financed out of general revenue in Australia, by special contributing schemes in other capitalist countries, and at the other extreme, are run by private funds in Chile.

Taxation systems are critical for the following reasons. As each national capitalist class must constantly innovate new commodities or techniques and sustain its private enterprises in the face of foreign competition and domestic working-class demands, the range of revenue options open to national and sub-national state administrations becomes critical in periods such as the last ten years when growth slows down or stagnates. Marx was wrong when he stated that 'No modification of the form of taxation can produce any important change in the relations of labour and capital'.[10] While taxation policies have not directly modified the relations between owners and workers, the levels of corporate taxation or income taxes in particular Credit Processes can have serious effects on class relations – especially on the rate of net profit and future investment decisions. For example, the proportion of tax revenue collected from corporations has declined significantly in countries such as the United States and Australia during the last thirty years. All other factors being equal, would profit levels of private businesses have remained as high in recent years if corporate taxation had not declined? We also know that there is a large discrepancy between the official tax rates and the actual amount of tax paid by many private corporations. The role of 'free trade zones' in countries such as the Philippines, South Korea and Malaysia also becomes irresistible for companies seeking refuge from OECD countries with relatively high tax levels (despite the prevalence of tax avoidance in such countries and massive subsidies to private enterprises).

The inability of OECD states substantially to reduce government expenditure and commitments (there is little fiscal flexibility left for most state administrators after pensions, interest payments on debt, and the sum total of ongoing administrative and infrastructural services are paid for) means that the ever-increasing demands by monopoly and competitive sector businesses for more subsidies, more protection and incentives creates a perpetual crisis in Credit Processes. Add to these business demands the impinging demographic factors of ageing populations, a smaller tax base due to the explosion in part-time workers, an increasing unemployment rate, a workforce extremely hostile to income tax increases plus near bankrupt social security funds and one can see why most OECD state administrators have sought to remedy revenue shortfalls via higher debt creation and a variety of *indirect taxes*.

Marx was, however, largely correct when he stated that 'indirect taxes conceal from an individual what he [*sic*] is paying to the state, whereas a direct tax is undisguised ... . Direct taxation prompts therefore every individual to control the governing powers while indirect taxation destroys all tendency to self-government'.[11] The growth of numerous local and national indirect taxes such as VAT or utility charges for electricity, gas and other public services, are all symptomatic of the attempt by state administrators to raise revenue by subterfuge, deception and seemingly soft options. However, various indirect taxes are detrimental not only to workers but also to many kinds of capitalist enterprises (particularly those in sales, tourism and entertainment industries). The difficulty of introducing VAT in Japan and Australia in recent years has been due to public awareness of the inequity of indirect taxes and fear of reduced profit rates amongst many capitalists. Those countries which introduced

VAT and other indirect taxes before public attention was focussed on taxes in the late 1970s, are better able to avoid the costly political conflicts which are bound to occur in any country which attempts to reduce revenue shortfalls by imposing new taxes. For example, attempts by governments to use increased oil prices as sources of extra revenue caused the defeat of the Canadian Conservative Party government in 1980 and the near-defeat of the Australian federal government in the same year.[12] The attempts by many local and regional state administrators to raise revenue by legalising gambling (in the form of lotteries, casinos, poker machines) have also created serious political headaches as a result of religious and other powerful social opposition.

Yet indirect taxes are among the few options left to state administrators given the ability of organised workers to seek higher wages from their employers in order to make up for any new direct tax deductions from their pay. Also, the general revenue process in many capitalist societies, whereby taxes collected from wage-workers and competitive sector businesses are redirected to monopoly sector enterprises (via a disproportionate allocation of subsidies for variable and constant capital used in these monopoly sector businesses) engenders new forms of scrutiny of government budgetary decisions by various social organisations fearing the multiple problems (already analysed in Production Processes) – i.e. bankruptcies, unemployment, cuts in the 'social wage' and elimination of state sector jobs, removal of tariff protection and so forth.

If inflation is partially caused by monopoly sector businesses increasing prices to make up for the overproduction of commodities (and the underutilisation of production capacity), state institutions contribute to it in a very different way, through Credit Processes. Instead of the overproduction of commodities in Production Processes, *a permanent scarcity of revenue within credit Processes is also partially responsible for fuelling the fires of inflation*. This scarcity is the historical legacy of class conflict and class compromise in OECD countries between 1945 and the mid-1970s (the so-called Keynesian 'welfare state' legacy). (Revenue scarcity has also been a permanent feature of most non-OECD capitalist countries ever since they were historically subordinated to one or more of the imperialist powers.) Those countries with free Electoral Processes have witnessed a rapid increase in 'fiscal crises' for reasons which writers such as O'Connor, and others have discussed in detail.[13] The growth in taxes *and* in public debt is a complex historical outcome of post-1945 social developments which Kalecki did not anticipate when writing in 1943. The organisational strength of unions, Left parties and community groups meant that they were able to win large state sector social expenditure via militant participation in free Electoral Processes (while capitalist classes resisted but compromised in the expansionary optimism of the 'age of affluence'). But the always-present shortfall in revenue mushroomed into crises of fiscal scarcity by the 1970s. It was in this stagnant climate that capitalists tended to close ranks and reverted to demanding tax and public expenditure cuts in unprofitable mass consumption, in just the manner described by Kalecki when discussing the 'political business cycle' of the 1930s and 1940s.

State institutions are quite unable to revert to pre-1945 expenditure and revenue levels without provoking major social conflict. The potential for large-scale social disruption and increased indebtedness is recognised by many bourgeois politicians and business leaders despite their private attraction to the kinds of ultra-conservative tax reduction schemes proposed by 'small government' ideologues (such as Arthur Laffer) in various capitalist countries. The situation is even more desperate in all those non-OECD capitalist countries without free Electoral Processes, e.g. Brazil, South Korea, Argentina, the Philippines. The governments in these countries have already savagely exploited and soaked workers of taxes; they are unable to generate sufficient credit internally, yet the continued growth of capitalist accumulation necessitates escalating foreign debt – as the vicious circle of credit scarcity threatens to get out of control. Given the inbuilt demand for ever-increasing revenue and loans, the existence of free Electoral Processes in countries such as Brazil or Indonesia would only exacerbate credit scarcity by making state administrators potentially more responsible to social expenditure needs. Conversely, the suspension of free Electoral Processes in OECD countries would be ineffective unless accompanied by a drastic reduction in working-class standards of living, an increase in taxation and the prohibition of campaigns for higher wages and improved state-run social welfare services. Such draconian measures against the working-class and welfare recipients would decimate hundreds of thousands of self-employed professionals and small businesses in OECD competitive sectors (because of major falls in working-class disposable income), drastically reduce profits or bankrupt many monopoly sector corporations, and do little to reduce company debt, personal debt and combined state sector debt (other than to possibly prevent it from increasing); ironically, these draconian measures would increase revenue scarcity because capitalist states would be able to collect less in taxes in the wake of a major slump in the private sectors of Production Processes, thus causing even greater unemployment.

Selective restrictions on component elements of free Electoral Processes (such as the banning of strikes), would do little to remedy the deep-seated malaise characterising most Production and Credit Processes in capitalist societies. Scarcity of revenue is only matched by the scarcity of 'economic cures' which can avoid killing the 'capitalist patient' in their attempts to halt or slow down a disease which is terminal in any case. Thus what we have been witnessing during the past decade has been a series of specific 'holding operations' in national Credit Processes whereby the restructuring of state institutions, cuts in social expenditure and the introduction of new taxes have been tried with minimal success. Inflation has not been eliminated, unemployment is worse, subsidies for private businesses are higher, growth (with the exception of a few industries and countries) is too low, and so the record repeats itself year in and year out. While Marxists have long recognised that crises in capitalist societies can result in either 'socialism or barbarism', conservatives such as Ludwig von Mises have also noted the negative consequences of prolonged crisis. As von Mises puts it: 'although inflation does indeed destroy Capitalism it does not do away with private property ... it cannot create anything, not even a socialist order of society'.[14]

Changing Practices within Credit Processes

In recent decades, there has been a proliferation of new forms of money and money-making. The intense competition between banks, finance companies, insurance offices, credit co-operatives and other finance capitalists has been manifested in the diversity of credit offered to individuals, companies and state institutions at local, national and supranational levels. With profit margins dependent on the volume of new credit loaned out, faced with the incessant logic of having to reduce liquidity and reserve deposits in order to maximise profit rates, finance capitalists are particularly vulnerable to crashes in areas of speculative activity like real estate, or recessions in commodity production and sales. The 'thin ice' which finance capitalists skate upon, and the actual and potential disasters which result have been well documented by writers such as Mandel – especially the crashes of 1974–5 and 1981–2.[15]

In leading capitalist countries there are substantial differences in the pattern of ownership of major commercial banks. They may be state-owned (as in France), highly concentrated in private hands (as in most countries) or more widely dispersed across a federal system as in the United States where there are about 14 300 banks – though the ten largest banks dominate over 30 per cent of American commercial banking. Not only does ownership of banks differ within various national Credit Processes, but the multiplicity of national regulations, or lack of regulations over banking, offshore activities, consumer finance, bond issuing, share speculation, insurance policies, investment trusts, building societies and foreign bank operations vitally effect profit rates. There are such major national and local differences in regard to controls over finance and credit, not to mention endless new forms of money or credit creation, that no standard notion of what defines 'money supply' (in monetarists' terms) is shared by capitalist countries. That is, various capitalist countries use M_2, M_3 or M_4 or as high as M_7 to try and define all the fiscal devices used by capitalists to evade government accounting and credit regulations.[16]

Although nationalised banks compete with privately-owned banks for similar customers they are not pressured by stockholders demanding higher profit rates and increased share earnings. This vital difference could prove to be critical in a period of prolonged stagnation. The effect of stockholders demanding constant quarterly or annual growth in profits is a problem upon which many analysts of corporate organisational structure and performance are reflecting. The need drastically to re-structure a business can often clash with the very short-term interests of executives eager to maintain their jobs by pleasing investors with quarterly or annual growth figures. It is in this sense that the forms of calculation used by enterprises have to be given more attention by Marxists.[17]

No other national Credit Process has such a disproportionate influence on other national and local credit processes as the Credit Process of the United States. The fluctuating fortunes of the American dollar since Bretton Woods in 1944 have been amply documented. Not only are American finance capitalists most important in the international arena, but the very size of the American domestic Credit Process and the cut-throat competition engendered within this market also has serious repercussions both domestically and on many other Credit Processes. For example, American banks dominate the personal credit field (such as travellers' cheques), with about 65–70 per cent of the approximately US $35 billion cheques sold in capitalist countries in 1979.[18] Also, during the 1970s, the explosion of plastic money saw roughly 600 million credit cards issued in the United States compared to about fifty million for the rest of the world. But inter-imperialist rivalry has seen the dominance of American banks challenged. Of the total deposits held in the non-Communist countries' top 100 banks, the share held by United States banks had fallen from 29.1 per cent in 1970 to 14.8 per cent in 1978.[19] By 1980 foreign banks had bought 109 American banks with assets of about US $77 billion – or twenty-six of the 300 largest American banks.[20] However, this massive sum is still small compared to the numerous banks which American finance capitalists control in other countries – with book assets of over US $300 billion (in 1980 figures).

The scramble to purchase foreign banks, foreign stocks, insurance offices and other forms of 'money-capital' – not to mention gold speculation[21] – is symptomatic of the need of large, monopoly sector finance capitalists to transcend their national Credit Processes in the quest for new markets and higher profits. No better indication of the desynchronisation between national Production Processes and supra-national Credit Processes is to be found than the dependence of leading banks on foreign earnings. For example, by the end of the 1970s, Citibank and Chase Manhattan came to rely on foreign earnings for a staggering three--quarters of their total profits.[22] The expansion of international loans and bank transactions is illustrated by the fact that in the past decade or so, international banking has grown at more than double the rate of domestic banking. By 1980 the Euromarkets involved over US $1000 billion, while total deposits in the international capitalist banking branches exceeded US $600 billion – approximately one-fifth of the size of the combined domestic money stocks of the seven major capitalist countries.[23] Nearly all the leading banks in the largest capitalist countries (whether private or state-owned) depend on roughly one-third or more of their profits from foreign Credit Processes. This is in marked contrast to the situation before 1970 when most banks (apart from leading American, British and a few other banks) operated within the confines of their own national Credit Processes.[24]

The rate of profit of finance institutions (especially banks) is thus determined by factors other than the quantity of commodities in circulation. While I have no wish to deny the inseparable relation of a large part of credit creation to profitable commodity production, sales and servicing, nevertheless, the important point to note is that a significant portion of finance capitalists' earnings are today derived from the provision of loans directly to domestic and foreign state institutions rather than just to capitalist commodity producers. Given the massive amounts borrowed by local, regional and national state institutions for non-profitable services, administration, infrastructure and so forth, banks are caught in the contradictory position of thriving on the deficits of the capitalist states, and yet depending on state borrowers not to damage private sector businesses – e.g. by excessive deficit budgeting, weakening national currencies and government bonds, by raising interest rates, applying credit restrictions, and worst of all, by defaulting on debts to private businesses.

The fragile relationship between private banks and government borrowers is particularly evident when examining the growing dependence of finance corporations on state institutions in non-OECD capitalist and Communist countries.[25] These countries now owe the major foreign commercial banks close to 40 per cent of their national debts – up from 17 per cent in 1970.[26] Between 1974 and 1978, leading capitalist banks expanded their international loans from US $280 billion to a staggering amount of approximately US $900 billion.[27]

Even if finance capitalists were able to avoid serious risks with Communist and capitalist state institutional borrowers (an unlikely development), the level of non-OECD capitalist countries' debt (which had grown from US $87 billion in 1971 to US $524 billion in 1981)[28] is sufficiently high to cast grave doubts on the possibility of maintaining the annual lending rates achieved during the 1970s without precipitating major financial defaults or crashes. Yet if banks reduce the volume of foreign lending, they face a cut in profits and create the possibility of slumps in Production Processes as international trade is strangled through lack of credit. Given the nature of this vicious circle, it is not surprising that central banks and key state institutions in various countries have intervened in recent years to try and regulate the level of foreign loans and to try and provide supra-national fiscal reserve cushions in the likely event of major credit defaults. There have already been major crises in the Canadian, Turkish, Italian, Mexican and other banking systems during 1982-3. When central bank governors warned (as early as 1980) about the real possibility of a financial crash affecting 'the international banking system as a whole',[29] it was clear by the end of 1982 that major rescue operations were unavoidable.

The instability of currency rates since the abandonment of the Bretton Woods system in 1971, has further complicated the fortunes of finance capitalists and borrowers. Private companies and state institutions have all geared themselves to short-term bonds, commercial paper, 'futures

markets' and other minimal risk, short-term, speculative money transactions. State administrations have also had to change their borrowing
procedures given the reluctance of investors to buy long-term bonds. For
example, in 1981-2, the West German federal government had only
4 per cent of its notes issued for longer than ten-year terms, while over
50 per cent of its notes were for four-year, short-term borrowings. Those
investment institutions which can invest or lend outside the limits of
local and national Credit Processes are better able to profit providing
they are not overextended or burnt by currency movements and foreign
debts.

The repercussions from major conflicts in national Electoral Processes,
falling rates of profit in national Production Processes and from credit
squeezes or inflationary state sector policies in national Credit Processes,
all reverberate across national boundaries – especially in Europe where
currencies are aligned to one another in the European Snake.[30] Thus,
crises in one country's Electoral, Production and Credit Processes are
exported into other national and local Processes. Few countries can
completely ignore currency changes and are most affected by the problems or booms of weaker or stronger capitalist societies. While local and
national Credit Processes are made up of many specific historical elements, there is no doubt that in areas such as currency rates and interest
rates, supra-national forces and conditions have become as important, if
not completely dominant in all cases. Nevertheless the difference between
national Credit Processes can be seen in such things as currency levels.
The current account deficits suffered by the United States are not equivalent to the deficits registered by many non-OECD countries. Marxists
such as Magdoff and Robinson[31] note that the use of the American
dollar as the principal currency of international trade has meant that
devaluations of the dollar benefitted American businesses by forcing
weaker countries to export goods in devalued American dollars. During
the 1970s attempts were made by particular states and private businesses
to divest themselves of American dollars; but no other country has been
able or willing to provide a reserve currency to replace the dollar and
every run on the latter only threatens to wipe out more of its value.
Moreover, there is extensive opposition to a multiple currency reserve
system; it is bad enough that the American dollar is unstable without complicating matters by having three or four unstable reserve
currencies.[32]

The desynchronisation of social practices in Credit Processes with
Electoral and Production Processes is evident in such things as speculative

activity carried on by profit-making financial institutions against their own home base currencies. Also, significant sections of commodity export-oriented businesses in national Production Processes have demanded that national inflation rates, interest rates and taxation rates be lower than other rival national rates. Yet conservative measures designed to achieve a lower national rate of taxation and inflation by reducing particular state sector 'social wage' expenditure, devaluing the national currency, etc. only created future problems by increasing debt, unemployment, lowering consumption levels of workers and increasing the cost of imported goods needed by businesses operating in local and national Production and Food Production Processes. Moreover, if national currencies are kept artificially high, or if the rate of interest has to rise in line with other national interest rates, investment in local production is deferred due to the high cost of raising loans compared to anticipated profit rates. Thus the fragility of key component elements of Credit Processes is witnessed daily as multiple announcements of changes in oil or gold prices, changes in levels of government expenditure or borrowing, wild fluctuations on stock exchanges, due to speculative investments, or natural disasters and changes in the political fortunes of parties or persons, trigger off further runs on currencies. About the only thing that has boomed in the past decade has been the industry of 'experts' – the crystal ball gazers whom businesses executives in their thousands flock to hear at rip-off prices, hoping to learn how to survive the stormy future or profit from the latest fashionable investment.

Finally, the profit rate of individual capitalist enterprises is difficult to estimate at face value because of the varying rates of inflation over lengthy periods and in different countries, and the method of public and private accounting procedures adopted. Within national Credit Processes a struggle developed in the 1970s over whether to adopt current cost accounting or retain historical cost accounting for businesses. Adoption of the former process would have devalued the assets and profit rates of companies in that it required calculation of stock and machinery replacement to be based on inflated current costs rather than earlier and original historical costs.[33] In other words, as nominal profit rates and company assets were actually eroded by persistent inflation, current cost accounting would place businesses in manufacturing, servicing, sales, finance or other industries at odds with their public accounts and share prices. This would affect their relations with state institutions (e.g. the calculation of rates of depreciation allowances and other tax subsidies). If accounting procedures convert what appear to be nominally attractive profit growth rates into real or adjusted lower rates (and even negative profit rates), then confidence in particular companies' shares is undermined, businesses are subject to takeovers or forced into raising larger capital funds to avoid critical debt/equity ratios. In the United States, the value of company takeovers and mergers (in the monopoly sector only) jumped from less than US $12 billion in 1975 to over US $82 billion in 1981.[34]

While radical analysts are correct in arguing that many monopoly sector businesses favour inflation as a means of solving crises of over-production (by reducing overheads and wage costs indirectly via higher prices), this solution is by no means beneficial to most businesses if the rate of inflation continues to grow or remains persistently high. It becomes difficult to calculate the real cost of borrowing money in local, national or supra-national Credit Processes. Instability becomes the order of the day as forward investment plans become risky propositions given the uncertainty over interest rates or the availability of credit when needed; saving becomes unattractive and the inbuilt struggle of classes wishing to protect their share of wages and profits increases. Within Credit Processes the incompatible needs of constituent elements at local, national and supra-national levels has witnessed the erosion of confidence and stability since 1971. Short-term options overshadow all the activities of lenders and debtors. The margin of flexibility and the room to manoeuvre becomes smaller each year.

Major Contradictions within Credit Processes

It would be wrong to believe that all the activities I have just discussed, constitute a sphere or process of chaos. But if we are to understand why problems such as 'stagflation' are not random events, it is necessary to grasp the multitude of conflicting activities within Credit Processes which exacerbate desynchronisation. The margin between the relatively smooth operation of private and state institutions and eruptions of crisis, are very small. The following conditions are becoming increasingly visible in most leading capitalist societies.

Competition exists between the sum total of domestic private enterprises and the local and national state institutions operating in national Production Processes, over the need for credit and the need for revenue. This competition is expressed via the entry of state institutions into the money markets, stock exchanges and public listings, in attempts to raise loans, fill bond issues and generally soak up those funds which are sought after by private companies. The interdependence of various Credit Processes means that national interest rates in major capitalist countries have spill-over effects on other national Credit Processes, forcing particular state institutions to alter local interest rates on government bonds issues in order either to prevent the outflow of money, or to soak up excess private credit creation by imposing various forms of monetary sanctions and controls. When state administrators are reluctant or unable to increase direct and indirect taxes due to Electoral Process pressures, they are forced into expenditure cut backs or greater competition with private businesses in the search for extra credit.

In capitalist societies the right to accumulate personal savings often clashes with the need of businesses and states to 'liberate' the individual of his or her assets in order to maintain sales or fill 'fiscal crisis'-ridden state coffers. The component elements (i.e. private businesses, state institutions and individuals) of each local and national Credit Process are at a different level of indebtedness; so it is difficult to estimate the specific cut-off points beyond which levels of private company or particular state debts become intolerable. There is no doubt that writers such as Mandel, Castells and others are correct when they point to the explosion of company, personal and state debt over the past forty years. The point of dispute is whether inflation has been mainly caused by increases in private rather than state debt, and whether the growth of indebtedness can be overcome without capitalist systems collapsing. Mandel argues that after 1945

actual state expenditures although still substantial, ultimately became of secondary importance in the dynamic of permanent inflation. Henceforward the main source of inflation became the expansion of overdrafts on current accounts granted by banks to the private sector and covered by the central banks and governments – in other words, production credit to capitalist companies and consumer credit to households (above all for the purchase of houses and consumer durables). Thus permanent inflation today is permanent inflation of credit money, or the form of money creation appropriate to late capitalism for the long term facilitation of extended reproduction (additional means for realising surplus value and accumulating capital).[35]

While Mandel is perfectly correct in pointing out the inseparable connection between credit creation and the dynamic of extended capitalist reproduction, I believe that he is mistaken in relegating the growth of expenditure by state institutions to a position of secondary importance. Here I would agree more with Rowthorn, O'Connor, Habermas and Gough in stressing the decisive role which class struggles have played in the size and nature of state sector services and in the creation of 'fiscal crises'.[36] Space prevents me from giving a historical survey of the rise in particular forms of state expenditure. However, the point to be made is not that combined local and national state apparatus debts are higher than private company and personal debts. Rather it is the persistent level of growth in local and national capitalist states' expenditures – especially during the 1960s and 1970s – which necessitated the extra creation of credit given the condition of revenue scarcity discussed earlier. Although it is clear that corporate and personal debts constitute the lion's share in most capitalist societies, nevertheless, state sector debts increased more rapidly than private debt. In the United States, federal government debts increased by almost 7000 per cent between 1946 and 1974 compared to between 1000 and 3500 per cent for corporate and personal debts over the same period.[37]

The significant variations in state expenditures and debt levels in capitalist countries are only explicable in terms of (a) the level of historical social struggles in free Electoral Processes, and (b) the historical development of private enterprises within local and national Production and Food Production Processes and their needs for state subsidisation of constant and variable capital. To reduce state expenditures to a derivative status is to fall into the erroneous analysis of Credit Processes by concentrating on the law of value in the private sector as the primary, if not sole dynamo underlying these Processes.

Turning to personal debt, demographic factors such as whether the person is a single white male in a skilled job or a sole female parent, or living in a two-income household, etc. will partially determine the potential amount of new taxes or consumer debt which can be negotiated without the eruption of class struggle or a fall in sales due to a drop in real disposable income. The growth in personal debt has also been determined by historical struggles over the eligibility of the poor, women, blacks and other 'credit risks' to borrow money – especially home finance.[38] Whether capitalist enterprises can facilitate an explosion in loans to workers and peasants in non-OECD countries – thus creating the conditions for extended commodity reproduction – remains unclear. At the moment it appears highly unlikely that most non-OECD countries could duplicate the experiences of OECD countries after 1945 – as it would be necessary dramatically to raise wage levels and real disposable incomes if credit obligations were to be met.

It became clear during the 1970s in OECD countries that corporate expansion depended heavily on the constant growth of personal debt[39] which in turn depended on the level of taxes cutting into disposable income and the growth in savings due to fear of unemployment. Persistent inflation and crises of profitability within enterprises in Production Processes triggered off speculation in material goods, particularly in private houses, thus exacerbating violent social conflict (e.g. squatters' struggles) directed at state institutions in West Germany, Holland and other countries (including demands for cheap public housing and rent controls); also home building construction was seriously affected by inflated home costs making mortgage payments prohibitively expensive for large numbers of working-class people.[40] With rising unemployment and part-time work, plus fundamental demographic changes in age and family structures, it is most doubtful that the rate of personal indebtedness witnessed during the past thirty years can continue at the levels necessary to solve overproduction crises, without fundamentally clashing with the needs of enterprises in Production Processes. That is, the attempts of capitalists to cut wages contradicts their need to sustain workers' consumption levels, if overproduction of commodities and credit default are to be avoided.

If we leave to one side the issues of limits to personal debts and the revenue scarcity experienced by capitalist state institutions, the role of credit creation also raises controversial arguments concerning crises in the production and circulation of commodities. Orthodox Marxists such as Mandel argue that credit creation disguises a fall in the rate of surplus-value by artificially extending sales and making credit available in recessions. This is certainly true for many businesses extracting surplus-value. It is not as relevant, however, to the numerous unproductive sales and service enterprises in Production Processes which depend on credit extension even though they do not extract surplus-value. But even those businesses which extract surplus-value are not necessarily experiencing crises because of a fall in the rate of surplus-value extracted. Many businesses may in fact be maintaining highly exploitative labour processes but suffer falls in profit either because of credit restrictions or realisation problems caused by a fall in sales. Crises in circulation due to fiscal restrictions in Credit Processes can create a disproportional gap between the rate of surplus-value extraction in the commodity-producing enterprises and the circulation and consumption of these commodities.[41]

Hence it is necessary to analyse struggles *within* the factories of particular Production Processes (e.g. struggles over the rate of exploitation) as being interrelated with, but *not reducible* to crises associated with the availability of finance, etc. in Credit Processes. The inherent contradictions of capitalist societies are very much exacerbated by the fact that most enterprises extracting surplus-value have more control over their *own* labour processes than they do over the innumerable institutions and other businesses required to guarantee a trouble-free circulation of commodities once they leave the site of production.

In conclusion, it can be shown that the ability of local, national and supra-national state administrators to *control* or eliminate problems associated with revenue scarcity, personal debt and company debt, are minimal. The profit-making interests of banks, brokers, insurance companies, accountants, etc. are seriously at odds with the needs of state institutions for extra revenue. Supra-national conflicts and transactions in the form of capital movements, currency rates, interest rates and speculative investments are almost impossible to 'rationalise', as the failure of Bretton Woods' regulatory mechanisms has shown. The internal desynchronisation of all the component elements of Credit Processes, makes any attempts to 'rationalise' these latter Processes utopian; to 'synchronise' these local, national and supra-national Credit Processes with Electoral, Production and Food Production Processes is even more utopian. One of the reasons for concentrating so much on developments in the 1970s here is that the rate of credit creation and credit scarcity assumed qualitatively now dimensions during this decade compared to the all previous historical experiences in capitalist societies. Much of the credit made available to businesses, individuals and states is made on strictly short-term bases, as is a large percentage of finance capitalists profit-making investments, speculations and loans. It is therefore difficult to avoid dramatic images of a 'time-bomb' ticking away in the form of major government or business defaults. There is also the potentiality for major social breakdown once outlets for expansion are seriously curtailed due to credit restrictions on commodity producers or scarcity of revenue for state institutions.

What is not clear is the level of fiscal resources and credit creation which leading capitalist countries can mobilise in a crisis as they did during two world wars. Certainly, the more far-sighted technocrats and crisis-managers who wish to save capitalist societies (e.g. prominent members of the Brandt Commission or the Brookings Institute) have called for serious modifications to Credit Processes in order to raise more revenue and prevent major debt defaults, the collapse of international trade, and worst of all, social revolutions.[42] Providing a paradoxical, but enlightening instance of the crises of desynchronisation between Processes, are those social forces dominating free Electoral Processes in key capitalist societies such as the United States, Britain and Japan which have embarked on heavy militarisation policies in recent years – thus making the prevention of subsequent crises within Credit Processes even more unlikely as deficits increase, etc. The emergence of what O'Connor called a 'social–industrial complex'[43] to replace the American 'military – industrial complex' is even more remote today than it was in 1972.

With each national government concentrating on minimising internal domestic problems, there is little prospect that Electoral Process pressures will permit altruistic supra-national agreements to be reached in the boardroom of the World Bank, EEC Commission, IMF or other agencies. *The inability to regulate Credit Processes is not due to the so-called anarchy of capitalist relations but rather to the very organised power of groups and individuals in private and state sectors who have too much at stake to let the 'invisible hand' of market forces run their course,* (In chapter 10 I will discuss the nature of 'organised anarchy'.) Each organised attempt to postpone crises by increasing debt, increasing or reducing taxes, altering currency rates, cutting social expenditure and so forth, only compounds the malaise and increases the possibility of future major collapses. The question then remains whether capitalist classes could survive the repudiation of debt, the devalorisation of capital on a gigantic scale – starting out afresh to accumulate new capital. This scenario cannot be ruled out, although the question of which capitalist enterprises and individuals would survive such a holocaust is too much of a nightmare for even the toughest capitalist to contemplate.

9
The Industrialisation of Food Production Processes: A Neglected Revolution

Most Marxists and non-Marxists are in broad agreement that the emergence of capitalist societies witnessed the depopulation of the land and the transformation of pre-capitalist social relations, e.g. the abolition of serfdom in Europe and the rise of commercial agriculture. But very few writers have paid much attention to the subsequent revolution in food production which capitalist production and social relations promoted – especially in the second half of the twentieth century. The very evenness of the historical transformation of pre-capitalist social relations into capitalist commodity production relations has already been discussed in relation to Electoral, Production and Credit Processes. The social forces struggling within these other local and national Processes have had a profound effect on the nature of Food Production Processes – in terms of technological changes in the production of food, the financing and retailing of food production and very importantly, changes in the nature of working-classes' diet due to class struggles over the standard of living. In the following pages I will explain the nature of Food Production Processes and why they have to be distinguished from Production Processes. But before doing this, I would like to explain why the notion of Food Production Processes is used in preference to other concepts such as 'Ecological Process'.

Just as the notion of 'Political Process' or 'Citizenship Process' are either too vague or too narrow to encompass the social relations within Electoral Processes, so too, the concept 'Ecological Process' fails to convey the specific role and importance of the production, exchange and consumption of food. While the decisive role of ecological relations is incorporated within the notion of Food Production Processes, the emphasis is very much on the effect of environmental destruction upon food production, rather than a more general concern for all forms of natural ecologies. It will be argued that specific social struggles within particular Electoral, Production and Credit Processes directly and indirectly affect both food production and general ecological phenomena. As with Credit Processes, the supra-national relations between different elements of local and national Food Production Processes in capitalist societies have become very important compared to the predominantly local and national social relations of Electoral Processes, e.g. the dependence of many countries on a few major food-exporting countries such as the United States. Also, the industrialisation of Food Production Processes is an historical phenomenon linked to the growth of capitalist societies and other contemporary societies; it is not applicable to pre-capitalist societies. In other words, the general term 'Ecological Process' may be applicable to all historical societies, but Food Production Processes are synonymous with the development of capitalist production relations.

Why, it may be asked, give prominence to Food as one of the four key Processes rather than the production and circulation of other natural and processed raw materials such as oil, copper, tin and so forth? It is certainly true that the availability or scarcity of key raw materials or 'world commodities' seriously affects numerous Production, Electoral and Food Production Processes. The strategic control of key commodities such as oil can definitely exacerbate difficulties in particular national Electoral, Production and Credit Processes – forcing the reorganisation of energy consumption, raising the price of manufactured goods and affecting Electoral and Credit Processes via such things as foreign policy changes and domestic Electoral struggles, increased debt, balance-of-payments deficits, tax increases and new subsidies. Yet ultimately the level of consumption of raw materials such as oil or copper is determined by the general health of elements within Production Processes in particular countries. The price and availability of raw materials may *appear* as a wholly autonomous or extraneous causal factor in economic crises (e.g. the pervasive belief of non-Marxist political economists, disseminated via the mass media in capitalist countries, that the rise in the price of oil after 1973 has been the main cause of 'world recession'). But, contrary to this appearance, the supply of and demand for oil and all other raw materials, are determined more by the activity within Production Processes rather than the other way round. Note the fluctuation in the price of oil and other raw materials in recent years; so-called scarcity has turned into glut and overproduction.

Raw materials might be seen as belonging in an autonomous Process in isolation from the fortunes of Production Processes. First, rises or falls in the price of raw materials definitely affect particular local and national Electoral, Production, Credit and Food Production Processes, especially those in Third World countries, for international prices (generally determined by cartels) can produce major internal socio-political problems and instability. Second, the potential exhaustion of finite resources or the disruption of supplies due to local war or political turmoil can lead to further serious strains in the existing Electoral, Credit and Production Processes of many countries. These latter factors could possibly justify the inclusion of a fifth Process (e.g. 'Raw Material Processes') as a further refinement of the notion of the crises of de-synchronisation. However, my notion of Food Production Processes includes all those ecological determinants associated with food pro-duction – e.g. environmental damage (oil spills, soil erosion, acid rain) caused by the production, processing and circulation of raw materials. It is also possible to incorporate most of the elements of so-called 'Raw Material Processes' into my notions of Production Processes or Electoral Processes (e.g. the relationship between levels of manufacturing and raw material production or the intensity of political conflicts which affect the supply of raw materials). Furthermore, the notion that Food Pro-duction Processes are worthy of separate attention, on a level similar to Electoral, Production and Credit Processes, can be justified on the grounds that, while there are overlaps with the other Processes (as is true of all of the four Processes), there are distinct and irreducible developments within Food Production Processes which are irresolvable within the framework of capitalist societies. Technically speaking, all food production could be fitted into Production Processes. But the production and exchange of food is in need of separate analysis because of the vital importance which food has to the continued existence of social stability let alone human survival.

Just as the level of class conflict and democratisation within particu-lar Electoral Processes influences the rate of private capitalist profitable accumulation, so too the very nature of the internal components of particular Food Production Processes vitally affect the level of class harmony or conflict. The destruction of irreplaceable ecological forces within Food Production Processes could spell the end of capitalist class domination regardless of whether social participants within Electoral Processes are class-conscious. Lack of class conflict within particular Electoral Processes will not guarantee capitalist classes trouble-free hegemony if the objective limits of ecological factors create barriers to accumulation beyond the control of both capitalists and workers. It is in this sense that Food Production Processes have the potentiality to determine the ultimate limits of trouble-free 'harmony' in capitalist countries. Ecological factors within particular Food Production Processes would also define limits to any alternative future social orders.

Historically, Marxists such as Kautsky, Lenin, Gramsci and Mao conceived food producers in narrow strategic terms, focussing on the conservative or radical nature of peasants and their role in revolutionary activity.[1] It was only after the old regimes fell that revolutionaries in Russia, China, Cuba, Vietnam and of course Cambodia had to deal with the horrendous dilemmas of Food Production Processes as the politics of scarcity. Revolutionaries have been mainly preoccupied with the task of implementing social revolution outside the towns without creating mass starvation due to peasant resistance. In contrast, the fundamentally different nature of Food Production Processes in most contemporary OECD countries (e.g. the absence of large peasant populations) has left radicals in these developed capitalist societies without an adequate understanding of the connections of complex capitalist Food Production Processes to Electoral, Production and Credit Processes. In the Russian and Chinese revolutionaries' programmes, the mere quantitative re-distribution of food to the masses involved a gigantic qualitative revolution. Today the egalitarian quantitative distribution of food is still a revolutionary dream for the countless millions of hungry people in the world. But the qualitative nature of Food Production Processes in capitalist societies completely rules out the adequacy of confiscations and redistributional solutions similar to those of earlier revolutions. Orthodox Marxists have generally conceived socialism as the unleashing of 'the forces of production' developed by capitalists but without the exploitative class relations which characterise bourgeois societies.[2] However, if the rest of the world's population were to consume food and non-edible products at prevailing OECD levels,[3] the necessary expansion in food production and consumer good production would most probably lead to ecological disasters.

Marx was partially correct when he argued that the ultimate reason for all real crises in capitalist societies 'always remains the poverty and restricted consumption of the masses'.[4] But leaving aside the technical debates concerning underconsumption theory, Marx's scheme of extended reproduction in volume 2 of *Capital* (see my critique in chapter 3) made no allowance for the ecological limits to mass consumption – even though he did discuss humanity's relation with nature in other writings and called for a balance between town and country. If one wishes to understand the interconnections between local, national and supra-national Production and Food Production Processes, it is necessary to recognise that it is not just the wage levels of the proletariat which could restrict capitalist accumulation. The very promotion of the mass consumption of edible and non-edible commodities by capitalist enterprises exacerbates contradictions within capitalist societies in ways that orthodox Marxists could barely foresee. Although the *relative* gap between the wealth of capitalist classes and the working-classes in most capitalist societies has remained the same during the past one hundred years (and even widened in some countries), there has nevertheless been a quantitative and qualitative transformation of proletarian consumption. The harmony of social classes, not to mention the potential growth of capitalist societies, is inextricably bound up with the delivery of a sufficient amount of *manufactured food* at prices which workers, welfare dependents, etc. can afford, and which environmental forces can bear. When one takes into account the critical effects of problem-ridden food production on Communist countries, plus the rapid transformation of Production and Food Production Processes in many non-OECD countries, it becomes clearer why Food Production Processes play such a pivotal role in capitalist societies. The complex social and ecological forces within Food Production Processes only exacerbate the desynchronisation of local and national Processes – especially as crisis-managers have even less chance of 'synchronising' climatic forces.

Critics of agribusiness and environmental abuse such as Susan George, Malcolm Caldwell, Colin Tudge, Barry Commoner, Alan Roberts[5] and many others have already written rich and comprehensive studies of the connections between food chains and the capitalist control over natural resources. Most of these studies are invaluable in highlighting the mounting dangers which stem from the irrationality of capitalist domination. With a few exceptions most of these authors say very little about the political economic implications of Food Production Processes on private accumulation and state institutions, apart from exposing all the horrors perpetrated by both capitalist enterprises and state administrations and revealing the need to fight for more rational domestic food policies. While it is unfair to criticise other writers for not conforming to my own notion of Food Production Processes, it is important to condemn the mutual ignorance and general hostility of numerous ecologists and Marxists towards each others' analyses (especially those in Europe); for all the limitations of Commoner, Caldwell, George, etc., they are still light years ahead of the traditional 'economistic' radicals unconcerned with what they incorrectly call 'petty bourgeois' environmental issues. I believe that the notion of Food Production Processes not only attempts to overcome the latter 'apartheid' between orthodox Marxists and environmentalists but also inserts 'food' once again into the centre of any analysis of class struggle and social reproduction.

The Three Key Aspects of Food Production

I have already indicated that Food Production Processes overlap with Production Processes and embrace more than what is usually classified as edible material. Let me elaborate. Within Food Production Processes one has to distinguish between (1) all those individuals (and their dependents) and enterprises working *directly* off the land or sea – e.g. farmers working for themselves or in varying social organisations – from pre-capitalist peasant communes to elaborate, mechanised multi-million dollar businesses; (2) all those individuals and enterprises *intermediately* concerned with the (a) manufacture and processing of food in its varying stages – from the production of flour to the growth of genetic engineering; (b) the wholesale and retail distribution of food – from cattle-yards to fast food outlets; (c) the manufacture of machinery and chemicals designed to grow, harvest, sell and store food (e.g. fertilisers, harvesters, weighing machines and refrigerators); and (3) the *indirect* determinants of Food Production Processes – the various forms of raw material production and consumption which determine the quantity and quality of water supply, air pollution, ozone layers, climatic patterns, carcinogenic content and numerous other general ecological problems.

It is difficult completely to separate most of the *intermediate* activities connected to the manufacture and sale of food (points 2a–c) as well as most of the *indirect* activities of raw material production and mining (point 3) from Production Processes. Consequently, struggles within Production Processes such as those between workers and capitalists, have important spill-over effects on all those enterprises which are also indispensable parts of Food Production Processes. Therefore the crises of profitability troubling enterprises within Production Processes also become crises of profitability for enterprises within Food Production Processes. Individual and corporate food producers are also subject to all the problems associated with Credit Processes as key component parts of Food Production Processes become more and more indistinguishable from the production, distribution and financing of *non-edible* commodities and services. In fact, manufactured or processed food is the largest industry group in most leading OECD countries' national Production Processes. Also, in countries such as the United States, food industries have purchased about two-thirds of total farm production in recent years.[6]

The historical changes within Food Production Processes have produced different problems compared to those visible in Production Processes. Could all those people currently classified as poverty-stricken, especially in Third World countries, ever be given jobs or incomes which would enable them to purchase the kind of expensive mass-manufactured food available to populations in OECD countries in recent decades? And if so, could this be achieved within capitalist societies without either inflating the cost of food to those populations who currently consume manufactured food, or more seriously, without destroying key ecological systems? At the moment, overproduction exists in both non-edible and selected edible commodities produced in Food Production Processes in EEC countries, North America and Australia. The difference is that while the industrialisation of countries such as South Korea, Brazil, Taiwan, Iran, the Philippines and Mexico has exacerbated overproduction of non-food commodities (by constituting new challenges to enterprises and employment levels in Production Processes in OECD countries), the transformation of Food Production Processes in the 'newer' capitalist societies has created extra demand for manufactured food. Domestic food production has also declined due to forced labour migration from country to city (e.g. in South Korea over seven million people migrated to cities between 1962 and 1977);[7] much nutritional local agriculture has been converted into the production of luxury export crops such as pineapples, bananas, coffee and so forth.[8] For political economists the question should not be how many non-OECD countries can repeat the rapid capitalist industrialisation of Japan but rather, how many countries can transform their whole social relations into capitalist relations which are viable only at the price of being seriously dependent on the importation of food and raw materials at manageable prices? Japan imports over 80 per cent of important food items[9] and South Korea already imports almost half its food needs – being one of the top five markets for United States agricultural products.[10] Yet, South Korea's transformation into a capitalist society like Japan is by no means complete.

The potential drain on ecological systems becomes apparent when we consider that in Britain, Canada, the United States and West Germany about three-quarters or more of the food eaten has been processed before it reaches consumers' kitchens.[11] According to an OECD report, 'all but 9 per cent of the food sold by American supermarkets had first been bought (or produced) and processed by a food firm'.[12] This staggering proportion has not been reached by other leading OECD countries such as France and Italy (where well below half the food consumed by 1980 was processed), let alone by populations in dozens of Third World countries. In Western Europe, North America, Japan, Australia, New Zealand, South Africa as well as among affluent minority populations in Latin American, Asian and Middle Eastern countries, the growth of manufactured food and take-away fast foods has been closely related to technological developments in freezing, packaging and chemical substitutes during the last ten years. Add to these technical changes, the explosion in manufactured pet food, plus the intense promotion of alcohol, tea and coffee, and one has not only a picture of the historical transition from non-processed to processed food, but also of the growth of manufactured cultural dependency upon 'junk food', and widespread addiction. Moreover, government budgets in many countries are affected by high tax revenues flowing from alcohol and tobacco sales; this budgetary dependence becomes more and more difficult to control or change. Where government restrictions upon tobacco sales have been implemented, it is no accident that large cigarette producers diversified into food production and other profit-making ventures.

In all the leading capitalist food producing countries such as Australia, the United States and Canada, there are ample statistics to show the steady decline in the number of farms during the past fifty years and the concentration of capitalist agricultural enterprises. In the United States for example, there were 5.6 million farms in 1950 but only 2.7 million by 1978 – of which a mere 2.4 per cent accounted for 40 per cent of the total US $117.4 billion in gross sales.[13] However, the average size of American farms was 400 acres in 1978 compared to the average size of most farms in EEC countries which were less than 25 hectares (about 62 acres) in 1975 (except British farms which were at least double the size of their European counterparts).[14] It is clear that while the formal statistics of countries such as Australia, the United States and various other leading capitalist societies show considerably less than 10 per cent of the labour force engaged in *direct* agricultural or food production, these very low figures disguise the large numbers of workers engaged in all the *intermediate* forms of processing, and mechanised, energy and chemically intensified food production which capitalist agribusiness has promoted. The socio-political implications of this tremendous variation in size of farms and the number of people *directly* engaged in Food Production Processes will shortly become evident.

The massive assistance given by capitalist state institutions to agribusiness and manufactured food (via research and development, subsidies and state marketing boards) reveals mixed results in terms of productivity increases – some of which are potentially alarming.[15] In countries such as Britain, food production doubled during the twentieth century but the yield per acre only increased about 50 per cent as opposed to the thirty-fold increase in the use of potassium and phosphorus.[16] It is difficult to estimate what long-term effects the use of chemically intensive agriculture will have on the growing of food. What is known is that significantly more food is produced on land in the early years of artificial fertilisation compared to those land areas long subjected to multiple forms of artificial soil substitutes.[17] We also know that chemical fertilisers create cancer by seeping into rivers and water supplies. The growth of chemical agriculture and agribusiness has impoverished many farmers while earning enormous profits for leading corporations. For example, in Latin American countries such as Brazil, agribusiness has produced a bonanza for corporations such as Exxon, International Harvester, Ford, W. C. Grace, Du Pont and others.[18] On the other hand, the price of mass-manufactured fertiliser and farm machinery critically affects food yields in all those countries where farmers and state institutions cannot afford to import such expensive commodities as fertilisers. A new form of dependency emerges as Food Production Processes undergo a transition from labour-intensive to capital-intensive methods. For example, in 1973–4 a change of investment by oil companies engaged in fertiliser production led to a doubling of prices which forced forty-three poor countries to cut back on imports – thus resulting in a serious drop in the level of food grown – a situation which undoubtedly cost the lives of many people.[19]

The transformation of Food Production Processes into capital-intensive manufacturing is most visible in the United States where the productive machinery used by the average farm has jumped from US $6200 in 1940 to US $165 000 in 1977.[20] With tractors and various elaborate harvesters each costing between US $30 000 and US $70 000 (in 1980), it is no surprise that hundreds of thousands of American farmers will cease producing food in the near future as capital costs force bankruptcies and an even greater concentration of ownership. Also, the close relationship between the cost of fertiliser, levels of debt incurred, tax allowances received and food grown, is converting food production into a high risk capital investment. If many American farmers, who are among the richest in the world, will be unable to stay in business due to the increased costs of constant capital, then what chance is there and what future lies in store for millions of farmers in dozens of other countries?! The gradual or rapid historical incorporation of each local Food Production Process in particular countries into national and inter-national patterns of food production and distribution, has been usually accomplished by the uprooting of the rural labour force and its trans-formation into wage labour, the breakdown and elimination of non-processed food production (e.g. farmers in many countries are unable to compete outside local areas with agribusiness), and the integration of *direct* food producers into the contradictions emanating from local, national and supra-national Electoral, Production and Credit Processes. Here are a few of the problems experienced in each of the four Processes with specific reference to Food Production Processes.

The Relationship between Food Production Processes and Electoral and Production Processes

The conflicts between social forces within Food Production Processes and Electoral Processes is particularly evident in all those capitalist societies with free Electoral Processes. In Australia, Japan, North America and Western Europe, conservative parties and politicians have relied heavily on rural areas as bastions of electoral support. I have already noted the influence of historical voting gerrymanders, consti-tutional provisions favouring non-urban populations in various legis-latures and class conflict between workers and farmers. Not only are rural populations over-represented in many national legislatures, but the price of food is a key barometer in the cost-of-living indexes in many capitalist countries. The power of forces within Food Production Processes is visible in the EEC where over 70 per cent of the European Commission's budget is allocated to various forms of agricultural sub-sidies, export incentives and food price support schemes in order to placate both farmers and consumers.[21] The lower the wage of workers, the higher the percentage of income which is taken up by food bills. Hence the delicate balancing act of sustaining profit rates of enterprises in Food Production Processes and profit rates of all other enterprises in Production Processes, is jeopardised once wage demands are heavily influenced by the need to be able to purchase increasingly expensive food.[22] In recent years, the Japanese and Swedish governments have embarked on a campaign of subsidies and imports to keep the cost of food from escalating. The Japanese government has imported vegetables from Taiwan and South Korea in order to prevent larger wage demands being made by workers. Food in Sweden is already amongst the most expensive in Europe and any anti-inflation policy depends on delicate balancing acts between governments and private food producers, and between workers in cities and private non-food corporations.[23] This is only a single example of the numerous interventions of state administrators in various countries to prevent food prices and food supplies playing a destabilising part in general macroeconomic policy and crisis-management. In the United States the food stamp programme involved about twenty million people prior to the Reagan presidency in 1981. It remains to be seen whether attempts by farmers to gain higher prices for their food, or government reductions in the number of people eligible for food stamps will have serious affects on social stability.

As the cost of *direct* and *intermediate* food production increases due to increases in the cost of variable and constant capital, the ability of governments to avoid major social struggles will be diminished. The strategic importance of North American, Australian, Argentinian, South African and Western European grain, meat and dairy production means that should capitalist developments in non-OECD countries result in higher purchases of food from these key producer countries, then it will be extremely difficult to avoid conflict within the Electoral Processes of these producer countries should domestic food prices increase as a consequence of higher exports. If farmers and food enterprises are able to obtain large foreign orders then state institutions in principal food-exporting countries will have to either increase local subsidies to keep domestic prices down, initiate more food production or face the internal consequences of inflationary policies. And if the 'optimistic' scenario of future capitalist expansionary developments involves the development of serious strains on Food Production Processes due to excessive demand, a stagnant or low-growth scenario will also involve pressures to increase food prices as declining sales are compensated for by monopoly sector agribusinesses increasing prices (in a manner similar to non-edible commodities). That is, unless lobbies within Food Production Processes manage to obtain greater subsidies for lost sales income from capitalist state administrators. Within the EEC, Food Production Processes have been perhaps the weakest link and the most problem-ridden area since the founding of the 'common market'. The political fortunes of parties in France, Ireland, Italy, Denmark, etc. depend upon, and are influenced by multilateral policy negotiations within the EEC (e.g. vetoes by other member countries and violent protests by farmers against supra-national and national food and drink policies).

While there has been no dramatic rocketing of food commodity prices in the early 1980s (net farm income has fallen in Australia, Canada and the United States compared to the escalation of food prices and earnings in 1972), it would be premature to believe that food prices in many countries will remain stagnant in the future. Perhaps the most serious problem confronting Electoral and Food Production Processes is the clear incompatibility between the availability and price of food and the nature of class power characterising Electoral Processes in Australia, Argentina, Canada, the United States, New Zealand, Britain, France, West Germany and other key capitalist food-producing countries. At the moment it is inconceivable that individuals and enterprises within the Food Production Processes and Production Processes of these countries will be subjected to stringent state-controlled, national food planning policies. The very opposite is in fact occurring. As enterprises within Food Production Processes become more capital-intensive, require added chemicals, and as private investment increases in luxury cash crops or fast foods, the capitalist corporations and workers in *direct* and *intermediate* food enterprises are unlikely to support legislation needed to prevent major food shortages, inflated food prices, unsafe food and ecological disasters. For any major attack upon the nature of food production would also entail an attack on the very structures of private ownership and private decision-making. It would require major challenges to constitutional and voting structures within Electoral Processes which are designed to enhance agribusiness and rural lobbies' interests. It would require a major redirection of tax revenue within Credit Processes from the present support of capital-intensive enterprises within Food Production Processes to alternative forms of food production.

To achieve greater control over the production of food so that it was both healthy and equitably distributed, would in itself necessitate a major counter-hegemonic conception of the very 'manufactured' cultural notions of existing Food Production Processes. This would require an awareness of the critiques of agribusiness produced by ecologists, womens' groups (e.g. critiques of artificial baby food), animal liberationists and anti-imperialists which emphasise the dangers of the historical development of Food Production Processes to humans, animals and environments. It would also require a major critique of the conservative gender and class relations governing food production, preparation and consumption which are inseparable from larger struggles over the nature of capitalist societies taking place in Electoral Processes. In so far as numerous technical developments are sustaining the flow of new food products, agribusiness methods will maintain the popular support of millions of people in capitalist countries. It is clear that the wage-labour system and the increasing commodification of food means that each attack upon the safety of food products, or each defence of species and ecological systems endangered, will meet with hostile and serious opposition from capitalist enterprises, and from workers and consumers who will lose jobs or pay higher prices for food. In OECD societies, the goals of the animal liberation movement and the production of safe, nutritional food would most likely result in higher food prices, compared to agribusiness methods of food production – given the continuation of all other capitalist institutions and relations, e.g. cost of non-food commodities used in food production and marketing, labour and so forth. Hence the contradictory tendencies within particular Electoral Processes; on the one hand we witness the historical apathy and ignorance of all those people who are either hostile to attacks upon capitalist Food Production Processes or who have become indifferent to all the warnings about cancer, sickness, pollution, destruction and starvation, and on the other hand, we see increasing signs of opposition to the continual growth of irrational forces within Food Production Processes as the social costs of agribusiness become more and more threatening. There is no conceivable way in which the production of food in capitalist societies is going to be problem-free in the future. Either movements seeking healthier food, animal liberation and environmental protection will be successful at the expense of private accumulation, or the continued expansion of agribusiness (with all its fuel, credit and labour costs) will invariably result in higher food prices without any of the improvements or eradication of suffering advocated by radical critics.

Regardless of whether social movements within particular Electoral Processes are able to impose more rational controls over all the elements involved in the production, distribution and consumption of food, there are certain tendencies appearing within Food Production, Credit and Production Processes (discussed in earlier chapters) which are bound to increase social conflict, pressures on profit rates and credit scarcity. Free Electoral Process struggles will certainly be decisive in many countries, but the transformation of Food Production Processes in all those societies without free Electoral Processes (both capitalist and Communist) will exacerbate production problems within all capitalist food-producing enterprises. As the manufacture of food (especially that of meat and dairy products required by changing diets) begins to necessitate increasing expenditure on imported feed grain, chemicals and heavy machinery, whole regions and societies begin to lose control over the quantity and quality of food produced. It is estimated that if the rest of the world were to be fed by the same methods used to produce food in the United States (e.g. a corn farmer uses an average of 135 pounds of nitrogen, 69 pounds of phosphates and 84 pounds of potash per acre[24]) then this change of methods would require 80 per cent of the world's total energy expenditure.[25] Obviously the rest of the world's population will not be fed in the near future at anywhere near the North American rate. But the fact that almost four-fifths of all American grain (which accounts for about 60 per cent of the total produced in capitalist countries) is fed to animals, that the bulk of grain imports to Eastern Europe is used for similar purposes rather than as food for direct human consumption, and that grain imports to Western Europe and other parts of the world are also used for manufactured food production, means that the energy needed for food production is bound to increase. Monopoly control over oil, coal and other energy sources, plus the high concentration of ownership in freight and transport (especially road and shipping companies), the multiple pressures flowing from artificial chemical and fuel costs needed to grow or catch food, together with the added cost of distributing it and packaging it (paper production costs) – all these factors will most likely ensure the upward movement of food prices.

The conflict between monopoly sector and competitive sector businesses is also strikingly evident in relation to Food Production Processes. Of the estimated 350 000 small retail outlets which went bankrupt in Western European countries between 1965 and 1975, about 300 000 were selling food.[26] While the majority of British consumers saw food prices go up after entry into the EEC, a tiny minority of large companies benefited from this move into the EEC – fifteen of the twenty-one top European food manufacturers were

British monopoly sector businesses.[27] The conflicts in Production Processes between private businesses and state apparatuses over tariff protection, access to foreign markets and import controls are also the perennial issues confronting monopoly and competitive enterprises in national Food Production Processes. Struggles over access to EEC markets by non-member countries; battles over fishing grounds in Asian, Australian, Latin American and European waters; fears of EEC member country food-lobbies concerning potential Spanish, Portuguese and other food-producing countries' entry into the EEC; attacks by Argentina, Australia, New Zealand and United States farmers on the dumping of food by EEC countries at cut-rate prices, etc; these are all examples of the deep-seated conflicts between and contradictory interests of local and national Food Production Process enterprises. Furthermore, the general crisis of overproduction and unemployment characterising major capitalist Production Processes has meant that one of the few areas where jobs have been created is in fast food retail outlets rather than in food growing or manufacturing. However, most of these jobs have been part-time, low-paid and filled by under-18-year-olds with no real prospect of continued employment. In Third World countries the unemployment situation has been critical for years as millions have been uprooted by agribusiness's planting of luxury cash crops, driven into the shanty towns on the fringes of major cities and left waiting for the next 'economic miracle' promised by authoritarian politicians in moments of self-delusion or blatant ideological deception.

The Relationship between Food Production Processes and Credit Processes

The interconnection of Food Production and Credit Processes is particularly visible in the level of subsidies for food enterprises and farmers coming from tax revenue, the scarcity of credit available to both small farmers, as well as many Third World nations dependent on private banks, supra-national agencies such as the IMF, and the effect of speculation (as a hedge against inflation) on fertile, food-producing land. If one examines the escalating support given by capitalist state administrators to agribusiness and small farmers alike, it can be seen that most tax support, tax exemptions, research and development benefits, fuel subsidies and so forth are appropriated in a disproportionate manner by the small percentage of giant agribusinesses. Whether large or small, farmers enjoy privileged positions in relation to credit advances and tax concessions. In Brazil, agricultural enterprises have received between one-fourth and one-third of total state credit since 1963-4.[28] Of West Germany's 840 000 farmers, two-thirds pay no income tax at all, and the other third pay very low rates compared to other tax-payers.[29] In the United States, 80 000 dairy farmers cost tax-payers and consumers about US $3.5 billion in subsidies and price supports during 1980/1 - of which about 50 per cent went to the largest 15 per cent of dairy farmers.[30] The price support for milk rose higher than the cost of production in America but the National Milk Producers' Federation, being a powerful political lobby group (like other farmers' organisations in national Food Production Processes), will resist cuts in subsidies. The struggles over tax subsidies manifest themselves in Electoral and Credit Process conflicts and in less food production if profits decline. Not only are many food enterprises dependent on subsidies from state institutions, but the level of indebtedness is particularly important because of the slim margin between profitability, survival and/or bankruptcy. The rapid increase of farming costs during the 1970s has witnessed the level of outstanding farm credit in the United States increase to a massive US $120 billion in 1978-9.[31] In previous historical periods, peasants, share croppers and other *direct* producers were driven off the land through debt, war or persecution. The contemporary nature of industrialised food will produce quite different fall-out consequences if businesses become unprofitable through debt or loss of tax support. Decreases in tax concessions and crop subsidies result in falling production. High interest rates and costs of capital equipment result in *direct* food producers buying less from *intermediate* enterprises: witness, for example, the crisis in farm equipment firms such as International Harvester in recent years.

Like many non-edible commodities produced, the growth of manufactured food necessitates increased subsidising of variable and constant capital costs in order to maintain profit rates. This in turn imposes more strain on tax collection and government expenditure policies as social struggles over budgetary priorities (given the shortage of revenue in many countries) make continued heavy subsidies of food enterprises very contentious issues. Similarly, at an international level, provision of credit to nations in the Third World or Eastern Europe and China are fraught with all the political difficulties discussed earlier in the chapter on Credit Processes. There is ample evidence of American and other capitalist state administrations using the carrot of food-aid (or stick of food-aid denied), credit provision for grain and fertiliser imports, as well as other strategic policies such as grain hoarding, in order to influence or control policies in various national Electoral Processes. The lack of a united front between capitalist grain exporters to Eastern Europe in recent years reflects the deep conflict between the United States, Canada, Western Europe, Argentina and Australia over support for American policies against the Soviet Union or other countries such as Iran. As countries such as Poland try to get out of the heavy debts they owe to banks in capitalist countries, the dilemma for banks and governments arises concerning the increasing risk of debt default; yet this fear of debt default is complicated by the dependency of many farmers on sales to Communist countries, e.g. American farmers earn over one-seventh of total agricultural export earnings from Communist countries.

The debt burdens caused by agribusiness imports in Third World countries (fuel, fertiliser, machinery), will be exacerbated the more Production Processes are organised along capitalist lines. As the growth of capitalist manufacturing increases already massive debt levels, the very possibility of continued capitalist development in South Korea, Mexico, Brazil, Egypt and other countries depends on overcoming credit scarcity. The industrialisation of Food Production Processes in these countries increases the chance of debt default or the need for more credit. Either workers are kept at starvation levels (a dangerous situation), or imported food bills force higher debt and increased commodity production (and thus higher exploitation of workers) to pay for extended credit – an equally dangerous scenario for many countries.

The recent explosion of speculative dealings in property and other assets (due to a fall in profit rates of many enterprises), also impinges directly on Food Production Processes. Prime farm land in countries such as the United States is being lost due to speculation in property developments. Extensive sales of the richest land near 242 large American cities (farm land can sell for more than ten times its value if subdivided for residential or commercial property) has dramatically reduced the availability of unexploited farm land which may be desperately needed in the future.[32] As interest rates on home mortgages remain high, the price of inner urban homes becomes too expensive and outer farm land is eagerly snapped up despite increased fuel costs for transport. The loss of valuable top-soil and millions of acres of good farming land to roads and other developments is also very costly. Whether land is used for food, property or other investments is thus determined by the nature of developments in Production and Credit Processes.

Food Production, Environmental Damage and Social Conflict

Space prevents me from going into all the *indirect* determinants of Food Production Processes such as the future prices and ecological costs of energy sources, e.g. oil, nuclear power, oil from synthetics and so forth. Similarly, it is difficult to estimate whether the so-called threat to ozone levels, the 'green-house' affect or other climatic alterations affecting food production will mean serious food shortages or nothing of the sort. There are no reliable estimates of finite resources or of the capacity of oceans, forests and farming land to withstand agribusiness techniques. Population projections and demographic analyses of age distributions, and predictions about dietary changes and patterns of income distribution are too volatile to be useful. Most radical critics of existing Food Production Processes are confident that sufficient land and water is available adequately to feed the whole world's population provided the nature of what is produced and how it is produced and distributed are changed. While it is obvious that the Eastern European countries and China cannot feed themselves if their existing political structures are maintained, the implications of these inadequate Communist methods have not received adequate discussion amongst radicals in capitalist societies. For if Food Production Processes are decisive to the future of capitalist and Communist societies, how do reformists and revolutionaries 'handle' the 'food problem' in any 'transitional' programme to socialism?

The interconnections of Food Production Processes with Electoral, Production and Credit Processes indicate that perhaps no other area of social life (as currently organised under capitalist and non-capitalist societies) will require such profound changes if greater equality is to be attained (and even the survival of human beings ensured). The affect of food shortages in Poland gave rise to mass struggles for democratic control. In capitalist societies the relation between social forces and institutional structures in both Electoral Processes and Food Production Processes have not been given the scrutiny they deserve. In those countries where Left parties are relatively strong (e.g. France and Italy) the need to gain allies (e.g. small farmers, shopkeepers) in particular Electoral Process struggles has meant the postponement of radical alternative Food Production Process policies. While struggles between workers and capitalists over economistic demands (such as wages) characterise those food enterprises in the *intermediate* part of national Food Production Processes, e.g. food and drink companies and chemical plants, there has been little thought given to the relation between *direct*, *intermediate* and *indirect* component elements of Food Production Processes. Thus the whole transformation towards an increasingly capital-intensive form of food production is being accomplished at the very moment when many opponents of capitalist social relations are still unaware that what they thought they were opposing (i.e. traditional forms of non-processed food production) is very rapidly being 'revolutionised' by capitalist classes themselves. The historical transformation of *direct* food production into *intermediate* or industrialised food began slowly in the seventeenth and eighteenth centuries. The acceleration of industrialisation within Food Production Processes during the last fifty years is now in full swing. It remains to be seen how far the restructuring and redefinition of eating habits can be carried while still remaining profitable for private corporations. One thing is certain, the transformation of Food Production Processes cannot be reversed or significantly modified without a social revolution in attitudes as well as in ownership.

Just as socialist movements cannot simply nationalise private military contractors and utilise those specialised and refined factories of destruction for humane needs, so too, large numbers of capitalist food enterprises are incompatible with environmental health standards and humane social values. Numerous *intermediate* Food Production Process factories would have to be completely 're-tooled', *direct* farming labour forces and food growing methods would have to be altered, and all those enterprises affecting food chains *indirectly* would have to be subjected to the most stringent environmental standards. Needless to say, the re-tooling of arms factories is considerably easier than the reorganisation of existing Food Production Processes – and the arms factories present immense difficulties. The momentous political implications of alternative Food Production Processes on Left 'alternative programmes' and notions of socialism will be taken up in Part III.

10
One 'World-System' or 'Organised Anarchy': The Crises of Desynchronisation

Having discussed the major characteristics of Electoral, Production, Credit and Food Production Processes as they interact with one another at local, national and supra-national levels, it remains for me to clarify several major aspects of what I call the desynchronisation of Processes. I have criticised existing monocausal explanations of crises in capitalist societies, the simplification of social reality in 'world-system' and 'world capitalist mode of production' analyses, and of course, the whole tradition of artificially separating 'the State', 'Civil Society' and 'the Economy'. It is now necessary to explain why the theory of crises arising from the desynchronisation of Processes is more comprehensive than earlier theories. It could be argued that orthodox Marxist analyses of crises emerging from the 'laws of motion' of capitalism have a clear structural hierarchy of causation which the theory of desynchronisation of Processes lacks. Certainly it is true that my analysis of Processes lacks a clear economic 'base' which the orthodox Marxian notion of the 'laws of motion' of capitalism claims to provide. But if we recognise the contradictory roles of state institutions in the reproduction and negation of exchange-value relations, then we cannot retain intact Marx's theory of crises in volumes 2 and 3 of *Capital*. If, as I believe, there is no separate realm of 'the Economy' apart from 'the State', then the hierarchical structure of crises causation must be drastically reworked within the context of local, national and supra-national interactions.

There are several main reasons for disavowing that the 'economic' is 'determinant in the last instance', and for refusing to specify whether one Process is intrinsically more important than another: either one works with notions of 'base' and 'superstructure' which are ultimately reductionist, no matter how supposedly non-mechanistic the account may try to be, or else one acknowledges that what were formerly designated as part of the 'superstructure' (e.g. state institutions) are in fact also part of the 'base'. As most contemporary Marxists acknowledge that states are vitally involved in the accumulation of private capital, it is not possible to subdivide all those activities within Electoral, Production, Credit and Food Production Processes into an equivalent of 'base' and 'superstructure' without also lapsing back into an economic determinism. The realms of the 'political' and the 'economic' are acknowledged by many Marxists to represent artificial divisions. It follows that one Process cannot be more important than another Process in causing a pre-revolutionary crisis, if social struggles determine the nature and role of all particular private and state institutions. Hence a Production or Credit Process cannot be more important than a Food Production or Electoral Process – for each Process involves social struggles within and between capitalist enterprises, state institutions and all those groups of people employed by or dependent on these latter institutions. Yet, while no one Process consistently overshadows or determines the others, this is not to deny that within particular societies it may well be that national or supra-national forces are much more vital in determining social conflicts compared with forces in many local or regional Processes. But even this situation is not a case of simple cause and effect – as mechanical models of social change attempt to argue. It is not possible to establish which Process or variable is more decisive once there are more than two variables involved. One has to analyse empirically the historical relations between each combination of local, national and supra-national Processes, in order to argue whether or not in a particular society the determining causes of social crises were precipitated or mediated by local, national or foreign factors.

Against both Orthodox Crisis Theory and the New 'Agnosticism'

Even if one were to elicit all the complex mediations between the various Processes, this in itself may not be sufficient to satisfy those who wish to know why 'desynchronisation' is more illuminating than traditional theories of 'economic crisis'. After all, Marx said that one cannot have a permanent crisis, and yet it may appear that I have rejected economistic crisis-collapse theories of capitalism only to substitute a theory of permanent crisis. I would like to stress that my analysis of Processes is not a relativistic theory which is based on endless varieties of 'crisis'. In so far as capitalist classes dominate most of the countries in the world, it is vital to recognise that the health of private capitalist enterprises is centrally related to the reproduction of contemporary social relations. In this sense, the crises which I have analysed in Electoral, Production, Credit and Food Production Processes are unintelligible if disassociated from particular forms of private capitalist class activities. But the whole theory of desynchronised Processes is designed to counter the fundamental misconception that there exists a 'capitalism' which is subjected to crises. In differentiating capitalist societies (with their complex private and state institutions) from 'capitalism' – which can mean everything from broad notions such as a mode of production or a world order, to narrow concepts such as private production as opposed to government-rung businesses – social reality, as manifested in Processes, can no longer be interpreted in simplistic or all-embracing categories. It is not 'capitalism' which is subject to crises, but rather the social institutions and forces which constitute particular Processes in capitalist societies. This I believe to be a crucial distinction.

If one believes that capitalist societies are reproduced by a healthy 'economy' (which is understood as only private capitalist enterprises), and that not only all other socio-political institutions, but the whole 'capitalist world' will collapse like a deck of cards once the 'base' goes into its final crisis, then it follows that I do not adhere to a 'crisis-collapse' theory. In contrast, the notion of a desynchronisation of Processes is an attempt to transcend the polarised positions of orthodox crisis theorists and 'agnostic' neo-Marxists. Donzelot, Piccone and others have attacked orthodox Marxists such as Mandel or Commoner for concentrating on the crises in capitalist societies.[1] Donzelot argues that 'sieve-like concepts such as "crisis" or "contradiction" are inadequate – inadequate because they make it possible to neglect crucial transformations by referring them to the terms of a simple but outmoded debate, . . . they lead one in the end to mistake for decisive breaks, for surfaces of confrontation (whether real or merely logical), what is in fact the emergence of new techniques of regulation'.[2] Or as Cutler *et al.* put it, 'there is no general problem of the survival and reproduction of capitalism and the fact that capitalist economies manage to survive does not justify surprise and bewilderment'.[3]

If Donzelot, Cutler *et al.* are merely criticising those mechanistic Marxists who await the 'final crisis of capitalism', or all those radicals who negate the specific historical differences of capitalist societies and postulate a 'general' notion of 'the capitalist world', then one has little with which to disagree. But it seems to me that these 'agnostics' have gone much further, and abandoned even the possibility of unmanageable contradictions and crises. If each new series of social problems is only 'the emergence of new techniques of regulation', or if the 'survival and reproduction of capitalism' is unproblematical, then capitalist social relations in their various specific historical manifestations are accorded an eternal life, as they appear able to survive any challenge. But if capitalist societies are not able to survive all possible challenges, then it is up to the 'agnostics' who devalue the notions of 'crisis' and 'contradiction' to specify what will *not* reproduce capitalist relations. Rather than adhere to a 'big-bang', crisis-collapse theory or go to the 'agnostics' other extreme, I believe that it is important not to identify all concepts of crisis with their unacceptable 'crisis-collapse' versions. Marxists such as Mandel have contributed much by their analyses of crises in capitalist societies (despite the limitations of their methods), and it is rather cheap of critics such as Hussain to dismiss crisis analysis as an 'exercise in astrology',[4] just because revolutions have not broken out. The problem which I have tried to tackle in the theory of desynchronised Processes is precisely that of grasping the limitations of social reproduction within capitalist societies, without believing that these limitations apply uniformly to *all* existing capitalist societies.

In reconceptualising the 'metamorphosis of circuits' which Marx analysed in volume 2 of *Capital*, I have deliberately broken with the notion that all crises follow the cycles derived from *private capitalist units* of production. For Marx there could be no permanent crisis, as depressions in the 'economic cycle' either resulted in revolutionary class struggle, or 'cleansed' the private market by devalorising inefficient capitals – thus enabling the 'circuits' of capital accumulation to resume in the hands of the larger capitalist survivors of the recently-ended 'cyclical' crisis. After seeing why Electoral, Production, Credit and Food Production Processes involve more than just private capitalist enterprises, it is not possible to conceive crises within each or all of these Processes as 'cleansing' devices. *One cannot devalorise state institutions, social morality or ecological habitats* as one can commodity capital. Crises within each Process can be only temporarily overcome by *negating* those social forces responsible for the original crises (e.g. either by repressing movements or making social concessions to groups within free Electoral Processes), or by *displacing* crises so that they manifest themselves in other forms or at later times (e.g. by inflationary budgeting), or by incurring social malaise and the non-reproduction of social values through such devices as increasing unemployment, cutting welfare services. The theory of the desynchronisation of Processes clarifies why there are permanent problems within one or more of the four Processes – permanent in the sense that there are few if any capitalist societies which have not had to strive constantly to eliminate or displace conflicts in Electoral, Production or other Processes at local or national levels. Desynchronisation refers to the permanent inability of representatives of capitalist classes to co-ordinate, regulate or 'synchronise' all four Processes. This does not mean that all social policy and crisis-management is unsuccessful or contradictory. Far from it. But the more planning and co-ordination attempted (especially by the numerous state institutions within each Process), the greater the opposition of class forces within capitalist societies; the inherent incompatibility of class interests cannot be overcome – hence the *conscious* attempt to 'synchronise' all four Processes is not only impossible at national levels but verges on utopianism when attempted at the international or supra-national level.

While recognising that dominant classes attempt to crisis-manage or 'synchronise' the multiplicity of contradictions within each Process, we should also note a definite historical tendency in recent years for the desynchronisation of Processes to develop into the 'synchronisation' of crises. That is, as particular local and national Processes become more affected by interdependent developments in other local and national Processes, the desynchronisation of each Process from other Processes is exacerbated by the growing *'synchronisation' of crises* in more than one Production Process or Credit Process. If one can understand deep-seated crises such as 'stagflation', as stemming from the inability to resolve inflation in Credit Processes without exacerbating unemployment in Production Processes and conflict in Electoral Processes – in other words, from the inability to crisis-manage successfully because of incompatible tendencies and the desynchronised movement of each Process – then one has moved closer to understanding the permanent disorder of desynchronised Processes. But if one then goes on to recognise that recent historical developments express the pervasiveness or increased incidence of similar crisis tendencies in the Electoral, Production, Credit and Food Production Processes of many capitalist countries, then the seemingly contradictory notion, that 'synchronised' or simultaneous crises arise precisely from the desynchronisation of Processes at local, national and supra-national levels, will become clearer. For example, the specific historical development of nuclear power industries in particular national Production Processes is partially dependent on the character of national Electoral Processes, e.g. the relative absence of opposition to new power stations in Taiwan compared with West Germany, or the vital difference between strong central government in France and federal checks and balances in the United States.[5] This is clear evidence of the historical specificity of forces within local and national Processes each desynchronised with one another. Yet the spill-over effects of problems in particular national Production, Electoral and Food Production Processes is also evidence of the growing 'synchronisation' of crises in the major national nuclear industries – as social forces in other national Processes resist nuclear programmes and create a slump in the construction of new stations.

To argue that the increasing interdependence and interconnectedness of Processes at local, national and supra-national levels is making possible a more general crisis in many capitalist societies is *not* to equate this growing tendency towards a 'synchronisation' of Processes with a crisis-collapse of the *whole* 'capitalist world'. As I have stated several times, there is no single *homogeneous* 'capitalist world' which can suddenly experience a single crisis. Crisis symptons will certainly manifest themselves in more than one capitalist society (because of the growing interdependence of most nations); but each capitalist society, or more importantly, the social forces within each Electoral, Production, Credit or Food Production Process within particular capitalist societies, are in a different historical state of strength or fragility – as the more generalised crises of 1929 or 1974–5 showed – thus invalidating all those notions of a single 'world capitalist mode of production' which can collapse as soon as the weak link in the chain is broken.

The inadequacy of earlier radical predictions that capitalism must collapse has produced a generation of 'agnostics', who believe that the 'stagflation' crises of the past decade are merely a 'transitional phase' to a future, newly re-consolidated state of capitalism.[6] While one cannot predict the transformation or collapse of any society, I would nevertheless argue that the onus is on the 'agnostics' to show how capitalist societies can survive all those internal contradictions in the four Processes which I have outlined. Perfect elasticity and complete flexibility cannot be attributed to capitalist societies on any better grounds than inevitable revolution. What *can* be documented are all those potentially and actually explosive developments and demands, within desynchronised Processes, which make the difference between peaceful reproduction and unstable disorder very marginal indeed. I am quite prepared to assert that capitalist societies are definitely developing in a direction which will make the continuation of profitable commodity production an historical impossibility for the vast majority of enterprises. This impossibility to maintain profitability will not affect all private enterprises in all Production, Credit and Food Production Processes simultaneously; but there are no social indicators at present to justify any 'optimism' – to justify the belief that crises in most enterprises could be resolved by capitalist classes' relying on the survival techniques of earlier depressions.

It is true that governments in major capitalist societies can still draw upon untapped resources (both domestic and those emanating from supranational institutions), impose heavier taxes and subject particular societies to quasi-wartime conditions in attempts to rescue capitalist enterprises from disaster; but all these potential forms of crisis-management cannot eliminate the fundamentally incompatible social forces which constantly express themselves within desynchronised Processes. If the social trends manifested during the 1970s (e.g. growing unemployment, increasing conflict between competitive and monopoly sector businesses at national and supra-national levels, credit scarcity and so forth) continue in the midst of low rates of accumulation or even dis-accumulation due to stagnation, then it is certainly up to the 'agnostics' to show what grounds capitalists have to be optimistic. Given the great variety of historical conditions in local and national Electoral, Production, Credit and Food Production Processes, it would be absurd to expect major crises to break out at the same time in all capitalist societies, let alone be resolved in an identical manner. As the rate of profit of enterprises, or the level of social expenditure by state institutions, depends on social relations rather than on 'objective laws', it is not possible to put a time limit on the level or nature of social tolerance. It must be remembered that the dynamics of accumulation in Production and Food Production Processes are not only at odds with each other, but also at odds with the social relations expressed in Credit and Electoral Processes. Also, as I argued earlier, the belief that capitalist societies may be saved through repression and the suspension of free Electoral Processes is not only short-sighted, but overlooks the vital point that 'fascist' measures will probably exacerbate the difficulties felt by most businesses rather than resolve deep-seated contradictions. It is also clear that any movement towards greater socialisation of Production, Credit and Food Production Processes via extended state institutions will also exacerbate crises for private enterprises. But this is to anticipate issues to be discussed in Part III.

Why the Desynchronisation of Processes is not a 'System' Theory

Although I have been critical of all those analyses which assume there is a single 'world capitalist mode of production' or a 'world-system' consisting of a 'core' and a 'periphery', it could be claimed that my notion of local, national and supra-national Processes is also a 'world-system' analysis. I would like to emphasise very strongly that the analysis of local, national and supra-national Processes is the very antithesis of a 'world-system' perspective. It is important to stress the *decentralised* relationship of one Process to another Process. In 'world-system' analyses, it is the 'system' which predominates over the parts. The whole notion of 'core' states dominating 'peripheral' states means that all social relations between the latter gain their meaning *only* as constituent elements of a 'world-system' or 'world economy'. Once it is accepted that a 'world-system' or a 'world mode of production' exists, it is only a matter of casting the appropriate 'core' (dominant) actors and 'peripheral' (subordinate) victims. History is then presented as a succession of hegemonic states from the 'core' who preside over unfolding stages within the 'world-system'. In contrast to this homogenising 'system' theory (or 'globology' as one 'world-system' theorist calls it[7]), the concept of Processes is based on the very lack of a clear-cut 'core'. To speak of local, national and supra-national Processes interacting across national borders is not to confuse these multiple Processes with a 'system' which defines how elements within each local or national Process will relate to one another. The growing *interdependence* of many elements of particular Processes is *not* to be read as the logical predominance of the 'whole' over the 'particular'.

In contrasting the disproportionate influence of OECD countries with that of non-OECD societies, it was not my intention to portray a model of 'core' and 'periphery'. There are just as many differences between the United States, Ireland and Greece (all OECD states), as there are between Mexico and Uganda as Third World countries. The notion of local, national and supra-national Processes admits the relative historical dominance of particular countries. But the dominance of the United States or Britain at different historical periods is not equivalent to the dominance of these imperialist powers over a whole 'world-system'. If one begins with the assumption that there has never been a 'world-system' or a 'world mode of production' (even though there have been empires and very powerful nation-states), then it is possible to analyse the recent historical tendencies which have given rise to the first truly supra-national forms of interdependency – an interdependency which 'world-system' theorists incorrectly presuppose existed for centuries.

In chapter 8 I commented that the desynchronisation of Processes was due not so much to the 'anarchy of the Market', as to the very organised or entrenched vested social interests that had too much to lose in abandoning their affairs to the 'invisible hand' of market forces. If one recognises the decentralised nature of historical development and social struggles, it will become clearer why the relations between local, national and supra-national Processes are quite different from those relations depicted in 'world' models. What I call 'organised anarchy' prevents the possibility of successful regulation and management of the 'capitalist world' in which 'world-system' theorists would have us believe. The notion of a crisis of desynchronisation is closely linked to the rejection of long-standing stereotypical images of 'the capitalist mode of production'. It is necessary to reaffirm that there is no unilinear development of societies through stages of pre-capitalism, capitalism and socialism; 'world-system' analysts overlook the number of societies which have either 'skipped' extensive capitalist production or developed a hybrid mixture of predominantly non-capitalist institutions, rather than passing into the 'capitalist phase' of this homogenising historical scenario. The vast majority of capitalist enterprises are not monopoly corporations interacting within the 'world-system', but are rather the millions of small enterprises which have no assembly lines and are vitally preoccupied with local or national interests rather than transnational politics; while most enterprises are organised along industry lines (e.g. clothing manufacture or steel-making) and monopoly corporations dominate most of these industries, it must not be forgotten that all these industries operate within different nation-states rather than within a 'world market'. Given that each Process is a combination of both private and state institutions, it is not possible to reduce nation-to-nation relations to the interactions of homogeneous subjects or actors struggling over a slice of the 'world capitalist mode of production'. The non-reducibility of state institutions to mere 'superstructures' precludes the conception of the world as simply a 'capitalist world'. The complexity of bilateral and multilateral political, military and other relations explodes the simple myth of a single 'core' and its 'periphery'.

The notion of 'organised anarchy' in a world full of desynchronised local, national and supra-national Processes, is the polar opposite of concepts in system-theoretical models, which are based on integral parts each locked into the overarching structure of the 'system'. To posit a world of infinite complexity is to challenge the prevailing neatness and symmetry of many existing analyses of capitalist societies. Consequently, the whole thrust of 'business cycles', long waves or crises in the 'base' and other models becomes meaningless if one accepts the complex dynamics of social reproduction and non-reproduction. While I believe that it is impossible for capitalist classes to 'synchronise' all the major Processes, it remains to be seen how each capitalist society copes with the historical tendencies I have analysed in previous chapters.

Weaknesses in Rationality Crisis Theory

It could be objected, however, that while my critique of orthodox crisis theories is persuasive, I have ignored the difficult problem of 'rationalisation' and 'corporatism' raised by Weberians and contemporary neo-Marxists. A strong version of this critique might argue that the whole notion of Processes fails to deal with the history of irreversible 'bureaucratisation' which both state institutions and private corporations are promoting; for all the social conflict emanating from the desynchronisation of Processes, individual freedoms have still been eroded by the 'rationalisation' of life. That is, the distinction between free and unfree Electoral Processes is not adequate because the vital difference between formal and substantive freedom and rationality is ignored. This critique could be specifically directed against my analysis of Electoral Processes. For example, it could be argued that the so-called demand for more democracy and participation is in conflict with the recent historical tendency of social movements to withdraw from, rather than participate in existing institutional bureaucracies. If this is true, then my thesis of the incompatibility of increased democracy and capital accumulation is being overshadowed by the bureaucratic strengthening of state institutions and the fragmentation of working-class parties into weak, decentralised social movements.

Space prevents me from answering these criticisms in detail. I reject the predominant place given to the 'bureaucratisation' of life as the central crisis of 'modern society'. It could be argued against liberals and radicals influenced by Weber that, compared to social relations during Weber's own lifetime, there has never been as much formal and substantive freedom as exists today in those countries with free Electoral Processes. That social freedoms have been won and lost after much struggle indicates there is no inherent tendency towards more 'bureaucratisation'. Electoral Processes are *not* to be seen as functional to the reproduction of capitalist and formal-legal relations. It is precisely the internal struggles within political parties, trade unions, schools, hospitals, welfare institutions – struggles within both private and state institutions – which exacerbate desynchronisation. These social struggles are nearly all related to substantive rational issues of equality and freedom, rather than the unquestioned adherence to formal-legal-rational structures – which are defended by ruling classes as manifestations of freedom and democracy. It is in this sense that I distinguish between those countries with relatively free Electoral Processes (where struggles for substantive freedoms can be waged more easily) and those societies which do not adhere even to formal rights such as free elections.

The idea of the uneven historical development of formal and substantive rationality in local and national Processes is an important antidote to the hypothesis of a universal 'rationalising' tendency in the world. The simple expansion of state institutions does not in itself denote 'bureaucratisation' nor tell us which roles and services or controls have been increased – clerical work, garbage collection, dental care or security police? It is for this reason that I believe the concept of Electoral and other Processes corrects the historically pessimistic and distorted notion of ever-increasing 'bureaucratisation'. In recent years, many Weberians who deny the existence of class conflict, have been faced with the difficulty of explaining why 'bureaucrats' have not been able to prevent the attack on the expansion of employment within state institutions. After all, 'the State' was supposed to be a self-seeking 'autonomous power' and state employees were supposed to be different from proletarians! In reducing the complexity of state institutions to the single phenomenon of 'bureaucracy' or treating state institutions as separate from 'the Economy', Weberians (and many neo-Marxian sympathisers with Weber), have locked themselves into a conceptual framework which conceives history as the unfolding of ever-increasing 'rationalisation'.

This Weberian exaggeration reveals itself as pessimism and depression in the Frankfurt School's theses of the 'Dialectic of Enlightenment' or 'One Dimensional Man'; the 'administration of life' closes the realm of critique and negativity. It reveals itself as utopianism in the desire for a stateless socialism where all 'bureaucratisation' or administration will be abolished as free individuals determine their own existence. The 1960s revealed the weakness of the pessimist version as mass opposition to capitalist relations erupted. The abstract utopianism of stateless socialism will be discussed in detail in Part III.

I believe the preoccupation with 'bureaucratisation' to be based on a failure to transcend the traditional dichotomy of 'the State' and 'Civil Society' (e.g. Marcuse saw 'total administration' as the loss of distinct realms of 'state' and 'society'[8]). Nearly all writers who wish to emancipate 'Civil Society' and 'the individual' from 'the State' reduce state institutions to spheres or structures solely governed by technical rationality. But, just as many Althusserians wish to equate certain structures with certain roles (e.g. 'ideological' roles for state apparatuses as opposed to 'economic' roles for capitalist firms), so too, many theorists of bureaucratisation see states as narrow, administrative structures. It is important to assert that I do not regard 'bureaucratic power' to be a non-issue or simply a matter of quantitative expansion. For it is one thing to treat 'bureaucratisation' as the central issue in modern history, and quite another to analyse specific social struggles against technical rationality and evaluate the possibilities for administration to be minimised and made subject to democratic control. The choice is *not* between Weber's strong leaders or self-regulating stateless socialism. Neo-Marxists have attempted to distance themselves from Weber's non-radical politics, while at the same time pursuing his theme of 'rationalisation' in relation to capitalist and Communist societies. For example, Habermas's reformulation of historical materialism is one of the most brilliant contributions to radical theory in recent decades. Although I am deeply indebted to many of his insights on a whole range of theoretical issues, I regard his work on 'rationalisation' as unnecessarily burdened with vestiges of Weber's theory. Habermas has never been able to throw off his ideal-typical notions of capitalist 'economy' or 'the State'. Consequently, he sees 'modern societies' (another vague abstraction) as having sub-systems based on money (the 'capitalist economy') and power (state administration in Weber's sense).[9] While each sub-system has numerous exchanges with other sub-systems, they are each subject to different crises – for example, scarcity of value in 'the Economy' and 'rationality crises' in 'the State'.

The adherence of the Habermas school to ahistorical ideal types based on the separation of 'the Economy' from 'the State' (where the latter is primarily concerned with administration), takes its most artificial form in the work of Andrew Arato – a strong admirer of Habermas and Offe. Applying Habermas's and Offe's theories to societies in Eastern Europe, Arato develops a set of ideal types which attempts to show that the 'organising principles' in Communist societies are the 'state planning systems' compared to the 'market economy' in capitalist societies.[10]

Whereas crises occur within the system of exchange-value in capitalist societies, it is the contradictions within 'the State' which give rise to 'system crises' in Communist countries. As Habermas puts it (while discussing Arato): 'Just as the capitalist economy is dependent on the organisational accomplishments of the state, the specialist planning bureaucracy is dependent on the self-steering accomplishments of the economy'.[11] Using these separate 'organising principles' as the basis for his fear of technical rationality, Habermas asks, 'What resistance does the life-world itself pose to such an instrumentalisation for imperatives either of an economy set loose in its own dynamic or of a bureaucracy rendered autonomous?'[12] But the discovery of a 'self-steering economy' in Eastern Europe is just as unreal as 'the Economy' set loose in its own dynamic in capitalist societies. Habermas and Arato could have avoided these ahistorical ideal types if they were prepared to recognise that state institutions (especially those in Eastern Europe and China) are not separate from 'the Economy'. In attacking the old mechanistic, economic determinism of orthodox Marxism, Habermas and Arato are still governed by the notion that the capitalist private sector *is* 'the Economy' - thus reducing all the activities in state institutions and other structures (read 'Civil Society') to the 'sub-system' of 'administration' and 'socio-culture'. However, the logic or 'organising principle' of the Soviet economy is not 'exchange-value', and it is not possible to treat a centrally planned society simply in terms of the relationship between an autonomous 'sub-system' of 'administration' and the subordinated 'Economy', which cannot freely operate according to the principle of market 'exchange-value'.

Despite his valuable analyses of legitimation and motivation crises, Habermas comes close to a reformulation of the old 'base' and 'super-structure' model - but infused with the Weberian thesis of 'rational-isation'. If 'the Economy' is governed by the 'organising principle' of 'exchange-value', while 'the State' remains the realm of 'administration', then it is not surprising to find Habermas analysing the separate phenomena of an 'economic crisis' and a 'rationality crisis'. But how can millions of state-employed workers, welfare dependents and unpaid family members all be reduced to the separate 'sub-systems' of 'economy', 'administration' and 'socio-culture'? If state institutions enter crucially into the production of exchange-value and non-exchange-value goods and services, as Habermas correctly says they do, how can it be that state institutions are subjected only to a 'rationality crisis' while 'economic crises' belong to the private sector?

No capitalist society has ever developed in conformity with these ideal-typical compartmentalised 'sub-systems' – each governed by a distinct 'rationality' or 'organising principle'. In no Communist society have the managers and workers in state enterprises existed in a distinct 'sub-system' known as 'the Economy', which 'steers' itself without the constant interference and interchange of policy and personnel. I believe that the theory of desynchronised Processes can incorporate many of Habermas's valuable insights into motivation crises and distorted communication while avoiding his ahistorical and schematic compartmentalisation of social life. As state institutions and private institutions are both constituent elements of each local, national and supra-national Process, *no* Process is subjected to a *single* 'economic' or 'rationality' crisis, because life itself is not organised into separate 'sub-systems'.

The Limits of 'Corporatist' and Social Movements Theory

But while theorists such as Habermas employ the concept of rationality to analyse crises in contemporary societies, other critics (such as Offe and Touraine[13]) stress the 'corporatist', 'programmed' nature of capitalist societies. Claus Offe, for example, devotes considerable energy to analysing all the forms of 'étatisation' – that is, the manner in which interest groups are controlled, 'corporatised' and deployed as 'parademocratic' instruments or agents to maintain social stability by diffusing conflict between groups and 'the State'.[14] In stressing 'corporatist' developments, Offe also challenges the orthodox Marxist view that democracy is not compatible with capitalism. Instead, Offe argues that the introduction of universal voting, mass political parties and the development of 'corporatist', 'parademocratic' institutions has well served capitalist interests – even though political parties are now exhausting their 'integrative' roles.[15] If Offe is correct in arguing that new social movements are seeking autonomy rather than participation in 'corporatist' and bureaucratised political parties and state institutions, would not this alternative perception of recent historical developments weaken my analysis of Electoral Processes? In reply, I must emphasise that the desynchronisation of Processes does *not* rest on the existence of free Electoral Processes. Those countries without free Electoral Processes have not been able to 'synchronise' Production, Credit and Food Production Processes to prevent crises. Furthermore, while free Electoral Processes exacerbate crises within other Processes, there is no inherent logic of inevitable democratisation governing social institutions within

Electoral Processes. In this sense, the concept of Electoral Processes enables one to distinguish pseudo or formal democratic institutions from substantive democratic control and participation.

However, the stress on 'corporatism' and 'étatisation' tends to create a false dichotomy between all those activities organised or controlled by 'the State' (which are functional to capitalism) and anti-statist social movements. Touraine, Offe and Habermas[16] analyse social movements as social forces opposed to bureaucratised state institutions, trade unions and political parties; social movements seek alternative gender, racial, environmental, physical and cultural relations to those technical rational, violent, exploitative and commodified relations which are dominant at the moment. Touraine has many valuable insights to offer in relation to the emergence of new social movements and the various forms of activity carried out by these movements. However, his whole analysis is not only characterised by endless ideal-typical models, as well as the misconception and reduction of social movements and state institutions (with their complex relations) to homogeneous 'actors' or subjects, but is couched within a Left version of 'post-industrial society' theory.[17] While Touraine is not arguing that class conflict is disappearing (quite the contrary), his main theme is the historical decline of old workers' movements – which were the main social movements in 'industrial society' – and the rise of new social movements in the planned, technical, rational 'programmed society'. Touraine constructs an ideal-typical model of the passage of old social movements through stages of decline, cultural crisis, rejection, community withdrawal, to the birth of new social movements (none of which have yet replaced the workers' movements as the main opposition) in 'programmed society'.

There is no doubt that the old-style Communist and Social Democratic parties of the Second and Third Internationals have declined or been transformed in many countries in the last few decades. The issue is whether the party system within many Electoral Processes is falling apart or becoming more 'corporatised' rather than becoming more democratised. Offe believes that the historical growth of free competitive party systems 'de-radicalised' parties as rank-and-file members lost control and parties succumbed to the influence of market forces in the quest for votes. Hence, social movements are bypassing parties and demanding autonomy rather than participation; 'corporatist' tendencies are also bypassing parliamentary politics, and 'democratisation' is threatened and reversed by the growing repression of civil liberties carried out by governments in response to new social movements. With the exhaustion of the other main pillar of stability – what Offe calls the 'Keynesian welfare state' – the prospect of conflict being avoided remains bleak.

Despite Offe's critique of orthodox Marxism, he does not undermine the belief that full and substantive democracy is incompatible with capitalist societies. Instead, Offe establishes that mass parties organised along hierarchical, non-democratic lines with passive voters *are* compatible with capitalist relations. Offe's analysis of the demand for greater equality and more control by people over their own lives complements my analysis of democratising struggles within Electoral Processes. Yet, the analyses of 'old' and 'new' social movements have an ahistorical quality about them, in so far as Touraine and Offe tend to extrapolate from particular examples in Europe and project these onto other capitalist countries. The transition from 'industrial' to 'programmed' society is not really applicable to North America, Australia, Argentina, South Africa, New Zealand and elsewhere; these countries have never really had mass Communist parties or Socialist parties as major *parliamentary* parties which were 'de-radicalised' by the competitive party system. The short life of Debs' American Socialist Party prior to 1914, the lack of a radical, non-Fabian socialist programme for most of the history of the British and Australian Labor parties, are just a couple of examples of the ahistorical nature of Offe's thesis. Analysing the historical specificity of movements within particular Electoral Processes is more important than constructing suggestive but limited ideal types.

While it is true that relatively small workers' movements (e.g. Communist Parties) in North America, Australia, Britain and other countries have lost substantial support over the last thirty years, it does not mean that most new social movements have continued to bypass the party system. Here, the specific historical structure of formal aspects of Electoral Processes is very important – e.g. the voting system, the presence of candidate politics in the United States as opposed to strict party control over politicians in Europe and Australia. The relationship between new social movements and bureaucratic political parties has not been clear-cut. One could argue that, as capitalist societies have become more crisis-ridden since the 1970s, new social movements have also sought to infiltrate or influence the main Left parties (e.g. the British Labour Party or French Socialist Party). It is the failure of social movements to replace the central role of traditional political parties (most evident in the United States and Canada) which perhaps leads people back into parliamentary party politics. This is itself a potentially destabilising phenomenon. In Britain the destabilisation of the old party system is largely the result of a move to make the Labour Party more socialist rather than the growth of social movements outside the party system. Even in West Germany, the formation and recent electoral success of the Alternative Green Party (although more democratic) illustrates the attempt of new social movements to *enter* parliamentary politics instead of completely withdrawing into autonomous activities. In short, it is not a question of the 'old' class party being replaced by non-party movements. The resistance of existing Social-Democratic and Communist parties to democratisation is matched by the very limited successes of social movements struggling without the support of these old parties. The large, bureaucratised parties and trade unions unfortunately dominate the 'vital space' within Electoral Processes thus perpetuating the 'disorganisation' of social liberation movements.

It is too early to predict whether mass parties will be replaced by new social movements. The evidence in most countries with free Electoral Processes is too contradictory to support Touraine and Offe unequivocally. I would argue that in those countries which have strong parties affiliated to strong trade union movements, it is more likely that attempts will be made to radicalise these Social-Democratic and Communist parties in order to solve unemployment, halt growing militarism, extend civil rights and so forth. Offe says that there has been 'an increase of the social character of politics within capitalism, a dissolution of the institutional separateness, or relative autonomy, of the state, the withering away of the capitalist state as a coherent and strictly circumscribed apparatus of power'.[18] While I would question how 'separate' 'the State' ever was, the notion of the realm of politics transcending state institutions, in some way describes the internal relations of Electoral Processes. Many radicals such as Gorz[19] still wish for an autonomous 'Civil Society'. But to attain freedom and equality is not to emancipate the individual, 'the family' and 'Civil Society' from 'the State'. Rather, social movements and political parties struggle over the social relations within state institutions – which interpenetrate the social relations of 'the family' and 'Civil Society'. 'Electoral Process' is not another name for 'Civil Society'. There is no separate realm of 'Civil Society'. To revolutionise Electoral Processes is to revolutionise *both* state and private institutions and relations. If there are to be any improvements in substantive freedom and equality, they will not come about without changes in the social relations within state institutions – changes in schooling, public transport, health, welfare and a multitude of services and relations – all of which make 'civil life' what it is, and what it can be. It is important to stress that freedom and equality are not enhanced simply because there is mass participation in Electoral Processes (e.g. millions of uncritical devotees of the Ayatollah Khomeini) or an extension of state-run Production, Credit and Food Production Process institutions which continue market practices and exploitation.

The theory of desynchronised Processes is not narrowly oriented to analysing the impersonal nature of institutional crises occurring in different societies. It also enables us to analyse the relationship between personal motivation problems (e.g. feelings of alienation, meaninglessness, etc.) and the manner in which these personal experiences are interpreted or dealt with by individuals, either on their own or via social movements, therapists, religious or political institutions. For it is the 'alternatives' to existing irrational and oppressive social relations which are just as much in need of scrutiny and critique. In conclusion, while it is highly doubtful that capitalist classes will find the demand for greater equality and freedom compatible with their own interests, it remains to be seen how well radical political movements understand, let alone deal with, the crises resulting from desynchronised Processes. This issue is the subject of the following chapters.

Part III
Recognising the Nature of State Institutions: Implications for the Future

11
Between Reform and Revolution: 'Alternative Programmes' and their Failure to Confront the Desynchronisation of Processes

Discussing the varying theoretical and strategic approaches of socialists in Europe, Perry Anderson notes that the

> continuity of the political ideas of Kautsky and Bauer with those of Berlinguer and Carrillo on the road to socialism in Western Europe is now virtually complete .... Thompson shares positions with his adversaries Althusser and Poulantzas, not to speak of Hirst and Hindess, within a broad spectrum that now stretches from Euro-communism to left Social Democracy. The great majority of the Marxist intelligentsia in the West has rallied to these perspectives of late, and much creative work has been done from their standpoint.[1]

While Anderson is more attracted to 'the tradition of Lenin and Trotsky', he correctly points to the peculiar situation which exists around a 'rough' consensus between so many 'schools' of Marxism and non-Marxism (concerning a parliamentary transition to socialism) despite the bitter methodological disputes over such concepts as class, mode of production, history and so forth.

Why is it that 'the great majority of the Marxist intelligentsia in the West' have placed their hopes in 'parliamentary roads' to socialism? How can so many Marxists legitimate a range of strategies which defy the very detailed analyses that many of these same Marxists have provided of capitalist state apparatuses and capitalist classes? In fact, many 'alternative strategists' cite previous historical experiences since 1917, in order to affirm the correctness of the difficult path between Stalinism and Fascism. According to the 'Eurocommunist Left', 'the parliamentary road' is the only realistic strategy available – given the inherent dangers and utopianism of insurrectionist and anarchist strategies – and the failure of far Left parties to mobilise mass movements. The notion of a 'parliamentary road' is also interpreted by many socialists to mean the mass mobilisation of people in extra-parliamentary struggles, and not simply a reliance on narrow, electoral and parliamentary strategies. According to Bob Rowthorn, 'creating and developing an Alternative Economic Strategy is an important exercise in self-education for socialists . . . . It compels them to confront the practical difficulties of administering a modern society and thereby helps to overcome the legacy of moralism and sloganism which has dogged the Left for so long'.[2]

My analysis of 'alternative programmes' and the far Left critiques of these programmes is not concerned solely with the usual polemics and accusations about 'reformism', lack of support for mass struggle, sectarian politics, reliance on the model of 1917 and so forth. There is no shortage of attacks upon and justifications of 'parliamentary politics'.[3] Rather, I wish to analyse the way in which particular Electoral, Production, Credit and Food Production Processes affect the viability of 'alternative programmes' and why these 'programmes' will not resolve the major problems emanating from the desynchronisation of Processes. In being critical of 'alternative programmes', I do not wish to appear oblivious to the enormous difficulties confronting Left parties trying simply to defend previous gains made by workers against the savage cuts imposed by conservative governments. The various attempts by socialists to devise alternative plans at local level or within particular industries deserve critical and qualified support. While the increasingly vital role of transnational corporations and supra-national institutions impose major constraints on the viability of 'alternative programmes', the non-existence of a homogeneous 'world capitalist mode of production' is evident in the varying social problems confronting particular national political parties. For example, to achieve the level of 'social wage' services and working-class organisational strength already in existence in Sweden would in itself constitute a major social victory in countries such as the United States, Japan, Australia or Britain. As each particular national Left party is confronting socio-economic crises with varying degrees of organisational strength and varying levels of natural, industrial and social assets, some 'alternative programmes' are better placed to achieve part of their goals compared with other parties. But having recognised the current difficulties and opportunities confronting Left parties, it is nevertheless important to subject 'alternative programmes' to a stringent and critical analysis.

It is important to recognise that there are also significant differences between the 'alternative programmes' developed between 1972 and 1978, and the 'alternative programmes' put forward in the early 1980s by authors such as Aaronovitch[4] in Britain and the government of President Mitterrand in France.[5] These latter policies have certain similarities with earlier 'alternative programmes' but they publicly reject the 'radicalism' of the earlier 'Eurocommunist' strategies. My analysis of 'alternative programmes' focuses mainly on the earlier 'radical' versions (Mark 1) and the current champions of this strategy. At the end of my discussion of the more 'radical' policies, I will compare the recent 'alternative programmes' (Mark 2) with the earlier models, in order to emphasise the inadequate nature of both models in dealing with the desynchronisation of Processes. While my discussion of the manner in which the desynchronisation of Processes affects 'alternative programmes' will be mainly confined to the European scene, particular criticisms will undoubtedly also be relevant to many non-European 'alternative programme' strategies.

Production Processes and 'Alternative Programmes'

Most 'alternative programmes' claim to be able to resolve the crisis of 'stagflation' by the reorganisation of private enterprises and state institutions. These 'alternative' policies, it is argued, will simultaneously: (1) solve unemployment and yet sustain or improve profit levels in *non*-monopoly sector enterprises; (2) promote workers' self-management and yet make public enterprises work efficiently according to a complex government plan; (3) regenerate and protect local and national industries which will not be at the expense of workers in other countries (and so promote a new socialist internationalism); and finally (4) shift consumption away from private, exchange-value commodities to public or use-value goods and services while preserving a capitalist society. Nearly all these proposals are advocated, in more radical or limited terms depending on the faction of a particular party or the country of origin. Although the financing of these proposals is particularly crucial, and will be examined in the section on the relation between Credit Processes and 'alternative programmes', it is possible to evaluate the plausibility of the above changes to Production Processes without the added complexity of all those contradictions within Credit Processes.

A common weakness of most 'alternative economic programmes' is their heavy emphasis upon monopoly sector firms (or the 'commanding heights of the economy') at the expense of 'alternative programmes' oriented to enterprises – both private competitive sector and state institutions – which employ approximately 60 per cent or more of the paid workforce in most OECD countries. I have no quarrel with all those analyses which show that a mere 1 or 2 per cent of industrial enterprises dominate approximately half the total private enterprise commodity output in Britain, France, West Germany and other leading OECD countries. Nor do I have any disagreement about the fundamental need to nationalise or control these leading capitalist enterprises if any 'alternative programme' is to succeed. What I am concerned about is the almost total lack of analysis of the other 98 per cent of private enter-prises – especially those involved in the circulation of commodities and the servicing of commodity production. One of the reasons for this neglect is that nearly all the 'alternative programmes' are based on 'workerist' notions of the class system – that is, a heavy emphasis on strategies involving manual, blue-collar workers who toil in factories governed by giant assembly lines at the expense of alternative strategies for all other workers and especially unpaid people. Proponents of 'alternative programmes' are fully aware that most wage-workers are to be found outside blue-collar, assembly-line environments, yet the applic-ability of alternative models such as the Lucas Aerospace experience to the vast majority of state institutions and private enterprises is rarely mentioned, even though 'democratisation' of state institutions is con-stantly invoked.

Assuming that the leading 'mesoeconomic' or monopoly firms were nationalised without the Left government being overthrown, how would this nationalisation eliminate unemployment, prevent thousands of competitive private businesses from collapsing or suffering heavy profit losses, and lead to the production of socially useful goods and services? The last decade has already witnessed the steady reduction of labour in nearly every large private firm, not to mention nationalised state in-dustries.[6] We also know that nationalisation does not in itself lead to more useful or efficient forms of investment. The changeover from private to government control can often lead to loss of efficiency in early years as management is preoccupied with reorganising structures. If an 'alternative programme' continues existing commodity production for a number of years until gradually switching to new, use-value pro-ducts, then any major increase in the workforce of these recently nationalised monopoly sector firms would require substantial state subsidies (in the form of extra taxes or state debt), as profitability would almost certainly be eroded. In certain industries such as steel, substantial increases in output could be realised without significant increases in the workforce.

It is not clear in many 'alternative programmes' whether nationalised industries will work according to capitalist criteria or be part of a new form of 'market-socialist' planning. Regardless of which organising principle is implemented, 'alternative programmes' will have to confront major obstacles in local and national Production Processes. In leading European capitalist countries, Production Processes are dominated by industries such as automobiles, steel, chemicals, electronics, machine tools, textiles and food processing; the implementation of 'alternative' Lucas-style corporate plans in the monopoly sector would have disastrous effects on employment in thousands of enterprises in the competitive sectors of these countries. For example, the production of public transport vehicles instead of private cars would mean that many of the millions of EEC workers employed in small parts plants and in selling and servicing private motor vehicles would almost certainly be rendered excess labour.[7] If one multiplies these figures by including the potential new use-value products in other giant industries which would no longer require the same promotional retailing and servicing (as most of the products would *not* be designed for planned obsolescence), then a truly staggering unemployment figure would emerge as a result of the shift to socially useful production.

The belief that a redirection of national resources in the monopoly sector will sustain the profitability of the rest of the private sector (once the 'mesoeconomic' firms are nationalised or subjected to strict investment guidelines), is based on an analysis of commodity-producing enterprises rather than all those private firms which do not extract surplus-value. The suggestion that small businesses would be given state credit and access to new technology is largely irrelevant to all such businesses in retailing, wholesale merchandising and servicing, which would be rendered obsolete once a significant shift occurred in the productive output of the nationalised 'commanding heights of the economy' – from existing exchange commodities to many non-marketable socially useful goods. All those workers employed in private or state enterprises which produce parts rather than finished commodities (or which produce no parts at all), would have serious structural difficulties devising 'alternative' products or job specifications once the existing capitalist division of labour was abandoned or drastically modified in large monopoly sector firms. The Lucas Plan[8] strategy is *vital* to all those enterprises which *can* redesign products – but not to the vast armies of sales, clerical, service and finance workers who out-number surplus-value-producing workers by at least three to one (if one also includes all state sector employees).

It is difficult to envisage how the nationalisation of monopoly sector firms will prevent the 'rationalisation' of these same large export-oriented industries if they continue to produce very similar commodities to those which they currently produce. The issue is not merely one of market competition (i.e. pressure to introduce labour-saving technology) or protection in the form of national import controls. Even if import controls proved to be compatible with EEC membership, they would do little to improve exports, let alone guarantee jobs (in export-oriented firms) in the event that particular countries retaliated against such protectionist policies.[9] However, a Europe-wide socialist plan (as advocated in some 'alternative programmes') would in itself necessitate serious restructuring of existing major industries to avoid duplication, excess capacity and yet also resolve regional and local neglect. It is simply not possible to produce socially useful goods for export to other capitalist national markets at the same *quantitative* or revenue earning levels as existing private exchange commodities. Furthermore, giant corporations in countries such as Britain and France earn massive amounts by servicing commodity exchange markets, e.g. insurance, freight, banking (which also form part of Credit Processes). An 'alterna-tive programme' would hardly remain socialist if these practices and in-comes were continued largely untouched.

If for the sake of argument, one assumed that import controls and other forms of protection for local and national enterprises survived all forms of internal and external opposition, these policies would still not resolve the major problem of what to do with subsidiary branch companies operating outside the national Production Process in which the 'mesoeconomic' parent had been nationalised. Not only are most European multinational companies engaged in some of the worst forms of exploitation in Third World countries and other OECD countries, but their level of dependency on profits earned abroad constitutes a revenue problem of gigantic proportions should they be nationalised. Socialist governments would not only have to disengage these national-ised giants from many of their outrageous imperialist excesses, but also bear the burden of rescuing those corporations once their lucrative overseas earnings were abolished or reduced. Consequently, any failure to alter existing multinational practices would tie a socialist government to existing production and exchange relations, not to mention the military and political relations emanating from arms exports, subversion, bribery and the operation of cartels in numerous commodities.

If nationalised industries extricated themselves from present forms of multinational, civilian and military export production, from imperialist exploitation and from dependency on foreign investment revenue, the affect upon national Production Processes would be to bring many of the remaining private enterprises to the point of collapse. This is because the newly nationalised industries would have to find self-financing, profitable domestic investment outlets which would not compete against, but instead sustain the viability of all those competitive businesses which would now be subcontracting to nationalised enterprises engaged in socially useful production. Either businesses are able to make profits, or socially useful production undermines existing profit rates. Even if this gigantic problem were overcome through gradual, slow implementation, thousands of private businesses would not survive the increased costs arising from the reduction of working hours, or from increased wages for women and increased taxes (see my analysis of Credit Processes following shortly). If existing Production Processes are characterised by overproduction, shortage of suitable areas of profitable investment in commodity production, substantial dependency upon capitalist state institutions for the underwriting of the increased costs of constant and variable capital, the growing inability of competitive sector businesses to survive import competition and so forth, then any serious qualitative improvement in the wages for women, general work conditions and level of control over what is now produced (through enterprise plans) would be the final nail in the coffin for thousands of businesses.

'Alternative programmes' promote worker democracy, improved standards of living, job creation and socially useful products, while ignoring or minimising the incompatibility of these goals with profitable capitalist production. Stuart Holland, for example, has called for job creation on the same page as he advocates that national enterprises implement 'newly embodied technology, raising output per worker'.[10] In national and supra-national Production Processes this invariably means further capital-intensive, automated technology if export markets are to be sustained or improved given the increasing use of labour-replacing technology in Japanese, United States and other capitalist

Production Processes. Otherwise, 'raising output per worker' is in most cases incompatible with the reduction of worker exploitation and increased democracy.

While it is true that many nationalised industries are under-capitalised due to government cut-backs and controls over competition with private corporations, the belief that nationalised industries should be 'unshackled'[11] and allowed to earn competitive 'market prices' for their commodities and services would be disastrous for numerous private businesses. As existing nationalised industries such as gas, electricity and transport already subsidise the organic composition of capital in private sectors, a significant increase in prices for nationalised industries would further erode profits of all those private businesses not nationalised in the 'alternative programme'. Furthermore, unless the prices for services and commodities produced by nationalised industries (e.g. electricity) were kept under strict control for all non-capitalist consumers, the cost of any new policy of 'unshackling' nationalised industries would be borne by the working-class.

Because most 'alternative programmes' are oriented towards overcoming the existing power of monopoly sector firms, there is an inadequate appreciation of the differences between surplus-value-extracting enterprises in the private sectors (and state sectors) of Production Processes in capitalist societies. Admirable goals such as reducing 'superfluous advertising', curbing certain specific types of consumption (i.e. those which endanger health) and spurious innovations of the 'me too' variety, reviewing 'certain selling techniques', 'extending consumers' rights[12] – all these also attack the basis of numerous non-monopoly businesses in the competitive sector if they are properly implemented.

Nearly all the 'alternative programmes' accord a decisive role to the expansion of employment and social services in state institutions. Yet the assumption still prevails that a 'mixed economy' will continue to exist rather than a full-scale socialist economy. Consequently, all the admirable policies are couched in a framework which seems blind to the existing incompatibility of expanded 'social wages' (let alone half the intended new social policies advocated in 'alternative programmes') with capitalist rates of profit. Authors like Holland talk about the need to create 'social profits' rather than 'private profits'[13] as if 'profit' was simply some kind of moral category rather than the outcome of social relations between workers and companies which an expanded socialist state sector would weaken and probably destroy. (I will elaborate on the illusions of an expanded state sector in relation to Credit Processes later on.)

What is particularly striking about most 'alternative programmes' is that they invoke the language of radical transformation while at the same time accepting a context of ongoing capitalist enterprises, gradualism and social tinkering. Planning is seen as the panacea to 'stagflation' but, ironically, the notion of planning is itself based on an eclectic mixture of Left Keynesian 'indicative planning' and Marxian political economy. Production Processes are conceived in terms of (1) a problem-creating monopoly sector; (2) a passive or pliable competitive sector; and (3) an unproblematic 'economic' state sector (in contrast to the recognised 'political' problems of states, e.g. the role of the military). Hence 'planning' will somehow iron out the contradictions of Production Processes because once the 'mesoeconomic' sector is nationalised and integrated with the largely unproblematic state or public sector, then the remaining passive, or secondary sector of small businesses will be successfully integrated or harnessed to the 'alternative economy'. But, in the words of Glyn and Harrison, 'a half-way house between free enterprise and central planning is impossible'.[14]

A detailed critique of the analyses which concentrate on monopoly firms would also show that too much is attributed to the role of giant firms in causing *all* the symptoms of 'stagflation'. In ignoring the vital role which the majority of private businesses play *together* with monopoly sector firms, most 'alternative programmes' fail to tackle the serious criticisms that both capitalists and revolutionaries have levelled at their proposals. The more limited or conservative the 'alternative programme', the greater the likelihood that present contradictions within Production Processes will be exacerbated rather than resolved – simply because the new policies will fail to eradicate the root causes of 'stagflation'. In contrast, radical 'alternative programmes' will only bring to a head all the existing incompatible class interests if an 'alternative' Production Process (where the public or state-run part of the 'mixed economy' was larger than the private) were implemented and seriously threatened capitalist class privileges and profits. But even the more 'radical' 'alternative programmes' are quite conservative in that they fail to challenge many of the existing forms of labour, production, service and consumption in both the private and state sectors of capitalist Production Processes. The largely uncritical conception of small businesses and state institutions (apart from a vague call to 'democratise' the latter) means that the full implications of many radical critiques of existing environmental abuse, pervasive forms of sexual and racial exploitation and wasteful consumption patterns will remain largely untouched. In Italy, France, Britain and other countries the major Left parties are far too conservative when it comes to existing forms of energy consumption, occupational hierarchies, exploitative unpaid labour[15] and commodity fetishism; much of the rhetoric about self-management and socially useful production barely touches on alternatives to dominant capitalist social practices. Far too many supporters of 'alternative programmes' uncritically worship bourgeois concepts of 'growth'[16] - i.e. an expanded national GNP which is barely indistinguishable from that which exists.

In conclusion, one could agree with many of the proposed 'alternative' ideas about restructuring Production Processes if they were *not* to be implemented in a 'mixed economy'. There is no shortage of jobs, services and creative ideas which could emerge if workers and communities were given a non-capitalist context in which to implement these 'alternatives'. But most 'alternative programmes' incorporate two explicitly petty-bourgeois idealistic beliefs; first, that 'genuine competition' between small non-monopoly businesses would be compatible with a socialist plan - assuming the innocence or even virtues of non-monopoly firms; and second, that of workers' co-operatives promoting socialist relations while operating according to the vicious conditions determined by market criteria.[17] Illusions are also promoted about the viability of a 'social-industrial complex' which would replace the 'military-industrial complex'.[18] The notion of a 'social-industrial complex' is based on the largely unconsidered retention of nearly all existing jobs in state sectors (regardless of whether they are socially useful or not), plus the enormous expansion of a public sector, job-creating economy, which would not only be self-financing, but would be able to absorb and sustain private businesses. Existing private market commodity production would be gradually replaced by profitable state contracts for the production and servicing of socially useful goods.

While there is no doubt that a large number of individuals could make a living providing goods and services for private consumption (this is already visible in Communist countries where both black-market and legal, simple commodity production and exchange flourish), it is an entirely different proposition to believe that hundreds of thousands of existing competitive sector businesses could be transformed into profitable but socially useful businesses. Not only is this model impracticable in terms of public financing (see my discussion of Credit Processes shortly), but numerous private businesses are structurally incapable of adjusting to a 'social–industrial complex' because their role is defined within a capitalist commodity-exchange process. The implicit and explicit idea of a profitable 'social–industrial complex' alongside, or as part of a planned state sector, is merely the logical extension of Left Keynesian theory which fails to acknowledge the parameters within which existing state institutions have to co-exist with private capitalist production. One cannot simply resolve the problems of unemployment, inflation and fundamental social injustice and neglect by idealistically grafting a set of updated Fabian policies, or a radical socialist programme, onto the structure and dynamics of existing local, national and supranational Production Processes.

Without an adequate appreciation of the inherent role of state institutions within Production Processes, 'alternative programmes' advocate utopian solutions – which ironically lack the imaginative and wonderful social relations conceived of by radical utopians. For decades, Fabians and other social evolutionists or gradualists constructed their programmes upon the notion of an expanding 'mixed economy' which could be milked by state institutions – thus redistributing wealth in a comfortable, non-violent way and providing social mobility without revolutionising social relations. In contrast, 'alternative programmes' at least have the virtue of being constructed with a view to ending widespread crises rather than merely assuming the background of a seemingly endless 'post-industrial' boom. It is of particular historical irony to note that Social-Democratic and Communist Parties are today much closer to Trotsky's original 'Transitional Programme' of 1938[19] which also called for the nationalisation of the top sixty to 200 capitalist firms, the opening up of business secrets to a workers' plan, state control of credit and banking, employment for all, and the protection of the social privileges of small business people and farmers who would become dependent upon transitional states rather than upon capitalist trusts (or 'mesoeconomic' firms in current language).

Despite these similarities with Trotskyism, 'alternative programmes' also retain residues of Fabianism in that they implicitly and explicitly assume that socialists can make capitalist society work better in the short run compared to existing bourgeois parties. Although 'alternative programmes' warn of violence, disruption and full-scale bourgeois opposition, they simultaneously pin their hopes on a smooth transition as they postulate evolutionary plans of five-, ten- or twenty-year durations. The question of social peace or violence will be taken up later on; here it is important to recognise that, even under optimum favourable conditions, the proposed reconstructions of Production Processes are either too conservative, in that they are locked into existing class contradictions, or else radically naive in assuming that the vast majority of small businesses will transform or destroy themselves in the quest for socialism.

Food Production Processes and 'Alternative Programmes'

Most 'alternative programmes' say very little on the *direct, intermediate* and *indirect* component elements of Food Production Processes,[20] in fact, recent books such as *The Alternative Economic Strategy* and *Manifesto A Radical Strategy For Britain's Future*[21] have no discussion whatsoever of agriculture or food in general. Most policies on Food Production Processes are even vaguer than those concerning 'alternative' policies for industry. Yet, the price of food has been a burning issue for British socialists since entry into the EEC blocked cheaper food imports from the British Commonwealth. In France, Italy, Spain and other countries with significant farmers' movements, the Left has promised to protect small farmers and give them a better deal. Very little, however, has been said on all the *intermediate* elements of Food Production Processes, i.e. the manufacture and sale of processed food, the production of chemicals and machinery for *direct* food producers, and the manufacture of food storage equipment – all of which overlap with Production Processes. The same is true of all the *indirect* elements of Food Production Processes with the notable exception of policies on energy resources where various Left parties are still extremely conservative and slow to change on issues such as nuclear power.

Given the significant differences between European Left parties concerning the role of the EEC in any 'alternative programme', it is difficult to estimate whether major elements within Food Production Processes will be left largely intact or be significantly altered to accommodate national strategic interests. Regardless of whether a Europe-wide food programme or a national solution is advocated, there remain several decisive problems which flow from the 'alternative' policies examined in relation to Production Processes.

The nationalisation of monopoly sector processed-food producers and the implementation of industrial democracy, raises the question as to whether workers' self-management will result in the manufacture of qualitatively different food items which are nutritional and safe. Is this transformation technically possible given the structure of existing capitalist food firms? How are agribusiness farms and factories going to continue existing food production, if workers' 'alternative plans' reject the continued production of environmentally damaging and cancer creating chemicals, additives, etc? As a great deal of *direct* food production is capital-intensive and depends on chemicals and marketing, how will the nationalisation of monopoly firms prevent an increase in costs of all these *intermediate* accessories to farmers, given the commitment to reduce workers' hours, and improve work conditions? Would farmers incur higher costs for energy, freight and service charges if nationalised industries are 'unshackled' and existing subsidies are withdrawn? Any one of these prospective changes could seriously increase the price of food, result in shortages and/or lead to major confrontations between a Left government and food producers or between consumers and farmers given the already militant attitudes of farmers within capitalist societies.

As the labour force is largely concentrated within urban Production Processes, it would be technically feasible to encourage a sizeable population shift to rural areas if farms were not privately owned. A socialist government could reduce unemployment and make possible a return to labour-intensive farming by subsidising the cost of extra labour on private farms; but this would increase the budgetary outlay on food subsidies and also meet with hostile opposition from those farmers resentful of losing their private residential and economic powers. 'Alternative programmes' constantly talk of 'the people' and play down the sharp differences and separate interests of urban residents and farmers which a more participatory decision making process might either resolve or deepen.

Most 'alternative programmes' fail to discuss several major problems connected with Food Production Processes.

If import controls were implemented to save jobs in local and national Production Processes, it is highly likely that continued profitable domestic production of manufactured commodities would mean higher food prices unless farmers abandoned the more expensive artificial chemical and machine methods upon which many of them currently depend – or suffered a drop in their standard of living if prices remained fixed at low levels.

A socialist government would most probably have to preside over an unstable and devalued currency (due to external and internal capitalist classes attempting to undermine the 'alternative programme'), resulting in potential food shortages or higher prices depending on the particular national levels of imported natural and processed food. A devalued currency would add to the cost of energy imports and would also seriously affect all those enterprises in the *intermediate* part of Food Production Processes dependent on imported component parts. The success of an 'alternative programme' in Production and Food Production Processes would partially depend on the degree of self-sufficient energy, food and commodity production in a country embarking on a radical 'transitional' strategy.

As competitive private sectors have a large number of retail and service outlets involved in Food Production Processes, the improvement of workers' wages and conditions would have serious affects on fast food outlets, shops, restaurants and other establishments dependent on cheap and casual part-time labour. If wages for women were raised as part of the programme to end oppression, then many retail food outlets and eating establishments could go bankrupt.

Given the fact that hundreds of thousands of European farmers are already having difficulty surviving on small incomes, on undercapitalised farms, with fixed prices determined by various state marketing boards, and so forth, there remains ample room for an 'alternative programme' to improve the standard of living of farm workers and raise the level of food production. However, these technical possibilities must be carefully balanced against the fact of significant differences between small farmers and large agribusiness enterprises, and the increasing dependence of *direct* food producers upon all the *intermediate* manufactured component elements which exist within Food and Production Processes.

Historical experiences show that political and social instability has resulted in disastrous food shortages. Hoarding and price increases occur as farmers (ever suspicious and fearful of losing their land or their incomes) cut back production, and use various means of resisting control by governments committed to social change. Left parties already face the problem that in most countries they have relatively little support in rural areas compared to their strongholds in the cities. Yet if output from particular *intermediate* factories (vital to present food production) were interrupted due to social struggles within Production and Electoral Processes, a new socialist government would face new forms of food shortages quite different from those earlier crises in Eastern Europe where most food was non-processed. Consequently, any socialist government which did not carefully evaluate the interconnections between 'alternative' policies in Electoral, Production, Credit and Food Production Processes, would unfavourably affect the level of food production and consumption.

To mobilise the electorate in favour of socialist objectives requires that the standard of living should not be dramatically disrupted by food shortages or price increases as there will be more than enough social disruptions in other areas. This can only be done if 'alternative programmes' either leave Food Production Processes alone in the first period of office – a strategy which could only work if large areas of Production Processes were also left untouched, given the interdependence of the two – or channel significantly increased state funds into food price support schemes, wage subsidies, rural reconstruction and imported food. The latter strategy is itself dependent on the availability of revenue – an issue to be examined in connection with Credit Processes.

If the problem of sustaining a sufficient amount of food is a major fiscal and organisational problem, the investment funds necessary to shift energy production away from nuclear and other environmentally dangerous methods is even more forbidding – given the potential explosion of demands for state funds from all social quarters eager to implement 'alternative' policies. As yet there are no detailed policies specifying the measures which an 'alternative programme' would implement in relation to alternative fuels and non-wasteful consumption as well as the safeguarding of *indirect* elements of Food Production Processes. If 'alternative programmes' permit the newly nationalised multinational firms and existing private enterprises to continue their rapacious destruction of environments – especially in other countries – then a 'transition' to the pollution and destruction of *indirect* Food Production Processes will be accomplished, rather than the 'transition' to an ecologically conscious population and balanced environment.

Credit Processes and 'Alternative Programmes'

In chapter 8 I tried to show that Credit Processes comprised both private component elements (e.g. banks and financial institutions which live off the expansion of credit and the needs of private and state units of Production Processes) and local and national state institutions which experienced an almost permanent scarcity of revenue sources. 'Alternative programmes' are concerned with providing jobs (mainly in proposed expanded state sectors), or creating new community services, resolving social crises in regionally depressed areas, and generally improving the standard of living for both wage-workers and all those dependent on government pensions and payments; the fundamental questions remain (a) where is the money going to come from?; (b) how is inflation going to be halted?; and (c) how will workers, capitalists and those living off fixed incomes be affected by policies implemented in response to (a) and (b)? Most 'alternative programmes' put forward detailed descriptions and analyses of 'stagflation', but contain few specific measures which would make 'alternative' policies within Credit Processes viable under an 'alternative programme'. With varying emphases, and a few national differences, the majority of 'alternative programmes' propose to resolve questions (a), (b) and (c) with the same policies: nationalising banks and insurance offices; price and monetary controls; an incomes policy and planning agreements which will protect workers' standard of living; the creation of extensive investment funds; a wealth tax and other forms of income redistribution while at the same time protecting the standard of living of small capitalists, farmers and 'intermediate strata' who are not part of the monopoly capitalist class. Once we begin to examine closely the short-term implications of these 'alternative' proposals on private and state enterprises it becomes extremely difficult to conceptualise how many contradictions can be overcome.

For example, a consistent theme of most 'alternative programmes' has been the attack upon multinational corporations which are able to avoid taxes, fuel inflation and increase profits through transfer pricing techniques, benefit from huge outlays of public revenue in the form of various subsidies, while directing large sums of money into lucrative foreign investments or subsidiary branch factories where cheap labour is available. The nationalisation of these mesoeconomic giants would affect revenue, prices and investment funds in a number of ways. Theoretically, massive resources and assets would be at the disposal of a socialist government providing that this government and the workers self-managing these industries did not alter the nature of commodities produced for domestic and export markets, retained the exploitative imperialist subsidiaries of these firms in other countries, and managed to survive the withdrawal of foreign multinationals and the various forms of sabotage unleashed by capitalists. However, if the 'alternative programme' involved large sums of compensation for the former private owners, the production of socially useful goods which could not be profitably sustained via former methods of transfer pricing or sold in foreign markets, and the loss of revenue from branch companies in other countries due to the abandonment of imperialist policies and so on, then it is highly likely that a socialist government would have to pump massive amounts of public funds into the reorganisation and rescue of many of these recently nationalised monopoly sector firms. It is true that a certain percentage of public revenue which currently subsidises monopoly profits could be redeployed in the task of restructuring these nationalised industries. But an 'alternative programme' which assumes that existing commodity production emanating from multi-nationals can be subjected to Lucas Aerospace alternative plans without being a potentially enormous drain on public revenue (rather than a supplement to investment funds and taxes) is in for a very rude shock. One can already see the need for capitalist state institutions to rescue large private corporations and underwrite huge losses in nationalised industries, without the proposed nationalisation of the whole meso-economic private sector, let alone the shift to manufacturing socially useful goods.

If one examines the specific activities of finance capital giants (such as banks and insurance companies), it becomes apparent that an 'alternative programme' would liberate massive funds and permit control over credit policy in the short-run. But what would happen to profitability if: banks vacated the lucrative Eurodollar and Eurobond markets, the newly nationalised banking and finance system refused to engage in the high profit areas which make up current Third World debts, or central fiscal policy combatted inflation by reducing such things as high interest rates on private borrowing, thereby eliminating a major source of current finance capitalists' profits? What if the redirection of massive amounts of insurance companies' funds into non-profitable state sector investments occurred, thus reducing or nullifying bonuses accruing to millions of middle- and upper-income insurance holders currently dependent on profitable investments? Would tens of thousands of bank, insurance and other finance capitalists' employees be retained (after nationalisation) despite the fact that previous profit levels were not being earned?

While price controls, currency and investment controls and general fiscal control are envisaged by 'alternative programmes', these policies do *not* in themselves necessarily generate revenue but rather are intended to prevent capitalist sabotage and lack of compliance with any 'alternative programme'. The need for magical powers arises when the commitment to improving the 'social wage', employing the millions of unemployed and to redistributing social wealth is made with the assumption that it will not affect all the businesses in the competitive sectors of Production Processes and all 'intermediate strata'. As a future wealth tax would not raise sufficient revenue for 'alternative programmes', new taxes must fall heavily on small and medium businesses, professionals, well-paid workers, farmers, the self-employed and all those living off rents, share dividends and so forth. These new taxes would be highly unpopular and could prevent the election or re-election of Left parties. Similarly, if deficit budgeting is embarked upon in a radical manner it is possible for a socialist government to create jobs, expand 'social wage' services and generally improve the life of non-capitalist classes by printing money and devaluing the nominal and real value of existing capitalist assets, e.g. the price of commodities, savings and shares – all without raising taxation to cover these egalitarian policies. But this de-valorisation of existing commodity values (like the new taxes) would not be possible in a 'mixed economy' without destroying the privileges and profits of capitalist and petty-bourgeois classes and/or creating large-scale unemployment (as businesses went bankrupt), black markets and social instability as businesses, farmers and investors all mobilised against redistribution of income and/or an explosion of revenue within Credit Processes. It is argued by radicals such as Glyn and Harrison that the printing of money by the British state would not be inflationary so long as purchasing power is kept in line with extra production.[22] This assumption is valid for a small reflation of a 'mixed economy' but overlooks the fact that most 'alternative programmes' propose to resolve unemployment by creating *non-commodity*-producing jobs in state institutions (e.g. all 'social wage' services) and by restructuring nationalised industries so that they manufacture socially useful goods rather than only private exchange commodities.

   If a very limited 'alternative programme' were implemented for fear of antagonising small businesses and 'intermediate strata' (that all-embracing term which justifies capitalist social divisions), it is highly likely that extra taxation would be levied on working-classes (and not just businesses) – a political tactic to indicate that all 'the people' were bearing the cost of reflating the economy against disruptions caused by 'monopoly capitalists'. As with most policies in 'alternative programmes' it will be the mobilisation of anti-capitalist forces and the level of class struggle which will determine the extent and manner of 'alternative' revenue raising and expenditure.

The notion that 'alternative programmes' could finance the national-isation of private firms by requiring capitalists to transfer up to 50 per cent of their share stock to workers (along the lines of the Swedish employee investment funds) has gained popularity in recent years.[23] This strategy is based on a ten- to sixty-year slow nationalisation pro-gramme and assumes that co-operation from private enterprises will be sustained. (Swedish capitalist enterprises are already in open revolt.) However, this method of financing socialism will work only as long as particular national bourgeois classes are politically weak or else depend on the infusion of public funds to prop up failing or undercapitalised businesses. The control by workers of company stock will not resolve the desynchronisation of Processes if existing commodity production and exchange is continued. Should workers succeed in implementing 'alternative' plans which produce unprofitable socially useful goods, then either investment funds will become depleted (as falling profit rates eat into working capital and require increased government sub-sidies), or private capitalists will bitterly resist the certain destruction of their power. In the unlikely event that workers' funds succeed in con-trolling capitalist enterprises (while retaining capitalist production and exchange with minor modifications), the achievement would hardly constitute a socialist economy.

Even in Sweden, where the labour movement has managed to win better 'social wage' conditions and the Swedish state sector is relatively more involved in a 'social-industrial' 'mixed economy', the private sector is dependent on a substantial amount of state subsidy and the largest Swedish firms are heavily oriented to foreign markets. Any significant fall in export markets would have a serious destabilising affect upon domestic class relations and the capacity of the government to sustain domestic profit rates and workers' standard of living. Capital-ists in countries such as Britain, which have experienced falling rates of profit, would be even less disposed to an investment fund strategy. This is because many capitalist firms are themselves reluctant to invest in low profit industries in the Production Process, let alone share their declining profits with workers eager to transform production in the direction of socialist use-value products.

One of the 'alternative' proposals is to review 'certain forms of bank lending and consumer borrowing, including credit cards etc.'[24] While this is an admirable objective, it is difficult to comprehend how the elimination of credit cards, bank loans – especially for luxury consumer goods, home purchasing and so forth will be possible without devastating the private sector. Ample figures are available to document the close relationships between individual and company debt and the growth in commodity production over the past thirty years. If an 'alternative government' were seriously to increase the production of public housing by nationalised industries (rather than private contractors), this area alone would create widespread loss of profits, bankruptcies and devaluation of private assets as property speculation suffered a major blow.

It is not possible to conceive how existing private capitalist production could sustain its level of growth and profits if the whole structure of finance and credit facilities were overhauled to eliminate existing inflationary debt structures. Any serious reorganisation of Credit Processes (rather than straightforward nationalisation of banks) would entail a potential writing off of existing state sector debt – for if banks and other monopoly sector giants were nationalised, so too would be the government bonds and securities they held. This could create havoc in the stock-market-aligned value of private company bonds, stocks and shares, leaving bourgeois and petty-bourgeois investors and businesses in a state of disarray.

I have not said anything about the relations between local and national component elements of Credit Processes and their future relations with supra-national institutions such as the IMF, EEC and other bodies. It is extremely difficult to make head or tail of most 'alternative programmes' because they assume on the one hand that international trade will continue much as before, yet on the other hand they plan to attack foreign investment and foreign multinationals within their national boundaries, and they plan to engage in the extensive tapping of banks, insurance companies and other private assets without drastically affecting the small business sector. It remains completely unclear how investment controls, currency and price controls, will not lead to the devaluation of currencies, personal savings, insurance and superannuation policies; it is also unclear how the billions spent by tourists within Europe as well as numerous other consumer practices dependent upon existing capitalist credit institutions can be maintained if sweeping reforms are implemented.

In short, how can numerous socialist policies be successfully implemented within the context of partially modified capitalist Credit Processes? While one can justify a certain secrecy about specific fiscal measures so that the likely forms of capitalist sabotage, investment strikes, etc. can be successfully countered, this in itself does not excuse the fundamental weaknesses of most 'alternative programmes'. The revenue scarcity which existing capitalist states suffer from will become acute if only half the 'alternative' policies concerning unemployment are implemented. Yet the belief that control over the monopoly sector will resolve revenue scarcity so that socialist governments will be popularly re-elected for as long as twenty or more years, is one of the most dangerous myths to be promoted. I have attempted to evaluate some of the implications of 'alternative programmes' on Production, Food Production and Credit Processes without taking up the usual questions raised concerning the role of the military and class opposition in Electoral Processes. The illusions and naïve assumptions concerning the viability of 'alternative programmes' in Production, Food Production and Credit Processes, are great enough without the extra problems posed by existing Electoral Process struggles and obstacles.

Electoral Processes and 'Alternative Programmes'

Most of the discussions about 'Eurocommunism', 'alternative economic programmes' and other 'alternative' parliamentary strategies have in fact been preoccupied with Electoral Processes rather than any detailed analyses of Production, Food Production and Credit Processes. There is no need to repeat in detail all the fears and problems surrounding the role of repressive apparatuses, the possibility of internal and external class destabilisation and the enormous problems associated with democratising existing capitalist state institutions. The hopes of supporters of 'alternative programmes' rest on the neutralisation of the armed forces, the election of sympathetic Left governments in other countries, the ability to halt unemployment and to reflate Production Processes, the spread of democratic anti-capitalist ideas at a pace which is controllable rather than fuelled by ultra-Leftist occupations, strikes and land and property seizures, as well as the neutralisation or defeat of bourgeois and petty-bourgeois classes without recourse to the suspension of pluralist Electoral Processes.

Given the massive problems which would arise from changes to existing Production, Food Production and Credit Processes, it becomes clear that Electoral Processes are envisaged to be almost 'above' all the 'economic' problems which I have discussed in previous sections. For example, Francis Cripps naïvely believes that the 'resolution of the crisis of corporate capitalism in Britain will be decided by media battles, not by Chilean-style destabilisation and coups. The Alternative Strategy could become a realistic option if it could establish its own resonance in the media'.[25] Leaving aside counter-revolution or revolutionary confrontation, it is important to draw attention to the following organisational features of free Electoral Processes which pose serious obstacles to the self-proclaimed 'parliamentary paths'.

The specific historical characteristics of local and national state institutions, political parties and trade unions are more than conservative enough to dampen any belief that 'alternative programmes' could reflate Production Processes at the same time as extending self-management and democratisation. One only has to look at the principal Left parties, such as the French and Italian Communist Parties, the British Labour Party and the leading trade union organisations, to see how far they are from allowing internal democracy, let alone from tolerating a non-corporatist workers' control movement which would actively participate in drawing up democratic planning agreements rather than being told what to do by party and union bureaucrats. It is not surprising that many people are fearful that 'alternative programmes' will become 'Euro-corporatism' instead of 'Eurocommunism'.[26]

The very notion of countering bourgeois hegemony requires extra-parliamentary rank-and-file activity for which electorally oriented parties such as the British Labour Party are not prepared or equipped. Even the more grass roots oriented parties such as the Italian Communist Party are faced with problems or organisational discipline (in opposition, and at local government level); if self-management were given more than lip service once the Communists entered a national government, difficulties would only be accentuated. Radical 'alternative programmes' are only possible if Left parties can mobilise mass grass roots activity – yet this mobilisation is a serious threat to the very rigid parties which themselves hope to benefit from such a strategy.

Many capitalist state orders are based on complicated structural branches of government, statutory authorities and executive organs which an 'alternative programme' would not be able fully to control short of major constitutional changes.[27] Hence the implementation of 'alternative economic programmes' would come up against the combined inherent conservativism of state administrators and Left organisational cadres. While numerous progressive changes could be implemented, and the climate of conservativism challenged – a major victory in itself – these significant gains would have to be evaluated in relation to the broader aim of improving social life via an extended state sector. If democratisation of state institutions in social welfare, health, housing and nationalised industries were implemented, this democratisation would involve either the dismissal of thousands of 'social-control' bureaucrats, or the extensive retraining of the latter for socially useful jobs. However, there would be little or no democratisation if the gross inequalities of hierarchically structured salaries were retained and the pervasive inequalities based on gender, race and mental/manual divisions within the trade union movement and occupational structure left untouched. Theoretically and practically, the notion of planning agreements, self-managed Lucas-style 'alternative' plans and other forms of workers' democracy are incompatible with a 'mixed economy', characterised by a large private sector. Either Braverman, Gorz, Marglin and Roberts[28] are correct about the inherent relation between hierarchy and capitalist production, or else an 'alternative programme' (spread over five to fifty years) would have to devise a 'new' form of production and control relations which simultaneously satisfies capitalist owners, senior government bureaucrats and socialist workers – a truly magical formula.

If 'alternative programmes' have to raise vitally needed revenue (for job creation and 'social wage' programmes) from all those 'intermediate strata' and skilled workers currently enjoying social and income privileges in the occupational hierarchy, there will need to be a very radical transformation of consciousness (among these privileged workers), if a truly 'alternative programme' has any chance of being implemented. Strategically there is little ground for believing that an 'anti-monopoly' coalition of workers, small businessmen, farmers and 'intermediate strata' could survive one election, let alone the number needed to implement twenty-year plans, given the objective consequences flowing from significant changes to Production, Food Production and Credit Processes. On the other hand, we have already witnessed the support given by the Italian Communist Party and Mitterrand's government to conservative austerity measures, so there is justified suspicion that 'alternative programmes' could be suspended indefinitely in the quest for electoral support from competitive sector capitalists and 'intermediate strata'. The strategy of extending political hegemony to all areas of Electoral Processes was seen as feasible in the mid-1970s before conservative bourgeois parties abandoned their neo-Keynesian policies. Once the ideological climate changed in favour of dismantling state sectors, it created a crisis within 'Eurocommunist' parties because the notion of a 'common programme' and 'historical compromise' would not work if one or more of the coalition partners refused to embark upon inflationary, expanded state sector policies let alone an extensive challenge to the monopoly sector.[29]

The hope that other countries would elect a Left government once the break through was made in one country echoes the 'weak link in the chain' strategy which the Bolsheviks pursued after 1917 but which was not successful because of the lack of successful revolutions in the West. While the chance of more than one Left government being elected is not entirely remote, the desynchronisation of national Electoral Processes with one another is sufficiently wide to isolate a Left government for one to three years. This would mean that the first Left government (e.g. France at the moment) might act very cautiously for fear of antagonising other conservative powers; be unable to resolve the crises emanating from desynchronised Processes, hence disillusioning or frightening the electorates in other neighbouring countries; or risk going it alone and frightening other electorates because policies were distributing wealth and challenging the power of bourgeois classes and 'intermediate strata'. One could imagine that every endeavour would be made by monopoly firms, conservative parties and conservative media in other countries to paint any radical Left government in the worst possible light if this government were really implementing an 'alternative programme'. Moreover, as recent conservative attempts to reverse working-class gains have succeeded in reducing expenditures on social welfare and produced higher unemployment in Britain and other countries, 'alternative programmes' are either forced to become more radical, or implicitly to accept more conservative objectives (e.g. 'reducing' unemployment rather than eliminating it, or supporting 'limited' public expenditure rather than 'irresponsible' increases in public spending). This brings me to the Mark 2 'alternative programmes' of recent years.

'Alternative Programmes' (Mark 2) – The Transition Away from Socialism

With the conservative onslaught by the Thatcher and Reagan governments, the failure of the Italian Communist Party to enter a coalition government and the attempted coup by sections of the military in Spain, the optimistic climate of the mid-seventies gave way to generalised conservativism, with aggressive capitalist attacks on numerous facets of post-war social developments, including those introduced by conservative parties. Although the election of Mitterrand, Papandreou, Palme and Gonzales may halt this reactionary trend, it is already abundantly clear that the 'alternative programmes' (Mark 2) have made significant concessions to the political Right. While it is too early to know exactly how the French capitalist order will be affected by Mitterrand's potential seven-year presidency (especially as his policies were presented in more traditional electoral terms rather than as part of the earlier joint Socialist and Communist Common Programme), it is not illogical to expect that the actual policies implemented will be even less radical than the already watered-down Socialist Party platform. After barely one year in office, Mitterrand had made significant concessions to employers, slowed social reforms to a snail's pace, maintained reactionary policies on nuclear power and done little to solve unemployment.

It is of particular interest in this context to recall the 'radicalism' of the 'alternative programmes' put forward in the 1970s by Jacques Attali and Jacques Delors (Mitterrand's senior advisor and Finance Minister) together with Franco Archibugi, Stuart Holland and other European socialists[30] – compared with some of the more recent 'alternative programmes' (Mark 2) not to mention Delors's own conservative policies as a French cabinet minister.[31] In Britain, for example, one of the most recent and comprehensive theoretical outlines of an 'alternative programme' is Sam Aaronovitch's *The Road From Thatcherism* (1981) – a title which in itself makes Stuart Holland's *The Socialist Challenge* (1975) appear radical. Aaronovitch's book is not only less radical than Holland's strategy, but it also openly disavows the link between an 'alternative programme' and socialist strategies (even though Aaronovitch still sees himself as a socialist). According to Aaronovitch, 'The Alternative Economic Strategy is and must be a programme of radical reform. It does not and should not require those who support it to be committed to a socialist reconstruction of Britain. If we are not clear on this we shall abandon one of its main sources of strength, namely that it is a "common programme" being constructed by many different groups and interests'.[32] Note that the concept 'common programme' is retained, but no longer in the 1970s French sense of a *socialist* Common Programme.

Overall, the 'alternative programme' as conceived by Aaronovitch is simultaneously more honest, yet also far less radical than earlier policies. Aaronovitch states quite boldly that the vast majority of businesses (80 per cent of manufacturing industry, all of farming, the entire commercial and commodity trading sector[33]) would remain in private hands. He is also opposed to central planning, favours high levels of public sector investment (up to recent West German levels) in industry – especially in capital-intensive, high-technology areas[34] – and generally argues that an 'alternative economic strategy' has to be able to 'offer support, encouragement and reward'[35] to private enterprise and not just controls. This openly class-collaborationist perspective is mixed with many policies advocated in earlier 'alternative programmes' such as price controls, planning agreements, controls over multinational corporations, a wealth tax and income redistribution. Aaronovitch, like other 'populists', aims to please 'all the people' – a recipe for almost certain failure.

Although Aaronovitch is critical of Keynesian theory, his policies virtually amount to a Left Keynesian reflation of the economy by the public sector rather than the private sector. Like Mitterrand, he is not committed to full employment but rather to an ambitious, but theoretically unsound scheme[36] which would, he hopes, create one million new jobs – a rather inadequate goal given the fact that overall unemployment levels would still leave at least two or three million people without work. Similarly, the abandonment of radical policies at the supra-national level is particularly evident in Rowthorn's analysis of international trade. While pointing to Britain's interdependence with EEC countries, it is difficult to find even the flimsiest suggestion that an 'alternative programme' would significantly alter the quantity and quality of existing commodity exports and imports or invisible trade.[37] The paradoxical situation is that the Mark 2 model is less ambitious precisely at a time when the symptoms arising from the crises of desynchronisation are much worse than a decade ago. While some of the 'moderate' Mark 2 'alternative programmes' could be implemented within a 'mixed economy', it is difficult to understand how these policies would advance the goal of socialism when a massive jobs programme would not even bring unemployment figures down to the (very high) 1970s levels, let alone significantly redistribute wealth or change social relations along socialist lines.

What Mark 2 policies will probably lead to is a period of mild reflation which would eventually relapse into deep recession thus requiring a Left government to either radicalise its policies (and confront capitalists in a dramatic sense), or face a split within the 'alternative programme' movement similar to that which characterised the disillusionment within Callaghan's Labour Party before and after 1979. One can already see how the Mitterrand government is bending over backwards to appear non-radical, and little change is expected in the capitalist control of French domestic and foreign businesses and in their practices (e.g. arms and nuclear fuel exports to repressive regimes in Asia and Africa will continue). On the key issue of militarism and nuclear weapons, Mitterrand's Socialist government is carrying on the worst tradition of 'Atlanticism'-cum-Gaullism (and Papandreou's Socialist government has abandoned its policy against American bases and NATO). So much for neutralism and international socialist solidarity!

In conclusion, one would have to say that both the Mark 1 and Mark 2 models of 'alternative programmes' are characterised by similar weaknesses. Should a Left government be able to survive one or more terms in office, it would almost certainly be unable to resolve the contradictions emanating from the crises of desynchronisation, short of rapid anti-capitalist socialist transformation. The more cautious and conservative the 'alternative programmes', the greater the likelihood that the material standard of living of the working-class would remain stagnant at best, or more probably deteriorate if unemployment remained at high levels and 'social wage' services were not significantly improved. The more radical the programme, the greater the short-term instability and potential critical shortage of goods and services due to the inability of a Left government to find adequate substitutes for the resources, revenue, skills and commodities withdrawn by hostile bourgeois classes.

Aaronovitch makes a number of pertinent criticisms of the revolutionary Left (to which I will return later). But one of the arguments used by proponents of 'alternative programmes' against those who advocate 'instant socialism' is based on the belief that repressive apparatuses will not intervene against a well thought out, patient, but radical Left movement. In my opinion, this 'patience' will become increasingly irrelevant given the reality of the increasing contradictions emanating from the desynchronisation of Processes. Either a Left government will deliver major social concessions to its supporters, thus exacerbating contradictions within Processes by threatening private enterprises through a mobilised, militant population, or be tossed out of office for presiding over minimal, defensive style policies, or perhaps retain office with the support of bourgeois classes after defeating and dividing radical opposition.

There can be no really 'alternative programme' without a mobilised electorate. There can be no successful long-term mobilisation without a conscious mass promotion of anti-capitalist policies. Even a very patient and cautious 'alternative programme' such as that which is advocated by the Bennites or 'Eurocommunists' is dangerous enough possibly to warrant military intervention (given the disclosure that an attempted coup was planned against even Wilson's government during the 1960s). And as other critics have pointed out, the failure of a future Left government to implement radical policies could be a demoralising experience to millions of people and could easily discredit 'alternative programmes' for a whole generation.

However, the gravest short-term danger to any 'alternative programme' is the widespread illusion that most of the key policies advocated are capable of eliminating the causes of 'stagflation' in a peaceful, class-collaborationist manner. Commenting on the British Communist Party's 'alternative programme', orthodox Marxists Dornhorst and Newman argued that in place of Marxism 'it has substituted petit-bourgeois eclecticism, a mish-mash of social chauvinism and common-or-garden liberalism, something eminently acceptable to the bourgeoisie'.[38] While there is no doubting the 'eclectic mish-mash' of most 'alternative programmes', it would be political naïveté to assume that this so-called 'reformism' would be 'eminently acceptable to the bourgeoisie'. My critique of the weaknesses and illusions of 'alternative programmes' is not based on the traditional orthodox Leninist position or on strategies of 'dual power' promoted by various Trotskyists. Rather, it derives from an analysis of the contradictory role and nature of complex state institutions which constitute part of local and national Electoral, Production, Credit and Food Production Processes.

Ultimately, any belief in the viability of 'alternative programmes' must rest on the basic premise that private capitalist enterprises are sufficiently profitable and 'flexible'[39] to be able to live with a 'transitional' strategy which demands higher taxes and greater controls over all facets of production and profits. This optimistic belief in the basic health of capitalists is also shared by non-socialists who argue that capitalist societies are merely in the midst of a transitional phase of restructuring, en route to another more prosperous phase – similar to the restructuring which took place in earlier historical periods. But, if one believes, as I do, that the contradictions flowing from the desynchronisation of Processes are not simply repetitions of earlier capitalist developments (i.e. if one rejects cyclical short and long waves), then it is difficult to ignore the deep-seated malaise which continually grows worse. While it is true that various leading capitalist societies can live with this stagnation and decay for some considerable time, 'alternative programmes' are based on a false belief that a breakthrough in the vicious circle of 'stagflation' is possible in a relatively continuous manner rather than as a disruptive 'break'. While conservatives put forward an *implicit* incomes policy (which means major wage cuts) and rely on market forces to end 'stagflation', many 'alternative programme' theorists present an *explicit* incomes policy (involving protection of workers' living standards) and rely on planning and a government-led investment recovery. (Yet all attempts to limit inflationary wage and price increases have not worked in countries such as Britain.) Both versions are oriented to recovery within capitalism rather than to socialist relations. Any temporary reflation of capitalist societies will make socialism less attractive to wavering voters if there is no critique of capitalist social relations. But the exacerbation of crises within Production, Credit and Food Production Processes will make the implementation of an 'alternative programme' so much harder without very radical short-term measures which would only outrage capitalist classes.

Overall, most 'alternative programmes' seem more oriented to an earlier 'historical moment' than designed to solve the social problems emanating from the current desynchronisation of Processes. The lack of adequate 'alternative' policies relating to most of the workers in non-surplus-value-extracting enterprises (private and state) matches the over-emphasis on plans based on the 'industrial worker'. In believing that 'alternative strategies' will eliminate unemployment within the context of a 'mixed economy', socialists are failing to confront the need to think about the maintenance of millions of people who will *not* find work within these limited 'alternative' schemes. The recognition that capitalist societies cannot be made to work equitably (the Fabian hangover), has unfortunately not registered itself deeply enough in the minds of 'alternative strategists'. It is true that 'alternative strategies' exhibit a strong radical analysis compared to the various Social Democratic governments of the past thirty-five years, but their whole strategy depends on the genuine belief that 'stagflation' can be overcome within a 'mixed economy'. This is particularly evident in the various alternative plans for the 'local state' or for certain industrial enterprises. While initiating new ideas and practices, these 'islands of socialism' in many ways fail to surmount the old critique that one cannot have socialism in one factory or in one city.

The non-existence of a single 'world capitalist mode of production' becomes evident when examining the 'internationalist alternative programmes'. There is an influential current of thought which argues that only a Europe-wide 'alternative plan' will get individual Western European nations out of the depression. This school of thought stresses the 'internationalisation of capital' and rejects the concept of a national economy as a Keynesian myth.[40] While it is certainly true that Western European countries are heavily interrelated with one another, it would be a serious error to overlook the large national and local sectors of Production, Credit and Food Production Processes – especially all those state sector and competitive sector institutions, enterprises and services. Even the monopoly sectors of leading countries are desynchronised with one another – witness the different historical levels of industrialisation, 'de-industrialisation', etc. The quite different export markets and commodities produced in West Germany, Britain, Italy and other European countries means that any possible reflation strategy would not necessarily benefit all countries concerned. The notion of West Germany and France as the 'locomotives' which pull the carriages of Belgium, Britain or Spain out of the depression, has little practical reality. The distribution of power within each local and national Electoral Process means that Left parties will be pressured to expand employment and production within state institutions – if the 'alternative' is not merely a reflation of production within capitalist enterprises. But state institutions are national rather than international institutions. It is in this sense that a national economy is not a species which has disappeared from the world stage. Up until now, Europe-wide strategies for certain industries (e.g. steel) have not saved jobs or increased production, but have only led to power struggles over the size of cutbacks. It would be naïve to believe that Left governments could get together and reflate 'mixed economies' while ignoring the powerful vested interests of their own national classes. Either one has Europe-wide socialist planning (unencumbered by dominant capitalist sectors within national Production Processes), or one is left with the weak tools of indicative planning. Five- to twenty-year plans for 'mixed economies' (involving the reelection of numerous governments), are much more difficult to achieve than even those highly optimistic national plans proposed by 'alternative strategists'.

The preoccupation of many Left activitists in Britain and other countries with building Left Labour or Social Democratic parties, overlooks the fact that strong cadre parties such as the PCI are equally under the influence of notions of market socialism as solutions to the current crisis. There is little point in building a Left party if this party is dominated by illusions concerning the viability of 'alternatives' within 'mixed economies' – either at a national or Europe-wide level. 'Alternative strategists' also put forward the example of post-war reconstruction after 1945 in order to show that the mass redeployment of labour is possible within a 'mixed economy'. The difference between the late 1940s and the 1980s is that leading OECD countries have an abundance of productive capacity (which does not have to be rebuilt) and many enterprises are still eager to continue shedding labour. While limited public works projects can be initiated, the mass relocation of the labour force (i.e. finding new jobs for millions of unemployed) can only be achieved at the expense of most capitalist enterprises – rather than with their willing co-operation as in the period after 1945. Similarly, all notions of state-sponsored high-technology industries and imitations of the 'Japanese model' (as pursued by the Mitterrand government) must confront the reality that massive expansion of new industries based on micro-chip technology eventually means a decrease in the number of workers employed in those jobs replaced by the 'electronic' office and factory.

Overall, many of the specific proposals within 'alternative programmes' are too oriented to social agendas originally devised by capitalist classes. The labour movement in capitalist countries has never really successfully challenged or altered the nature of capitalist commodity production. The vital gains made by workers have been in the areas of distribution (e.g. 'social wage' goods and services) plus civil rights legislation. But the prolonged phase of 'stagflation' requires a decisive break in the sphere of *production*, not just in the sphere of distribution. Those more radical 'alternative programmes' which stress the change to socially useful production are unfortunately still tied to believing that these changes are possible within a 'mixed economy'. Many socialists still believe that it is possible to continue current levels and forms of consumption, maintain occupational, income and social divisions, and yet gradually move to a more egalitarian and fully employed non-capitalist social order. The reluctance to come to terms with scarce resources – fiscal, ecological, etc. – fuels the illusions of achieving major social change within the ongoing conservative structures of everyday life.

Thus, most 'alternative strategists' misunderstand the 'historical moment' which we are witnessing – especially the restructuring of

Production Processes and Food Production Processes. Their solutions are more suitable for a period of growth in capitalist countries rather than the current phase of labour shedding, overproduction and general restructuring. What are the 'alternative policies' for millions consigned to welfare relief, structural unemployment and so on? Where are the policies for a restructuring of income maintenance policies and the effect these will have on Production and Credit Processes? In short, nearly all 'alternative programmes' are characterised by a failure to propose policies which will eliminate the misery caused by the radical restructuring of local, national and supra-national Production and Credit Processes carried out by capitalist classes. They are also characterised by a profound conservatism when it comes to alternative policies for Food Production Processes and challenges to prevailing social relations within Electoral Processes.

12
A Socialist Stocktaking: Against Stateless Socialism and Market Socialism

I have tried to establish why most existing 'alternative programmes' will not resolve the deep-seated crises emanating from the desynchronisation of Processes. The problem with 'alternative programmes' is not just the policies which they propose for the immediate future, but the highly dubious assumptions about how future socialist societies will work, e.g. the popularity of market socialism. The widespread disillusionment with the Soviet and Chinese 'models' of a 'planned society' has produced confusion within the ranks of socialists concerning viable alternatives to both capitalist social relations and the repression and malaise of 'actually existing socialism'. The theoretical and organisational vacuum created since the discrediting of Stalinism and Maoism, together with the major deficiencies and illusions of recent 'alternative programmes', makes it all the more difficult, yet no less imperative, to confront socialists with the painful and sober truths concerning the role of state institutions and why they will not wither away – no matter how attractive alternative ideas of a 'stateless' society may look on paper. Socialist theory and practice has been preoccupied with trying to theorise and implement an alternative to existing capitalist and Communist societies which would maximise equality and freedom. After seeing the inadequacies of existing notions of 'the State' and 'Civil Society', and the resulting confusion, it is important to examine critically the assumptions underlying notions of decentralised, self-managed, pluralist, worker-council-controlled states and concepts of altogether stateless socialist societies.

It is possible to identify three broad trends of thought concerning socialist alternatives. The first trend stresses the need to break with all notions of 'state socialism' based on central planning, which is seen as inevitably leading to a 'monolithic state' and the crushing of all forms of decentralised, self-managed, pluralist institutions. The second trend favours central planning (but not the form it takes in 'actually existing socialism'), and recommends various alternative paths to socialism – from the vanguard party to self-managed participation in central planning. The third trend favours varying forms of 'state socialism' but stresses the need for combinations of pluralist, market socialism and central planning.

While the 'anti-statists' attack both the central planners and the market socialists as bureaucrats and authoritarians, the central planners and the market socialists attack each other as either hangovers of Stalinism or restorers of capitalism. Each school of thought sincerely proclaims its commitment to equality and freedom, and yet they all cannot maximise *both* equality and freedom as the many processes involved in redistribution and in extending freedom are not complementary. Ultimately, each particular version of socialism must resolve its position on the questions of planning and pluralism if it is to reckon seriously, not just rhetorically or philosophically, with the role of state institutions and the objectives of freedom and equality. Instead of retracing in detail the voluminous expositions by Eastern and Western socialists of the respective merits and weaknesses of central planning and market socialism, I will focus on certain aspects of this old debate – especially the role which state institutions are accorded. After examining some of the main arguments for and against market socialism and central planning, I will discuss the relative merits of decentralised socialist planning in order to see whether this 'third way' avoids the problems inherent in the former schemes.

Advocates of Market Socialism

In his valuable discussion of market socialism and central planning, Alec Nove argues that

> in a modern integrated economy, the lower levels will have nothing to guide them except instruction from the higher levels, *unless* they base their activities on some objective criterion such as might be provided (though imperfectly) by price-and market signals. The invisible hand *might* be consistent with workers' self-management. The visible hand *must* imply a vastly complicated system of instruc-

tions and administrative allocation, operated by a large and complex group of people whose role and function incline them to bureaucratism.[1]

It is worth exploring these two tendencies of the 'invisible' and 'visible hand' more closely. For example, it is quite common to find many anarchists and socialists advocating what has been called 'socialist anarcho-liberalism' – a conception of socialism which is based on the 'invisible hand' of spontaneous, self-managed groups.[2] According to the critic Stojanovic, 'every distributive understanding of justice is excluded in advance as statism, parasitism, and an effort to alienate surplus value from the direct producers. 'Socialist' anarcho-liberalism rejects collectivism as the ideology of statism, but it does so from the standpoint of individualism and self-governing group egoism rather than from the standpoint of Marxist humanism'.[3]

The similarity between some forms of anti-statist, anarcho-socialism and of anti-statist liberalism is readily visible in Evan Luard's recent book *Socialism Without the State*.[4] Having exhausted existing historical sources of bourgeois theory, defenders of 'the mixed economy' such as Luard have begun to borrow concepts from the socialist tradition in order to justify small-scale, market-based social relations. But the convergence of liberal and socialist traditions (from an anti-capitalist perspective) is also demonstrated by 'alternative programme' theorists in Western Europe, as well as by some Eastern European dissidents. It is important to note that, while the following people do not advocate a stateless society, they draw upon liberal traditions in their critique of 'despotic egalitarianism' in the East and monopoly capitalism in the West.

According to Feher and Heller's model of socialism, 'the predominant place will be occupied by the property held by democratic groups and by state property authorised to take independent economic initiative. Although we presuppose a society where these two forms of collective ownership prevail, we are still operating within a world of symmetrical market relations, since the market remains as the basis of economic calculation'.[5] Or in the words of the Italian socialist Ruffolo, 'a socialist society would not eliminate the regulation of the market, but would liberate it from monopolistic elements through decentralisation and a new power balance between associations of producers and consumers. Such theoretical liberal conditions can only be made real through a democratic socialist order'.[6]

If we examine some of the assumptions underlying the market socialism of Feher, Heller, Ruffolo and many other supporters of 'alternative programmes', we find a belief that socialism should extend rather than discard various political principles first developed by liberalism (a matter to which I will return to in the next chapter), as well as the notion that the market is a mechanism or social relation which does not necessarily give rise to private capitalist property relations. In their desire to avoid any new one-party dictatorships, Feher and Heller oppose central planning because 'the State' becomes the enforcer of the public interest which *it* alone represents. (Note that they work with a conception of both 'the State' and 'the party' as subject.[7]) As an alternative to what they label 'despotic egalitarianism', 'dictatorship over needs' or the 'hyper-rationalism' of the planning elites in Eastern Europe, they propose that 'the State' be only one of many collective forms of ownership. Thus, while 'the State' can 'and should be the administrative organ of redistribution' it will 'be the "representative of general interests" and not "generally" itself'.[8] Or in the words of another Hungarian Ivan Szelenyi, 'I am not against planning by governments, I am against government by planners'.[9]

The critique of existing central plans is also articulated by 'Left Eurocommunists' such as Claudin, who puts forward the vision of a socialist system based on self-management at every level 'co-ordinated by a *flexible general plan* which sets out basic options that have been *scientifically* delineated and democratically decided'[10] [my emphasis]. A similar view is advocated by Raptis (a critic of both vanguard parties and 'Eurocommunism') who argues that 'there is no *absolute* incompatibility between self-management, the plan and the necessary utilisation of, not exactly the 'market' in the capitalist sense, but *the methods of the money market economy'.*[11] Despite their different conceptions of political strategy, Feher, Heller, Ruffolo, Claudin and Raptis represent a 'broad Left' vision of socialism as a society based on decentralised self-management, co-ordinated by a 'flexible' or non-rigid plan which will be democratically worked out by the people. They all implicitly recognise, and rightly, that 'state ownership' or nationalisation of private property is insufficient in itself to be called socialism. This 'statist' vision of socialism (e.g. as nationalisation) is attacked by Raptis in the general proposition that 'New property relations can only become new social relations if there are also new forms of management'.[12] This is true, but there immediately arise some questions which have to be pursued in more depth. What are these new forms of management? How 'flexible' and how 'general' must the plans be, in contrast to both rigid central planning and market freedom? Will the democratically-decided plans be enforced if enterprises refuse to adhere, and if so, by whom and with what sanctions?

It seems to me that when discussing the weaknesses and strengths of planning, market socialism or self-management, people like Feher, Heller, Claudin, Raptis, etc. appear well-intentioned but naïvely evasive of organisational problems. This is apparent in their level of analyses and their philosophical assumptions, especially by comparison with analyses of the same questions by Nove, Bahro, Brus or Mandel. Because the latter political economists (with the exception of Bahro, and to a lesser extent Mandel) have devoted more space to the technical problems of planning than to questions concerning culture and general social relations, they are able to avoid much of the naïvety shown by socialist philosophers and political activists on the practical questions arising in Production Processes, Credit Processes and Food Production Processes. On the other hand, Nove, Brus, Mandel and most political economists could greatly benefit from the writings of socialist philosophers and social analysts who focus much more perceptively on problems of socio-cultural relations and moral values. In making this distinction between philosophers and political economists I would like to stress that both perspectives have their limits. Yet in order to transcend the confines of the existing discourse over planning, it is first necessary to confront some of the harsh and unpleasant propositions put forward by the political economists.

Instead of talking about planning or self-management in essentially ethical terms only, political economists such as Nove and Bahro also examine the systemic or structural strengths and weaknesses of these political values. For example, Bahro correctly dismisses the possibility of self-sustaining communes all co-existing horizontally and sharing information and resources in a stateless, non-hierarchical manner. This vision of non-selfish, socialist self-management (which infuses a great deal of anarchist and anti-bureaucratic thought) is 'inconceivably purely from the standpoint of information theory; we can imagine the confusion of channels linking each commune with all others, and the constant to and fro flow of information that the diversity of the reproduction process involves. The association necessarily develops an obligatory vertical dimension'.[13]

While Bahro advocates the need for planning (which I will discuss shortly), Nove, as one of the most trenchant critics of central planning, represents the market-socialist perspective. Attacking a common Left view that 'real' planning could exist in a non-bureaucratic, mass-democratic form if only alienation and lack of democracy were overcome, Nove argues that central planning is inherently wasteful and bureaucratic. 'Democratic procedures are indeed essential,' he says, 'but these cannot be meaningfully applied to multiple-millions of microeconomic decisions; an elected assembly can vote on broad priorities (e.g. more for primary education, or housing, or developing a region), but hardly on whether three tons of constructional steel should be allocated to this or that building site, or that production of red dyestuffs be increased by 3%.'[14]

Not only is democratic participation unable to determine the millions of microeconomic decisions but, in Nove's view, central planning is inherently incompatible with self-management or workers' control. According to Nove, centralised planning systems in Eastern Europe already suffer from 'informational indigestion', and democratic participation would most probably exacerbate this 'indigestion' as thousands of communes made their views known from below. The coordination and processing of this mountain of information by central planners would reduce self-management to a meaningless exercise, if workers could not determine their production according to market signals and instead had to rely upon distant information (as to what to produce).

Nove does to democrats who believe in a non-Stalinist central plan what Bahro does to anarchists and socialists who believe in a stateless, non-hierarchical system of self-managed communes. While I disagree with Bahro's political alternative, i.e. a democratic League of Communists rather than a pluralist system, I am much more in sympathy with some of his notions of planning than with the market-socialist scenario advocated by Nove. Bahro, Nove and especially Feher and Heller (in their analysis of the 'dictatorship over needs') make unarguably valid criticisms of the glaring waste, irrationality and general weaknesses of central plans in Eastern Europe. But it is important to distinguish the debate over central planning/market socialism in Eastern Europe from the larger question as to whether democratic central planning or market socialism is a desirable alternative for capitalist societies suffering from the crises of desynchronisation. In Eastern Europe the whole debate of plan or market is carried on against a background of dictatorship, deeply entrenched forms of corruption, cynicism, fear and privilege. Equally important, the social and industrial development patterns (except in East Germany and Czechoslovakia) are significantly different from those of major OECD capitalist societies – especially in the percentage of people working in agriculture or in non-commodity production. Consequently, there is no way that existing forms of 'command' plans or limited markets are going to solve major social problems in Eastern Europe, short of social revolution. The viability of democratic socialist planning or of market socialism is not to be judged solely against the experiences of Eastern Europe. While important lessons can certainly be learnt – especially the negative aspects of undemocratic planning and the growth of inequality as market forces increase – still, it cannot be said that democratic planning or unrestricted market socialism have ever been implemented.

Nove and other critics of central planning in Eastern Europe do not ignore the various problems arising from market socialism – e.g. income inequalities and uneven regional development, particularly as manifested in Yugoslavia. However, there is a tendency either to project the weaknesses of central planning in Eastern Europe onto planning *per se*, or conversely, to *minimise* the negative social consequences arising from the implementation of market-socialist practices in any future post-capital societies. Given the limited space available, let me briefly indicate why a socialist society which lacks democratic central planning will not be able to maximise the attainment of equality and freedom. I will address myself both to existing weaknesses manifested in market socialism, and to hypothetical scenarios put forward by authors such as Feher, Heller, Nove and Raptis.

The Failure of Market Socialism Adequately to Deal With All the Non-'Direct Producers'

The questions as to how much autonomy enterprises should be given, which areas of social life should be planned or which resources should be redistributed by state institutions have been answered in different ways by socialists who wish to see an alternative to existing forms of central planning. The example of market socialism as practiced in Yugoslavia militates against any future market-socialist alternative just as much as the example of the USSR used by Nove and others militates against the notion of democratic central planning. Of all the Communist countries in existence up until 1982, Yugoslavia has consistently had the highest rate of unemployment (resulting in mass emigration), the highest inflation rates, apart from Poland (over 30 per cent in recent years compared to minimal rates in the USSR), extensive disparities between regions, widespread unequal ownership of sizeable amounts of private property, the greatest dependence on capitalist enterprises (especially those from EEC countries) and a minimal degree of genuine workers' self-management because of the real control vested in the hands of managers and party officials. Raptis argued against Mandel in 1969 that it was 'not the "excesses" of self-management which create the inconveniences of the Yugoslav system, but the centralist bureaucratic impediments preventing the spread of self-management to all levels and all spheres'.[15] There is no doubt that one-party bureaucratic dictatorship has combined with market socialism to exacerbate social inequalities in Yugoslavia. But Raptis is still assuming that self-management as a mechanism could prevent the social inequalities that result when enterprises operate according to price and profit criteria determined by market exchange. Twenty years ago, Mandel wrote that if

> all enterprises are given an extensive, if not complete, autonomy, and encounter each other on the market as competitors free to seek the maximum income, then collective and egalitarian sharing of the income *within the enterprise* will not prevent social inequality and economic wastage from spreading *within the economy as a whole*. The factories which are technically best equipped and the most advanced parts of the country, will inevitably 'exploit' the backward enterprises and less developed areas. *Any exchange on an equal footing between groups whose economic power is unequal increases the inequality between them and gives rise to inevitable economic fluctuations.*[16]

Carlo, Vuskovic and members of the *Praxis* group have confirmed Mandel's analysis in recent years, without being Trotskyists.[17]

It is not just the Yugoslav model which is in dispute here; the fundamental problem for self-management socialists is how to maximise the internal democracy and autonomy of each production unit without market mechanisms giving rise to social inequalities. For example, Feher and Heller reveal the traditional preoccupation of socialists with the 'direct producers'. In their model of socialism, where property is held in a pluralist way by democratic groups and 'the State', market mechanisms somehow co-exist with state redistribution. Now one of the principal goals put forward by Feher and Heller is the abolition of wage-labour. Yet this admirable socialist objective is naïvely seen to be attainable within the framework of market relations. According to Feher and Heller, the collective owners decide their own income which will be determined by free discussion in order to avoid gross social inequalities.[18] The secret of how wage-labour can be abolished within the framework of market relations, which operate according to criteria of price (for labour and materials), is not revealed to us.[19] Nor do they (along with many other socialists) confront this most important fact, that in leading OECD capitalist countries the vast majority of wage-workers do not produce commodities – that is, they are *not* 'direct producers'. How these millions of workers in Production and Credit Processes (e.g. most workers in state institutions, and all in private services) are to be 'revolutionised', in order that their appropriate income can be determined (in socialist collective property units), is not clearly explained by the advocates of market socialism.

For the problem is not merely one of defining 'direct workers' in terms broad enough to include all those who work for wages (e.g. teachers or clerks) rather than just commodity producers. Any model of socialism which is based on notions of collective property units earning income for the 'direct workers' must fail to confront the contemporary historical division of labour existing in leading capitalist societies: the vast majority of workers perform labour which could not earn income if their present employers (whether capitalists or governments) were removed. Not only do many jobs not directly earn income (e.g. social welfare, social control jobs, etc.), but their bureaucratic or wasteful forms would have no place in a socialist society lacking present forms of state administration and of private sales, advertising and commodity production. If the abolition of wage-labour is to be placed on the agenda of a socialist society, then it must be clearly understood that exchange-value criteria cannot be one of the principal regulatory mechanisms. Even in a planned social system the abolition of wage-labour would remain a distant goal – let alone in a society which is forced to calculate according to a mixture of 'symmetrical market relations'!

What the championing of self-management by the 'direct producers' rests upon is the traditional 'workerist' image of the proletarian as a blue-collar industrial worker. This conception is prevalent amongst a whole range of socialists – from Maoists and Trotskyists right through to anti-Leninists such as Feher and Heller, and especially among non-socialists who fill conventional sociology books with notions of the working-class which exclude the vast majority of wage-workers simply because they do not work in factories. Self-management is based upon an extension of Marx's theory of the alienation of the worker from the *product* of his or her labour. As such it is premised on a worker who produces commodities – which, in a socialist society, would change to use-value commodities rather than marketable commodities as under capitalism. Although self-management market socialists recognise that millions of people will not be involved in 'direct production' but will be working in communal structures and services, this vital factor does not seem to find adequate expression or analysis in their critiques of central planning. Their emphasis is overwhelmingly on *commodity-producing enterprises*, rather than on the reality of the division of labour already established within leading capitalist societies. It is no good for Szelenyi to criticise Bahro in terms of the polarised situation in Eastern Europe, where undemocratic central planners confront and exploit 'direct producers'.[20] To side with the 'direct producers' may be justified, but it does not tell us how the surplus they produce will be consumed by or distributed to the vast majority who are *not* 'direct producers'. Marx's championing of equality was based on the need to end the exploitation of the surplus-value-producing proletariat. But the real issue for contemporary socialists is how to establish egalitarian institutions which also safeguard the interests of those millions of paid *and* unpaid workers who are not directly producing surplus-value.

As most people in a socialist society cannot be 'direct producers' – unless there were a reversion to an agricultural society – the problem of state institutions becomes central; the admission of some form of 'representation of the general interest' *must* inevitably erode the degree of autonomy which self-management socialists advocate – whether in a market-socialist or non-market society. Before discussing an alternative to models of market socialism and stateless socialism, let me first outline some of the problems and inequalities which would result from various market-socialist models.

To begin with, analysts such as Nove, Feher and Heller argue the need for state institutions or a central authority to prevent gross inequalities of income and provide non-marketable goods and services – e.g. public parks and education. How then can the self-management organs be autonomous? Nove also argues that central planning is preferable in areas such as electricity, energy resources and so forth.[21] If this is true, how can one expect workers in those institutions and enterprises operating on non-market criteria to tolerate central planning, when their colleagues in most other commodity-producing enterprises will be free to determine their own conditions? Either one has autonomy in *all* spheres of labour, or else enterprises cease operating according to market criteria as they become receptive and are ultimately persuaded to accept a general non-market plan.

The belief that market socialism will minimise the waste and irrationality of existing, rigid and undemocratic plans is based on two considerations: the material incentive it gives the 'direct producers', and the enterprises' ability to respond to those customer preferences which Soviet central plans ignore or regard as secondary. But self-management would be able to function only in those enterprises which workers take over from their previous private or government owners (in capitalist societies), or from the state planners (in Eastern Europe). The existing inequalities of each enterprise – in terms of location, size, resources and products manufactured – will either be allowed to continue (thus perpetuating inequalities), or be redistributed by some form of central or national institutional arrangement.

When the vast majority of the population are not 'direct producers', then, with all the greater efficiency and customer satisfaction that market socialism supposedly promises, the wealth produced will have to be taxed or redistributed to all non-'direct producers', if the material incentives which operate in private capitalist markets are not to lead to glaring income and material inequality. This massive redistribution away from the minority of 'direct' commodity producers is bound to affect the level of worker productivity, efficiency and social or moral involvement, unless a strong socialist communal ethic prevails. I would like to argue that this communal ethic cannot develop and flourish, if enterprises are operating according to competitive market criteria.

For if key industries such as energy were planned, and credit, currency controls and other fiscal arrangements centralised, then the 'direct producers' would have only token self-management. If prices for materials, products and labour are not fixed by planning, if scarcity prevails in many areas, if enterprises are permitted to export and import according to 'customer preference' and so forth, then market socialists are relying solely on 'moral incentives' to prevent social inequality, privatisation and parochialism. It is naïve to believe that all countries would simultaneously 'go socialist', thus eliminating 'temptation' or the influence of capitalist morality on socialist countries. Market socialists such as Nove insist that, while self-management may be compatible with the 'invisible hand', the 'visible hand' of planning reduces workers' control to a state of dependence on information from above. If this is true, how can market socialists believe that self-management can survive if, as they themselves advocate, key co-ordinating and controlling mechanisms will be necessary to prevent the negative features of 'socialist-anarcho-liberalism'?

In short, market relations guarantee that there is a greater inbuilt structural possibility that inequalities will proliferate, as compared to a centrally-planned society. Market socialists and self-management socialists need to tell us very clearly: what would happen to those autonomous enterprises which refused to participate in communal plans, sought alternative investments or went on strike because they resented redistribution to non-'direct producers'? (This situation could also arise under democratic central planning, and has already occurred on a massive scale in Poland under *undemocratic* planning.) How would market-socialist mechanisms prevent false information being fed into planning agencies by all those enterprises eager to earn bonuses and other material incentives? In other words, how does material competition foster communal solidarity?

Under a democratic central plan, the 'direct producers' would begin with the conception that a particular factory was *not* solely their property, but rather communal property. However, it is difficult to persuade workers operating on market criteria that they are not the sole 'owners', but merely control the enterprise on behalf of a larger community, when their primary reference point must be market viability rather than planned social production. For the non-profit-ability of an enterprise could result in closure or the sacking of workers, unless the factory were subsidised by other enterprises or out of a general fund run by state institutions. It is not enough to cite the likeli-hood of numerous unprofitable enterprises (given the increased produc-tion of *non-marketable use-value goods* in a socialist society); the question remains of how socially useful production and services will be maintained under market socialism. It is relatively easy to criticise the glaring weaknesses of undemocratic Soviet planning. But it is another matter to show how a mixture of plan and market will maximise ef-ficiency, social equality, genuine self-management *and* a socialist ethic.

When one examines the alternative models of socialism put forward by Raptis, Heller, Nove, etc., the only thing that really separates them is the degree of radical self-management which they accord to the 'direct producers'. All of them favour some mix of market mechanisms with 'redistribution' or planning. All of them argue that a communal ethic or social mechanism must prevent gross inequalities. None of them tells us how this redistribution or 'flexible plan' leaves self-management intact or fully in control of investment and production decisions. None of them tells us how the vast majority of *non-'direct producers'* will earn an income or obtain social goods and services, other than through complete decentralisation so that the communes live (unevenly) off the profitability of their 'own' enterprises, or through 'equalising' administrative 'redistribution' by state apparatuses (which involves precisely the 'visible hand' so deplored by anti-central planners). Ultimately the problem of market socialism versus planning boils down to the relative role of spontaneous knowledge (which the market provides through the 'invisible hand' of supply and demand) versus that of planned, conscious knowledge.

It is inconceivable that a new socialist society will immediately consist of people all imbued with a socialist ethic, who have shaken off deeply socialised commodity-fetishist beliefs and practices. Market socialism would run the major risk of perpetuating former income, investment and social inequalities simply because a self-managed, spontaneous information process would not of necessity promote inter-enterprise and inter-communal solidarity. On the other hand, a 'mixture' of plan and market would not succeed if the plan were merely a form of 'indicative' planning (as in capitalist countries), where enterprises were still left to rely upon their own narrow interests, prejudices and judgements. The moment that 'indicative' planning becomes significantly binding over enterprises rather than voluntary (in response to social pressure for non-marketable goods or for redistribution to non-'direct producers'), the 'visible hand' of conscious planning clashes with local market forces.

Given the need for any radical alternative to confront the problem of how to sustain material existence for the vast majority of non-'direct producers', the problem for self-management supporters is to spell out the limits and mutual responsibilities which will govern and constrain the groups of 'associated producers'. It is the existing crises of de-synchronised Processes in capitalist societies which have to be overcome. Market socialism with minimal planning offers no guarantee that desynchronisation will be resolved – in fact, it could be restored or even exacerbated if enterprises went their separate ways. Only a planned society which minimised or eliminated the 'organised anarchy' of private capitalist enterprises (and the class conflict this produced) would overcome the desynchronisation of Processes. Market socialism is inherently anti-planning, for the plan may restrict market mechanisms which have a logic of their own. While it would be dangerously naïve to believe that democratic planning could create a wonderful balance or equilibrium between all inputs and outputs (the illusions and hopes of the super-planners or plano-maniacs as Trotsky called them), there is no doubt that planning could solve the fundamental problems of un-employment, poverty, inflation, regional and social imbalances. For democratic central planning can overcome the deficiencies of market mechanisms; it is *not* built around structural features which presuppose the successful profitability or income-earning capacity of each enter-prise or social unit.

Hence the moral safeguard against social inequalities (which is supposed to make the market 'socialist' rather than 'capitalist' ac-cording to the market socialists) can be more effective under *market-less* planning, simply because competition between enterprises can be minimised. Very importantly, if a socialist society were to seek the introduction of new use-value products, ecologically-balanced tech-nology, nutritional food and so forth, market socialist mechanisms could in fact frustrate these socially desirable ends, if workers in particular factories rejected the production of environmentally safe goods – because they required more labour perhaps, or earned little or no profits. The advantage of democratic planning is that it *depends* on an active socialist morality but is free of the structural negativities which market mechanisms (and undemocratic planning) could easily promote.

The long-term goal of abolishing wage-labour is compatible only with a democratically-planned society. As the percentage of national income and resources allocated for the production of goods and services *in kind*, i.e. the 'social wage' or social consumption fund increases, the reliance upon paid money wages decreases. An *adequate* and extensive guaranteed minimum income is ultimately destructive of market relations (a factor capitalist classes recognise even if well-intentioned social-democratic 'mixed economists' do not). Market socialism could not survive if a minority of 'direct producers' had to labour excessively in order to supply an increasing percentage of social consumption funds. Given the internal contradictions of Production, Credit and Food Production Processes within existing capitalist societies, any alternative socialist society that did not implement an extensive social consumption fund, sustaining the majority of the people with non-wage income, would probably be unable to increase employment, end the discriminatory division of labour and ensure useful social investment. An extensive social consumption and income fund would enable millions of people to be redeployed from existing state sector and private sector jobs which are wasteful, destructive and linked to unnecessary control functions. It would also permit reductions in working hours, and involve non-wage income recipients in communal self-managed services. These options would be severely limited in a 'market-socialist' society, which depended on enterprise profitability rather than on mutual planning allocations.

Plan and Market – A Problem-ridden Mixture

Socialists are caught in a major theoretical and practical 'double bind', when they seek to explain the nature of an alternative to capitalist societies. If they formulate an ahistorical 'blueprint' of socialism, then they transform the active process of social creation into a model which predetermines subsequent action; if they say nothing about the future, they are severely criticised for having no plan. Yet in capitalist societies the vast majority of people (including economists) have only the flimsiest understanding of how capitalism works – as opposed to elaborate ideas about how they think it works. The inability of socialist societies to maximise equality and freedom, without a widely dispersed knowledge of resource allocations and social strategies, poses a massive problem which minority ruling classes in capitalist societies do not face. Consequently, the whole dispute over market or plan involves the vital dimension of mass democratic control, which the regulators of private capitalist production constantly attempt to minimise or repress. The same entrenched hostility to democracy is practised in Communist countries, whether it is the Soviet Union with its 'command' planning or Yugoslavia with its 'market socialism'.

So far I have discussed some of the differences between proponents of market socialism and of central planning. Three related questions have to be discussed. First, can one have market mechanisms which are free of the social relations inherent in capitalist market societies? Second, can one have central planning which is free of the social relations currently evident in Communist countries? Third, can one have decentralised socialist planning which avoids the weaknesses of both market socialism and central planning?

In contrast to Heller, Feher and Ruffolo, who would like to see socialist societies where market mechanisms work without the distortions created by 'monopoly capitalism', Wlodzimierz Brus is much more cautious in his advocacy of a mix between planning and market mechanisms. He shares with other advocates of market socialism the belief that exchange relations are secondary to property relations – that is, if private property were not dominant then market exchanges could co-exist with socialist planning.[22] However, Brus is a pluralist in the sense that he is not an opponent of central planning. On the contrary, Brus believes that planning must be the 'principal regulator' in a socialist society with the market playing a vital but secondary role.[23] According to Brus, market socialism means that the market becomes the 'principal regulator' – which is not what he advocates. It appears that Brus is walking a tight-rope in his attempt to balance planning and market mechanisms. Against central planners he warns that it is not possible to eliminate a labour market, an inter-enterprise market or a consumer market – unless one wants centralised, coercive job allocations, physical plant controls and consumer rationing.[24] Against advocates of self-management (who oppose market socialism) he warns:

> Complete elimination of a market mechanism means the total sub-ordination of all economic units to direct co-ordination methods, to commands. This is frequently overlooked by people who on the one hand favour self-management on the shop-floor and on the other hand are opposed to any form of regulated market mechanism as a tool of coordination. Autonomy must mean the introduction of self-regulation, obviously connected with the operation of the market (which should be controlled).[25]

While Brus recognises that there will be no ideal solutions in any socialist society, it is difficult to avoid the fear that the planning and market mechanisms he advocates may give rise to all the negative features associated with market socialism. Market mechanisms will remain secondary only if 'formal' guidelines are not subverted by growing in-equality and competitiveness – a very difficult condition to achieve, given that market mechanisms encourage competitiveness. But if one does not opt for Brus's mix of plan and market, it is still necessary to confront the polar opposites of coercive allocation or market mech-anisms. It seems to me that what Brus calls market mechanisms are not necessarily competitive exchange relations, simply because labour or goods are not allocated by a central authority. The joint control over labour resources (at central and numerous decentralised levels) does not have to be seen as the *free* selling and buying of labour. The self-regulation which Brus advocates can be compatible with democratic grass-roots inputs *vis-à-vis* labour needs. But it would be wrong to believe that a socialist society can approve labour exchange or mobility which permits extensive individual job rotation at the expense of the group, or the dismissal of individuals for the sake of temporary enterprise 'efficiency'. If Brus is advocating that labour allocation be solely or largely in the hands of individual enterprises, then it will not be too long before market-socialist mechanisms take over and labour scarcity and unemployment appear, as richer enterprises or regions attract labour and leave the poorer units or localities with a surplus of unemployed people. The choice should not lie between Stalinist job coercion or a so-called free labour market.

Turning to the role of a consumer market, it is possible to both agree and disagree with Brus's analysis. In so far as no society will become socialist overnight, it is perfectly reasonable to expect, for a long transition period, the existence of a small private sector of simple commodity exchange based mainly on individuals, families or craftspeople. However, this market sector would have to constitute a very small proportion of total output and labout within a Production Process, if it were not to negate overall planning and social policy oriented towards equality. The existence of market mechanisms within Food Production Processes in socialist societies is very much dependent on the percentage of population involved in *direct* production, rather than in the manufacture of food within the *intermediate* parts of Food Production Processes. This will undoubtedly be a major problem for any socialist society to resolve effectively. However, I do not agree with Brus that a general consumer market (for edible and non-edible products) is the alternative to poor goods, lack of choice, shortages or rationing. In a democratic socialist society the creation of local, regional and national consumer councils, as well as genuine consultation and input into production plans, will dramatically influence both the quality and quantity of goods and services. Once again, the market is not the only alternative to 'command' planning.

As for scarcity, in capitalist societies commodities are permanently rationed, though the mechanism is called 'freedom of choice', which is freedom to purchase goods that one can *afford*. Even Brus admits the need for price controls and other regulations to prevent market mechanisms getting out of control. Ultimately, the adequacy of material resources and the prevalence of a socialist ethic will determine how close to a bare minimum the informal, unofficial provision of labour, commodities, etc. is kept. No capitalist market society has eliminated black markets, 'moonlighting', tax avoidance and other 'underground' activitiess. It would be naïve to believe that a democratically planned socialist society will be immediately free of these 'informal channels'. But it is very important to emphasise that the size of particular black markets and of other 'underground' activity, is directly and indirectly related to the degree of corruption and injustice which the population believes to exist. The 'formal' mechanisms of no production system can survive undamaged, if cynicism and systematic corruption eat away from within.

Brus argues for an inter-enterprise market in the light of all the negative experiences arising out of 'command' planning in Eastern Europe. But once again, it is not clear how much autonomy Brus would allocate to individual enterprises to deal with one another (thus bypassing planning regulations), and whether this market mechanism would not eventually replace planning as the 'principal regulator'. Brus argues against Ticktin and other critics of market socialism that one should not make a fetish out of the term 'market'.[26] But it is very important to clarify what is meant by market mechanisms. In capitalist societies, despite the inseparable linkage of state institutions with private enterprises in Production, Credit and Food Production Processes, market mechanisms imply certain things: (a) minimal controls over what, when, where and how much private enterprises will produce; (b) minimal controls or minimal planning decisions as to how many people, and what kind of people, will be employed; and (c) minimal controls over the quantity and quality of goods individuals may purchase or sell without reference to group, regional or national priorities.

When I said earlier that the choice was not between coercive Stalinist allocations or the market, I had in mind the need to maximise democratic control without the twin evils of either 'command' planning or the 'invisible hand of the market'. Either market mechanisms means individualised exchanges according to the 'invisible hand' of supply and demand (involving both individual people and individual enterprises), or we are talking of conscious, deliberated planned exchanges. The problem is that people wrongly identify the exchange of goods, labour or services as the market, simply because there is no coercive, commanded allocation. However, it would be stretching the concept of market too far if we thought a 'labour market', 'consumer market' and 'inter-enterprise market' could remain governed by unplanned laws of supply and demand once people had consciously decided to subject all these elements to the 'principal regulator' – central planning. Once Brus advocates or concedes that in a socialist society people will need conscious inputs, feedback, regulation, redistribution mechanisms, local and national co-ordination and general planning priorities, the only spheres which will retain market mechanisms are the 'underground economy' and the small, private, simple commodity sphere. For how can 'invisible' market mechanisms co-exist in a role complementary to visible planning decisions? Either the planning is merely 'indicative' and the market becomes the 'principal regulator', thus entailing the weaknesses associated with market socialism, or else labour, consumer and inter-enterprise exchanges are co-determined at local and central levels. This raises two related questions: whether one can have decentralised planning without market mechanisms, and whether one can have central planning free of the coercive irrationality which Brus and others so rightly condemn.

Strengths and Weaknesses of Decentralised Planning and Central Planning

If one agrees with Brus that 'there is no automatic connection between non-market forms of distribution and the weakening of vertical stratification',[27] it is important to evaluate whether centralised or decentralised planning can minimise inequality without market mechanisms. One of the fullest and best descriptions of decentralised socialist planning is to be found in Michael Albert and Robin Hahnel's recent work *Socialism Today and Tomorrow*.[28] As strong critics of both market socialism and central planning, Albert and Hahnel put forward an elaborate alternative consisting of parallel pyramids of local, regional and national workers' councils, consumer councils and industry councils. These producer and consumer councils would be organised along decentralised lines, but linked vertically within federal structures as opposed to the centralisation of decisions in contemporary 'command' planning. The whole notion of decentralised planning is based on pluralist political and social practice, intricate consultative and redistributive mechanisms between the numerous social units and, very importantly, the fundamental notion of socialism as an active, discursive process of conscious planning.

I find the concept of decentralised socialist planning very attractive and challenging. It is very attractive because it goes a long way to reconciling the perennial values of equality and freedom. It is challenging because the viability of decentralised planning necessitates coming to terms with the desynchronisation of Processes without lapsing back into 'command' planning. Albert and Hahnel attack existing Communist societies because the 'co-ordinator class' dominates decision-making at the expense of socialist democratic participation.[29] Central planning, they argue, is inherently authoritarian and perpetuates the undemocratic division of labour, social stratification and anti-socialist values. I would argue that these characteristics are unquestionably true of undemocratic central planning but not inherently part of central planning. However, I would be only too happy to endorse Albert and Hahnel's decentralised socialist planning if some major problems could be resolved or accounted for adequately. For example, their entire discussion of decentralised planning takes place within the confines of a nation-state and with no thought for how international relations would be managed. They fail to specify whether the whole world would be socialist or whether the decentrally planned socialist society would co-exist alongside capitalist societies. If the local, regional and national units are not self-sufficient, then how is international trade to be organised without resorting to either market mechanisms or central control? After all, the existing federal systems – whether the United States or the USSR – have central control over currencies, trade regulations, budgetary policy, military forces, and over numerous other social areas.

One could say there is nothing inherently democratic, egalitarian, non-stratified, etc. in decentralised institutions, let alone federations. Conversely, central planning does not inherently mean 'big' institutions or enterprises as one can centrally plan small units. Albert and Hahnel argue that a central computer will provide information for all units, and that higher workers' and industry councils will have the power of sanction or command over local units if consultation leads nowhere or the consensus is violated by a minority of selfish people.[30] But how are local and regional units to prevent the concentration of policy-making powers in the hands of federal councils? Will there, or will there not, be a co-ordinating administration, military personnel, external relations personnel? Will the judicial system operate according to universal norms or according to decentralised values? Furthermore, if decentralised planning strongly opposes any introduction of market mechanisms along the lines of enterprise profitability as well as central redistributive mechanisms, how will the large number of non-direct producers obtain their sustenance in money and/or kind? It is quite likely that the majority of people will be found in consumers' councils rather than in workers' councils, so that major decisions are made within the former councils rather than the latter. Most importantly, because Albert and Hahnel do not discuss the transition period in any detail, it is not clear how decentralised control would lead to a fundamental redistribution of material and human resources in order to remedy gross inequalities between localities and regions. If geographically-based workers' councils simply forwarded (to national councils) requests for supplies which could not be met locally or regionally,[31] then the wealthy geographical areas would orient towards self-sufficiency while the poor areas suffered continued deprivation. The rectification of major inequalities would require increased co-operation at central level – the very tendency which decentralised planning opposes. It is also unclear how non-market mechanisms can create maximum social equality if price mechanisms do not govern the relationship between councils, and central co-ordination and redistribution is opposed – i.e. will there be simple barter between councils if prices and central co-ordination are opposed? While the authors discuss the issue of long-term research and development planning, it is difficult to imagine how five-, ten- or twenty-year projects will not limit decentralised unit inputs and outputs when formulating *annual* planning targets. The balance between decentralised and central co-ordination will indeed be precarious.

Although the notion of decentralised planning has many features which would be compatible with democratic central planning (as opposed to 'command' planning), it is the failure of Albert and Hahnel to confront the desynchronisation of Processes in capitalist societies which ultimately leaves their alternative proposals incomplete and fragile. If it could be shown how decentralised planning would prevent incompatible local and regional interests from restoring desynchronised social practices, then decentralised control deserves full support. The very recognition of the desynchronisation of local, national and supranational Processes means that socialists can no longer put forward tidy symmetrical images of socialism as alternatives to their equally ideal-typical concepts of 'capitalism' and 'the capitalist state'. The age of utopian planning is over. Democratic social order presupposes disorder and multiple levels of human interaction and needs. Yet any planning in a socialist society must be able to overcome and prevent the social crises emanating from the desynchronisation of Processes without promoting the dictatorial and wasteful features of 'command' planning. Planning will become tyrannical if it reduces people to objects, regards local needs as secondary and generally carries on the tradition of 'revolution from above'. Instead, planning has to be based on the reality of heterogeneity – a plurality which can be neither left completely un-touched nor subjected to unquestioned commands.

Nevertheless, planning involves administration and this is unavoidable in any socialist society. Self-management should be seen as the control over local and communal institutions, production facilities and so forth. As most people will *not* be producing commodities, but will rather be involved in the self-administration and provision of socio-cultural services or 'social wage' goods and services, there should be ample room for the direct self-management of everyday social relations, which is almost totally absent from existing capitalist and Eastern European regimes. Certainly millions of people are involved in these activities in Eastern Europe, but they are tightly constrained by one-party bureaucratic dictatorships. In contrast, democratic central planning does not entail the central control of all non-commodity services and facilities. The inability to permit genuine decentralisation of the vast majority of *non-commodity-producing* social institutions is directly related to the absence of pluralism (which I will discuss in the following chapter). But the critique of bureaucracy put forward by Nove and other market socialists would be just as relevant to any notions of a socialist society having a 'mix' of centrally-planned enterprises (in energy, etc.) and market enterprises. This is because all the market-socialist proposals for a 'central authority', redistributing goods and services, would also involve the 'visible hand' of administration – one of the main dangers which Nove *et al.* criticise.

The problem of controlling the 'visible hand' of administrators (whether centralised or decentralised, whether in a democratically planned system or in a variation of market socialism) is not directly related to how commodities are produced. It is rather a question of how much say all members of a socialist society will have in what is produced and in the nature of distribution – a decision-making process which is currently dominated by a small percentage of 'visible' adminis-trators. Since the vast majority of people (including most paid workers) will *not* be 'directly' producing commodities, the decision-making structure of a socialist society must *not* be based on 'workerist' models where the production enterprise *is* the central focal point. Self-manage-ment conceptions must be updated so that the actual division of labour and the profile of paid and unpaid labour in capitalist societies is recognised when thinking of alternatives to current practices.

I would agree with Bahro when he says:

> The assortment of goods supplied, as opposed to the *conditions* of production, cannot and must not be freely chosen by the individual branch and factory, by any internal criterion of utility . . . . *The interests of the producers are particular interests among other particular interests*, and as long as they have their pivot in *producer* co-operatives, they are therefore fundamentally incapable of producing any plan that can satisfy the overall social requirement, no matter how democratically they are synthesised from the bottom upwards.[32]

This is why central planning must be based on producers acting as *social* individuals rather than as *individual* producers. Any central plan must be based on 'labour-time accounting' which conceives workers or 'labour' as human beings, as opposed to financial accounting which treats 'labour' as a commodity ruled by price.[33] Nove argues that an advantage of market firms is that they have surplus capacity with which to work, free from the political pressures applied by Soviet central planners who try to calculate in terms of maximising unreal targets. In contrast, Bahro argues that planning should not set down the rate of growth[34] (which is hardly ever fulfilled anyway), and that labour-time accounting should work on the basis of an adequate reserve of labour power and surplus capacity. These surplus reserves would be built into the plan, thus permitting room for bottlenecks and unforeseen crises, without the existing corruption, exploitation and tension in rigid Societ planning.[35]

Although Bahro does not say a great deal about non-'direct producers', it is clear that his conception of planning is compatible with a society where the vast majority of people relied on planned redistribution (rather than enterprise profitability), and could have a say in the *conditions* of their everyday institutions, services or enterprises. The possibility for commodity-producing workers to influence the design and creation of socially useful products would be matched by the possibility for individuals to design and create more humane services and social relations in the whole network of *non-commodity-producing* institutions. The degree of participation achievable in these areas is tied inseparably to the level of democratic tolerance which exists and the level of solidarity which can be forged out of common objectives.

Consequently, the belief that one can do away with all state institutions is not only naïve but goes squarely against the realisation of egalitarian principles. The attempts to minimise administration will depend on how many non-commodity-producing institutions are controlled at local level, and how well federal structures are balanced with central co-ordinating bodies. Central planning *will* involve waste and inefficiency; it will also have inbuilt mechanisms tempting planners to exceed their duty as advisers and usurp the role of dictators. The benefits of *democratic* planning and the struggle to decentralise decision-making as people become more active will clearly outweigh those dangers of market socialism, provided that wherever practically possible 'there should *never be less than two* independently prepared "plans" '.[36] Raymond Williams puts it well when he argues:

> It is not just the practical point that we have had more than enough experience of expert plans which turned out to be wrong (the switches from coal to oil, and from rail to road, are only the most obvious examples). It is, more fundamentally, that the preparation of at least two plans, while fulfilling the necessary conditions of effective and where necessary specialist knowledge, provides, in its practical alternatives, genuine conditions for the actual as distinct from the appropriated exercise of public interest and rationality. Moreover, it is inherent in the requirement of detailed and practicable alternatives that decision is neither appropriated nor mandated but is each time actively and generally made.[37]

However, it is crucial to stress that no form of planning or variety of plans to choose from is infallible. One can never perfect the future, but people can democratically learn to minimise group mistakes.

Unfortunately, the people living in 'actually existing socialist' societies will most likely opt for variations of market socialism, given their experiences of undemocratic central planning. Although I agree with Kuron's view that 'the Finlandisation of Eastern Europe'[38] would represent a historical step forward in terms of democratisation, it is almost guaranteed in advance that greater independence from the USSR will not eliminate social inequality in Poland or any other Communist country if variations on the Yugoslav model of market socialism are adopted. Whereas the belief in democratic central planning is held by only a minority in Eastern Europe, it is the task of socialists to try to persuade those in capitalist societies attracted by 'alternative programmes', based on market-socialist principles, that these principles and the programmes built upon them cannot provide the resolution so urgently needed to current crises of desynchronisation.

Concluding Summary

In evaluating the strengths and weaknesses of various models of market socialism, 'mixes' of plan and market, decentralised or central planning and self-management with and without socialist state institutions, I have kept in mind the following problems: (a) how to prevent the re-currence of social crises emanating from the desynchronisation of Processes; (b) whether models of market socialism, etc. will provide the bases for the long-term growth and reproduction of socialist relations or degenerate into new forms of inequality and social alienation; (c) whether alternative socialist models deal adequately with the majority of non-'direct producers' rather than just with commodity-producing enterprises; and (d) whether models of socialism pay more than lip service to the immense material and social inequality confronting a new society – thus clearly stating what mechanisms of redistribution will be needed, and whether this new society will be organised along local, national or world scale.

I find all proponents of societies based on self-administered, stateless councils or communes to be utterly unconvincing. The highly desirable goals of self-managed, anti-bureaucratic control cannot be secured, let alone reproduced, if socialists cannot tell us how alternatives to wage-labour, revenue collection, market mechanisms or central planning can be instituted. Many advocates of self-management actually call for general plans and social institutions which are in fact new socialist state institutions of co-ordination and redistribution. But most advocates of self-sufficient communes, co-operatives, regions or whatever, fall back on the 'new socialist morality' rather than any coherent or plausible notion of social reproduction and exchange. As for advocates of market socialism or 'mixes' of plan and market, their proposals seem to be short-term responses to Soviet 'command' planning or Western capitalist depressions, rather than long-term solutions to the desynchronisation of Processes. I see no convincing arguments from market socialists about how to finance and develop institutions for the majority of unpaid and non-surplus-value-producing workers. There is no real prospect that 'direct producers' will or should, bear the burden of carrying the rest of the population; socialist 'responsibility' will soon lose its attractiveness when successful market-socialist enterprises are heavily taxed in order to pay for social consumption and other use-value funds and investments needed to maximise equality. More importantly, there is little prospect that market-socialist plans will provide enough employment (let alone maximise equality) if implemented at the national level in a world full of other capitalist or market-socialist societies – each trying to maintain growth by market competition.

Market socialism is incompatible with the long-term creation and survival of socialist relations; it is too heavily oriented to criteria of technical rationality, and is already historically obsolete when one considers market pressures to increase automation. With many industries operating well below full capacity, low growth in international trade, not to mention very high levels of unemployment and poverty, it is absurd to believe that 'alternative programmes' – based on versions of radical or moderate market socialism – will be able to counter existing competitive trends, let alone resolve massive problems confronting both capitalist and Communist countries. All those Communist governments which have tried to counter 'command' planning with various market mechanisms, have only imported problems from capitalist countries without transcending either the irrationality of one-party dictatorship or the causes of 'stagflation' in capitalist societies. There is very little prospect that a pluralist socialist society would fare any better with market mechanisms, as competition between political parties is itself part of the 'organised anarchy' manifested in desynchronised Processes, rather than a 'natural' panacea to undemocratic 'command' planning.

While I am very sympathetic to the concept of decentralised planning, I cannot see this being successfully implemented without the existence of socialist state institutions. The balance between the degree of central co-ordination and decentralised planning will depend on the demographic and geopolitical factors involved. Decentralised planning is probably most feasible within the boundaries of a nation-state, but central planning will be required in relation to all external trade and most likely in the vital areas of revenue raising for social funds. Moreover, it is difficult to see how wage-labour could be abolished in the early life of a socialist society – even as the proportion of payment-in-kind or the 'social wage' increased. But this move towards non-wage-labour would only be possible in a society which had clearly established nation-wide institutions of redistribution and planning. The transformation of existing forms of paid and unpaid wage-labour is dependent on the establishment of Production Processes which are capable of being planned for periods longer than one or two years. This will necessitate – at the very least – central co-ordination if not central planning (via federal or other structures) and a mutual recognition – at all levels – that self-management and national co-ordination are limited mechanisms rather than ahistorical polar absolutes. However, I am not optimistic that central co-ordination can co-exist with decentralised planning; it is most likely that democratic central planning will be implemented to counter the weaknesses in decentralised planning. That is, the 'visible hand' of administrators which Nove and others warn against is unavoidable in any transitional society. The social struggle over how many of the millions of micro-decisions will possibly be in the hands of an army of central planners or decentralised in regional planning offices cannot be *a priori* established. It is important to stress, however, that decentralisation does not mean the introduction of market mechanisms. There is also no automatic connection between decentralisation and democratic control, just as there is little validity in the principle that all 'small' (or all 'big') units are inherently better.

A socialist society requires mass participation, honest information and material exchange, social struggle against inequality and privilege as well as constant self-reflection and active learning mechanisms (issues I will discuss in the next chapter). But democratic participation and control are only the prerequisites to greater equality and freedom rather than intrinsic solutions to the questions of market or plan. Deep-seated radical beliefs that workers' control will solve everything – and that questions about planning are merely 'technical' issues – are recipes for disaster. It is most likely that any new socialist society would have to be constructed out of the chaos and disintegration of capitalist societies and Communist regimes. Societies suffering from 'de-industrialisation', food shortages, useless state apparatuses and private businesses which will have to be abolished or severely restructured (thus creating the need for alternative employment for millions of workers) – are hardly favourable environments in which democratic control in itself can resolve all problems. Priorities will have to be established in relation to which industries are needed, whether they can be self-sufficient within national boundaries, how long it will take to restructure the 'old' division of labour allocations, what minimum and maximum rates of social consumption and investment funds will be implemented across the society and so forth. We have already seen that shortages of material resources in countries such as Vietnam or Angola could not have been remedied by democratic control alone. As for models based on workers' co-operatives and councils, radicals must confront the reality that most co-operatives (i.e. those producing commodities) would involve market competition (and hence work against socialist values in the long-run) or, without co-ordinating state institutions, be reduced to some form of self-sufficient economy based on primitive barter.

Finally, it may be objected that my desire to overcome and prevent the re-emergence of crises emanating from the desynchronisation of Processes betrays the old desire for a perfectly co-ordinated society which leads to 'totalitarianism'. Let me simply say that I do *not* believe that socialist societies will bring about the end of social conflict, that certainty will replace doubt and that any form of social planning can predict let alone confidently control the future. To try and overcome the 'organised anarchy' of capitalist societies, as well as the absence of free Electoral Processes in Communist countries, does not mean that the democratic and conscious attempts to plan material resources and institutions within Production, Credit and Food Production Processes leads to the elimination of socialist pluralism. All those who criticise utopian and non-utopian thought for advocating large-scale social planning must also confront the utopian element within their own images of socialist pluralism. For if one rejects ideologies of 'the good life' and advocates notions of democracy as being synonymous with uncertainty and social diversity, how are the material resources of particular societies to be organised so that these admirable concepts can be realised? Without a corresponding theory of the social co-ordination of material resources, all notions of socialist pluralism must remain highly dubious or utopian. We already know the inequalities and lack of socialism existing in market socialist societies such as Yugoslavia. Advocates of stateless socialism and 'mixes' of plan and market must also convince us that they are not the real utopians. For if alternatives to the irrationality of Soviet command planning and 'organised anarchy' in the West either appear to be too close to that which exists (and hence constitute no alternative at all) or are so utopian that material resources cannot be adequately co-ordinated and redistributed, then all notions of democracy and pluralism will have a short life. In short, there are very good reasons for believing that a non-market planned society with socialist state institutions offers the best hope of avoiding the desynchronisation of Processes or the disintegration of any future revolutions into new forms of barbarism.

13
The Impossibility of Socialist Pluralism without State Institutions

Socialist pluralism has developed from socialists' desire to avoid the horrors of Stalinism and also from the need to placate the fears of electorates in capitalist countries worried about the 'dictatorship of the proletariat' and the Stalinist implications of other policies of 'Eurocommunist' and 'Eurosocialist' parties. On the one hand we have a concept of socialist pluralism which is put forward by radicals as the basic organisational principle of a socialist society. On the other hand we have the concept of socialist pluralism as a political process, as a constituent element of 'alternative programmes' designed for the slow transition from capitalism to socialism within the framework of a 'mixed economy'. In rescuing the concept of pluralism from its ideological use by American pluralists and other Cold War warriors – who used the term to cover up the class-divided social inequalities existing in capitalist countries – contemporary socialists have yet to agree on the character or vital aspects of socialist pluralism in theory and practice. In recent years many socialists have agreed that economic equality does not equal political equality (Bobbio),[1] or as Habermas puts it: 'Liberation from hunger and misery does not necessarily converge with liberation from servitude and degradation'.[2] The widespread critique of the idea that the nationalisation of private property and simple material redistribution was synonomous with socialism, grew out of the experiences of women, ethnic minorities and millions of workers discriminated against and oppressed by the new 'masters' – who supposedly administered the peoples' nationalised property in a 'socialist' manner.

Yet the demands of numerous social movements to have their own identities, organisations and strategies (in contrast to the traditional control monopolised by vanguard parties) has resulted in radicals confusing the nature of bourgeois political pluralism with socialist pluralism. Discussing the differences between liberal democracy and social democracy, David Beetham argues that there

> are five main dimensions that one can envisage pluralism assuming in a socialist democracy: division of power between centre and locality; division within the economic sphere between plan and market; separation between different sectors or functions of public administration; division between political authority and the legal system; division between political authority and the means of communication. These are not all mutually exclusive dimensions, but overlapping or intersecting ones.[3]

Beetham acknowledges that these five dimensions appear similar to liberal democracy, but goes on to outline the significant differences between the latter and socialist pluralism – especially in relation to the role of popular democracy, private property and self-management. My interest in Beetham's five dimensions of socialist pluralism is related to his discussion of the role of state institutions. For while he believes in self-management, he also sees socialist pluralism as resting on a 'mix' of plan and market. In this respect he joins a majority of contemporary socialists who erroneously believe that market socialism or plan and market can maximise equality and democracy.

Having argued in the previous chapter that popular notions of stateless societies run by workers' councils or self-managed communes were just as unlikely to achieve socialist objectives as the various mixtures of state plans and market mechanisms, I will now try to explain more fully why socialist pluralism cannot survive without the development of socialist state institutions. Rather than using Beetham's five dimensions, I will try to discuss his conceptions of socialist pluralism within the broader perspective of the historical desynchronisation of Processes. For if we are to distinguish between bourgeois pluralism and socialist pluralism, we must consider whether the latter is able to resolve and prevent the crises associated with the historical desynchronisation of Processes within capitalist societies. Most importantly, although I will discuss socialist pluralism in general terms, each society will have to construct its own version of socialism. Just as there is no single form of capitalism, so too, there can be no one ideal-typical form of socialism. Hence, any theory of socialist pluralism will have to confront the following basic problems: the territorial size of socialist institutions at local, national or supranational levels; the institutionalisation of socialist morality through mechanisms which are communicable, not only throughout a new society, but also beyond one generation; the social division of labour which must be able to reconcile 'direct producers' with the rest of the population; the role of military and paramilitary forces in relation to the fundamental issues of domestic law and order and defence against external threat; and finally, the traditional problem of how to achieve socialist pluralism in the 'realm of necessity' as opposed to in the 'realm of freedom'.

Socialism and the Nation-state: The Geopolitics of Socialist Pluralism

When radicals speak of the need for a socialist society, several perennial questions arise: will this society exist within national borders or will it be world-wide?; will it emerge throughout the world simultaneously, or will socialism be implemented unevenly through a lengthy process?; will there be one co-ordinating centre or self-managed decentralisation?; how will inequalities in material and social resources be overcome? Within Marxism the relationship between capitalism and socialism has often been conceptualised in the following schematic terms: bourgeois 'Civil Society' gives rise to the 'capitalist state'; as the capitalist market or 'Civil Society' becomes a 'world market', the overthrow of capitalist society becomes an international struggle; socialism on a world scale is necessary to replace 'world capitalism'; after an appropriate 'transitional period', all the national state apparatuses 'wither away' and a world socialist 'Civil Society' replaces bourgeois 'Civil Society'. As Trotsky put it so clearly, 'the completion of the socialist revolution within national limits is unthinkable .... The socialist revolution begins on the national arena, it unfolds on the international arena, and is completed on the world arena. Thus, the socialist revolution becomes a permanent revolution in a newer and broader sense of the word; it attains completion only in the final victory of the new society on the entire planet'.[4]

Trotskyists and other proponents of 'world revolution' have consistently argued that revolution will not occur simultaneously on a world scale, but only after a process of struggle. The critical factor is that the time gap between the outbreak of revolution on the national arena, and its final completion on 'the entire planet', could be anything from one year, ten years, to twenty, fifty, one hundred or more years. How would the revolutionary forces in one or more nation-states organise the new transitional society in the crucial intervening years? Would not this effectively mean 'socialism in one country' despite the support given by victorious socialists to revolutionaries in other countries? Even if we accept the need to make revolution beyond national borders, the theorists of 'world revolution' still have to explain how they think this transition from national revolution to a 'world socialist society' will be organised. Upon the completion of 'world revolution', would the world be full of workers' councils and federal states? Would 'world socialism' work according to an international super-plan, or market socialism based on regional and national plans or a world parliament of workers' councils?

The existence of desynchronised local, national and supra-national Processes cannot be ignored when considering the short- and long-term implications of national and international strategies and concepts of alternative societies. Despite increasing national interdependence, the enormous growth of international trade and all forms of cultural, financial, scientific and other exchanges between societies, it would be romantic to believe in the possibility of 'world revolution' in the forseeable future. Trotskyists and other proponents of 'world revolution' are constantly citing incidents and struggles in various countries as evidence of increased international solidarity when, in most cases, these events are merely examples of fairly restricted struggles confined to local or national Processes. But the possibility of 'world revolution' is an entirely different question from the fundamental question as to whether socialist pluralism is viable within a 'world socialist society' should this 'world revolution' occur. There are more than enough obstacles confronting the implementation of socialist pluralism within national boundaries, without the added complexity of working out the nature of a 'world society'. One can get the impression from 'world revolutionaries' that the overthrow of capitalism in all countries will, in itself, make socialism viable. While one can readily acknowledge the massive obstacles confronting socialists isolated in one country, this does not mean a 'world socialist society' would be any more successful simply because opposition from 'foreign' capitalist classes were removed. To remove major obstacles is not a substitute for devising alternative institutions which are capable of promoting freedom and equality on a world scale. The successful overthrow of capitalist forces in Russia, China, Vietnam, Cambodia, Ethiopia, etc. has not resulted in peaceful co-operation; and radicals cannot attribute the ensuing conflicts solely to capitalists and Stalinists.

The old debate over permanent revolution of socialism in one country has to be abandoned. Instead, the issue of nationalism or internationalism has to be posed in terms of the desynchronisation of Processes. Can the crises emanating from the desynchronisation of Processes be over-come at the national level? Would an internationally planned world – one which overcame desynchronised Processes – be a realm of freedom or a new 'world tyranny'? The answer to these questions is possible if we first differentiate between two dimensions of nationalism/inter-nationalism: (a) consciousness and morality – that is, the social bases of national and parochial prejudices as opposed to an internationalist or universalistic consciousness and set of moral principles; (b) the geopol-itical bases of internationalism – that is, the institutionalisation of inter-nationalist values and whether national territorial social institutions would prove to be incompatible with 'world socialism'.

If we look at the dimension of consciousness and morality, we can agree with the 'world revolutionaries'' attacks on the deeply entrenched national chauvinistic ideas, so evident in many Social Democratic, Labour and Communist parties. For universalistic values to become hegemonic would, in itself, constitute a revolutionary breakthrough. But the absolute necessity of an internationalist perspective, does not in itself guarantee the maintenance and reproduction of international solidarity if the proposed institutional structures are incompatible with local needs. Universalism and internationalism do not mean monolithic, world-wide control; but all opponents of socialism in one country must be able to show that internationalism can be instituted in a manner which enhances socialist pluralism. Although it cannot be discounted, the chance of a simultaneous world-wide collapse of capitalist production (apart from world war) is remote. I also do not believe that a radical, internationalist consciousness will sweep the world before any possible world-wide collapse of capitalist production. Hence the scenario confronting radicals is one which involves pursuing strategies at national levels which combat the mass popularity of non-universalistic norms based on chauvinistic, sexist and racist practices.

Any real chance of radical social change is most likely to occur at the national level with the possibility of outside support coming from one or more other societies. Therefore it is necessary to work out alterna-tive national and regional institutional structures and policies (which can deal with desynchronised Processes), rather than aim at some pure internationalist 'world society'. More importantly, I do not believe that a 'world socialist society' would survive (if by some chance it emerged very quickly), without the creation of local and national socialist state institutions. The primary task for socialists is therefore to work out alternatives to existing capitalist and Communist societies which are not based on the illusions and weaknesses of models of stateless socialism or versions of market socialism and 'mixes' of plan and market. I have already discussed the dangers of subscribing to these 'alternatives' at the national level. To believe that these stateless socialist or market-socialist plans are viable at the world level, is to believe in a 'socialist' mythology which is both dangerous and illusory. Let me explain.

Let us, for the moment, assume that revolutions have overthrown all existing regimes, so that we can examine the proposed global socialist society. If all national state institutions were replaced by workers' councils, would they all meet in one world-centre after organising all their delegates in a federal or decentralised manner? How would these stateless socialist institutions resolve or overcome the enormous gap between well-endowed and deprived nations or regions? Would there be self-managed local autarchy instead of nationally organised levels of surplus material goods and services for export? If market mechanisms were introduced, how would all the competitive features of market socialism not lead to a re-emergence of the crises of desynchronised Processes? On the other hand, if there was a single central plan for the 'entire planet', this would undoubtedly be the blueprint for a nightmare rather than a pluralist socialist society. Put starkly, all the problems of social redistribution and inequality at a national level would be magnified a thousand times in any unplanned, self-managed stateless 'world socialist society' or one with 'mixes' of market and plan. But a centrally planned world, no matter how democratically constructed, would guarantee the suppression of social diversity, local control and the goal of greater freedom and equality. What will itself be a constant struggle – namely, balancing self-managed social control at decentralised levels with a democratic *national* central plan – would most likely be impossible in a world with billions of people and infinite numbers of parties and social movements all wishing to make decisions. It is one thing to hope for a united federation of national socialist states, each co-operating with one another, yet based on national and local self-administrated plans. It is quite another thing to aspire to an internationalism which postulates a single world society without socialist state institutions – a 'self-managed global village' or alternatively, a 'world socialist market' without capitalist multinational corporations.

The geographical realities of nation-states, especially countries such as Japan, Indonesia or Australia, physically isolated by sea and ocean, make national state institutions a territorial necessity. In Europe, with supra-national movements and structures, the chance of transcending national institutions is perhaps greater than anywhere (especially in relation to the heavy interdependence of Production Processes). But even in Europe, geographical proximity is overshadowed by cultural and institutional rivalry – a critical factor in balancing pluralism with one central European plan. Existing national boundaries may not retain their present form, but it is difficult to imagine that a centrally planned Europe would necessarily be a better than nationally planned socialist countries cooperating and increasing interdependence in a federal socialist Europe. North America and Latin America appear linguistically more homogeneous (apart from significant French- and Portuguese-speaking minorities), but major social inequalities as well as the lack of mass socialist movements makes 'socialism in one country' (apart from Central American states) a remote possibility let alone a pan-continental American socialism. Most of the traditional radical images of how the advanced industrialised countries will help less developed countries to 'skip' historical 'stages' after the 'world revolution' are premised on the belief that socialist institutions in the advanced countries will be relatively unproblematical. But it is not clear whether large industrialised societies will try to be self-sufficient, operate according to plan or market and so forth.

The desynchronisation of Processes directly negates the whole theory of the 'weak link in the chain'. Once the notion of a single 'world capitalist mode of production' is revealed as historical fiction, the strategy of 'world revolution' must confront the reality of historically uneven and desynchronised local and national Processes. Even if the theorists of 'world revolution' were to convince us of the possibility of this revolution, the goal of a 'world socialist society' in which 'the State' withered away would most likely be the negation of socialism. Therefore, it is necessary to invert and modify Trotsky's statement that the socialist revolution 'attains completion' only after the 'world revolution', I would argue that the success of socialist societies throughout the world is unthinkable without the prior construction of alternative socialist state institutions (free of market mechanisms and dictatorial parties) which help to create and reorganise local and national social relations in a manner which is accessible, accountable and reproducable. If national, regional and local solutions are continually relegated to secondary status, or rejected as impossible without 'world revolution', the prospects for new socialist societies emerging are very bleak.

One of the reasons for the popularity of national 'alternative programmes' (despite their glaring weaknesses) is that they are able to escape the abstract and utopian notions of a 'world revolution' which relies on a 'world party' and its member parties, e.g. the Fourth International. If one believes that there is little option but to adopt national strategies (which does not preclude support for international causes wherever possible), then abstract internationalism becomes a liability. For example, given the struggles within local, national and supra-national Production, Credit and Food Production Processes, it is imperative that policies such as import and export controls be implemented – regardless of whether one calls it 'state monopoly of foreign trade'[5] or something else. The dispute over import controls should not be over whether there should be any or not, but rather, which class is to benefit from these controls, and how to prevent them from simply becoming a device to protect profit levels of private enterprises. It is correct for Trotskyists to criticise import controls if these controls are presented in chauvinistic terms, e.g. 'buy British goods'. It is quite another thing to advocate an abstract internationalism which envisages a national trade union movement 'pursuing capital wherever it goes, building an international workers challenge from which it cannot escape'.[6] This romantic championing of international 'combat' conveniently overlooks the military regimes and dictatorships in South Korea and dozens of capitalist countries where capitalist enterprises escape from the pressures exerted in free Electoral Processes.

In recognising that most workers in local and national Production and Food Production Processes are not assembly-line workers in the global 'new international division of labour', that most businesses are small local and national enterprises, and that millions of people work within, or are dependent upon national state institutions which have little to do with other national state institutions, it becomes clear why national solutions must take precedence over an unlikely 'world revolution'. It must be emphasised that I do not believe that all those supra-national problem-elements of various Processes can be smoothly resolved within single national boundaries. This is the bitter reality which radicals must face. Mutual assistance and alliances will have to be built up with other socialist nations or relatively friendly non-socialist societies. There will be no easy path. But not to advocate and struggle for radical change at local and national levels is to resign oneself to an even worse future for the increasing numbers of poor, unemployed and victimised. Above all, radicals must not ignore the basic historical facts that unemployment levels, social welfare policies, social laws, wage levels and so forth, are all related to national policies rather than 'world policies'. Of equal importance, many existing nation-states contain within their boundaries significant national minorities such as the Scots, Catalans, Corsicans, etc. If socialists do not work out socialist pluralist institutional structures within existing countries, then one can forget about the chance of 'world revolution' succeeding. In short, 'internationalism' must first be implemented at home. To postpone the formulation of radical national policies and social institutions for the sake of revolutionising the fictitious 'world mode of production' is to maintain an abstract and illusory purity while immobilising national social struggles.

From Revolution to the Next Generation: The Reproduction of Socialist Values

It appears to me that there is a fundamental gap between the many detailed radical analyses of how capitalist relations and ideologies are reproduced (through a miriad of social institutions), and the relatively few analyses (which are based on simplistic notions) of how socialist relations will supposedly be reproduced in an alternative society. If one believes, as I do, that social relations are not reproduced solely by face-to-face interactions, or spontaneously, then socialists cannot ignore the major issues of how solidarity, equity, universalist norms and other non-parochial relations and values are communicated and reproduced. Many of the alternative radical conceptions of socialism based on decentralised communal control, the absence of national legal, educational, media and political-party structures, assume that socialist values will be cultivated successfully in the context of a radical micro-pluralism. But for diversity to be safeguarded and reproduced, there must be institutions which mediate, consolidate, adjudicate, facilitate, redistribute and hence reproduce not merely local, but also universal values.

Without the creation of new socialist state institutions at local and national levels, it is difficult to comprehend how socialist values of equity and co-operation could survive. Just as market relations in capitalist societies are not solely reproduced by the 'invisible hand', so too, in a socialist society there is a need to face up to the task of how many, and what kind of 'visible institutions' are needed to promote universalistic values. While it is not possible to determine whether people in a socialist society will wish to preserve a distinct set of educational institutions, national print and electronic media outlets, national and/or local cultural institutions and so forth, it is not difficult to imagine the negative aspects of a purely local set of pluralist institutions. One only has to look at the history of Christian churches to see that the local parish as a site of face-to-face conservatism and stagnation gives meaning to the term 'parochialism'. If the various Christian parishes have by and large stagnated, even though they have existed within the framework of national and international organisations, what life-expectancy could we expect of 'socialist parishes' each existing without larger national and international socialist institutions? One could protest that the comparison of religious institutions existing in class societies with socialist communities is irrelevant and unfair. But one does not have to make a literal comparison of Christian and socialist 'parishes' in order to confront the immense problem of how to preserve commitment and growth of socialist values in one generation of people after another.

Diversity and freedom to participate cannot be guaranteed solely by written laws and formal representative structures. But it is more likely than not, that unless egalitarian, non-racist, non-sexist, non-authoritarian and environmentally sensitive values are communicated in more than oral form or immediate practice, then spontaneous, local conceptions of these new values will be in great danger of being misconceived, abused, violated and watered down. It is absolutely essential that legal and representative institutions of a *non-local* stature co-exist with organs of local democracy and participation. As socialists do not believe that disputes between people, groups or regions will disappear, it will be up to citizens to create new socialist state institutions which transcend local councils, communes, factories, offices and farms, so that appeals can be heard, rights preserved and most importantly, a common ethic constructed. If one does not wish to risk having a single vanguard party once again becoming the 'intermediary' between the infinite number of local councils (thus nullifying their power), then it is essential to construct over-arching regional and national state structures which facilitate and guarantee the participation of all parties and organisations.

A number of socialists (such as Heller, Hirst and Poulantzas)[7] have discussed the need for institutions which would protect individual rights in a socialist society. While writing from different methodological and political perspectives, Heller, Hirst and Poulantzas argue against socialists who believe that workers' councils will be adequate to express the wishes of 'the people' and protect them from abuse and threat of dictatorship or Stalinism. Paul Hirst makes a number of pertinent criticisms of those who rely solely on either direct democracy or representative democracy.

He also warns against the danger of misconceiving 'the State' as a homogeneous legal subject (when there are an infinite number of state institutions, each responsible for different social practices). According to Hirst: 'The 'people' *as such* cannot act. Indeed, what the 'people' as a political entity *is* must be defined by specific organisations and by laws.'[8] Heller and Poulantzas also wish to preserve the gains made by liberals and working-class parties within capitalist societies (relating to personal and social freedoms and rights) without defending the private capitalist class system. Hirst, on the other hand, makes some major criticisms of radicals who wish to defend civil rights on the basis of 'natural' or 'absolute' rights. Arguing against 'absolute' rights as a form of individual 'possessiveness', Hirst believes that rights should only be seen in relation to specific historical social practices; that is, individual capacities, sanctioned by laws, can be recognised as rights so long as these rights are not unconditional claims made by one subject against other subjects.[9] In other words, individual rights must be grounded in the context of social practice, rather than legitimised by the appeal to ahistorical, 'natural' or 'absolute' conditions.

While I would agree with Hirst's overall analysis of rights and the need for social laws which go beyond the vague generalities of 'the State' or 'the people', I would, nevertheless, like to stress the difference between 'absolute' rights and universalistic principles. If 'rights' are not to be completely relativised or simply reduced to current social practice, it is important that particular notions of eligibility to participate in institutional decision-making, or the principles determining the operation of social institutions be *explicitly* committed to universalist values rather than exclusive or discriminatory principles based on race, gender, age, etc. Universal values do not have to be grounded in ahistorical, 'natural' or 'absolute' terms. One can justify universal as opposed to parochial values in terms of the need to overcome actual historical practices based on discrimination, exploitation and oppression. Universal values are not absolutes; they are moral constructs which all people in a socialist society would need to uphold if new forms of toleration and democracy were not to be threatened by any form of irrational or exploitative social practice legitimised under the banner of 'pluralism'.

The need to distinguish between universal rights and 'absolutes' is vital if socialists are not to persecute individuals under the banner of 'socialist morality'. Gorz correctly criticises Marx for believing that it was possible for individuals to coincide totally with their social being. As Gorz puts it:

Individual existence can never be entirely socialised. It involves areas of experience which, being essentially secret, intimate, unmediated and incapable of mediation, can never be held in common ... . Insofar as they have postulated that individuals exhaustively coincide with their social being, and that social being realises the full wealth of human capacities, the theories, utopian visions and political practices of socialism have led to a straightforward negation of the individual subject. By negating singularity, doubt, and that area of silence and incommunicability peculiar to affective life, they imply the repression of everything ... . This repressive, inquisitorial, normalising and conformist quality is something that socialist morality has had in common with the social moralities of religious communities, catholic fundamentalism, and military and fascist societies. This has been so because any morality which takes the universal (and the good) as a given, deducing from it what individuals must do and be, is bound to be oppressive and dogmatic.[10]

While I share the general thrust of Gorz's critique, nevertheless, the issue is not as simple as he puts it. It is one thing to criticise all those who believe in a naïve or 'totalitarian' psychology or anthropology which seeks to impose absolute truths for the sake of the 'common and individual good'. But how does Gorz justify the struggle for a democratic socialist society if he is not committed to universal rights? For without universal (as opposed to absolute) categories which transcend the particular and specific manifestations of inequality, unfreedom, etc., how does one ground a commitment to democracy and equality of opportunity? Furthermore, it would not be possible for people to define irrational or 'anti-socialist' practices if prior commitments to the defence of universal rights for women, blacks, etc. were not articulated. While 'socialism' and 'socialist values' are not ready-finished, ideal types or ahistorical 'absollutes' which socialists merely translate into practice, it is inconceivable that social groups wishing to construct a form of socialist pluralism would be able to do so without a minimal commitment to certain universalistic principles. For if socialist pluralist institutions and practices were merely justified on pragmatic grounds (e.g. let everyone 'do their own thing' so long as faction-fighting or social conflict can be minimised), then it would be impossible to tell the difference between bourgeois, laissez-faire pluralism and socialist pluralism.

Within Electoral Processes in capitalist societies, the majority of people are excluded from decision-making in administrative, legal, trade union, media and other cultural, educational, religious and sporting institutions – whether they be state-run, voluntary organisations, private or state-subsidised, privately controlled institutions. The difference between state-run or privately-run institutions is often determined by the degree to which administrative control is either immune from or accountable to public pressure. Depending on the specific history of social struggles, many state-run organisations are often more susceptible to civic lobbying than privately-run institutions. The distinction is not, I have argued, between 'the State', 'Civil Society' and 'the Economy' as separate realms. State institutions are inseparably part of the reproduction of social relations in what has been called 'Civil Society' and 'the Economy'. This will be even more true of socialist societies which abolish all private enterprises (except a tiny minority of simple-commodity producers, crafts people, etc.) When socialists such as Heller argue that it 'the State' swallows society there will be no space left for the exercise of individual rights, she is either perceiving 'the State' as a monolithic subject (with a will and interest of its own) or confusing one-party dictatorship with what she calls 'the State'. For in actuality, state institutions cannot swallow anything. Rather, particular people, or a political party, or a military organisation, may dominate all state institutions, thereby negating pluralism and creating a tyranny.

Any new socialist society will have to be a constant process of creating universal values, while defending and mediating between local and national interests. If wide discrepancies occur between one educational facility and another, between one communal form of settling disputes and another, between levels of income, entitlements to 'social wage' goods and services, or in the nature and form of election, local administation or delegation, then the dynamics of diversity could easily result in new forms of class structures and socially privileged groups. It is for this reason that local control and minimal outside bureaucratic interference must be balanced by the institutionalisation of mechanisms which guard against local tyranny, parochialism, intolerance and income inequalities. Consultation, interdependence and residential movement between one community and another requires explicit written laws, rights and obligations – rather than reliance solely on informal exchanges and personal delegation. It is inconceivable that the construction of a socialist society would be carried out by people all immediately committed to universal values and free of desires to settle old scores or stamp out institutions they personally disliked (e.g. religious institutions). The transition from capitalism to socialism is most unlikely to be accomplished without the creation of nationally co-ordinating, adjudicating and representative bodies.

It is necessary to insist that the fear of 'State' and 'society' being dissolved into one another cannot be alleviated by clinging to the artificial notion of 'Civil Society'. There is no way of comprehending communal resources as being 'outside' 'the State' once large-scale private capitalist property is abolished. Of course, one can subscribe to a naïve belief in spontaneously self-co-ordinating stateless communes, or advocate autonomous market-socialist enterprises (with all their weaknesses) where 'the State' will supposedly be separate from 'the socialist Economy'. But if one recognises the artificial nature of traditional notions of 'the State' and 'Civil Society' (by acknowledging that states are not 'outside' the so-called 'Economy'), and the fact that 'administrative' and 'political' functions will all co-exist with the 'economic' in future state socialist institutions, it becomes clearer why state institutions cannot, and should not 'wither away'.

In arguing that the 'economic', 'administrative' and 'political' will all be part of state institutions, I am not saying that 'political democracy' will be reduced to 'economic democracy' as Bobbio fears. This reduction would make the division of pluralist powers impossible to achieve and would simply be another version of workers' councils or stateless socialism. While it is to be hoped that most of the people who work will also be the decision-makers, it is necessary to recognise that the two roles will not overlap in many instances; decisions will have to be made at several levels, involving both the 'direct' participants as well as non-producers. Yet all of these varying commodity- and non-commodity-producing institutions, community structures, etc. will be part of an expanded socialist state – rather than institutions in 'Civil Society' or 'outside' socialist states. The difficulty in explaining these new forms of socialist institutions is related to our deeply ingrained misconceptions of states as things or subjects; hence it is common to see 'the State' confused with the governing party or regime in references to and warnings about the 'Behemoth State'. In overcoming these misconceptions, it is necessary to recognise the bureaucratic nature of existing pluralist institutions – whether state-run or private – rather than fearing that all-embracing culprit and demon 'the State'.

The problems of constructing structures of participation and control, thereby redefining conventional notions of 'public' and 'private', does not depend on preserving that which does not exist – namely, a separate and distinct sphere of 'Civil Society'. Instead, it has a great deal to do with the social division of labour and the corresponding subdivisions of collectively-owned facilities and resources into local and national institutions which simultaneously promote co-operation and yet maintain checks and balances on one another. In the American or Madisonian concept of checks and balances, the object was to prevent tyranny rather than to promote social equality. Socialist pluralism can be attempted with market socialism, but the consequences will be guaranteed social inequality and very little socialist morality to be admired by the next generation. The difficulty of implementing socialist pluralism (based on checks and balances) with a non-market planned social process, is inseparably related to the power relations between 'direct producers' and the general population and the new social division of labour.

Socialist State Institutions and the Division of Labour

In a critique of Bahro's advocacy of the separation of the League of Communists from the state apparatus, Miliband argues that this simplistic analysis of power 'leaves *the state* in a position of *independent power*, which is precisely what needs to be overcome'.[11] Once again, 'the State' is conceived as a subject – an actor who can accumulate 'independent power' for itself. Bobbio, Miliband, Heller and many others, actually reduce 'the State' to the 'political–administrative machine' and are concerned that 'the bureaucracy' will not act as a coherent 'independent power' *above* the 'will' of the people or the party. Bahro also subscribes to the image of 'the State' as a homogeneous 'bureaucratic subject' which needs to be checked by the League of Communists. In reality, it is rare to find bureaucrats working at all local, regional, federal or central levels (in both capitalist and Communist countries) burying their jealously guarded specific interests for the sake of a common 'bureaucratic interest'. The problem of 'bureaucracy' is not one of an abstract power conflict between two or three homogeneous subjects – for example, 'the State' against 'the party' (both bureaucratic subjects), or 'the State' against an unbureaucratised 'Civil Society'.

As all institutions in a socialist society will be local, regional or national state or public institutions – whether a factory, child-centre, theatre or legislative council – the possibility of a single bureaucracy or party standing over all institutions can only be effectively countered by radically democratising the social division of labour and instituting structural checks and balances. In capitalist societies the constitutional processes of checks and balances are constantly undermined or rendered irrelevant by massive inequality due to private-property ownership, the lack of democracy in Production, Credit and Food Production Processes, and exclusive or limited professional access to many state and private institutions within Electoral Processes – based on qualifications, social hierarchy, income differentials and restricted voting and candidate procedures. All these factors contribute to the desynchronisation of Processes – a situation which checks and balances in socialist institutions must aim to avert. But a socialist society could only institute radical checks and balances (in order to maximise self-management and make it compatible with a national plan) if social inequality and existing divisions of labour were drastically changed.

Many of the obstacles to full social equality in Production, Credit and Food Production Processes can be eliminated by eliminating private property used to employ and exploit wage-labour. But it would be naïve to believe that many of the specialised divisions between mental and manual labour will be quickly overcome. Some may never be overcome. Socialist pluralism, on the other hand, would degenerate into bourgeois pluralism if wide income differentials were maintained, and material inequalities and privileges prevailed. Market socialism would almost certainly maintain many existing occupational and social divisions, as competitive 'socialist' enterprises would be aiming at profitability and technical efficiency. Only a non-market, socialist-planned society could significantly and consistently reduce hierarchical and occupational wage and power differentials without exacerbating internal contradictions – e.g. promoting social equality without worrying about material incentives associated with competitive, market-socialist enterprises.

Despite the necessity of any socialist society breaking with the 'logic' of capitalist productive forces and relations, dismantling major industries, eliminating millions of bureaucratic jobs in existing private and state-run institutions, reorganising millions of unemployed and unpaid people into communally useful roles and services and so forth, this revolution in the existing social division of paid and unpaid labour will *not* reduce all jobs to interchangeable occupations and tasks. The transition from wage-labour to payment-in-kind will be closely related to the degree of local democratic control which tries to overcome major inequalities in job structures and counters tendencies to relapse back into hierarchically exclusive role structures. Without a long period of redistributing resources from well-endowed areas to poor cities and regions, without voluntary or imposed controls on the possible congregation of residents in popular cities or regions (for climatic or cultural factors) at the expense of other geographical areas, there can be little justification for advocating a policy of radical, decentralised self-sufficiency. Theoretically, self-sufficiency would possibly offer the best chance of overcoming hierarchy, bureaucracy and material inequality, through self-regulated balance and minimal external interference – if ecological resources were not abused and if social diversity made possible the dynamic expansion of communal reciprocity and tolerance. But local self-sufficiency is not on the forseeable historical agenda given the likelihood that any socialist society would only emerge from the chaos left behind in capitalist and Communist societies. Therefore, it is necessary to conceive an institutional arrangement where extensive self-management and checks and balances are made compatible with a national plan which at least aims at maximising national self-sufficiency, if not local self-sufficiency.

What should be aimed for is a plurality of overlapping powers (structured vertically and horizontally) which allocate responsibilities and tasks – and yet ensure that these tasks are *not held exclusively* or permanently by the same people, e.g. in representative bodies or in specialised adminstrative centres. These overlapping structures of power must be specified in written constitutions which establish *dual control* by local and national communal institutions so that channels of communication and administration cannot be monopolised by permanent administrators or a vanguard party – no matter how much the latter are committed to democratic principles.

Just as the 'direct producers' must not be permitted to monopolise decision-making (e.g. which goods they would like to produce), so too, the majority of non-'direct producers' must be prevented from administering the 'direct producers' in the everyday workings of an enterprise. Ultimately, the prevention of the tyrannical politicisation of all facets of everyday life by one-party bureaucrats (who lay down the 'correct line'), can be achieved only if the formal powers of *dual* or overlapping control are acted upon and defended by the people. The 'checks' of local interests will be 'balanced' by the need to co-operate with national plans. Planning bodies will be checked by a plurality of social movements as well as the constitutional requirement that they democratically construct at least two national plans which can in turn be subjected to widespread grass-roots debate. Just as the 'direct producers' must see their role as 'associated producers' rather than narrow collective owners, so too, local and national administrators must become 'associated consumers' (either by job rotation or grass-roots pressure), thereby identifying their tasks with the fulfilment of social consumption needs at local and national levels.

At the moment, most proponents of democratic planning are not pluralists, e.g. Trotskyists who advocate 'workerist' solutions or people like Bahro (in *The Alternative*) who believe in pluralist groups within one party rather than multiple organisations. Hence there is a pressing need to promote the idea of democratic central planning which combines with alternative conceptions of state structures at local and national levels; such a broader conception of central and decentralised control must take into account that most people are not 'direct producers' and that pluralistic organisations are needed which guarantee *dual control* over all facets of everyday life. It is important not to confuse the notion of *dual control* with the traditional Leninist strategy of 'dual power'. The strategy of 'dual power' was devised for a pre-revolutionary crisis which is supposed to give rise to numerous workers' councils acting as an alternative power to 'the capitalist state'. It is the vanguard party which links up all these workers' councils and institutes a prolonged period of contestation (as long as several years according to Mandel)[12] within capitalist society. Once the bourgeoisie is defeated, 'dual power' theorists conceive of the need for a 'dictatorship of the proletariat' which will actually consist of numerous councils. How democratic central planning will be implemented by these councils is not revealed. To imagine a *stateless* network of workers' councils spontaneously re-producing the *dual controls* of checks and balances, is to believe that each succeeding generation will be just as aware of the original dangers as the first generation of revolutionaries.

Repressive State Apparatuses and the Dangers to Socialist Pluralism

The strategy of neutralising or gaining the support of military forces in order to implement 'alternative programmes' has to be clearly differentiated from the role of coercive apparatuses in any future socialist society. While I do not believe that one can adequately discuss the role of repressive apparatuses without also taking into account the social background against which a revolution or radical restructuring of society would possibly occur, it is nevertheless possible to analyse long-term objectives as opposed to the constraints (which I will discuss later) arising from 'the realm of necessity'. These long-term objectives have much to do with the preconceived ideas which radicals have about the nature of law and order, e.g. the belief that armies, police, prisons and secret services should either be abolished or retained in different forms. If coercive forces were retained, how would they remain accountable to pluralist institutions; are military and paramilitary apparatuses (which have nearly always been organised along anti-democratic lines) compatible with socialist pluralism? One of the greatest problems facing any socialist movement is the incompatibility of existing forms of highly centralised military weapons systems and apparatuses with the socialist goal of democratic control and decentralisation.

Given my earlier assumptions about socialist societies having to survive within national boundaries rather than depending on a 'world revolution', it is almost certain that some organisation of defence forces will be necessary. While certain countries surrounded by seas, such as Australia, Japan, Britain, etc., may choose effective self-defence by organising mass civil disobedience against any potential invaders, these tactics may prove inadequate against rapid cross-country land invasions. The case for pacifism is only plausible if one believes that socialism can be brought about peacefully and that internal and external counter-revolutionary forces can be neutralised without implementing martial measures. But assuming that the socialist society had a military force, no new socialist society could adequately justify acquiring or retaining nuclear, chemical and bacteriological weapons (given the inherent spiralling effect of arms races), as these are all aimed at other territories rather than for strictly defensive use against external invasion. In any event, it is most unlikely that there could be socialist societies with minimal non-nuclear forces before the contemporary threat of nuclear war was overcome and extensive Europe-wide (and possibly international disarmament) implemented.

The existence of national military forces poses major problems for all supporters of socialist pluralism. In capitalist societies with free Electoral Processes, the military are theoretically kept in check by parliamentary representatives. But the best that democrats can hope for in capitalist countries is that military forces remain constitutional; reform parties are constantly looking over their shoulder, as the intervention by the military in 'civilian affairs' is a well-known historical phenomenon. It is difficult to argue that a local peoples' militia is inherently less threatening than a national military force. The possibility of local 'war lords' emerging in alliance with foreign governments is just as probable as a national military coup d'état. Whether the armed forces are organised along decentralised local lines or at national level, the issue of accountability still remains. A full-time, standing military force – whether made up of volunteers or conscripts – must be made to be morally and institutionally committed to socialist pluralism. Socialist morality could be instilled by integrating armed personnel into the everyday workings of social production and services (when not in training or on border duty). Mechanisms could be devised which divide service duty between 'civilian' and 'defence' duties; a national legislature or federation of council delegates (representing all parties and groups) could hold ultimate sovereign authority. Full- or part-time armed personnel would be eligible to sit on this national council or legislature. The very process of opening up all military units to elections, and of limiting the number of commanding personnel from any one party (e.g. by proportional voting or other such democratic measures), would integrate the armed forces more closely with the socialist pluralist practices existing in the rest of society. All secret service and intelligence organisations would be prohibited. The risk to internal democracy is far greater from security police than from any external threats via subversive agents.

The danger of military forces grasping power – whether they are organised in centralised or decentralised structures – cannot be overcome so long as military forces remain separate, non-democratic institutions. Just as 'direct producers' must become 'associated producers', so too, all people serving in military forces must become 'associated defenders' in that they will be fully integrated as citizens first, and soldiers second. Finally, all military alliances with other countries, as well as exchange of professional military personnel, profitable arms exports and joint military satellite or other such communications would be prohibited. This policy of defensive neutrality would permit direct aid to other national liberation or revolutionary movements (if agreed to by democratic procedure) but would consist of volunteer fighters rather than conscripted soldiers such as Soviet and Cuban troops in Angola or Ethiopia. On the positive side, socialist societies would actively promote regional and international nuclear-free and conventional demilitarised zones. The outrageous militarist and national chauvinist policies of contemporary Socialists and Communist parties in countries such as France, would never make possible the creation of defence forces which were compatible with socialist pluralism. As long as radicals do not successfully attack the interlocking bases of military-industrial production, high technology and authoritarian stuctures, socialist pluralism will remain a utopian vision or a truncated version of bourgeois pluralism.

In capitalist and Communist countries all military, police and other coercive institutions are called repressive apparatuses by radicals. It is clear that any change of name of these armed institutions – e.g. com-

mittees of public safety, peoples' liberation army or workers' courts –
will not in itself transform the role of these apparatuses from institutions
of repression to agents of genuine democratic service and organs to be
used only in the absolute last resort. Most images of stateless socialism
are based on the belief that penal sanctions and all forms of military
forces will be unnecessary in a society committed to resolving issues by
discussion, re-education and tolerance. It is true to say that any future
socialist society which does not strive to maximise these peaceful solutions, will hardly advance democratic values or egalitarian relations.
But all these peaceful solutions presuppose a revolution in consciousness,
the absence of external enemies and the attainment of internal material
equality. While the majority of people would have to believe in radical
universalistic values (if socialism were to be democratically constructed),
this does not account for a significant minority who would continue to
believe in old practices. Moreover, the widespread commitment to radical
domestic practices would not guarantee peaceful international relations.

Supporters of vanguard parties can avoid confronting the problem of
the compatibility of coercive apparatuses with socialist pluralism. This
is because the strategy of 'dual power' puts forward the notion of all
power to local councils, while at the same time falling back on the co-
ordinating and vanguard role of the party. Issues of democratic accountability, relations between individual councils and national forces of the
'dictatorship of the proletariat' are all subsumed under the role of the
party as the organ of proletarian democracy and consciousness. Pluralism
is assumed to exist within the party and the so-called powers of local
councils are suitably invoked by the central committee if these do not
clash with the policies of the vanguard party. In other words, legality,
the use of coercion and the very organisation of democracy are all
accounted for in circular terms via the interpenetration of the party
with the masses.

However, in a society which is based on a plurality of parties and
social movements, clear checks and balances have to be placed upon all
individuals and institutions capable of armed coercion. Domestic law
creation and enforcement should not be solely in the hands of either
local or national institutions. Police forces or other such institutions,
should preferably be organised only at the local level. In contrast to
national institutions of material redistribution, organisations of policing
should be decentralised. This grass-roots form of policing must guard
against the creation of a national police force with its corresponding
forms of hierarchy, career structures, separation from local populations

and potential as a national strategic force. Policing of conflict situations should wherever possible be carried out by local populations in the form of full- or part-time jobs subject to regular replacement (e.g. annual rotation). These part- or full-time police should be kept to a bare minimum in numbers and supplemented by voluntary reinforcements in an emergency.

The potentiality of wide discrepancies in the quality and quantity of local policing can only be checked by the creation of national and regional legal structures and legislatures. Maximum communication between one commune and another over social relations, common problems and so forth, must still be supplemented by socialist state institutions (at higher levels) which hear appeals concerning locally unresolved disputes, police or vigilante abuses as well as appeals resulting from institutional conflicts and clashes over authority rights and material assets. These higher appeal bodies and legislatures could mobilise other local and regional police bodies to enforce laws in the event of a breakdown in local order or a stalemate between local authorities. I have already argued that citizens rights and equity in society as a whole, require legal reference points beyond the local commune. Similarly, local policing must be guided by non-parochial norms. On the other hand, national intervention must be checked by the option of local resolution of problems within a defined time period, followed by external intervention should the injustices or stalemate remain as before. National and regional adjudicating bodies are necessary to counter the harm which could well arise from over-zealous public displays of 'proletarian justice' in workers' courts or other such open forums.

The problem of prisons also transcends the local arena. While the prison population would not be anything near its existing levels in capitalist and Communist countries, there would still remain a tiny hard-core element of murderers, rapists, armed robbers and other violaters of individual and social bodies. If local communities had no appropriate facilities or desire to enforce sentences, then regional or national detention centres would have to be supervised by appropriate national or regional authorities. The protection of prisoner rights, the implementation of educative and rehabilitatory programmes would all have to transcend variations in local standards and prejudices. A prison officer group would have to be strictly separated from any local police forces and kept under constant check by outside social organisations if prisons were not to become once again what they are at the moment. As to the incidence of violent crime, just as schools cannot change a social formation on their own, so too violent crimes such as rape cannot be over-come by education alone. Only a transformation in the power relations and social practices between gender, race and age groups will create a social context where violence and abuse is minimised. The degree of non-violent crime will proportionally diminish as the level of communal solidarity increases – thus making many forms of detention obsolete or counter-productive. On the other hand, failure to implement grass-roots democratic control balanced by national co-ordination and solidarity, will be quickly manifested in the rise of corruption, private interests, token public moralising and widespread black-marketeering and cyni-cism – the hallmark of existing undemocratic 'socialist' republics.

Socialist Pluralism in the 'Realm of Necessity'

The conditions influencing the transition from existing capitalist and Communist societies to any future socialist societies will make the task of implementing socialist pluralism very difficult to say the least. I have distinguished between 'alternative programmes', which advocate socialist pluralism in the context of capitalist 'mixed economies', and socialist pluralism in a non-market, planned society with socialist state insti-tutions. Pluralism, whether bourgeois or socialist, has the greatest chance of success in peaceful conditions. But the crises emanating from the desynchronisation of Processes makes the prospect of a peaceful transition to socialism almost utopian. We must be clear about the potential and actual obstacles confronting advocates of pluralism as a strategy for overthrowing capitalist classes.

First, most 'alternative programmes' accept the broad 'rules' of bourgeois pluralism because these programmes are based on a strategy of forging an anti-monopoly class alliance between workers, competitive sector businesses and others. This anti-monopoly strategy is based on the mistaken belief that the non-monopoly sector bourgeoisie and petty bourgeoisie will at best benefit from 'alternative programmes' or at worst be neutralised into reluctant support. Such illusions discourage extra-parliamentary activity, foster unnecessarily narrow electoral policies and an excessive commitment to existing legal principles and regulations. To believe that a transition to socialism is possible in a parlia-mentary process which permits the rotation in office of conservative parties and socialist parties, is science fiction. The only form of 'pluralism' which is possible in capitalist societies is one which requires all parties and groups to accept those minimal social values compatible with existing private-property requirements. For one cannot have workers' and citizens' control of enterprises and community institutions if the 'formal' constitutional structure of bourgeois pluralism protects private property and corporate body rights. In so far as 'alternative programmes' schizophrenically advocate mass participatory democracy on the one hand, and yet defend bourgeois property rights and laws on the other, it is highly unlikely that socialist pluralism would ever triumph over existing bourgeois pluralism.

Yet if 'alternative programmes' pursued a radical, but peaceful strategy, they would quite likely have to deal with the following anti-pluralist forces and adverse social conditions: (a) the emergence of violent Right-wing movements attempting to create havoc or even stage a coup; (b) the outside chance that nuclear war could be triggered by fanatical Right-wing military or political leaders seeking to destroy radical social movements as 'Russian agents'; (c) the collapse of currency, property, wage and 'social wage' values – thus requiring drastic emergency laws to put an end to potential riots, food hoarding, factory and property occupations and general disorder; and (d) sabotage and subversion by domestic and external anti-radical forces seeking to create disunity among radical social movements by deploying all kinds of 'tricks'. All these frightening prospects are enough to make one think twice about radical action. Unfortunately, all these threats are continually with us, regardless of whether radical action is pursued or not. Those who wish to follow the 'safe and moderate' non-radical line must be able to convince us that bourgeois pluralist relations will not be seriously eroded – if Left reforms are carried out in conditions of serious social depression. For either one surrenders all those policies necessary to combat unemployment and inequality (for the sake of preserving bourgeois pluralism), or one recognises that socialist pluralism can not be constructed within the context of a fragile free Electoral Process constantly threatened by authoritarian and violent social forces.

People are understandably alarmed if one rejects bourgeois pluralism, as the alternative is usually conceived of as military dictatorship or as Stalinist terror. However, an alternative conception of pluralism – a non-bourgeois pluralism – can be developed from the very ideas of 'alternative programme' theorists. For example, 'alternative economic' theorist Giorgio Ruffolo has called for the transformation of a potential coalition of isolated workers, womens' groups, ethnic groups, youth and so forth into an actual coalition. Using the Marxian notion of a 'class in itself' and a 'class for itself', Ruffolo sees the difference between a potential coalition and an actual coalition as the difference between a 'coalition *in* itself' and a 'coalition *for* itself'.[13] Obviously a coalition *for itself* would have to share a minimum consensus while retaining the organisational and social plurality of each original member or party to the coalition. Those parties and groups which refused to be part of the 'coalition for itself' would be allowed to exist after the defeat of major conservative forces providing they did not attempt to violate the minimal conditions agreed to by the coalition movement. Supporters of 'alternative programmes' may immediately reply that the threat of repression against opponents of 'the coalition' would invariably frighten the masses away; or that an intolerance of capitalist class parties and organisations would lead to one-party dictatorship. One can only answer that the 'alternative programme' strategy is itself a major threat to capitalist classes, and it would be stretching credibility too far to argue that the implementation of an 'alternative programme' would not give rise to violent confrontations once bourgeois and petty-bourgeois social forces were increasingly threatened.

Ultimately the prevention of one-party dictatorship depends on the degree of education, toleration and democratic solidarity of a pluralist coalition engaged in social struggle against capitalist relations. Despite all the 'formal' commitments, constitutional documents and promises made by Socialist and Communist parties, there is no reason to believe that these parties would necessarily tolerate disruptive conservative forces or far Left activists (if the Left government had large, popular support). The same is particularly true of military forces together with national bourgeois parties who would also 'overcome' their so-called respect for bourgeois pluralism if an 'alternative programme' were seen to be dangerous. The advantage of non-bourgeois pluralism is that it advances the notion of socialist democracy beyond the notion of bourgeois rights. After all, it has been the 'Eurocommunist' parties who have correctly promoted the view that parliamentary democracy and civil liberties are achievements of the working-class rather than generous gifts bestowed upon society by bourgeois classes. A revolutionary 'coalition for itself' would build upon the historical achievements of social struggles by raising the consciousness of socialist democratic pluralism to a level which went beyond the inherent property and constitutional limits of bourgeois pluralism.

There are two main alternatives to a strategy of building a socialist 'coalition for itself'. These are the old strategies of either building a vanguard party or pursuing gradual reforms. It is true to say that there are powerful arguments in favour of a vanguard party. These arguments are mainly technical arguments. Most revolutions in the twentieth century have been carried out by vanguard, non-pluralist parties organised along military or paramilitary lines. While the vanguard party is able to make quick, tactical changes in strategy in order to counter enemy attacks, the absence of major revolutionary vanguard parties has not resulted in more effective radical opposition from a plethora of competing and hostile social movements. While the discipline and coherence of a vanguard party is very difficult to achieve in a pluralist 'coalition for itself', the price for such discipline is far too high when one looks at the repressive consequences of successful vanguard parties in existing Communist countries. Maybe a 'coalition for itself' will never come into being without a major party playing a central or pivotal role. But the need for major parties is not in dispute. It is the democratic centralism of such parties which is incompatible with a pluralist 'coalition for itself'. Given the major criticisms of vanguard parties and Left parties made by many feminists[14] and other individuals and groups, it would be politically regressive to ignore the positive role which group autonomy can play in achieving social change. A 'coalition for itself' would have to incorporate structures of autonomy and co-operation. However, if a coalition cannot be built before revolutionary change is carried out, the prospects for socialist pluralism after the revolution are very poor.

The other major alternative to a socialist 'coalition for itself' is to believe that (a) bourgeois pluralism will not be eroded; (b) small reforms will resolve the enormous suffering experienced in the world today; (c) piecemeal reforms are better than 'revolutionary chaos', even if they do not resolve major crises; and (d) bourgeois and socialist notions of pluralism will somehow develop in harmony if socialists 'extend' the definition of democracy. I can only regard these positions as recipes for exacerbating the desynchronisation of Processes, or at best, presiding over tiny reforms which perpetuate stagnation – and ultimately extreme measures from either the Right or the Left. If people are ever to build socialist institutions and relations, there is no possible shortcut or by-passing of what is called the 'realm of necessity'. Perhaps the tasks of preventing nuclear holocaust, or the potential collapse of key institutions within national Production, Credit and Food Production Processes, or the need to combat repressive coercive apparatuses, will all make democratic pluralism an impossible luxury in a world struggling to survive? I would like to argue that any democratic alternative which resolves the crises emanating from the desynchronisation of Processes, will only be attainable through the development of mass social movements organised within a 'coalition for itself'. Whether the so-called 'realm of freedom' can ever be attained, is not immediately relevant. But those people who believe socialist pluralism can be achieved peacefully within a 'mixed economy', will find that faith alone is not enough in any historical period – especially the period confronting us all.

Conclusion

So what remains as the alternative to the strategies proposed in 'alternative programmes' traditional strategies of insurrectionism and 'dual power', spontaneous anarchist action or, at the other extreme, elitist terrorist attacks carried out against capitalist institutions and prominent individuals on behalf of 'the proletariat'? In OECD capitalist countries with free Electoral Processes, one of the main tasks is to convince the majority of existing labour and social liberation movements to go beyond 'alternative programmes' without lapsing back into traditional insurrectionist strategies. It would be disastrous to leave people with a choice between the false optimism and naïvety of 'alternative programmes' and the 'workerist' traditionalism of sectarian parties or grouplets. If 'alternative programmes' are not going to resolve the crises emanating from the desynchronisation of Processes, it is up to socialists to attack these limited and unrealistic strategies instead of waiting to be disillusioned (as millions were during the 1960s and 1970s with social-democratic governments).

Major confrontations with capitalist classes in national Electoral, Production, Credit and Food Production Processes cannot be avoided. It is therefore necessary to build a broad 'coalition for itself' which will fight through all the existing local and national parliamentary channels as well as mobilise a mass movement (beyond single-issue oriented politics such as opposition to nuclear war) via extensive extra-parliamentary activities. The strategy of building a 'coalition for itself' should not be confused with the strategy and policies proposed by 'Eurocommunist Left' people such as Claudin, Buci-Glucksmann, Poulantzas and Trentin. It is similar in the sense of endorsing and encouraging extra-parliamentary struggles within Electoral Processes rather than relying solely upon 'respectable' electoral images in order to attract the support of the 'intermediate strata' and small capitalists. Yet it differs from the 'Eurocommunist Left' position on several important grounds. The 'Eurocommunist Left' position is based very heavily on a 'class-theoretical' analysis which almost completely lacks a detailed analysis of the nature of activities within desynchronised Processes. The theory of the 'relative autonomy of the State' has been used to justify the long-term occupation of positions within state institutions (by the pro-letariat) – a 'political space' relatively autonomous of 'the Economy'. However, I argued in chapter 11 that there can be no successful manage-ment of capitalist state institutions (for ten to twenty years) if a radical 'alternative programme' is pursued. Either one adopts the naïve optimism of 'alternative programme' policies (which are prepared to tread very carefully, i.e. conservatively), or one recognises that the successful long-term occupation of positions within state institutions is not solely a 'class-theoretical' issue.

Many of the 'Eurocommunist Left' analyses concentrate on criticising the 'strategic' positions adopted by 'moderate' 'alternative programme' leaders such as Berlinguer and Marchais, e.g. criticisms of the 'watering down' of radical objectives in the quest for electoral success. Rather than putting forward a clear alternative to the anti-monopoly strategy (advocated in 'alternative programmes'), the 'Eurocommunist Left' have said very little about the 'non-industrial working-class' – especially on questions concerning the oppression of women, ecological questions and social welfare alternatives. The lack of critique of 'alternative economic strategies' means that the 'Eurocommunist Left' position appears to espouse the incompatible positions of market socialism and democratic central planning or decentralised self-management. This is because the 'Eurocommunist Left' is torn between believing that 'alternative programmes' based on 'mixed economies' or market socialism can work, and recognising that if capitalist classes do tolerate these reforms they will not be socialist. The 'Eurocommunist Left' has paid little attention to Production, Credit and especially Food Production Processes; hence there is hardly any alternative analysis concerning the need to change consumption patterns (especially those involving the nature of Food Production Processes). Instead we have a 'class-theoretical' analysis of the need for extra-parliamentary structures (which is fine) but hardly any real analysis as to why existing Processes within capitalist societies cannot be used to transform consumption patterns or initiate participatory democracy, within a framework of the 'mixed economy'.

Until recently, the 'Eurocommunist Left' have contributed to the illusory strategy of 'alternative programmes', while the far Left have posed no alternatives other than traditional notions of council democracy, vanguard parties and 'dual power' strategies. One of the main purposes of this book it to point out why misconceptions of 'the State' lie at the base of so many dubious political strategies and alternative conceptions of socialism. Recognising the nature of state institutions as constituent elements of Electoral, Production, Credit and Food Production Processes, involves a comprehensive analysis of the multiple political–economic and socio-cultural roles and relations connecting state institutions to all other social institutions. Most vanguard parties or theorists of 'dual power' work on the assumption that the working-class will confront 'the capitalist State' as an external or separate force. This is also true of radical anti-statists who see social movements as radical forces 'outside' 'the State' and in direct opposition to the parliamentary party system. These perspectives contain a germ of truth, but are fundamentally flawed. The reason for this is that contemporary working-classes and social movements are already part of state institutions – as employees, students, welfare recipients, etc.; they contest existing policies made by other state administrators in the public institutions of local and national Electoral Processes – e.g. in the legislatures, colleges, hospitals, public transport systems, nationalised industries and so forth. The struggle for socialist pluralism is, therefore, not a struggle of 'Civil Society' against 'the State', but a complicated internal struggle within many state institutions, as well as a struggle within private institutions and between state-run and private institutions. It is a struggle to eliminate the dominance of private capitalist enterprises, to extend the public domain within society and thus subject this extended sphere of public institutions to radical democratic control.

If we are to have a better informed and more realistic Left, then it is up to each national 'coalition for itself' to confront the task of specifying in detail (a) which pluralist, *dual controlled* regional and national state structures and forums will have to be created beyond the rudimentary grass-root levels of workers' councils; (b) how self-sufficient, dependent or interdependent democratically planned local and national Production and Food Production Processes (within national boundaries) can become – given the almost certain disruption and instability created by other national and supra-national capitalist classes; (c) how Food Production and Production Processes can be restructured away from the present disastrous trends, given the likelihood that foreign aid and co-operation will be minimal; (d) what type of income support schemes, community welfare services, alternative labour processes and work options will be needed for millions of unemployed and unpaid workers in order to revolutionise existing social conditions.

A radical socialist manifesto requires years of mass mobilisation by a 'coalition for itself'. The respective parties and social movements of this 'coalition' are too weak to achieve success on their own. But their single- or multiple-issue campaigns form the basis of a socialist pluralist programme. Struggles for some of the policies currently advocated in 'alternative programmes' should be actively encouraged. But the struggle for jobs, anti-discriminatory social legislation, nationalised industries, improved 'social wage' services and so forth, should be stripped of all their surrounding illusions. In contrast to 'alternative programmes', it must be recognised that most of these reforms *will exacerbate the crises of desynchronised Processes* rather than provide solutions to contemporary social problems. A radical socialist pluralist programme cannot be implemented within the framework of existing Processes. State and private institutions within Electoral, Production, Credit and Food Production Processes can serve as models and examples of what have to be changed; their specific social relations and organisation of material resources (e.g. existing social laws, industrial structures, etc.) are the starting point of local and national alternative plans. Each active member in a radical 'coalition for itself' must become aware of how short- or long-term proposals for change either contribute to existing desynchronisation of Processes or form the basis for a resolution of these crises. Such an overall understanding of the relation between local, national and supra-national Processes will, I hope, lead to closer collaboration between individual and group members of any national coalition.

Ultimately, a mass-based 'coalition for itself' would either win a national election and implement a sweeping revolutionary programme, or else precipitate major confrontation well before any election is possible. This may appear as abstract 'ultra-Leftism' to many supporters of 'alternative programmes', but one can only reply that 'alternative programmes' are already depicted as 'extremist' by bourgeois parties, the media and employers' federations. There has been a marked tendency in recent years for many socialists to become less radical precisely at that point in time when conditions require far more than existing 'alternative programmes' have to offer.

The optimism of the Left during the early 1970s has been replaced by a sense of despair, *ad hoc* responses (signifying the phenomena of pessimism and drift) and near paralysis in the face of what is depicted as the power of 'international capital'. For example, Barry Hindess criticises even 'alternative programmes' for being too radical and out of step with conservative electorates. According to Hindess, 'The successful management of the British economy is an important and worthwhile objective for the Labour Party and one that will be difficult enough to satisfy.'[1] This latter view is also widely held within Left parties in other countries. Yet the aim of 'successfully managing capitalism' represents 'dead-end politics'. Once socialist movements lose any sense of replacing capitalist institutions with socialist alternatives, it is only a matter of time before small piecemeal alternatives come to resemble the stagnant policies of Callaghan and Schmidt. While there is no doubt that Left reform parties have had a much greater commitment to civil liberties, social consensus and social welfare than recent conservative governments, nevertheless both Left and Right governments have done very little to reverse the tide of de-industrialisation and general stagnation. Hindess may be correct in saying that Left activists are out of step with the masses, but when was this ever not the case. The main difference between the Left of today and the Left of the 1930s is that the contemporary Left lacks the certainty of a new-found faith which the Left of earlier decades possessed. Having justifiably rejected many of the old Left views and practices, the contemporary Left are faced with the choice of either adjusting to social agendas already largely determined by existing capitalist domination of institutional life, or promoting new alternatives which break the downward spiralling effects of desynchronised Processes. One thing is for sure, the next decade will sorely test the capacity of Socialist, Communist and Labour parties. It is difficult to see how, in deteriorating social conditions (especially the erosion of large sections of the industrial workforce through unemployment) these parties can be spared from internal disruption and major conflict. If they adhere to cautious 'alternative programmes' they will lose support in subsequent elections for failing to resolve major social crises; yet if these parties respond with much more radical policies they will be attacked by capitalist classes for being 'revolutionaries'. The political position known as 'ultra-Leftist' may soon lose its claim to be an exclusive label.

As for the near paralysis of reform-oriented governments in the face of supra-national pressures, these obstacles will continue to exist regardless of whether policies pursued are conservative or radical. To wait for 'world revolution' is to wait a very long time indeed. To pursue a

'Euro-Keynesian' reflation of more than one country is to postpone temporarily confronting the underlying causes of contemporary crises as well as shifting the problems on to other countries. Many conservative-and reform-oriented plans for overcoming 'stagflation' are based on developing new industries which can compete in international markets. If the greater part of new productive capacity is built for supra-national rather than national consumption, it is highly likely that the failure of export-led recoveries to eventuate will leave individual national Processes in a much weaker state than at present. Without a clear policy specifying the creation of new industries that will be primarily oriented to local and national consumption, the restructuring of present national industrial capacity along supra-national lines will make any alternative national plans almost impossible to implement.

Given the unlikely occurrence of 'world revolution', this means that the Left must pursue neo-autarkic policies if little or no co-operation or assistance is forthcoming from other societies. This means openly espousing and preparing people for policies which would most likely result in many existing consumer goods becoming scarce; it would also mean developing plans which involved shifting the heavy reliance upon money wages to new and more extensive forms of payment in kind (e.g. more 'social wage' goods and services') to compensate for any reduction in wage levels. The significant (but by no means total) reduction in export income would inevitably mean less imported goods and the need for greater reliance upon national resources. While such a radical pro-gramme would be extremely difficult to promote, it nevertheless con-stitutes one of the few alternatives to the current phenomenon of fatalistic 'mechanical-socialism' which immobilises people until the power of 'international capital' is overthrown or 'harnessed'. The more people begin to rely upon a short-term international solution or reflation, the less likely are we to see radical alternatives to existing forms of life-style, stagnation and oppression. Until radicals apply themselves to thinking about the feasibility of neo-autarkic alternatives, we shall not know whether particular nations are capable or incapable of pursuing such a strategy – depending on the availability of natural and industrial resources, skills and other social assets. Nearly all the existing 'alternative programmes' stress the need for caution in order to avoid the twin horrors of Stalinism and new forms of 'fascism'. Yet the continuation of current levels of consumption enjoyed by populations in OECD countries is already paid for by the oppressed millions in the Third World. Social democratic support for parliamentary democracy in countries such as South Korea or Indonesia will not overcome deep-seated exploitation if little change occurs within OECD countries – especially if reform governments pursue the existing forms of production, growth targets and export-led recoveries at the expense of Third World countries. In proposing a neo-autarkic strategy, the Left would be forced to evaluate which industries, resources, income and export commodities could be compatible with non-exploitative social relations. Radical solutions at the national and local level should not be confused with indifference and national chauvinism.

I am acutely conscious of the unpleasant options confronting those who come to terms with the nature of desynchronised Processes. Generally speaking, Marxists analyse capitalist societies with a view to pointing out evidence which might indicate future crises or even collapse. Apologists for capitalist relations are often characterised by the opposite perspective – that is, the self-confidence that major problems will be ironed out because capitalist societies will somehow last forever. If my analysis is much closer to the former rather than the latter, it is only because it is impossible to ignore the overwhelming evidence which points to a lengthy period of bitter confrontation. The fact that 'alternative programme' theorists can acknowledge many signs of de-synchronisation, and yet remain optimistic about their non-confrontationist strategy, is something which, perhaps, cannot be explained by reason alone.

One thing is certain, those who argue that capitalist societies can survive temporary 'cyclical' downturns, and those who argue that the current crisis is historically and qualitatively different to earlier recessions, cannot both be right. Empirical research and endless statistical pronouncements show that a number of important indices such as over-capacity in key industries, falling profits rates in leading OECD countries, persistently high inflation rates, revenue scarcity, increasing unemployment and poverty, etc., etc. cannot be ignored by proponents of reforms. There is a rough consensus between nearly all bourgeois and radical theorists and politicians, that the 'room' available to capitalist classes to sustain profitable production is shrinking, and that expanded state services and 'social wage' goods cannot be accommodated without shifting the balance of social power in favour of national proletarian classes. Conservative parties respond by cutting existing levels of state expenditure, Right-wing Social Democrats content themselves with conservative policies with a 'human face' and radicals call for the overthrow of capitalist societies. It is only the supporters of 'alternative programmes' who defy the general consensus and believe that major reforms can be instituted within capitalist 'mixed economies'. If one believes that 'window-dressing' reforms by Right-wing Labour and Social-Democratic parties will be utterly inadequate in relation to the enormity of suffering and social problems, then the only choice is between 'alternative programmes' or radical transformation beyond the 'mixed economy'. To believe, as many bourgeois, and some radical writers, that the next long wave – supposedly to commence at the end of the 1980s – will resolve the current crises of desynchronisation, is to subscribe to secular versions of the fairy godmother who will solve everything 'tomorrow'.

There can be no successful restructuring of capitalist societies without a restructuring of state institutions. This reorganisation of Electoral, Production, Credit and Food Production Processes is mainly being carried out by Right-wing political forces. In so far as existing Left parties, trade unions and social movements fail to appreciate the constituent roles which state institutions play within local, national and supra-national Processes, we face either the repetition of earlier mistakes and narrow misconceptions, or else one of false optimism about the possibility of a smooth transition to socialism. But if we become increasingly aware of the dominant misconceptions of state institutions, of the need to redefine and thoroughly restructure the role and nature of these institutions in an alternative society, rather than simply hope that all these institutions will 'wither away', then the preliminary steps to a new form of radicalising practice may emerge. It is for these reasons that the 'recognition' of states is long overdue. To go 'beyond' the generality of 'the State' is to become critical of traditional Left theories, to engage in struggle and to devise strategies for the creation of humane and rational societies.

Notes and References

1. Identifying the Problems

1. B. Brecht, 'The Other Germany' (1943), *Gesammelte Werke*, vol. XX (Frankfurt: Suhrkamp, 1967) pp. 283-9.
2. P. Valery, *History and Politics*, trans. D. Folliot and J. Mathews (London: Routledge & Kegan Paul, 1962) pp. 219-20.
3. A. Gramsci, *Selections from the Prison Notebooks*, ed. and trans. Q. Hoare and G. N. Smith (New York: International Publishers, 1971) p. 276.
4. H. Marcuse, *An Essay on Liberation* (Boston, Mass.: Beacon Press, 1969).
5. C. Lasch, *The Culture of Narcissism* (New York: Warner Books, 1979).
6. M. Foucault, *Discipline and Punish*, trans. A. Sheridan (London: Allen Lane, 1977).
7. R. Miliband, *The State in Capitalist Society* (London: Weidenfeld & Nicolson, 1969); and N. Poulantzas, *Political Power and Social Class* (London: New Left Books, 1973), first published in France in 1968.
8. J. O'Connor, 'The Fiscal Crisis of the State Revisited', *Kapitalistate*, no. 9, 1981, p. 47.
9. Ibid.
10. For a full discussion of misconceptions of 'the State' as ideal type, subject, thing and derivative part of capital, see my 'Identifying Dominant Misconceptions of States', *Thesis Eleven*, no. 4, 1982, pp. 97-123.
11. See, for example, G. Therborn, *What Does The Ruling Class Do When It Rules?* (London: New Left Books, 1978).
12. See, for example, S. Wilhelm, 'The Rise of State Rule: An Exploratory and Interpretative Essay', *Catalyst*, no. 9, 1977, pp. 1-58.
13. See, for example, G. Esping-Andersen, R. Friedland and E. Wright, 'Modes of Class Struggle and the Capitalist State', *Kapitalistate*, nos. 4-5, 1976, pp. 186-220.

14. See J. Holloway and S. Picciotto (eds), *State and Capital* (London: Edward Arnold, 1978).
15. See Lasch, *The Culture of Narcissism*; M. Foucault, 'On Governmentality', *Ideology and Consciousness*, no. 6, 1979, pp. 5–21; and J. Donzelot, *The Policing of Families*, trans. R. Hurley (New York: Pantheon Books, 1979).

2. Against the 'Holy Trinity' of 'The State', 'Civil Society' and 'The Economy'

1. K. Marx, *The German Ideology*, reprinted in L. Easton and K. Guddat (eds), *Writings of the Young Marx on Philosophy and Society* (New York: Anchor, 1967) p. 469.
2. A. W. Gouldner, *The Two Marxisms* (London: Macmillan, 1980) p. 371.
3. A. Heller, 'Past, Present, and Future of Democracy', *Social Research*, vol. 45, no. 4, Winter 1978, p. 882.
4. See A. Arato, 'Civil Society Against the State: Poland 1980–81', *Telos*, no. 47, Spring 1981, pp. 23–47.
5. See ibid for quotations from Kuron, Smolar, Rupnik and others. Also see M. Markus, 'Understanding Poland', *Thesis Eleven*, no. 3, 1982, pp. 41–51.
6. For an example of the misconception of 'the State' and 'Civil Society' as subjects, see A. Arato, 'Empire vs Civil Society: Poland 1981–82', *Telos*, No. 50, Winter 1981–2, pp. 19–48 – especially p. 26 where Arato discusses the events in terms of the unstable situation which 'must lead to either society or state moving to abolish the other's institutions'.
7. See N. Poulantzas, *Political Power and Social Classes* (London: New Left Books, 1973) p. 128 and L. Althusser, *Lenin and Philosophy and Other Essays* (London: New Left Books, 1971) pp. 121–73.
8. For further discussion and critique of 'Ideological State Apparatuses', see my 'On the State of the State', *Theory and Society*, vol. 7, nos 1–2, 1979, pp. 199–242.
9. See J. Habermas, 'The Public Sphere', *New German Critique*, no. 3, 1974, pp. 49–55 and E. Knodler-Bunte, 'The Proletarian Public Sphere and Political Organization: An Analysis of Oskar Negt and Alexander Kluge's *The Public Sphere and Experience*', *New German Critique*, no. 4, 1975, pp. 51–75. Habermas's seminal book on the 'Public Sphere' remains untranslated in English as does most of the German debate on this important area.
10. See Knodler-Bunte, 'The Proletarian Public Sphere and Political Organization' for one of the few accounts of Negt and Kluge's book, *Öffentlichkeit und Erfahrung; Zur Organisationsanalyse von bürgerlicher und proletarischer Öffentlichkeit* (Frankfurt am Main, 1973).
11. P. Anderson, 'The Antinomies of Antonio Gramsci', *New Left Review*, no. 100, 1977, pp. 5–78.

12. J. Urry, *The Anatomy of Capitalist Societies: The Economy, Civil Society and the State* (London: Macmillan, 1981).
13. Ibid, p. 106.
14. Ibid, p. 153.
15. V. Navarro, 'The Nature of Democracy in the Core Capitalist Countries: Meanings and Implications for Class Struggle', *The Insurgent Sociologist*, vol. X, no. 1, 1980, p. 9.
16. Ibid, pp. 5-6.
17. Urry, *The Anatomy of Capitalist Societies*, pp. 102-5.
18. See E. M. Wood, 'The Separation of the Economic and Political in Capitalism', *New Left Review*, no. 127, May-June 1981, p. 1.
19. Ibid, p. 89. Another typical example of the continued separation of 'the Economy' from 'the State' is S. Aaronovitch, R. Smith, J. Gardiner and R. Moore, *The Political Economy of British Capitalism: A Marxist Analysis* (London: McGraw-Hill, 1981) in which the authors draw a model to show how 'the Economy' is separate from 'the State' (p. 93).

3. From 'Civil Society' to 'World Capitalism: The Reduction of State Institutions to Non-Economic Superstructures'

1. See R. Luxemburg, *The Accumulation of Capital* (London: Routledge & Kegan Paul, 1963). For more recent discussions of Marx's schema, see D. Harris, 'On Marx's Scheme of Reproduction and Accumulation', in M. C. Howard and J. E. King (eds), *The Economics of Marx* (Harmondsworth: Penguin Books, 1976) ch. 20, and M. Morishima, *Marx's Economics* (Cambridge University Press, 1973); also see E. Mandel, *Late Capitalism* (London: New Left Books, 1975) ch. 9, and P. Baran and P. Sweezy, *Monopoly Capital* (Harmondsworth: Penguin Books, 1968) on military production and accumulation.
2. I. Gough, *The Political Economy of the Welfare State* (London: Macmillan, 1979) Appendixes B and C.
3. See K. Marx, *Capital*, vol. 2 (New York: International Publishers, 1967) p. 395.
4. Ibid.
5. Ibid, pp. 402-11.
6. Ibid, p. 458.
7. Ibid, p. 348.
8. See Gough, *The Political Economy of the Welfare State*, pp. 158-66.
9. See Mandel, *Late Capitalism*, ch. 9.
10. For a list of key military contractors to the United States Pentagon see M. Reich and D. Finkelhor, 'Capitalism and the Military-Industrial Complex', in R. Edwards, M. Reich and T. Weisskopf (eds), *The Capitalist System* (Englewood Cliffs, NJ: Prentice-Hall, 1972) pp. 392-406.
11. M. Aglietta, *A Theory of Capitalist Regulation*, trans. D. Fernbach (London: New Left Books, 1979).

12. See ibid, pp. 99–110.
13. Ibid, p. 32, where Aglietta reduces the whole United States state sector to 'a part of the very existence of the wage relation', i.e. as a 'consumer' of Department II.
14. E. Mandel, *The Second Slump*, trans. J. Rothschild (London: New Left Books, 1978) p. 169. Also see Mandel's 'flexible' analysis of the origins of crises in Departments I or II, in Introduction to *Capital*, vol. 3 (Harmondsworth: Penguin Books, 1981) p. 50.
15. See E. Mandel, Introduction to *Capital*, vol. 2 (Harmondsworth: Penguin Books, 1978) p. 28.
16. Ibid, p. 29.
17. Ibid, pp. 29–30.
18. See E. Mandel, 'The Industrial Cycle in Late Capitalism', *New Left Review*, no. 90, 1975, p. 8.
19. J. O'Connor, *The Fiscal Crisis of the State* (New York: St. Martin's Press, 1973) chs 4, 5 and 6.
20. See Gough, *The Political Economy of the Welfare State*, p. 160.
21. R. Rosdolsky, *The Making of Marx's 'Capital'* (London: Pluto Press, 1977) p. 467.
22. Ibid, pp. 467–8.
23. See B. Fine and L. Harris, 'The Debate on State Expenditure', *New Left Review*, no. 98, 1976, p. 105. Also, in their work, *Rereading 'Capital'* (London: Macmillan, 1979) p. 71, they attack other orthodox Marxists such as Mandel for trying to document empirically the fall in the rate of profit. Fine and Harris argue that Marx's law 'refers to an abstract tendency not an empirical tendency'! If this is the case, then Aglietta, Mandel and others are wasting their time trying to show empirically that the rate of profit depends on a particular equilibrium or disequilibrium between Departments I and II.
24. M. Folin, 'Public Enterprise, Public Works, Social Fixed Capital', *International Journal of Urban and Regional Research*, vol. 3, no. 3, 1979, p.356.
25. L. Trotsky, *The Permanent Revolution and Results and Prospects* (New York: Merit Publishers, 1979) p. 146.
26. See F. Frobel, J. Heinrichs and O. Kreye, *The New International Division of Labour* (Cambridge University Press, 1980) ch. 2, p. 33. There are far too many articles and books by radicals on the 'global factory', the 'world economy' and other such ideal-typical or general boundaryless concepts. Here are a few examples of the different exponents of this simplified approach. (a) Orthodox Marxist: L. Harris, 'The Balance of Payments and the International Economic System', in F. Green and P. Nore (eds), *Economics: An Anti-Text* (London: Macmillan, 1977) ch. 8; (b) radical non-orthodox Marxist: R. J. Barnet, *The Lean Year: Politics in the Age of Scarcity* (New York: Simon & Schuster, 1980); (c) Wallerstein's 'world-system' theorists: C. Chase-Dunn and R. Rubinson, 'Toward

a Structural Perspective on the World System', *Politics and Society*, no. 4, 1977, pp. 453–76. This latter school divides the world into stereotypical patterns: 'The industrial–commercial block in core states produces strong states, while the export-oriented block in peripheral states produces weaker states' (p. 470). In recent years radicals have strongly criticised the weaknesses of Frank's 'dependency' theory, Amin's 'accumulation on a world scale', Wallerstein's and Emmanuel's 'world-system' and 'unequal exchange' theories not to mention the 'classic' theories of imperialism put forward by Lenin, Bukharin and Kautsky. One of the major reasons for the convulsion in 'imperialist' studies is the growing recognition of the complexity of state institutions and their interaction with private capital in the accumulation processes of so many modes of production. Despite the rejection of many of their arguments on epistemology, history, classes, etc., I am largely in agreement with the points made by Cutler, Hindess, Hirst and Hussain concerning the nature of the 'national economy', in *Marx's 'Capital' and Capitalism Today*, vol. 2 (London: Routledge & Kegan Paul, 1978) pp. 243–53. After completing this book, I noted Michel Aglietta's article, 'World Capitalism in the Eighties', *New Left Review*, no. 136, 1982, pp. 5–41, which pointed to the decisive role of uneven national economies – despite the inappropriate title of his article.

27. See, for example, N. Harris, 'Crisis and the Core of the World System', *International Socialism*, no. 10, 1980-1, p. 25.
28. See S. Amin, 'The Class Structure of the Contemporary Imperialist System', *Monthly Review*, January 1980, pp. 9–26; also C. Palloix, 'The Self-Expansion of Capital on a World Scale', *Review of Radical Political Economics*, vol. 9, no. 2, 1977, pp. 1–28. For a perceptive critique of Amin's work, see S. Smith, 'The Ideas of Samir Amin: Theory of Tautology? ', *Journal of Development Studies*, vol. 17, no. 1, 1980, pp. 5–21.
29. A. de Janvry and C. Garramon, 'The Laws of Motion of Capital in the Center–Periphery Structure', *Review of Radical Political Economics*, vol. 9, no. 2, 1977, pp. 29–38. This quote is from p. 29 and is the opening to another example of 'world capitalist' analysis which blurs and reduces social relations and state institutions to uniform processes.
30. See N. Harris, *Of Bread and Guns* (Harmondsworth: Penguin Books, 1983) for a simplistic analysis of 'the State' and other topics. For Wallerstein's view, see the quotation used by S. Jonas and M. Dixon, 'Proletarianization and Class Alliances in the Americas', in T. Hopkins and I. Wallerstein (eds), *Processes of the World-System* (London: Sage, 1980) p. 238. For a strong critique of 'world-system' theory, see V. Navarro, 'The Limits of the World Systems Theory in Defining Capitalist and Socialist Formations', *Science and Society*, Spring 1982, pp. 77–90.

31. See, for example, S. Amin, G. Arrighi, A. Gunder Frank and I. Wallerstein, *Dynamics of Global Crisis* (London: Macmillan, 1982) p. 236.
32. N. D. Kondratieff, 'The Long Waves in Economic Life' (1926) reprinted in *Review*, no. 4, Spring 1979, pp. 519-61.
33. E. Mandel, *Long Waves of Capitalist Development* (London: Cambridge University Press, 1980) p.11.
34. Ibid, p. 7.
35. Mandel, *Late Capitalism*, p. 120.
36. Research Working Group on Cyclical Rhythms and Secular Trends, 'Cyclical Rhythms and Secular Trends of the Capitalist World Economy: Some Premises, Hypotheses and Questions', *Review*, Spring 1977, pp. 483-500.
37. A. Bergesen, 'Cycles of Formal Colonial Rule', in Hopkins and Wallerstein (eds), *Processes of the World-System*, p. 122.
38. See W. W. Rostow, *The World Economy: History and Prospect* (London: Macmillan, 1978) ch. 54 where Rostow discusses the fifth Kondratieff upswing which nevertheless involves serious problems getting off the ground. Also see I. Wallerstein, 'The Future of the World-Economy', in Hopkins and Wallerstein (eds), *Processes of the World-System*, p. 179, and E. Hobsbawm, 'Looking Forward: History and the Future', *New Left Review*, no. 125, 1981, p. 14. Hobsbawm is, however, not so confident that a new long wave has already started. See E. Hobsbawm, 'The Development of the World Economy', *Cambridge Journal of Economics*, vol. 3, September 1979, p. 317.
39. See Rostow, *The World Economy: History and Prospect*, pp. 298-9.
40. Mandel, *Long Waves of Capitalist Development*, p. 8.
41. K. Barr, 'Long Waves and the Cotton-Spinning Enterprise 1789-1849', in Hopkins and Wallerstein (eds), *Processes of the World-System*, p. 87.
42. N. Bousquet, 'From Hegemony to Competition: Cycles of the Core?', in Hopkins and Wallerstein (eds), *Processes of the World-System*, p. 46.
43. Wallerstein, 'The Future of the World-Economy', pp. 167-80.
44. J. E. Cronin, 'Stages, Cycles and Insurgencies: The Economics of Unrest', in Hopkins and Wallerstein (eds), *Processes of the World-System*, p. 112.
45. A. Bergesen, 'Cycles of Formal Colonial Rule', p. 123.
46. See Mandel, *Long Waves of Capitalist Development*, pp. 51-5.
47. Mandel, *Long Waves of Capitalist Development*, p. 21.
48. Ibid.
49. Ibid, pp. 127-8 and Mandel, *Late Capitalism*, pp. 115-22.
50. Mandel, *Long Waves of Capitalist Development*, p. 9.
51. B. Rowthorn, 'Late Capitalism', *New Left Review*, no. 98, 1976, p. 79.
52. Mandel, *Long Waves of Capitalist Development*, p. 29.
53. Rowthorn, 'Late Capitalism', pp. 63-9.

54. Mandel, *Long Waves of Capitalist Development*, p. 65.
55. Ibid, p. 49.
56. See D. Gordon, 'Stages of Accumulation and Long Economic Cycles', in Hopkins and Wallerstein (eds), *Processes of the World-System*, p. 14. For Gordon, 'the structure of the state' is only one of other variables necessary for accumulation. In distinguishing 'the State' from 'economic' variables such as 'the financial structure', etc. Gordon merely subscribes to the old dichotomy of 'the political' and 'the economic'.
57. See Wallerstein, 'The Future of the World-Economy'.
58. See R. B. Day, 'The Theory of Long Waves: Kondratiev, Trotsky and Mandel', *New Left Review*, no. 99, 1976, p. 78.
59. The most comprehensive non-Marxist analysis of long waves is J. J. van Duijn's book *The Long Wave in Economic Life* (London: Allen & Unwin, 1983); van Duijn displays a highly positivistic and narrow economistic analysis of social change.

4. Electoral Struggles: The Limits of 'Political Business Cycle and 'Class-Theoretical' Analyses

1. See, for example, S. Menshikov, *The Economic Cycle: Postwar Developments* (Moscow: Progress, 1975).
2. A. Neuberg (alias O. Piatnitsky), *Armed Insurrection* (1928) trans. Q. Hoare, republished (London: New Left Books, 1970) p. 37.
3. B. Ollman, *Alienation: Marx's Conception of Man in Capitalist Society*, 2nd edn (Cambridge University Press, 1976) pp. 213-14, first published 1971.
4. Ollman is not alone in confusing or reducing surplus-value to an activity or condition outside the labour process. Paul Robinson attempted the same faulty equation with Marcuse's notion of 'surplus-repression' - see P. Robinson, *The Freudian Left* (New York: Harper & Row, 1969) p. 203. However, surplus-value is not equivalent to 'surplus repression' in that both are produced or conditioned by quite different social relations; also, surplus-value extraction will not disappear in a socialist society, rather the manner of extraction will change as will the distribution of the surplus - from private capitalist appropriation to one of social distribution based on need and equity.
5. C. Offe, 'Advanced Capitalism and the Welfare State', *Politics and Society*, Summer 1922, p. 484.
6. See J. D. Stephens, *The Transition from Capitalism to Socialism* (London: Macmillan, 1979) chs 4 and 5; G. Esping-Andersen, 'Comparative Social Policy and Political Conflict in Advanced Welfare States: Denmark and Sweden', *International Journal of Health Services*, vol. 9, no. 2, 1979, pp. 269-93; G. Esping-Andersen, 'Social Class, Social Democracy, and the State', *Comparative Politics*, October 1978, pp. 42-58; F. Castles and R. D. McKinlay,

'Public Welfare Provision, Scandinavia, and the Sheer Futility of the Sociological Approach to Politics', *British Journal of Politics*, vol. 9, 1979, pp. 157–71.

7. See M. Kalecki. 'Political Aspects of Full Employment', republished in *Selected Essays on the Dynamics of the Capitalist Economy 1933–1970* (London: Cambridge University Press, 1971).

8. Ibid, p. 141.

9. Ibid, p. 143.

10. Even those few radical analyses such as R. Boddy and J. Crotty, 'Class Conflict and Macro-Policy: The Political Business Cycle', *Review of Radical Political Economics*, vol. 7, no. 1, 1975, pp. 1–19 and D. A. Hibbs, 'Political Parties and Macro-economic Policy', *American Political Science Review*, vol. 71, 1977, pp. 1467–87 have either concentrated on labour/capital relations or narrow econometric evaluations of political parties in government *vis-à-vis* such things as the Phillips curve. There have been no analyses of the effects upon the internal structure of state apparatuses and the level and range of state sectors' roles by social movements in free Electoral Processes. Thus, Boddy and Crotty concentrate on the 'business cycle' rather than telling us much about either the nature of politics or the nature of state institutions. Hibbs, on the other hand, merely carries out a survey of Left or Right parties in office and their policies on higher unemployment or higher inflation options rather than treating state institutions and struggles in private institutions in a comprehensive manner.

11. See W. D. Nordhaus, 'The Political Business Cycle', *Review of Economic Studies*, vol. 42, 1975, pp. 169–90; B. Frey, *Modern Political Economy* (Oxford: Martin Robertson, 1978); B. Frey and F. Schneider, 'An Empirical Study of Politico-Economic Interaction in the United States', *Review of Economics and Statistics*, vol. LX, May 1978, pp. 174–83; C. Duncan MacRae, 'A Political Model of the Business Cycle', *Journal of Political Economy*, vol. 85, no. 2, 1977, pp. 239–63; S. Brittan, 'Inflation and Democracy', in F. Hirsch and J. Goldthorpe (eds), *The Political Economy of Inflation* (London: Martin Robertson, 1978) ch. 7.

12. See Frey, *Modern Political Economy*, p. 136.

13. See Ibid; also Nordhaus, 'The Political Business Cycle', p. 187.

14. See Brittan, 'Inflation and Democracy'.

15. For a good discussion of these Italian analysts of the 'social factory', see H. Cleaver, *Reading 'Capital' Politically* (London: Harvester Press, 1979).

6. Overcoming the Dichotomy of 'The State' and 'Civil Society': The Importance of Electoral Processes

1. See T. H. Marshall, *Citizenship and Social Class* (Cambridge University Press, 1950) and R. Bendix, *Nation Building and Citizenship* (New York: John Wiley, 1964).

2. See R. Dahrendorf, *Class and Class Conflict in an Industrial Society* (London: Routledge & Kegan Paul, 1959).
3. M. Kalecki, 'Political Aspects of Full Employment', in *Selected Essays on the Dynamics of the Capitalist Economy 1933-1970* (London: Cambridge University Press, 1971) p. 141.
4. For a biting critique of Lenin's position on trade unions see R. Hyman, *Marxism and the Sociology of Trade Unionism* (London: Pluto Press, 1971). Also worth noting is the twist of events in Poland in 1980 which has witnessed the first demand by workers in Eastern Europe for their own political organisation outside a ruling Communist Party. This, as Ivan Szelenyi has commented (ABC Radio, 13 November 1980) is an ironic rebuff to Lenin's belief that workers could only develop a limited trade union consciousness. In actuality, there is never a situation of 'pure spontaneity' as workers already possess varying degrees of consciousness which is either more or less developed.
5. For an outline of some of the historical differences in the attainment of democratic rights, see G. Therborn, 'The Rule of Capital and the Rise of Democracy', *New Left Review*, no. 103, 1977, pp. 3-41.
6. For a good analysis of the political and social obstacles which American workers faced, and why the union movement is relatively weak, see M. Davis, 'Why the US Working Class is Different' and 'The Barren Marriage of American Labour and the Democratic Party', *New Left Review*, no. 123, 1980, pp. 3-44 and no. 124, 1980, pp. 43-84, respectively.
7. For an analysis of the all-embracing business activities of the Israeili Histadrut, see F. Zweig, 'The Jewish Trade Union Movement in Israel', in S. Eisenstadt, R. Josef and C. Adler (eds), *Integration and Development in Israel* (New York: Praeger, 1970) pp. 162-84.
8. See 'Who Controls Pension Funds?', *Dollars and Sense*, no. 44, February 1979, pp. 6-7.
9. Trotsky's analysis of trade unions was determined by the social struggles up until the end of the 1930s. Consequently, he believed unions could serve as 'secondary instruments of imperialist capitalism for the subordination and disciplining of workers and for obstructing the revolution, or, on the contrary, the trade unions can become the instruments of the revolutionary movement of the proletariat'. L. Trotsky, 'Trade Unions in the Epoch of Imperialist Decay (1940), reprinted in T. Clarke and L. Clements (eds), *Trade Unions Under Capitalism* (London: William Collins, 1977) p. 87. This either/or analysis is inadequate in that many unions are neither revolutionary instruments nor loyal 'secondary instruments of imperialist capitalism'. In many capitalist societies with free Electoral Processes, the trade union movement is very much divided between right-wing, social-democratic or varying communist or independent political perspectives. For a range of union activity

in Europe, see C. Crouch and A. Pizzorno (eds), *The Resurgence of Class Conflict in Western Europe Since 1968*, vols 1 and 2 (London: Macmillan, 1978).

10. An editorial in *The Economist* deplored 'Belgian Roulette' because the multi-party system exacerbated by Flemish and Walloon divisions prevented urgent decisions from being made (such as cutting public spending and allowing American cruise missiles to be based in Belgium) – see *The Economist*, 18 October 1980, p. 17.

11. For a political economic analysis of the complexity of American budgetary control, see J. O'Connor, *The Fiscal Crisis of the State* (New York: St. Martin's Press, 1973) ch. 3; and for a critique of Mandel's and Poulantzas's views of the EEC, see S. Holland, *The UnCommon Market* (London: Macmillan, 1980) ch. 6.

12. For a survey of the extent of poverty in centralised states such as France or Italy, see V. George and R. Lawson (eds), *Poverty and Inequality in Common Market Countries* (London: Routledge & Kegan Paul, 1980).

13. See R. Lubar, 'Making Democracy Less Inflation-Prone', *Fortune*, 22 September 1980, p. 82.

14. See S. Leibfried, 'US Central Government Reform of the Administrative Structure During the Ash Period (1968–71)', *Kapitalistate*, no. 2, 1974, pp. 17–30.

15. For a non-Marxist survey of the historical complexities of local state apparatuses, see S. Tarrow, P. Katzenstein and L. Graziano (eds), *Territorial Politics in Industrial Nations* (New York: Praeger, 1978).

16. See E. Mandel, *Late Capitalism* (London: New Left Books, 1975) pp. 496–7. The OECD estimated that, in 1976, about 1 per cent of GDP in OECD countries and about 2 per cent of United States' GDP were on investment in pollution controls – high enough for capitalist classes to attack the increasing costs of regulation. OECD figures cited by W. Kaspar *et al.*, *Australia at the Crossroads* (Sydney: Harcourt Brace Jovanovich, 1980) pp. 100–1. The attack on regulatory controls is one of the principal themes of Milton and Rose Friedman, *Free to Choose* (London: Macmillan, 1979).

17. Protests, legal action and regulatory agency scrutiny have all increased the costs of nuclear power station construction (as with other capitalist projects) in that loan repayments, inflationary cost of fixed capital inputs are all serious burdens on potential profit rates if construction orders face lengthy delays or even cancellation.

18. A number of studies in Australia, Britain and the United States have revealed the persistence of major forms of wage and social oppression of women and blacks despite legislative changes in the 1960s and 1970s – see, for example, the survey in B. Campbell, 'Women: Not What They Bargained For', *Marxism Today*, March 1982, pp. 18–23.

19. G. Esping-Andersen, 'Comparative Social Policy and Political Conflict in Advanced Welfare States: Denmark and Sweden', *International Journal of Health Services*, vol. 9, no. 2, 1979, pp. 269–93.

20. G. Esping-Andersen, 'Social Class, Social Democracy and the State', *Comparative Politics*, October 1978, pp. 42-58.
21. See N. Chomsky and E. S. Herman, *The Political Economy of Human Rights, vol. 1* (Boston, Mass.: South End Press, 1979) for a detailed account of United States government support for many regimes which violated human rights.
22. See G. Therborn, *What Does the Ruling Class Do When It Rules?* (London: New Left Books, 1978) pp. 190-5; also N. Poulantzas, *State Power and Socialism* (London: New Left Books, 1978) pp. 232-41.
23. For accounts of the vital roles played by military regimes in the administration and accumulation of capitalist production in Latin American and other Third World countries, see J. Petras, *Critical Perspectives on Imperialism and Social Class in the Third World* (New York: Monthly Review Press, 1978) ch. 3 and R. Luckham, 'Militarism: Force, Class and International Conflict', *Institute of Development Studies Bulletin*, vol. 9, no. 1, July 1977, pp. 19-32. A good example of the 'relative autonomy' of the military (unencumbered by the 'checks and balances' of a free Electoral Process) is the forced amalgamation of private companies in South Korea during late 1980 in order to overcome serious problems in accumulation.
24. For an analysis of the residues of pre-capitalist social values and practices which capitalist societies parasitically depend upon – racism, sexism, religious and social bigotry – see J. Habermas, *Legitimation Crisis* (Boston, Mass.: Beacon Press, 1975) pt 2.

7. Production Processes: Beyond the Separation of 'The State' from 'The Economy'

1. K. Marx, *Capital*, vol. 3 (New York: International Publishers, 1967) p. 484.
2. For a full account of these three sectors see J. O'Connor, *The Fiscal Crisis of the State* (New York: St. Martin's Press, 1973) and J. Habermas, *Legitimation Crisis* (Boston, Mass.: Beacon Press, 1975) pt 2.
3. For a brief survey of the great variations in the size and nature of state-owned enterprises in non-OECD countries, see M. Gillis, 'The Role of State Enterprises in Economic Development', *Social Research*, vol. 47, no. 2, 1980, pp. 248-80.
4. It would take pages to list the flood of books and articles on these topics which have been published in recent years. A survey of journals such as *New Left Review, Capital and Class, Monthly Review, AMPO, Socialist Review, Feminist Review, Radical America, Telos, URPE, Kapitalistate, Theory and Society, The Insurgent Socialist, Race and Class, Economy and Society*, would provide extensive bibliographies for any readers wishing to gain extra information.

5. For example, see the discussion over the classifications of Poulantzas, Wright, Carchedi and others in P. Walker (ed.), *Between Labour and Capital* (London: Harvester Press, 1979). Poulantzas, Carchedi and Wright (to a lesser extent) all tend to analyse state sector employees in terms of the 'global functions they perform for capital', or as New Petty Bourgeoisie, or as occupying contradictory class locations. These conceptions of state sector workers are all couched in 'derivative terms' – for all jobs and roles are measured in terms of their functionality for capitalists – rather than recognising the manner in which many roles and state services are not comprehensible in exchange commodity terms and thus negate or weaken capitalist commodity production. Wright has recognised these non-derivative or contradictory aspects but, nevertheless, postulates a highly schematic and rigid typology of state sector positions – e.g. (a) bourgeois position in state institutions = top bureaucrats; (b) contradictory location = teacher; (c) proletarian position = clerk or typist. This derivative typology reduces state institutions to political and ideological 'superstructures' (the strong influence of Althusser) and thus fails to come to terms with the 'economic' role of state sectors – especially all those non-exchange-value goods and services. See E. O. Wright, *Class Crisis and the State* (London: New Left Books, 1978) pp. 94–6. It is a pity Wright's typology of state employees is so schematic as he does recognise the importance of non-exchange-value goods and services (following Claus Offe's work); see, for example, G. Esping-Andersen, R. Friedland and E. O. Wright, 'Modes of Class Struggle and the Capitalist State', *Kapitalistate*, nos 4–5, 1976, pp. 186–220.
6. D. Yaffe, 'The Crisis of Profitability: A Critique of the Glyn–Sutcliffe Thesis', *New Left Review*, no. 80, 1973, p. 52.
7. See E. Mandel, *Late Capitalism* (London: New Left Books, 1975) ch. 12.
8. The number of retail and wholesale businesses in a national Production Process varies considerably. Japan has the most with one retailer and wholesaler per sixty-nine people compared to one per 117 in the United States and one per 180 in West Germany. Matsushita Electrical appliance manufacturer has about 60 000 retail outlets – typical of the numerous shops which depend on large industrial corporations. For full figures on retailers see *The Economist*, 19 September 1981, pp. 88–9.
9. Erik Wright attempts to defend the orthodox Marxian notion that the rate of surplus-value affects the rate of profit. While conceding important points to the 'revisionists', his arguments are not persuasive in that he constantly shifts between the concept of 'surplus-labour' (which may *not* produce surplus-value) and 'surplus-value'. One can analyse the labour process in supermarkets or state institutions where workers are controlled and disciplined in a way which minimises loss of labour power even though these latter workers produce *no* value given the nature of their jobs. Therefore the

concept 'surplus-value' is not necessarily equivalent to 'surplus-labour' performed. See E. O. Wright, 'The Value Controversy and Social Research', *New Left Review* no. 116, 1979, pp. 53–82.

10. See, for example, E. J. Nell, 'Value and Capital in Marxian Economics', *The Public Interest*, Special Issue 1980, p. 195. Also see Marco Lippi's discussion of the limits of Marx's naturalistic assumptions behind surplus-value and socially embodied labour-time, in *Value and Naturalism in Marx* (London: New Left Books, 1980). I agree with Lippi that one does not need to get bogged down in endless mathematical disputes (between orthodox and 'revisionist' Marxists) over value theory. The more important objective is to illuminate the workings of contemporary capitalist societies, rather than salvage the honour of problematical concepts. This means that we have to recognise the differences between surplus-value-extracting enterprises and non-surplus-value-extracting businesses and state apparatuses.

11. See Mandel, *Late Capitalism*, chs 6–8 for a rich statistical and analytical survey of changes in production techniques.

12. For example, in non-communist countries ship building (which is an important indicator of whether international trade is growing or not), reached a peak of 34 million gross tons in 1975 but slumped to 12 million tons in 1980 – the bulk of which was produced in Japan, South Korea, Brazil and Taiwan. Also, sales of American-made cars fell to 6 578 305 units in 1980, the lowest registered figure since 1961 when 5 556 102 were sold: see *Motor Business*, no. 105, 1st quarter 1981 (United States of America: *The Economist Intelligence Unit*). Lack of growth in the car industry is critical in that car manufacturers made up eleven of the top fifty industrial corporations in capitalist countries in 1980 and oil companies totalled another twenty – making thirty-one companies highly dependent on automobiles. When one adds steel, rubber and other accessories, a truly alarming picture emerges given the deterioration in production and sales since 1980.

13. See Howard Sherman, 'Inflation, Unemployment and the Contemporary Business Cycle', *Socialist Review*, no. 44, vol. 9, no. 2, 1979, p. 94.

14. Of course it is important to recognise that in every capitalist society workers' wages are attacked on the grounds of undermining 'export competitiveness'. While wage levels are not irrelevant to profit rates, the belief that wages of 'greedy workers' are the *major* cause behind the relative drop in production and exports is not sustainable even on figures produced by conservative organisations. For example, the Institute of the German Economy reported that total wage costs per hour in manufacturing industry in 1979 were 21.14 Deutsche Marks for West Germany (the largest capitalist commodity exporter) and only 10.20 DM for British workers – a figure making it very difficult to sustain British capitalists' ideological attack on wage levels as the cause for the historical decline of British export

levels. See German figures cited in *Socialist Review* (Britain) 18 September 1980, p. 4.

15. Although productivity figures are not equivalent to rates of surplus-value extraction, they do give some indication of the health of capitalist enterprises. In the largest capitalist nation which has tried advanced managerial techniques for decades, the rate of productivity growth in the United States has declined from an average 3.3 per cent growth per year between 1948 and 1966, to 2.1 per cent between 1966 and 1973, and a very low 1.2 per cent per year between 1973 and 1977. See C. McConnell, 'Why is US Productivity Slowing Down?', *Harvard Business Review*, March–April 1979, pp. 36–60. Declining productivity figures have been subjected to critical evaluation by the editors of *Monthly Review* – see 'Productivity Slowdown: A False Alarm', vol. 31, no. 2, June 1979 and 'The Uses and Abuses of Measuring Productivity', vol. 32, no. 2, June 1980. Sweezy and Magdoff are concerned to attack the ideological notion that lagging productivity is behind the cause of inflation in America. They are correct to point out the false comparisons of industries and the dubious manner in which productivity rates are supposed to be applied to state sector workers such as teachers. However, I think it would be wrong to dismiss capitalists' concern over lagging productivity rates in commodity production as simply a device to hide huge levels of overproduction. Despite all the problems in productivity statistics, they are still used by capitalist enterprises as partial indices with which to compare labour rates in various countries – so as to help them to decide where to invest. If radicals completely deny the effect of wage struggles and labour struggles, alienation, sabotage, etc. on profit rates or productivity rates, then the notion of class struggle will itself become meaningless.

16. For a full discussion of limited planning capacities of capitalist states, see Habermas, *Legitimation Crisis*, pp. 97–102; C. Offe, 'The Theory of the Capitalist State and the Problem of Policy Formation', in Lindberg *et al.* (eds), *Stress and Contradiction in Modern Capitalism* (New York: Heath, 1975); also C. Offe, 'Crises and Crisis Management Elements of a Political Crisis Theory', *International Journal of Politics*, Fall 1976, pp. 29–67; C. Offe and V. Ronge, 'Theses on the Theory of the State', *New German Critique*, no. 6, 1975, pp. 137–47.

17. The dramatic growth of part-time workers during the 1970s is particularly visible in countries such as Australia and the United States. In Australia, approximately 20 per cent of the paid workforce were in part-time employment by 1981 (mainly women), thus disguising the official unemployment figures. For an analysis of the large number of American workers experiencing very low wage rates or working casually and part-time, see J. O'Connor, 'Capital Accumulation, Economic Crisis and the Mass Worker', *Social Praxis*, vol. 6, nos 1–2, 1979, pp. 5–18.

18. Not only is American manufacturing industry operating well

below capacity (within the United States) but the ratio between sales by foreign affiliates of United States firms and export sales by domestically based United States firms has grown from 1.9 in 1960 to 2.8 in 1976. Thus in 1976 sales by United States firms located abroad totalled US $212.8 billion compared to only US $76.6 billion exported by domestically based American firms. Of the US $212.8 billion sold by United States affiliates, US $161 billion worth of manufactured goods were sold in the countries in which the affiliates operated – US $14.1 billion was exported back to the United States and US $37.7 billion exported to other countries. See United States Presidential figures cited by H. Magdoff, 'The US Dollar, Petrodollars and US Imperialism', *Monthly Review*, vol. 30, no. 8, 1979, p. 12; also R. P. De Witt, Jr, 'The Multinational Corporations, State Policy and its Impact on the United States Economy', *Social Praxis*, vol. 5, nos 3–4, 1978, pp. 207–33 and B. Berberoglu and M. Landsberg, 'Transnational Production and the Worldwide Contradictions of Advanced Capitalism', *Social Praxis*, vol. 5, nos 3–4, 1978, pp. 181–205 for full figures and bibliographies of material covering the 'deindustrialisation' of the United States rather than a growth of domestically based export-oriented industries. Also see M. Green and R. Massie, Jr, *The Big Business Reader* (New York: Pilgrim Press, 1980) for a collection of material covering the massive and diverse social costs of recent capitalist restructuring in the United States. Similarly, in EEC countries 2.5 million industrial jobs were lost in the four years between 1974 and 1978, bringing the number of people employed in manufacturing industries in countries such as the Netherlands back to levels reached in 1950. See EEC statistics reproduced in 'Europe's Vanishing Factories', *The Economist*, 15 September 1979, p. 54; and for the Netherlands, see C. A. van den Beld, 'Deindustrialisation in the Netherlands?', in F. Blackaby (ed.), *De-industrialisation* (London: Heineman, 1979) ch. 6.

19. See 'Shifts in World Trade Soften Global Impact of US Slump', *International Herald Tribune*, 28 December 1981, p. 7.

20. See 'The Japanese Supertraders', *Far Eastern Economic Review*, 1 February 1980, pp. 39–40.

21. See J. Halliday, 'Capitalism and Socialism in East Asia', *New Left Review*, no. 124, 1980, pp. 8–10.

22. A. Carlo, 'Unemployment', *Telos*, no. 38, Winter 1978–9, pp. 5–31.

23. See OECD report on investment summarised in *The Economist*, 23 February 1980, pp. 78–9. Of the largest capitalist countries only Japan and France increased public investments since 1974 while Britain and Italy have slashed state sector public works by 30 and 15 per cent respectively.

24. A study by the Massachusetts Institute of Technology showed that 88 per cent of new jobs created in the United States between 1969 and 1976 were provided by competitive sector businesses – 66 per cent by firms employing less than twenty people and 80 per cent

by firms which were less than 5 years old – see *The Economist*, 29 September 1979, p. 104.

25. See the multilateral trade re-negotiations of GATT in Geneva 1979–80 which involved compromise deals between the United States, Japan and the EEC over tendering by foreign firms, e.g. the opening of state-owned Nippon Telegraph and Telephone to tenders by American private telecommunications giants and the agreement that only contracts worth more than US $167 000 will be open to foreign tendering.

26. See, for example, Y. Fitt, A. Faire and J. P. Vigier, *The World Economic Crisis: US Imperialism at Bay*, trans. M. Pallis (London: Zed Press, 1980) and E. Mandel, *The Second Slump*, trans. J. Rothschild (London: New Left Books, 1978) for extensive figures concerning the rivalry between imperialist powers.

27. See 'The New Wave Foreign Capital Investment in the United States: A Survey', *The Economist*, 26 October 1980.

28. In 1981 the New York Stock Exchange released a report entitled 'US Economic Performance in a Global Perspective' which documented the key areas in which the United States was slipping behind its main rivals: see *The Economist*, 25 April 1981, pp. 109–11.

29. See invisible world trade figures reported in *The Economist*, 5 July 1980, p. 77. Direct United States foreign investment abroad earned parent companies US $3.6 billion in 1960 compared to an estimated US $41 billion in 1981. See 'US Company Investors Abroad Now Bring Home the Bacon', *Australian Financial Review*, 13 March 1981, p. 50.

30. See *Fortune*, 11 August 1980, p. 204 for figures on top 500 companies.

31. For an indication of the social imbalances and suffering caused by capitalist enterprises moving in and out of regions, etc., see 'Special Issue on Uneven Regional Development', *Review of Radical Political Economics*, vol. 10, no. 3, Fall 1978.

32. See C. Offe and V. Ronge, 'Theses on the Theory of the State', *New German Critique*, no. 6, 1975, pp. 137–47.

8. From Abundance to Scarcity: Contradictions within Credit Processes

1. See S. De Brunhoff, *Marx on Money*, trans. M. Goldbloom (New York: Urizen Books, 1976) and M. Aglietta, *A Theory of Capitalist Regulation*, trans. D. Fernbach (London: New Left Books, 1979).

2. See K. Marx, *Capital*, vol. 1 (New York: Modern Library Edition, 1936) p. 130.

3. See A. Cutler *et al.*, *Marx's 'Capital' and Capitalism Today*, vol. 2 (London: Routledge & Kegan Paul, 1978) chs 1–6.

4. For a full discussion of the importance of different forms of enterprise calculation, see ibid, vol. 2, chs 7–11.

5. See A. Glyn and J. Harrison, *The British Economic Disaster* (London: Pluto Press, 1980) pp. 155–6.

6. See A. Sbragia, 'Borrowing to Build: Private Money and Public Welfare', *International Journal of Health Services*, vol. 9, no. 2, 1979, pp. 207–26 for an analysis of differing conditions of local borrowing in leading capitalist societies.

7. See J. Chubb, 'Naples Under the Left: The Limits of Local Change', *Comparative Politics*, vol. 13, no. 1, 1980, pp. 53–78 and A. Davidson, 'Italian Communism, the City and Participatory Democracy', paper presented to Australasian Political Science Association Conference, August 1978.

8. See 'Stopping Japan Going Bust', *The Economist*, 9 August 1980, pp. 74–5 and 'Japan's Multi-Billion Bond Issue Nearly Equals Big Four's Total', *Australian Financial Review*, 19 September 1980, p. 20. Also see A. Rowley, 'Tokyo's Tidal Wave Builds', *Far Eastern Economic Review*, 3 February 1983, pp. 42–5.

9. It is estimated that public sector borrowing requirements in Britain during 1980 were about 4.7 per cent of GNP. Translated into United States terms this would have meant a deficit of about 120 billion dollars – or double the actual deficit proposed by Carter in that year. For figures, see *The Economist*, 11 October 1980, p. 32.

10. K. Marx, 'Instructions for the Delegates of the Provisional General Council of the First International in 1866', quoted in M. Linder, *The Anti-Samuelson*, vol. 1 (New York: Urizen Books, 1977) p. 170.

11. Ibid.

12. For a survey of gasoline taxation prior to the 1980 elections, see A. Tait and D. Morgan, 'Gasoline Taxation in Selected OECD Countries 1970–79', *International Monetary Fund Staff Papers*, no. 2, 1980, pp. 349–79.

13. See J. O'Connor, *The Fiscal Crisis of the State* (New York: St. Martin's Press, 1973); M. Castells, *The Economic Crisis and American Society* (Princeton University Press, 1980); I. Gough, *The Political Economy of the Welfare State* (London: Macmillan, 1979); E. Mandel, *Late Capitalism* (London: New Left Books, 1975) and *The Second Slump*, trans. J. Rothschild (London: New Left Books, 1978); P. Mattick, *Economic Crisis and Crisis Theory* (London: Merlin Press, 1981) and *Economics, Politics and the Age of Inflation* (London: Merlin Press, 1980); and J. Habermas, *Legitimation Crisis* (Boston, Mass.: Beacon Press, 1975) pt 2.

14. L. von Mises, *Socialism: an Economic and Sociological Analysis*, trans. J. Kahane (London: Jonathan Cape, 1974) pp. 495–6.

15. See Mandel, *The Second Slump*, ch. 2.

16. For conservative analyses of the problems involved in working-out how the Eurodollar and Eurocurrency markets affect national statistics, see A. Crockett, *International Money* (Sunbury-on-Thames: Nelson, 1977); also see G. Johnston and A. Ball, 'The Euromarkets and Monetary Expansion', *Barclays Review*, vol. LV, no. 1, 1980, pp. 9–12 for an extensive diagram showing all the

intricate interconnections. For a less extensive diagram but useful introduction, see 'Big Bucks in Offshore Banks', *Dollars and Sense*, March 1980, pp. 6–7 and 19.

17. For an analysis of the various forms of calculation, profit and organisational structure of firms, see G. Thompson, 'The Firm as a "Dispersed" Social Agency', *Economy and Society*, vol. 11, no. 3, August 1982, pp. 233–50.

18. See 'Travellers' Cheques Take Wing', *The Economist*, 2 August 1980, pp. 72–3.

19. See 'The Foreign Grab for American Banks', *The Economist*, 30 August 1980, pp. 72–3.

20. See ibid and 'The New Wave Foreign Capital Investment in the United States: A Survey', *The Economist*, 26 October 1980, for a breakdown of foreign penetration of the American market.

21. See E. Mandel, 'Behind the Soaring Price of Gold', *Intercontinental Press*, 11 February 1980, pp. 120–7 for many points concerning speculation in gold in recent years.

22. See 'The Calm Before the Storm', *International Currency Review*, vol. 12, no. 3, 1980, pp. 28–33 and 'International Banking: A Survey', *The Economist*, 31 March 1979, for full statistics on American bank loans and profits derived from abroad.

23. See *The Economist*, 29 December 1979, p. 44.

24. Ibid.

25. By 1981, Western banks had lent Communist Comecon countries approximately US $88 billion. See *The Economist*, 13 February 1982, p. 13.

26. See S. Griffith-Jones, 'The Growth of Multinational Banking, the Euro-currency Market and their Effects on Developing Countries', *Journal of Development Studies*, vol. 16, 1980, pp. 204–23; also see 'Merchant Banking '80', special supplement in *Far Eastern Economic Review*, 19 September 1980.

27. See 'Recyclers' Recession', *The Economist*, 7 August 1982, pp. 10–11.

28. See 'A Nightmare of Debt', special survey in *The Economist*, 20 March 1982, p. 100. For a critical view of the role of the IMF, see R. Frenkel and G. O'Donnell, 'The "Stabilisation Programs" of the International Monetary Fund and their Internal Impacts', in R. Fagen, *Capitalism and the State in US–Latin American Relations* (Stanford University Press, 1979) pp. 171–216.

29. Quoted in 'Alarm Bells Are Ringing over the Massive Debt Crisis', *Far Eastern Economic Review*, 2 May 1980, p. 41.

30. Multiple problems created for businesses due to currency changes are recognised by conservative writers; see, for example, P. L. Gilibert and M. Monti, '"Weak" Currencies and the "Weaknesses" of the European Monetary System: An Italian View', *Three Banks Review*, no. 127, September 1980, pp. 57–72. The authors cite the difficulties associated for Italy in trying to adjust to West German economic policies.

31. See H. Magdoff, 'The US Dollar, Petrodollars, and US Imperialism', *Monthly Review*, vol. 30, no. 8, 1979, pp. 1-13 and H. Robinson, 'The Downfall of the Dollar', *The Socialist Register*, 1973, pp. 397-449.
32. See J. J. van Belle, 'How a Multi-currency Reserve System Unsettles Exchange Rates', *Euromoney*, January 1981, pp. 105-9.
33. For the effect of inflation on company profits, see 'How 1980 Profits at 370 Companies were Hit', *Business Week*, 4 May 1981, pp. 58-72.
34. See *The Economist*, 10 April 1982, p. 83.
35. Mandel, *Late Capitalism*, p. 417.
36. See B. Rowthorn, 'Review of Late Capitalism', *New Left Review*, no. 98, 1976, pp. 59-83; O'Connor, *The Fiscal Crisis of the State*; Habermas, *Legitimation Crisis*, pt 2; Gough, *The Political Economy of the Welfare State*, chs 5 and 6.
37. Castells, *The Economic Crisis and American Society*, p. 118. He notes that total United States debt has jumped from US $400 billion in 1946 to US $2.5 trillion in 1974 - of which US $1 trillion was corporate debt. It took fifteen years (1945-60) for the United States debt to double, but only ten years (1960-70) to double again.
38. For an excellent analysis of the difficulty in obtaining finance for homes in the United States, see M. Stone, 'The Housing Problem in the United States: Origins and Prospects', *Socialist Review*, vol. 10, no. 4, 1980, pp. 65-119.
39. See Mandel, *Late Capitalism*, chs 12 and 13.
40. See New York Times News Service Report, *Australian Financial Review*, 7 October 1980, p. 33. In the United States prices for existing homes rose 41 per cent faster than prices generally in the years 1968-79. The large amount of speculative capital being invested in housing has prompted liberals to call for the reduction of tax advantages for property investors so that more capital can be diverted to productive enterprises and energy sources. See A. Downs, 'Too Much Capital for Housing?', *The Brookings Bulletin*, vol. 17, Summer 1980, p. 4.
41. See Michael Lebowitz's analysis of crises caused by the asymmetry of circulation and production processes in Castells, *The Economic Crisis and American Society*, p. 23.
42. See E. Steinberg, J. Yager and G. Brannon, *New Means of Financing International Needs* (Washington D.C.: The Brookings Institute, 1978) for proposals such as a general tax on international trade, oil and raw materials trade, polluters, etc., in order to raise new sources of finance to cover the gap between the 'rich and the poor' countries. These proposals would only put extra pressure on profit rates and meet with bitter resistance from multinationals in particular. For a critical examination of the relation between debt, oil and banking, see H. Wachtel, 'A Decade of International Debt', *Theory and Society*, vol. 9, no. 3, 1980, pp. 503-18.
43. See O'Connor, *The Fiscal Crisis of the State*, ch. 9.

9. The Industrialisation of Food Production Processes: A Neglected Revolution

1. For an in-depth discussion of Kautsky's, Lenin's and revolutionaries' views of agriculture, peasants, etc., see A. Hussain and K. Tribe, *Marxism and the Agarian Question*, vols 1 and 2 (London: Macmillan, 1981).
2. See J. Mathews, 'Marxism, Energy and Technological Change', *Politics and Power*, no. 1, 1980, pp. 19‑37 for a critique of Marxists such as Stedman Jones and Balibar who defend Marx against ecologists. 'What Marx could not see, but what is now all too evident, is that freedom from nature (i.e. the decoupling of humankind's wants and activities from their material surroundings) implies enslavement to machines.' (p. 29.) For a sympathetic reading of Marx (as opposed to orthodox Marxists), see H. Parsons, *Marx and Engels on Ecology* (Westport, Conn.: Greenwood Press, 1977).
3. For an evaluation of the disproportionate resources used by leading OECD countries compared to the rest of the world, see M. Caldwell, *The Wealth of Some Nations* (London: Zed Press, 1977).
4. K. Marx, *Capital*, vol. 3 (New York: International Publishers, 1967) p. 484.
5. See R. Burbach and P. Flynn, *Agribusiness in the Americas* (New York: Monthly Review Press, 1980); S. George, *How the Other Half Dies* (Harmondsworth: Penguin Books, 1976); Caldwell, *The Wealth of Some Nations*; C. Tudge, *The Famine Business* (Harmondsworth: Penguin Books, 1979); B. Commoner, *The Closing Circle* (New York: Bantam, 1971); A. Roberts, *The Self-Managing Environment* (London: Allison & Busby, 1979); R. J. Barnet, *The Lean Years: Politics in the Age of Scarcity* (New York: Simon & Schuster, 1980).
6. See 'The Food Industry Innovation and Industrial Structure', *The OECD Observer*, no. 106, September 1980, pp. 18‑23.
7. See P. Kim, 'Saemaul Agriculture', *AMPO Japan Asia Quarterly Review*, no. 1, 1980, pp. 2‑11.
8. For the mass conversion of land-use into luxury cash crops see R. Burbach and P. Flynn, *Agribusiness in the Americas*, pt 3; and Ho Kwon Ping 'Profits and Poverty in the Plantations', *Far Eastern Economic Review*, 11 July 1980, pp. 53‑7.
9. See M. Goro, 'How to Deform Agriculture in the Name of Development: the Case of Japan', *AMPO Japanese Asia Quarterly Review*, no. 1, 1979, pp. 46‑51.
10. See Burbach and Flynn, *Agribusiness in the Americas*, p. 67; and Kim, 'Saemaul Agriculture', pp. 2‑11.
11. See 'Europe's Processed Cuisine', *The Economist*, 9 August 1980, pp. 88‑9.
12. See 'The Food Industry Innovation and Industrial Structure', *The OECD Observer*, no. 106, September 1980, pp. 18‑19.
13. See 'American Farming', *The Economist*, 5 January 1980, p. 5 for a special survey; for a detailed analysis of ownership, tax subsidies

and general conditions of farming in the United States, see I. Vogeler, *The Myth of the Family: Farm Agribusiness Dominance of US Agriculture* (Boulder: Westview Press, 1981).

14. See 'Farming in the EEC', *The Economist*, 1 November 1980, p. 53.
15. See R. van den Bosch, *The Pesticide Conspiracy* (Dorchester: Prism Press, 1978) for an analysis of the differences between the use of pesticides and 'controlled farming'.
16. See Tudge, *The Famine Business*, p. 12.
17. For an analysis of the increasing use of energy in agriculture between 1945 and 1970, see D. Pimentel *et al.*, 'Food Production and The Energy Crisis', *Science*, 2 November 1973, pp. 443-9.
18. See Burbach and Flynn, *Agribusiness in the Americas*, pp. 112-5.
19. See ibid, ch. 3 and George, *How the Other Half Dies*, pt 3.
20. See 'American Farming', *The Economist*, 5 January 1980, p. 12.
21. See S. Holland, *The UnCommon Market* (London: Macmillan, 1980) pp. 27-33.
22. See B. Rowthorn, 'Late Capitalism', *New Left Review*, no. 98, 1976, pp. 74-5 for a discussion of the effect of food prices on capitalists and workers.
23. See 'Vegetable Prices: A Key to Inflation', *Australian Financial Review*, 9 February 1981, p. 23 and 'Swedish Prices', *The Economist*, 10 October 1981, p. 89.
24. See 'US Farm Produce Predicted by Fertiliser Usage', *Australian Financial Review*, 23 October 1981, p. 67.
25. See Caldwell, *The Wealth of Some Nations*, pp. 125-6 and Tudge, *The Famine Business*, p. 12.
26. See *The Economist*, 29 December 1979, p. 52.
27. 'Europe's Processed Cuisine', *The Economist*, 9 August 1980, p. 89.
28. See Burbach and Flynn, *Agribusiness and the Americas*, p. 97.
29. See 'Farming in the EEC', *The Economist*, 1 November 1980, p. 61.
30. A. Critterden, 'How a "Sacred Cow" Milks the US Treasury', *New York Times* reprint, *Australian Financial Review*, 18 February 1981, p. 27.
31. See S. George, *Feeding the Few: Corporate Control of Food* (Washington D.C.: Institute for Policy Studies, 1979).
32. W. Blundell, 'US Finds its Best Farmland is Disappearing under City Sprawl', *Australian Financial Review*, 18 November 1980, p. 42. For an opposing view, see J. L. Simon, 'Are We Losing Our Farmland?', *The Public Interest*, no. 67, Spring 1982, pp. 49-62.

10. One 'World-System' or 'Organised Anarchy': The Crises of Desynchronisation

1. See, for example, A. Hussain, 'Symptomatology of Revolution', *Economy and Society*, vol. 9, no. 3, 1980, pp. 348-58 and Report on 'The Totally Administered Society Conference', *Telos*, no. 35, Spring 1978, pp. 181-3, for Piccone's attack on Commoner.

2. J. Donzelot, *The Policing of Families*, trans. R. Hurley (New York: Pantheon Books, 1979).
3. A. Cutler *et al.*, *Marx's 'Capital' and Capitalism Today*, vol. 2, p. 88.
4. See A. Hussain, 'Symptomatology of Revolution', p. 348.
5. See J. Falk, *Global Fission The Battle Over Nuclear Power* (Melbourne: Oxford University Press, 1982) for a good discussion of national differences in the opposition or support for nuclear power.
6. See, for example, D. Plotke, 'The United States in Transition: Toward a New Order?', *Socialist Review*, no. 54, vol. 10, 1980, pp. 71–123.
7. See A. Bergesen, 'The Emerging Science of the World-System', *International Social Science Journal*, vol. XXXIV, no. 1, 1982, pp. 23–36.
8. See H. Marcuse, *One Dimensional Man* (London: Routledge & Kegan Paul, 1964).
9. See J. Habermas, 'A Reply to My Critics', in J. B. Thompson and D. Held (eds), *Habermas: Critical Debates* (London: Macmillan, 1982) p. 279.
10. A. Arato, 'Critical Sociology and Authoritarian State Socialism', in Thompson and Held (eds), *Habermas: Critical Debates*, pp. 196–218.
11. Habermas, 'A Reply to My Critics', p. 283.
12. Ibid.
13. See A. Touraine, *The Voice and the Eye*, trans. A. Duff (Cambridge University Press, 1981).
14. C. Offe, 'The Attribution of Public Status to Interest Groups: Observations on the West German Case', in S. Berger (ed.), *Organising Interests in Western Europe* (Cambridge University Press, 1981) pp. 123–58.
15. See ibid and C. Offe, 'Competitive Party Democracy and the Keynesian Welfare State', unpublished paper delivered at Griffith University, Australia, July 1981.
16. J. Habermas, 'New Social Movements', *Telos*, Fall 1981, pp. 33–7.
17. See Touraine, *The Voice and the Eye* and *The Self Production of Society* (University of Chicago Press, 1977) for endless ideal types and ahistorical speculations.
18. C. Offe, 'Notes on the Future of European Socialism and the State', *Kapitalistate*, no. 7, 1978, p. 36.
19. See A. Gorz, *Farewell to the Working Class*, trans. M. Sonenscher (London: Pluto Press, 1982) p. 112.

11. Between Reform and Revolution: 'Alternative Programmes' and their Failure to Confront the Desynchronisation of Processes

1. P. Anderson, *Arguments Within English Marxism* (London: New Left Books, 1980) pp. 196–7.

2. B. Rowthorn, 'The Politics of the Alternative Economic Strategy', *Marxism Today*, January 1981, p. 6.
3. For some critiques of Eurocommunism and 'alternative strategies', see H. Weber, 'Eurocommunism, Socialism and Democracy', *New Left Review*, no. 110, 1978, pp. 3-14; C. Boggs and D. Plotke (eds), *The Politics of Eurocommunism Socialism in Transition* (London: Macmillan, 1980); Red Notes, *Working Class Autonomy and the Crisis* (London: CSE Books, 1979); E. Mandel, *From Stalinism to Eurocommunism* (London: New Left Books, 1978); D. Coates, 'Labourism and the Transition to Socialism', *New Left Review*, no. 129, 1981, pp. 3-22. For critical supporters of 'alternative programmes', see F. Claudin, *Eurocommunism and Socialism* (London: New Left Books, 1978); P. Ingrao, 'Eurocommunism and the Question of the State', reprinted in *Eurored*, no. 9, 1978, pp. 12-17; D. Purdy, 'The Left's Alternative Economic Strategy', *Politics of Power* (London: Routledge & Kegan Paul, 1980) pp. 55-80; F. Laclau and C. Mouffe, 'Socialist Strategy: Where Next?', *Marxism Today*, January 1981, pp. 17-22; A. Cutler *et al.*, *Marx's 'Capital' and Capitalism Today*, vol. 2, pp. 269-93; G. Therborn, 'Eurocommunism - Can it Regain the Initiative?, *Marxism Today*, April 1980, pp. 14-20; and P. Hain (ed.), *The Debate of the Decade, The Crisis and the Future of the Left* (London: Pluto Press, 1980).
4. S. Aaronovitch, *The Road from Thatcherism* (London: Lawrence & Wishart, 1981).
5. For a sympathetic analysis of Mitterrand's first year, see K. Dixon and D. Perraud, 'The French Experiment', *Marxism Today*, May 1982, pp. 15-21.
6. For an analysis of British nationalised industries and the manner in which they have been restricted by capitalist production criteria, see B. Fine and K. O'Donnell, 'The Nationalised Industries', in D. Currie and R. Smith (eds), *Socialist Economic Review 1981* (London: Merlin Press, 1981) pp. 265-85 and comments by K. Cowling, pp. 287-9.
7. See W. Wolf, 'Big Shake-Out Nearing for World Auto Industry', *Intercontinental Press*, 19 November 1979, p. 1138 for figures on employment in European car industries. Both the Italian Communist Party and other socialists such as Stuart Holland make much political capital over the development of the Alfa Romeo car plant at Naples - as an example of an 'alternative' policy which resolves regional unemployment - see M. Prior, 'Problems in Labour Politics: Interviews with Stuart Holland, Frank Field and Michael Meacher', *Politics and Power*, no. 2 (London: Routledge & Kegan Paul, 1980) p. 17. While car production has certainly created jobs in the South it is hardly an example of socially useful non-commodity production. Also it must be remembered that the Christian Democrats were behind the expansion of Italian public enterprises (IRI State Holding Company) and the latter should be seen in the con-

text of Italian Production Processes rather than as a 'model' to be admired by socialists like Stuart Holland. For an analysis of Italian public enterprises, see M. Maraffi, 'State/Economy Relationships: the Case of Italian Public Enterprise', *British Journal of Sociology*, vol. 31, no. 4, 1980, pp. 507–24.

8. See M. Cooley and H. Wainwright, 'The Lucas Plan: its Lessons for Labour', *New Socialist*, November–December 1981, pp. 13–16.

9. For a defence of import controls, see T. Ward, 'The Case for an Import Control Strategy in the UK', *Socialist Economic Review 1981*, pp. 93–108; for an opposing view see 'The Socialist Case Against Import Controls', *Socialist Review*, 19 May – 14 June 1980, pp. 18–20.

10. S. Holland, *The Socialist Challenge* (London: Quartet Books, 1976) p. 180.

11. Ibid, p. 149.

12. See F. Archibugi, J. Delors and S. Holland, 'Planning for Development', in S. Holland (ed.), *Beyond Capitalist Planning* (Oxford: Basil Blackwell, 1978) p. 188.

13. See Holland, *The Socialist Challenge*, p. 170.

14. A. Glyn and J. Harrison, *The British Economic Disaster* (London: Pluto Press, 1980) p. 161. The authors make a number of biting critiques against the British Alternative Economic Programme. Stuart Holland cites the Soviet NEP programme during the 1920s and the Chinese experience between 1961 and 1964 as evidence for the viability of an 'alternative programme' within a 'mixed economy'. See Holland, *The Socialist Challenge*, pp. 165–6. These are poor examples as both the Bolsheviks and the Chinese Communists dominated the repressive state apparatuses of their respective societies and were not in the disadvantaged position that any potential Left 'alternative movement' would be in capitalist 'mixed economies' – i.e. confronting entrenched and hostile capitalist class forces and state apparatuses.

15. For a critique of 'alternative programmes' neglect of women and all related forms of child-care, unpaid labour, etc., see A. Coote, 'The AES: a New Starting Point', *New Socialist*, November–December 1981, pp. 4–7 and J. Gardiner and S. Smith, 'Feminism and the Alternative Economic Strategy', *Marxism Today*, October 1981, pp. 24–30.

16. For a critique of 'growth' see V. Anderson, 'Has Economic Growth got Anything to do With Socialism?', unpublished paper delivered at Alternative Strategies Conference in London on 17 October 1981.

17. See J. Wajcman, 'Workers' Co-operatives – a Middle-class Ideal?', unpublished paper delivered at Alternative Strategies Conference in London, 17 October 1981.

18. The notion of a 'social-industrial complex' was actually used by leading businessmen in the United States and not just reformers wishing to move the United States economy in the direction of

Swedish patterns – see J. O'Connor, *The Fiscal Crisis of the State* (New York: St. Martin's Press, 1973) ch. 9. In Europe the 'military-industrial complex' is not as great as that in the United States, but the idea of transforming the 'mesoeconomic' sector has many similarities with the desire to build a 'social–industrial complex'.

19. See L. Trotsky, *The Transitional Program for Socialist Revolution* (New York: Pathfinder Press, 1973).
20. There are a few brief policy statements and pamphlets, e.g. the British Communist Party pamphlet, W. Page, *Farming to Feed Britain* (London: Farleigh Press, 1976) which is quite uncritical of chemical agriculture. In contrast, the Agenor Co-operative (based in Brussels) is more sensitive to environmental questions and promotes a Europe-wide alternative agricultural policy in opposition to existing EEC farm policies and agribusiness. See, for example, *The Great Milk Robbery* (Brussels: Agenor, 1981).
21. CSE London Working Group, *The Alternative Economic Strategy* (London: CSE Books, 1980) and F. Cripps *et al.*, *Manifesto: A Radical Strategy for Britain's Future* (London: Pan Books, 1981).
22. Glyn and Harrison, *The British Economic Disaster*, p. 172.
23. This idea is promoted by people such as John Stephens, see *The Transition From Capitalism to Socialism* (London: Macmillan, 1979) ch. 6, and by political leaders such as Tony Benn, see *Arguments for Socialism* (Harmondsworth: Penguin Books, 1980) p. 150.
24. See Archibugi, Delors and Holland, 'Planning for Development', p. 188.
25. See F. Cripps, 'The British Crisis – Can the Left Win?', *New Left Review*, no. 128, 1981, p. 87.
26. For lack of internal democracy in the PCF, see G. Ross and J. Jenson, 'Conflicting Currents in the PCF', *The Socialist Register 1979* (London: Merlin Press, 1979) pp. 139–71. Also see L. Panitch, 'Trade Unions and the Capitalist State', *New Left Review*, no. 125, 1981, pp. 21–43 for an analysis of the tendencies leading to 'Euro-corporatism'; and R. Hyman and T. Elger, 'Job Controls, The Employers' Offensive and Alternative Strategies', *Capital and Class*, no. 15, 1981, pp. 115–49.
27. This is well illustrated by B. Hindess, 'Democracy and the Limitations of Parliamentary Democracy in Britain', *Politics and Power*, no. 1, 1980, pp. 103–24.
28. See H. Braverman, *Labor and Monopoly Capital: The Degradation of Work in the Twentieth Century* (New York: Monthly Review Press, 1974); S. Marglin, 'What Do Bosses Do? and A. Gorz, 'The Tyranny of the Factory: Today and Tomorrow', both in A. Gorz (ed.), *The Division of Labour* (London: Harvester Press, 1976); and A. Roberts, *The Self-Managing Environment* (London: Allison & Busby, 1979).
29. See E. Altvater and O. Kallscheuer, 'Socialist Politics and the 'Crisis of Marxism'', *The Socialist Register 1979* (London: Merlin

Press, 1979) pp. 101–38 for an analysis which traces the mixed fortunes of the PCI and their economic strategy.

30. See Holland (ed.), *Beyond Capitalist Planning.*

31. In contrast to his advocacy of controls over foreign capital, nationalisation and socialist policies in earlier years, Delors now proclaims that 'We want France to remain a country where foreign capital can be placed and invested in complete security', *The Economist*, 30 May 1981, p. 64. Although he was never very radical, Delors, like other 'alternative programme' theorists, was easily diverted away from even his own 'theoretical' policies once he reached government.

32. S. Aaronovitch, *The Road from Thatcherism* (London: Lawrence & Wishart, 1981), p. 108.

33. Ibid, p. 61.

34. Ibid, pp. 56 and 34–5.

35. Ibid, p. 63.

36. See ibid, p. 128. For example, Aaronovitch calculates that 460 000 jobs would be created by a 5 per cent reduction in the length of the average working week. This faulty assumption is based on the belief that 80 per cent of private enterprises would hire extra labour without being compelled by legislation – an unlikely development given the possibility of increasing production without extra labour.

37. See B. Rowthorn, 'British and Western Europe', *Marxism Today*, May 1982, pp. 25–31.

38. R. Dornhorst and P. Newman, 'Which Way Forward for Comunists?: critique of the British road to socialism' *Revolutionary Communist*, no. 7, November 1977, p. 21.

39. In his defence of 'alternative programmes', Geoff Hodgson criticises the 'zero-sum concept of class struggle' – i.e. the view that 'if the position of the workers is to rise, that of the capitalists must fall'. See 'On the Political Economy of Socialist Transformation', *New Left Review*, no. 133, May-June 1982, p. 57. While Hodgson makes a number of valid points against those Left people who see struggles in 'zero-sum' terms, he nevertheless gives the impression that the rate of profit is quite 'flexible' and that capitalists can generally benefit from major gains made by the working-class!

40. See, for example, H. Radice, 'The National Economy – A Keynesian Myth', in *Conference of Socialist Economists 1982 Conference Handbook* (London, 1982) pp. 102–5.

12. A Socialist Stocktaking: Against Stateless Socialism and Market Socialism

1. A. Nove, *Political Economy and Soviet Socialism* (London: Allen & Unwin, 1979) p. 130.

2. S. Stojanovic, *Between Ideals and Reality*, trans. G. S. Sher (New York: Oxford University Press, 1973) pp. 125–8.

3. Ibid, p. 127.
4. E. Luard, *Socialism Without the State* (London: Macmillan, 1979).
5. F. Feher and A. Heller, 'Forms of Equality', *Telos*, no. 32, Summer 1977, p. 17.
6. G. Ruffolo, 'Project for Socialist Planning', in S. Holland (ed.), *Beyond Capitalist Planning* (Oxford: Basil Blackwell, 1978) p. 78.
7. F. Feher and A. Heller, 'Forms of Equality', p. 12.
8. Ibid, p. 18.
9. I. Szelenyi, 'Prospects and Limits of Power of Intellectuals under Market Capitalism', unpublished paper, p. 129.
10. F. Claudin, *Eurocommunism and Socialism* (London: New Left Books, 1978) p. 129.
11. M. Raptis, *Socialism, Democracy and Self-Management*, trans. M. Serrie and R. Sissons (London: Allison & Busby, 1980) p. 145.
12. Ibid, p. 134.
13. R. Bahro, *The Alternative* (London: New Left Books, 1978) p. 447.
14. A. Nove 'The Soviet Economy: Problem and Prospects', *New Left Review*, no. 119, 1980, p. 7.
15. Raptis, *Socialism, Democracy and Self-Management*, pp. 102 and 134.
16. E. Mandel, *Marxist Economic Theory*, trans. B. Pearce (London: Merlin Press, 1971) p. 645, first published 1962.
17. See, for example, A. Carlo, 'Capitalist Restoration and Social Crisis in Yugoslavia', *Telos*, no. 36, 1978, pp. 81–110 and B. Vuskovic, 'Social Inequality in Yugoslavia', *New Left Review*, no. 95, 1976, pp. 26–44. Branko Horvat, *The Political Economy of Socialism* (London: Martin Robertson, 1982) also proposes an elaborate scheme of regulating mechanisms in a federal structure to prevent the development of monopolies and other abuses in market-socialist practice. Yet he does not adequately deal with serious criticisms made of market socialism.
18. Feher and Heller, 'Forms of Equality', p. 19.
19. I. Szelenyi and G. Konrad, *The Intellectuals on the Road to Class Power*, trans. A. Arato and R. E. Allen (London: Harvester Press, 1979) fill in the social and political background in Hungary which partially explains the 'philosophical' approach to concrete problems manifested in Heller's and Feher's work. 'A kind of philosophical resignation has replaced the analysis of broad economic and social conflicts ... Social and political radicalism has here given way to a sociopsychological radicalism dedicated to the analysis of radical needs.' (p. 243.) Although Feher and Heller continue to analyse broad social conflicts, their analyses are notable more for their abstract generalisations than for their familiarity with political economic problems.
20. See I. Szelenyi, 'Whose Alternative?', *New German Critique*, no. 20, 1980, pp. 117–34.
21. Nove, 'The Soviet Economy: Problem and Prospects', pp. 5 and 16. Also see A. Nove, *The Economics of Feasible Socialism* (London: Allen & Unwin, 1983) pt 5.

22. See W. Brus and H. Ticktin, 'Is Market Socialism Possible or Necessary?', *Critique*, no. 14, 1981, p. 22.
23. Ibid, p. 33.
24. Ibid, pp. 22–5.
25. Ibid, p. 25.
26. Ibid, p. 26.
27. Ibid, p. 34.
28. M. Albert and R. Hahnel, *Socialism Today and Tomorrow* (South End Press, 1981).
29. Ibid, see p. 38 and pt 3.
30. Ibid, pp. 318–21.
31. Ibid, p. 313.
32. Bahro, *The Alternative*, p. 441.
33. Ibid, pp. 434–5.
34. Ibid, p. 416.
35. Ibid, p. 419. Nove attacks East German plans which allow for reserve capacity because there 'is no place in this version for meaningful workers' participation' – A. Nove, *Political Economy and Soviet Socialism*, p. 157. While it is true that undemocratic planning in East Germany makes workers' participation meaningless, this could not be said of 'reserve capacity' as conceived by Bahro in a democratic participatory society. As I have noted before, it is not clear what degree of meaningful participation workers could have under Nove's 'mixture' of market socialism and central planning. Also, Nove seems to be well-disposed to anti-radical Social Democrats such as Richard Löwenthal, and clearly reveals a preference for pragmatic and empiricist notions of morality – see, for example, his vulgar critique of Habermas's concept of 'distorted communication' in *Political Economy and Soviet Socialism*, ch. 13.
36. R. Williams, 'Beyond Actually Existing Socialism', *New Left Review*, no. 120, 1980, p. 13.
37 Ibid.
38. Quoted by J. Pelikan, 'Bahro's Ideas on Change in Eastern Europe', *International Journal of Politics*, Summer–Fall 1980 (special edition ed. V. Wolter, *Rudolf Bahro: Critical Responses)* p. 182.

13. The Impossibility of Socialist Pluralism without State Institutions

1. N. Bobbio, 'Are there Alternatives to Representative Democracy?', *Telos*, no. 35, 1978, pp. 17–30.
2. J. Habermas, *Theory and Practice*, trans. J. Viertel (London: Heinemann, 1974) p. 169.
3. D. Beetham, 'Beyond Liberal Democracy', *The Socialist Register 1981*, p. 200.
4. L. Trotsky, *The Permanent Revolution and Results and Prospects* (New York: Merit Publishers, 1969) p. 279.
5. This is Glyn and Harrison's alternative to 'import controls'; see

A. Glyn and J. Harrison, *The British Economic Disaster* (London: Pluto Press, 1980) p. 162.

6. N. Harris, 'Daydreaming about "Our" Britain', *Socialist Review*, 16 February - 13 March 1981, p. 27.
7. See A. Heller, 'Marxist Ethics and the Future of Eastern Europe', *Telos*, no. 38, 1978-9, pp. 153-74; P. Hirst, 'Law, Socialism and Rights', in P. Carlen and M. Collison (eds), *Radical Issues in Criminology* (Oxford: Martin Robertson, 1980) pp. 58-105; and N. Poulantzas (interviewed by H. Weber), 'The State and the Transition to Socialism', *Socialist Review*, no. 38, 1978, pp. 9-36.
8. Hirst, 'Law, Socialism and Rights', p. 83.
9. Ibid, p. 104.
10. A. Gorz, *Farewell to the Working Class*, trans. M. Sonenscher (London: Pluto Press, 1982) pp. 90-1.
11. R. Miliband, 'A Commentary on Rudolf Bahro's Alternative', *The Socialist Register 1979*, p. 283.
12. E. Mandel, 'A Political Interview', *New Left Review*, no. 100, 1977, p. 111.
13. G. Ruffolo, 'Project for Socialist Planning', in S. Holland (ed.), *Beyond Capitalist Planning* (Oxford: Basil Blackwell, 1978) p. 81.
14. See, for example, S. Rowbotham, L. Segal and H. Wainwright, *Beyond the Fragments* (London: Merlin Press, 1979).

Conclusion

1. B. Hindess, *Parliamentary Democracy and Socialist Politics* (London: Routledge & Kegan Paul, 1983) p. 156.

4. Clive and J. Stephen, *The Urban Predicament* (Boston: London:
    Pluto Press, 1980) p. 152.

5. B. Harris, 'Between the good times: Britain's spending Review',
    IEE Times, 19 March 1981, p. 27.

6. See K. H. Kee, 'Mutual Funds and the Future of Welfare State',
    Choice, no. 50, 1973, n. pp. 123–145; J. Hirsh, 'Law, Accident and
    Rights', in T. Carlen and M. Collison (eds), *Radical Issues in
    Sociology* (Oxford: Martin Robertson, 1980) pp. 58–105; and

7. *Published* (Interviewed by H. Welsh), 'The State and the
    Transition to Socialism', *Capital & Class*, no. 16, 1978, pp. 9–30.

8. Ibid, *Law, Socialism and Rights*, p. 42.

9. Ibid, p. 110.

10. A. Gorz, *Farewell to the Working Class*, trans. M. Sonenscher
    (London: Pluto Press, 1982) pp. 90–4.

11. R. Miliband, 'A Commentary on Ralph Dahrendorf', *Alternative
    for Socialist Register*, 1973.

12. Mandel, 'A Political Interview', *New Left Review*, no. 100,
    1976, p. 121.

13. See further, 'Project for a Social Planning', in *Socialism and
    Nation* (in *Left Politics*), Oxford: Basil Blackwell, 1983) ch. 8.

14. See, for example, A. Rose, 'Jane Labour' and H. Wainwright,
    Beyond the Fragments (London: Martin Press, 1979).

Conclusion

1. T. H. Marshall, *Citizenship and Social Class and Other* (Harmondsworth:
    Penguin, 1950) ch. 4.

Index